An OUTBREAK OF WITCHCRAFT

LITTLE, BROWN AND COMPANY
NEW YORK BOSTON

For Lisa Goodfellow

—DN

An OUTBREAK OF WITCHCRAFT

A Graphic Novel of the Salem Witch Trials

Written by
Deborah Noyes

Illustrated by
M. Duffy

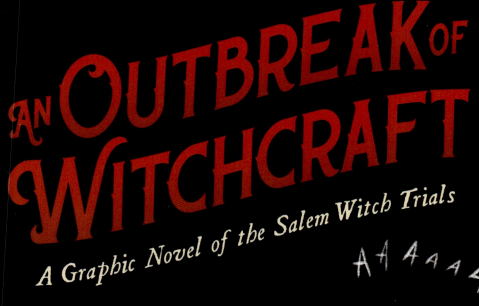

ABOUT THIS BOOK

This book was edited at various times in its life span by Patrice Caldwell, Heather Crowley, Rotem Moscovich, and Andrea Colvin, and it was designed by Megan McLaughlin. The production was supervised by Kimberly Stella, and the production editor was Jake Regier. The text was set in Dominican and 17C Record Print.

This is a work of historical fiction. While the characters in this account were real people, and the events are based on archival materials and documented facts, for reasons of narrative flow and coherence, the author has taken the occasional literary license with certain details and timelines.

Little, Brown Ink
Hachette Book Group
1290 Avenue of the Americas, New York, NY 10104
Visit us at LBYR.com

First Edition: June 2024

Little, Brown Ink is an imprint of Little, Brown and Company. The Little, Brown Ink name and logo are registered trademarks of Hachette Book Group, Inc.

The publisher is not responsible for websites (or their content) that are not owned by the publisher.

Little, Brown and Company books may be purchased in bulk for business, educational, or promotional use. For information, please contact your local bookseller or the Hachette Book Group Special Markets Department at special.markets@hbgusa.com.

Library of Congress Cataloging-in-Publication Data
Names: Noyes, Deborah, author. | Duffy, Melissa, illustrator.
Title: An outbreak of witchcraft / story by Deborah Noyes ; illustrated by M. Duffy.
Description: New York : Little, Brown and Company, 2024. | Audience: Ages 12 & up | Summary: "A graphic-novel retelling of the Salem witch trials in 1692, creating a narrative out of the historical context and what we can imagine of those accused." —Provided by publisher.
Identifiers: LCCN 2021021217 | ISBN 9780759555587 (hardcover) | ISBN 9780759555594 (trade paperback) | ISBN 9780759555600 (ebook)
Subjects: LCSH: Graphic novels. | CYAC: Trials (Witchcraft)—Fiction. | Witchcraft—Fiction. | Salem (Mass.)—History—Colonial period, ca. 1600–1775—Fiction. | LCGFT: Historical comics. | Graphic novels.
Classification: LCC PZ7.7.N75 We 2023 | DDC 741.5/973—dc23
LC record available at https://lccn.loc.gov/2021021217

ISBNs: 978-0-7595-5558-7 (hardcover), 978-0-7595-5559-4 (pbk.), 978-0-7595-5560-0 (ebook), 978-0-316-39562-5 (ebook), 978-0-316-56534-9 (ebook)

PRINTED IN CHINA

APS

Hardcover: 10 9 8 7 6 5 4 3 2 1

Paperback: 10 9 8 7 6 5 4 3 2 1

Such was the darkness of that day...that we
walked in the clouds, and could not see our way.
And we have most cause to be humbled for error
on that hand, which cannot be retrieved.

—John Hale, *A Modest Enquiry into the
Nature of Witchcraft*

The Afflicted

Abigail Hobbs
Wild teenage girl originally from Casco Bay, Maine, who confesses and accuses many, including Reverend George Burroughs

Deliverance Hobbs
Abigail's stepmother; confessed witch and energetic accuser

Elizabeth Hubbard
17-year-old grandniece of Dr. Griggs

Margaret Jacobs
Confessed witch who accuses her grandfather George Jacobs Sr. and Reverend George Burroughs

Mercy Lewis
17-year-old servant in the Putnam household and survivor of Native American raids in Maine

Betty (Elizabeth) Parris
*9-year-old daughter of
Reverend Samuel Parris*

Ann Putnam Jr.
*12-year-old friend of Betty and Abigail;
daughter of Thomas Putnam and
Ann Putnam Sr.*

Ann Putnam Sr.
*Mother of Ann Jr. and wife of
Thomas Putnam*

Mary Warren
*20-year-old servant of Elizabeth
and John Proctor*

Abigail Williams
*11-year-old niece of Reverend Samuel
Parris; orphaned in a Native American
raid in Maine*

The Accused

Bridget Bishop
*Bold, outspoken resident of Salem Town
who fancies red dresses and showy lace;
married three times*

Reverend George Burroughs
*Burly former minister of Salem Village;
now a minister in Wells, Maine*

Sarah Cloyce & Mary Easty
Rebecca's well-respected sisters

Giles Corey
*Martha's third husband;
a pugnacious farmer*

Martha Corey
*Churchgoing woman with
a "past"*

Philip & Mary English
Wealthy Salem merchant and his wife

Mercy & Dorothy Good
*Sarah Good's infant and
4-year-old daughter*

Sarah Good
Surly beggar

John Indian
*Tituba's husband; enslaved in the
Parris household and
an accuser as well*

George Jacobs Sr.
*80-year-old farmer with rheumatism
and a wry sense of humor*

Rebecca Nurse
Pious 71-year-old grandmother

John & Elizabeth Proctor
*Successful Salem Village farmer and
tavern keeper, and his pregnant wife*

The Accused (cont.)

Sarah Osborne
*49 years old; ostensibly
bedridden, long absent from
the church*

Tituba
*Enslaved Arawak woman in the home
of Reverend Samuel Parris*

Family Members of the Accused

Peter Cloyce
Sarah's husband

Francis Nurse
Rebecca's husband

Witch Hunters and Men in Power

Ezekiel Cheever
Court recorder and village schoolmaster

Jonathan Corwin
Town merchant and justice of the peace

Thomas Danforth
*Magistrate and acting governor of the
Massachusetts Bay Colony before the arrival
of William Phips; he is ultimately critical of
the trial proceedings*

Judge John Hathorne
*Magistrate and interrogator during the
preliminary witchcraft investigations*

Increase & Cotton Mather
*Influential father-and-son ministers from
Boston who write sensational books about
witchcraft but ultimately call for an end to
spectral evidence during the trials*

Nicholas Noyes
*Salem Town pastor; official minister
of and avid participant in the juried
trials held at the court of oyer and
terminer in Salem Town*

Witch Hunters and Men in Power (cont.)

Reverend Samuel Parris
Salem Village's minister

William Phips
Royal governor of the
Massachusetts Bay Colony

Edward Putnam
Thomas's brother; a church deacon

Thomas Putnam
Father of Ann Jr. and top supporter of
Reverend Parris; he makes some 140
accusations of witchcraft

Judge Nathaniel Saltonstall
Oyer and terminer judge who steps
down before the court begins to meet

Judge Samuel Sewall
*Oyer and terminer judge who repents
in 1697*

Judge William Stoughton
*Chief justice of the special court of oyer
and terminer formed to try witchcraft cases*

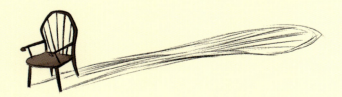

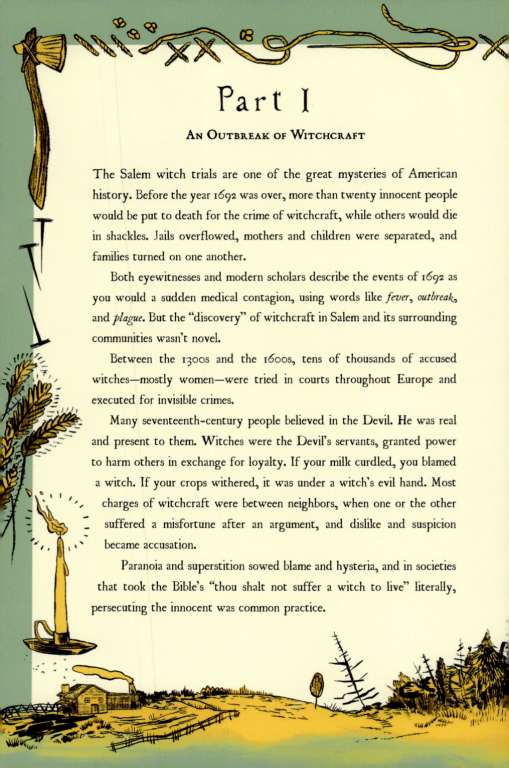

Part I

An Outbreak of Witchcraft

The Salem witch trials are one of the great mysteries of American history. Before the year 1692 was over, more than twenty innocent people would be put to death for the crime of witchcraft, while others would die in shackles. Jails overflowed, mothers and children were separated, and families turned on one another.

Both eyewitnesses and modern scholars describe the events of 1692 as you would a sudden medical contagion, using words like *fever*, *outbreak*, and *plague*. But the "discovery" of witchcraft in Salem and its surrounding communities wasn't novel.

Between the 1300s and the 1600s, tens of thousands of accused witches—mostly women—were tried in courts throughout Europe and executed for invisible crimes.

Many seventeenth-century people believed in the Devil. He was real and present to them. Witches were the Devil's servants, granted power to harm others in exchange for loyalty. If your milk curdled, you blamed a witch. If your crops withered, it was under a witch's evil hand. Most charges of witchcraft were between neighbors, when one or the other suffered a misfortune after an argument, and dislike and suspicion became accusation.

Paranoia and superstition sowed blame and hysteria, and in societies that took the Bible's "thou shalt not suffer a witch to live" literally, persecuting the innocent was common practice.

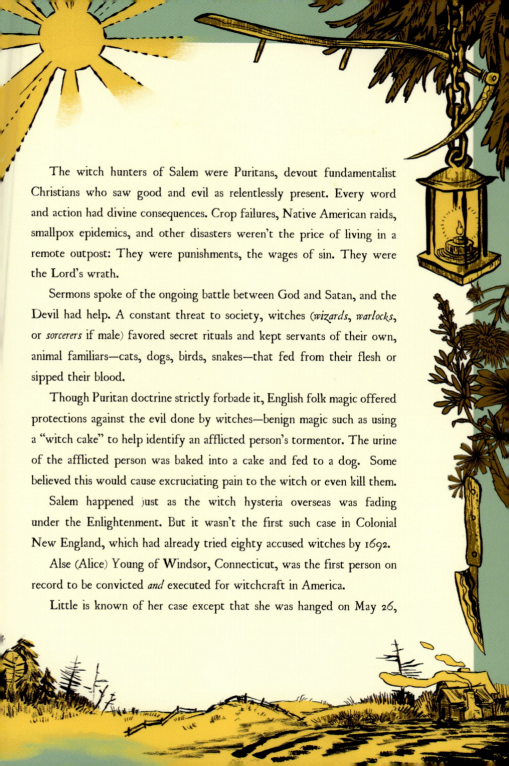

The witch hunters of Salem were Puritans, devout fundamentalist Christians who saw good and evil as relentlessly present. Every word and action had divine consequences. Crop failures, Native American raids, smallpox epidemics, and other disasters weren't the price of living in a remote outpost: They were punishments, the wages of sin. They were the Lord's wrath.

Sermons spoke of the ongoing battle between God and Satan, and the Devil had help. A constant threat to society, witches (*wizards*, *warlocks*, or *sorcerers* if male) favored secret rituals and kept servants of their own, animal familiars—cats, dogs, birds, snakes—that fed from their flesh or sipped their blood.

Though Puritan doctrine strictly forbade it, English folk magic offered protections against the evil done by witches—benign magic such as using a "witch cake" to help identify an afflicted person's tormentor. The urine of the afflicted person was baked into a cake and fed to a dog. Some believed this would cause excruciating pain to the witch or even kill them.

Salem happened just as the witch hysteria overseas was fading under the Enlightenment. But it wasn't the first such case in Colonial New England, which had already tried eighty accused witches by 1692.

Alse (Alice) Young of Windsor, Connecticut, was the first person on record to be convicted *and* executed for witchcraft in America.

Little is known of her case except that she was hanged on May 26,

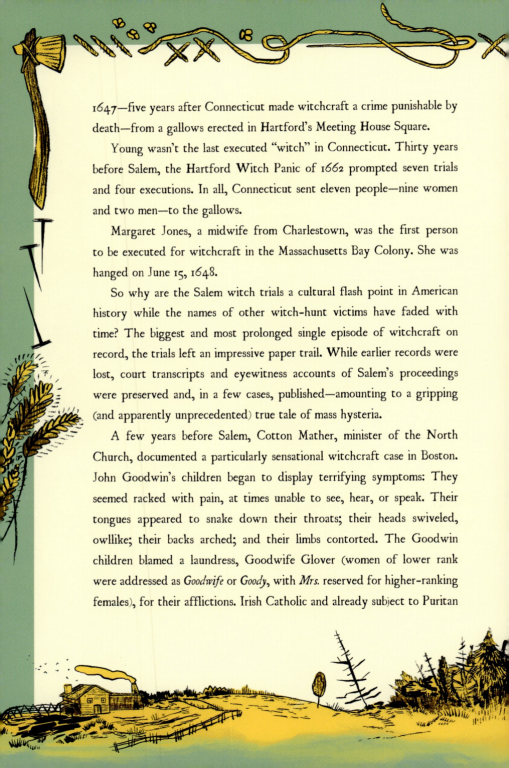

1647—five years after Connecticut made witchcraft a crime punishable by death—from a gallows erected in Hartford's Meeting House Square.

Young wasn't the last executed "witch" in Connecticut. Thirty years before Salem, the Hartford Witch Panic of 1662 prompted seven trials and four executions. In all, Connecticut sent eleven people—nine women and two men—to the gallows.

Margaret Jones, a midwife from Charlestown, was the first person to be executed for witchcraft in the Massachusetts Bay Colony. She was hanged on June 15, 1648.

So why are the Salem witch trials a cultural flash point in American history while the names of other witch-hunt victims have faded with time? The biggest and most prolonged single episode of witchcraft on record, the trials left an impressive paper trail. While earlier records were lost, court transcripts and eyewitness accounts of Salem's proceedings were preserved and, in a few cases, published—amounting to a gripping (and apparently unprecedented) true tale of mass hysteria.

A few years before Salem, Cotton Mather, minister of the North Church, documented a particularly sensational witchcraft case in Boston. John Goodwin's children began to display terrifying symptoms: They seemed racked with pain, at times unable to see, hear, or speak. Their tongues appeared to snake down their throats; their heads swiveled, owllike; their backs arched; and their limbs contorted. The Goodwin children blamed a laundress, Goodwife Glover (women of lower rank were addressed as *Goodwife* or *Goody*, with *Mrs.* reserved for higher-ranking females), for their afflictions. Irish Catholic and already subject to Puritan

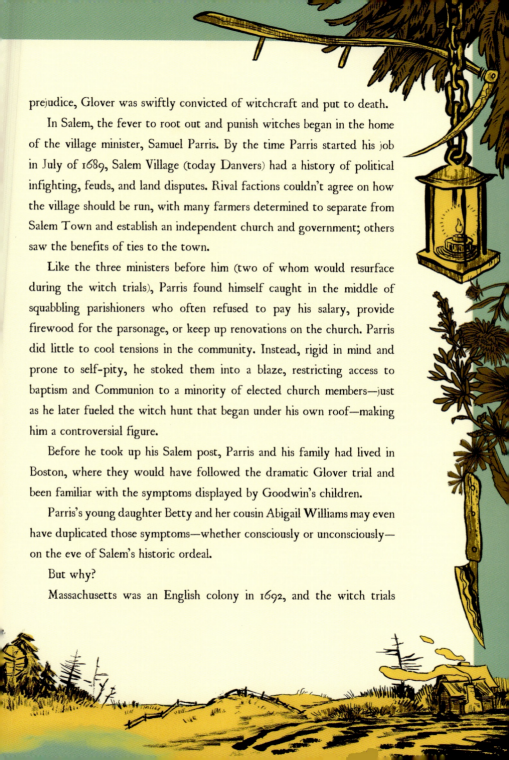

prejudice, Glover was swiftly convicted of witchcraft and put to death.

In Salem, the fever to root out and punish witches began in the home of the village minister, Samuel Parris. By the time Parris started his job in July of 1689, Salem Village (today Danvers) had a history of political infighting, feuds, and land disputes. Rival factions couldn't agree on how the village should be run, with many farmers determined to separate from Salem Town and establish an independent church and government; others saw the benefits of ties to the town.

Like the three ministers before him (two of whom would resurface during the witch trials), Parris found himself caught in the middle of squabbling parishioners who often refused to pay his salary, provide firewood for the parsonage, or keep up renovations on the church. Parris did little to cool tensions in the community. Instead, rigid in mind and prone to self-pity, he stoked them into a blaze, restricting access to baptism and Communion to a minority of elected church members—just as he later fueled the witch hunt that began under his own roof—making him a controversial figure.

Before he took up his Salem post, Parris and his family had lived in Boston, where they would have followed the dramatic Glover trial and been familiar with the symptoms displayed by Goodwin's children.

Parris's young daughter Betty and her cousin Abigail Williams may even have duplicated those symptoms—whether consciously or unconsciously—on the eve of Salem's historic ordeal.

But why?

Massachusetts was an English colony in 1692, and the witch trials took place during King William's War, a bloody conflict between New England and Canada (known as New France at the time) with its Native American allies.

Small, scattered English settlements to the north in Maine (*the frontier*, at the time, or *eastward*) were especially vulnerable to attack by French and Native forces. After violent raids, displaced and orphaned English settlers flooded into Essex County, with many finding their way to Salem Village. Mercy Lewis, Reverend George Burroughs, and others involved in the witch trials had survived a devastating 1689 raid on Casco (now Portland), Maine.

Roughly the same week that Betty Parris and Abigail Williams began to suffer strange fits in the Salem parsonage, a French war party padded through deep snow to gather at the perimeter of York, Maine. Native combatants attacked before dawn, killing or capturing 150 English settlers and torching the village.

Word of the raid reached Salem just as witch fever was taking hold, and many historians believe that the added fear and stress—the news, for some, triggered traumatic memories of earlier raids—fed the flames of the witch hunt. Puritan ministers, including Parris, had long demonized Native American "heathens" from the pulpit, aligning them with the Devil and evil magic. Tituba, an Arawak woman enslaved by Parris, was among the first women in Salem to be charged with witchcraft.

Strong-minded women were often subjected to accusations as a means of control, and most of the accusers at the trials were young, female, and powerless. Their daily lives, managed by distracted parents or masters,

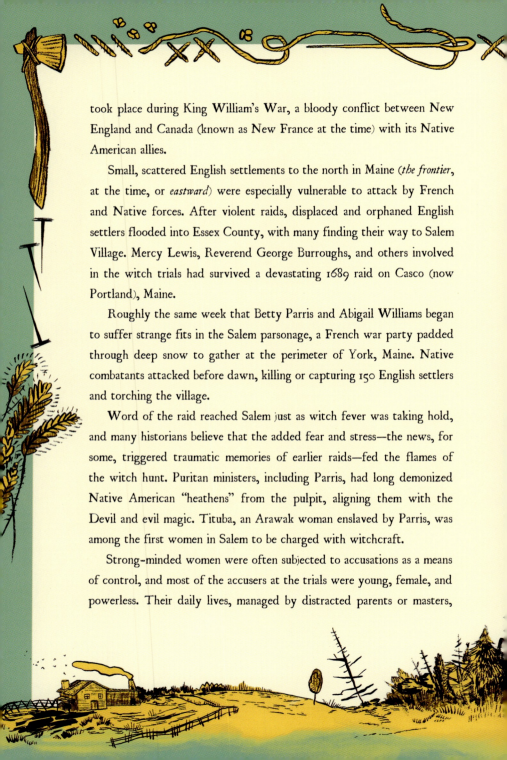

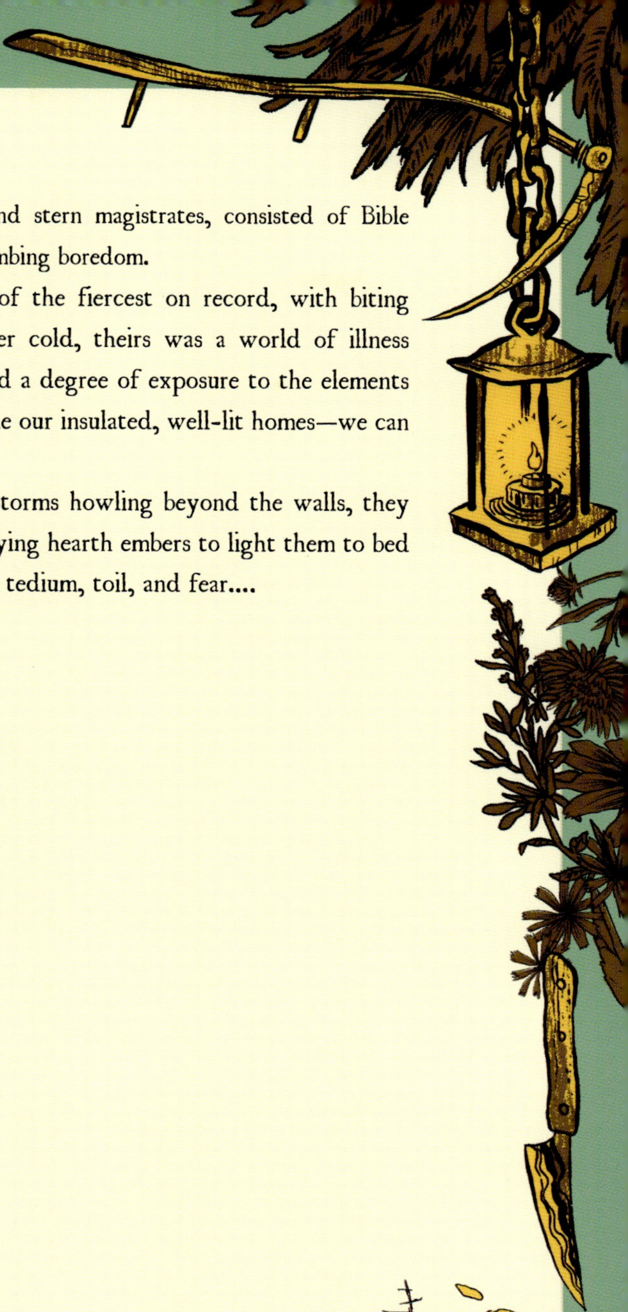

fire-and-brimstone ministers, and stern magistrates, consisted of Bible study, relentless chores, and numbing boredom.

That fateful winter, one of the fiercest on record, with biting winds, heavy snow, and bitter cold, theirs was a world of illness and war, dread and shame, and a degree of exposure to the elements and darkness that today—inside our insulated, well-lit homes—we can only imagine.

With wolves and winter storms howling beyond the walls, they had only a stub of candle or dying hearth embers to light them to bed at night—and little relief from tedium, toil, and fear....

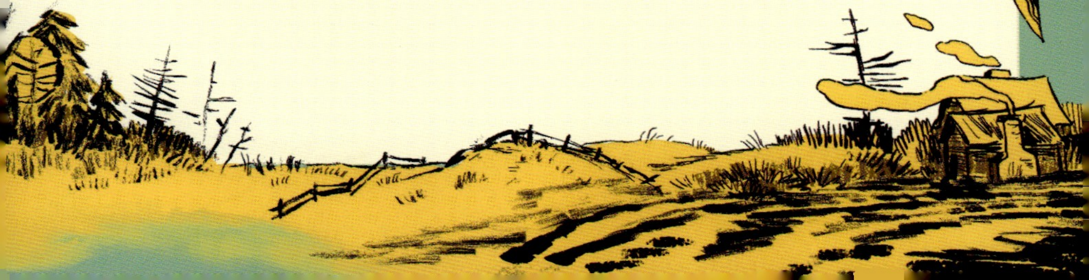

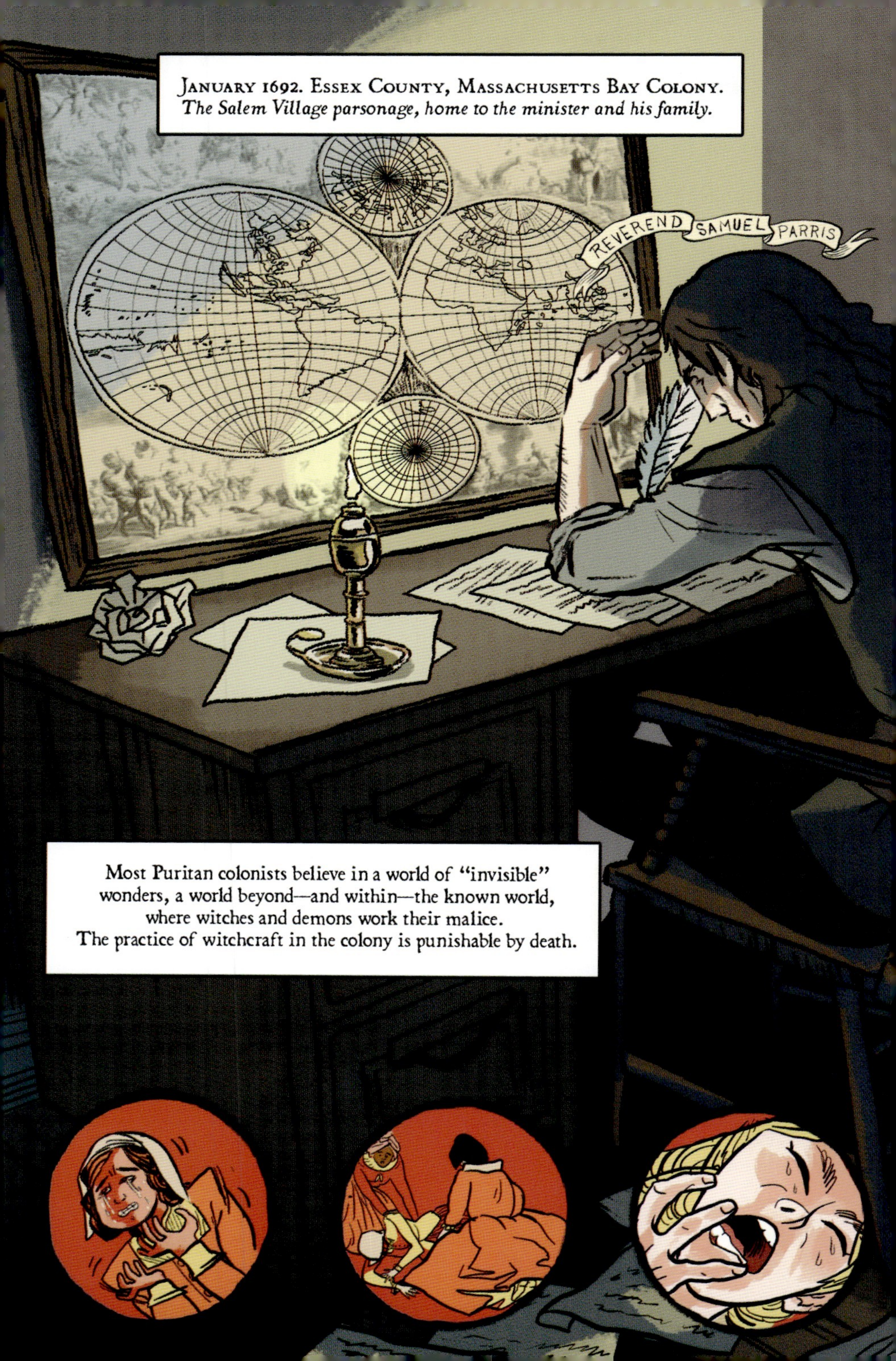
JANUARY 1692. ESSEX COUNTY, MASSACHUSETTS BAY COLONY.
The Salem Village parsonage, home to the minister and his family.
REVEREND SAMUEL PARRIS
Most Puritan colonists believe in a world of "invisible" wonders, a world beyond—and within—the known world, where witches and demons work their malice.
The practice of witchcraft in the colony is punishable by death.

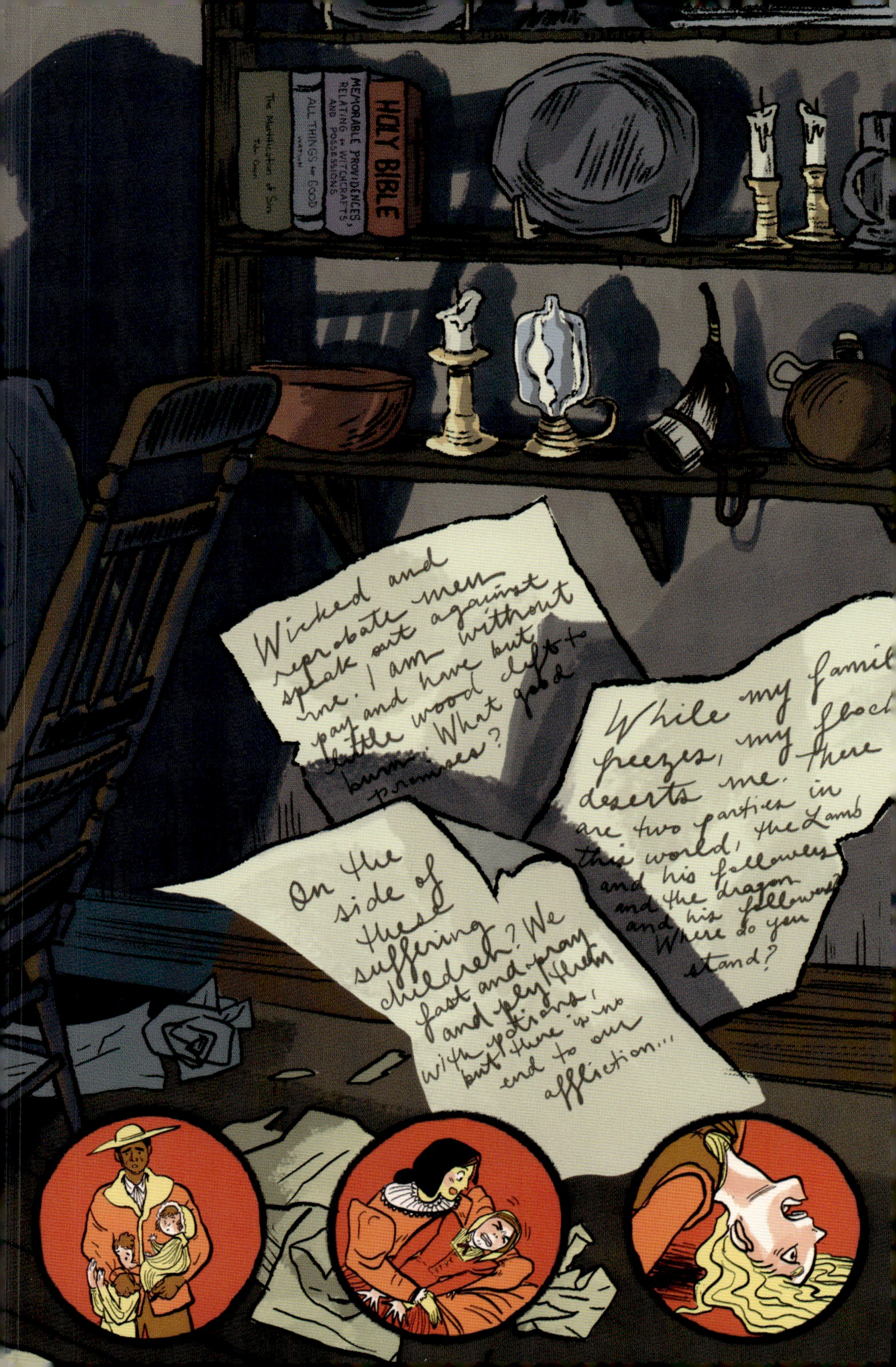
HOLY BIBLE
MEMORABLE PROVIDENCES, RELATING to WITCHCRAFTS AND POSSESSIONS
ALL THINGS for GOOD
The Mortification of Sin
Wicked and reprobate men speak out against me. I am without pay and have but little wood left to burn. What good promises?
While my famil freezes, my floc deserts me. There are two parties in this world, the Lamb and his followers and the dragon and his followers. Where do you stand?
On the side of these suffering children? We fast and pray and ply them with potions, but there is no end to our affliction...

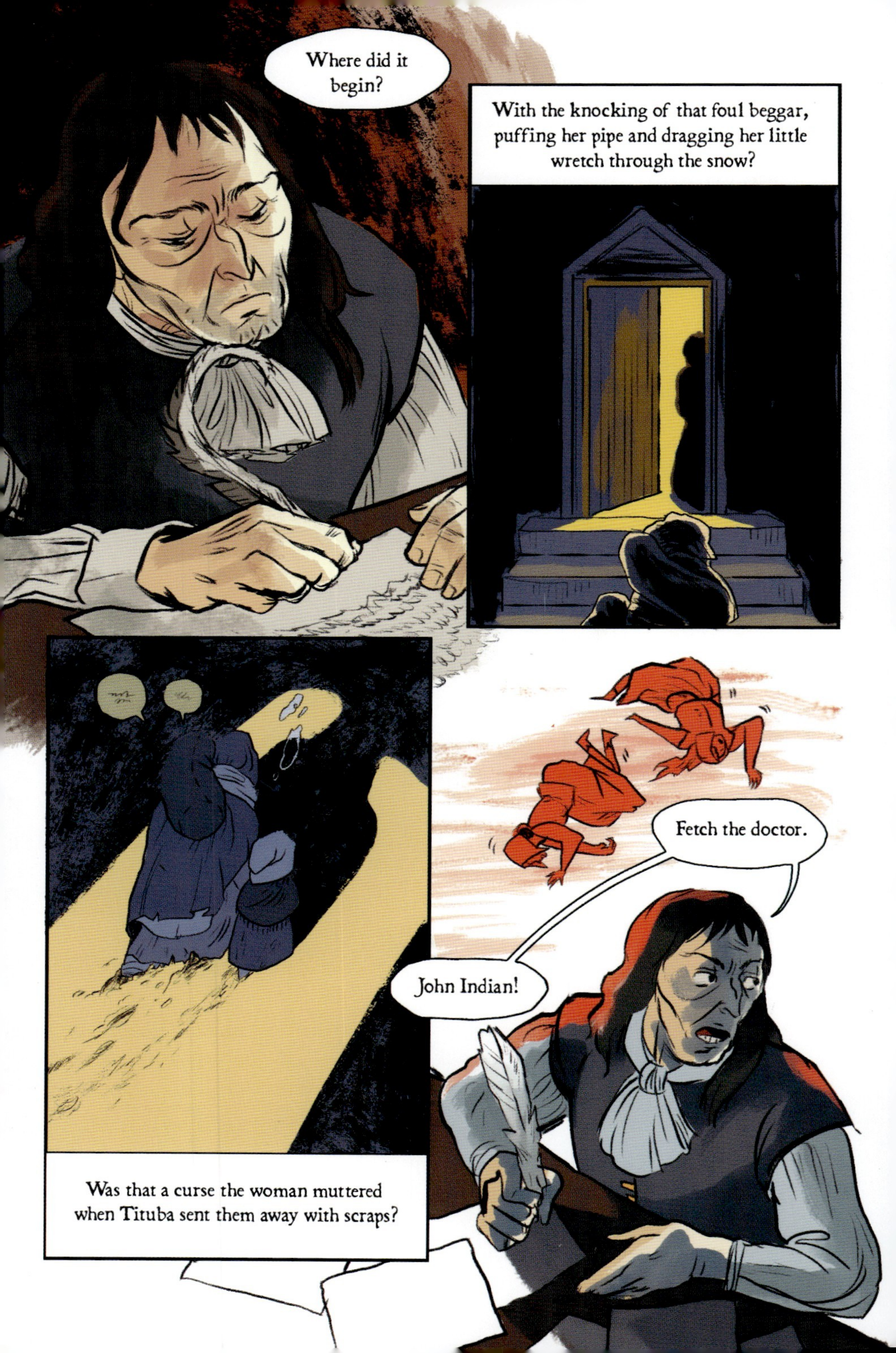
Where did it begin?
With the knocking of that foul beggar, puffing her pipe and dragging her little wretch through the snow?
Was that a curse the woman muttered when Tituba sent them away with scraps?
John Indian!
Fetch the doctor.

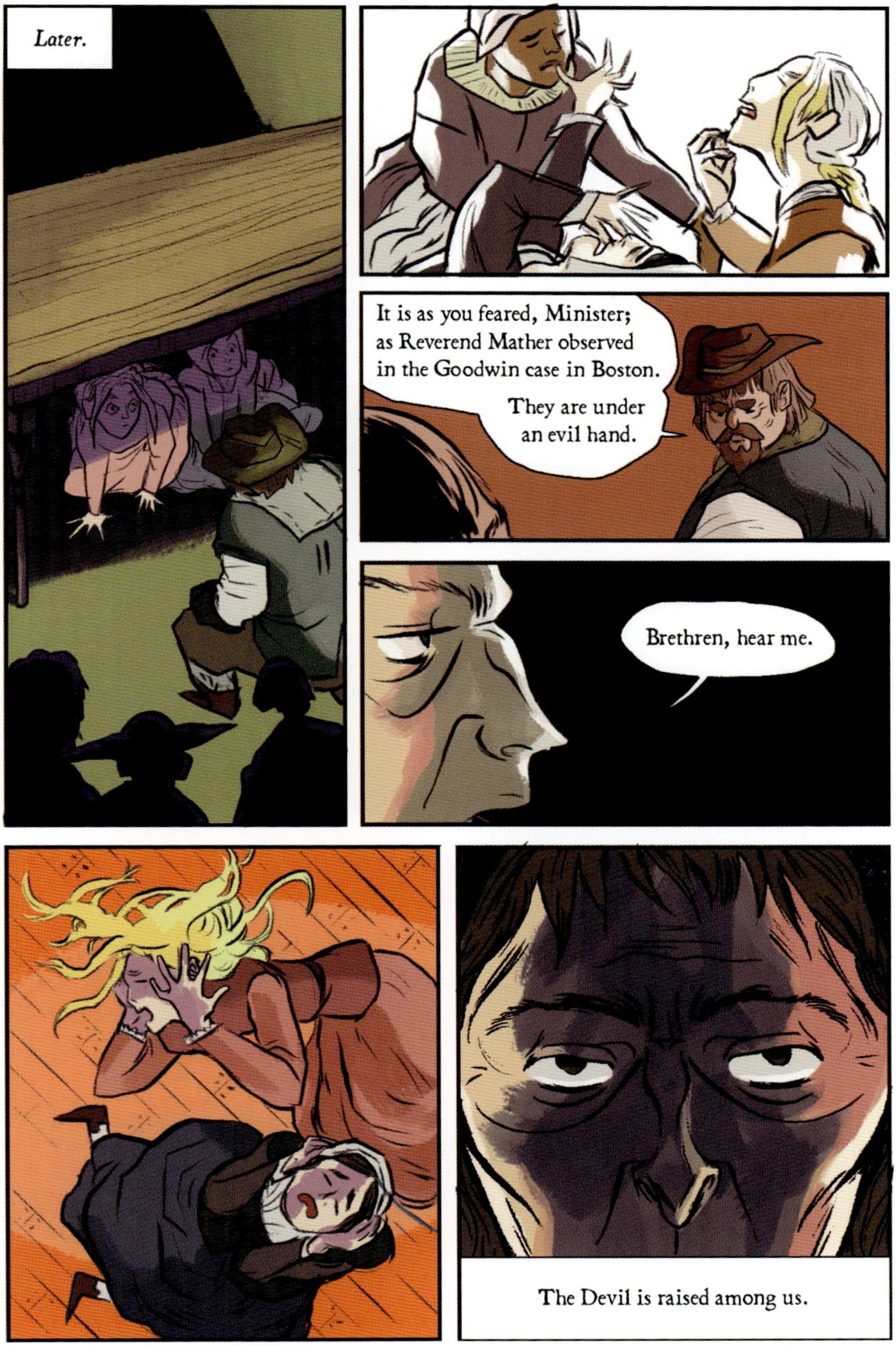
Later.
It is as you feared, Minister; as Reverend Mather observed in the Goodwin case in Boston.
They are under an evil hand.
Brethren, hear me.
The Devil is raised among us.

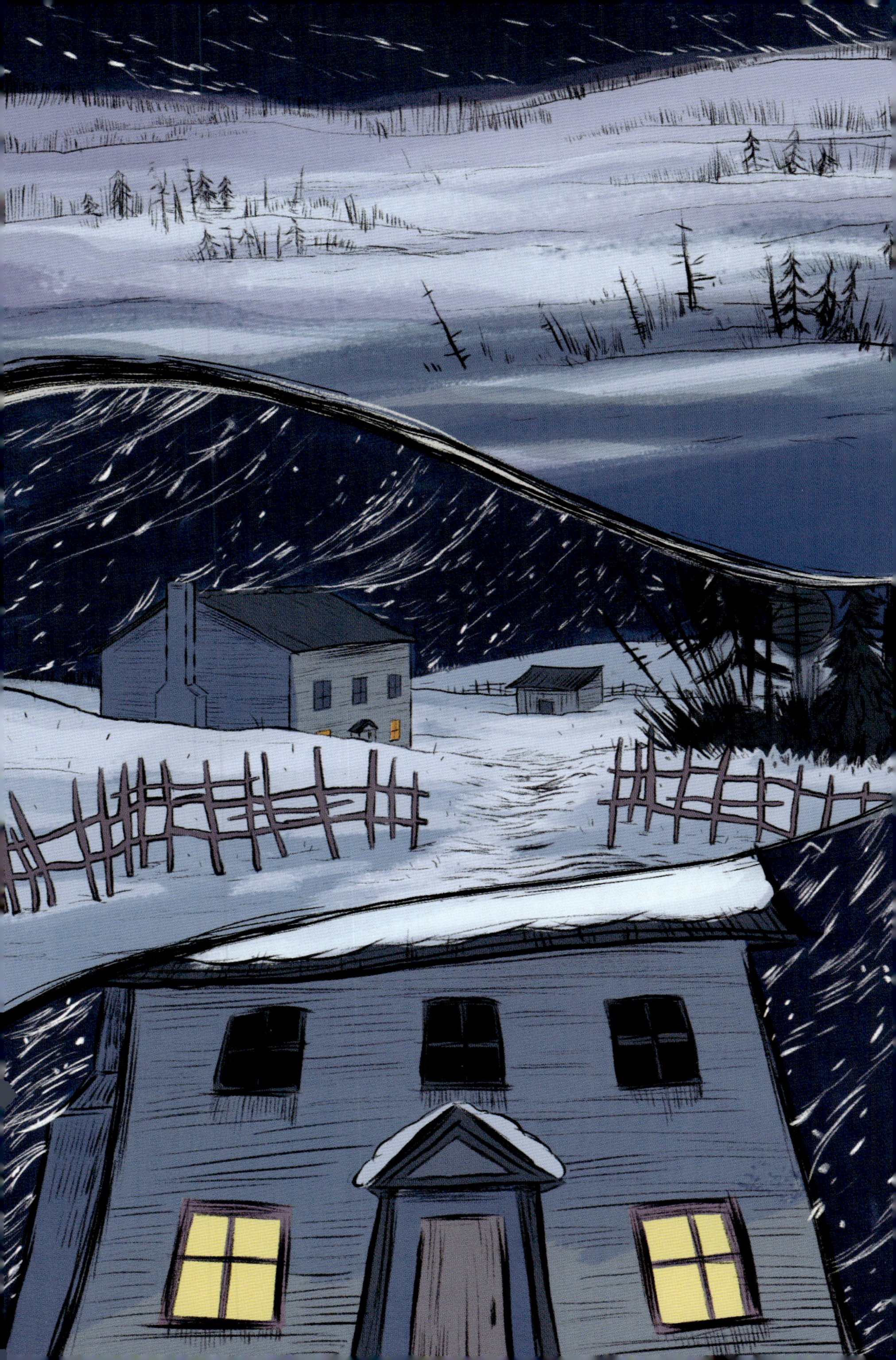

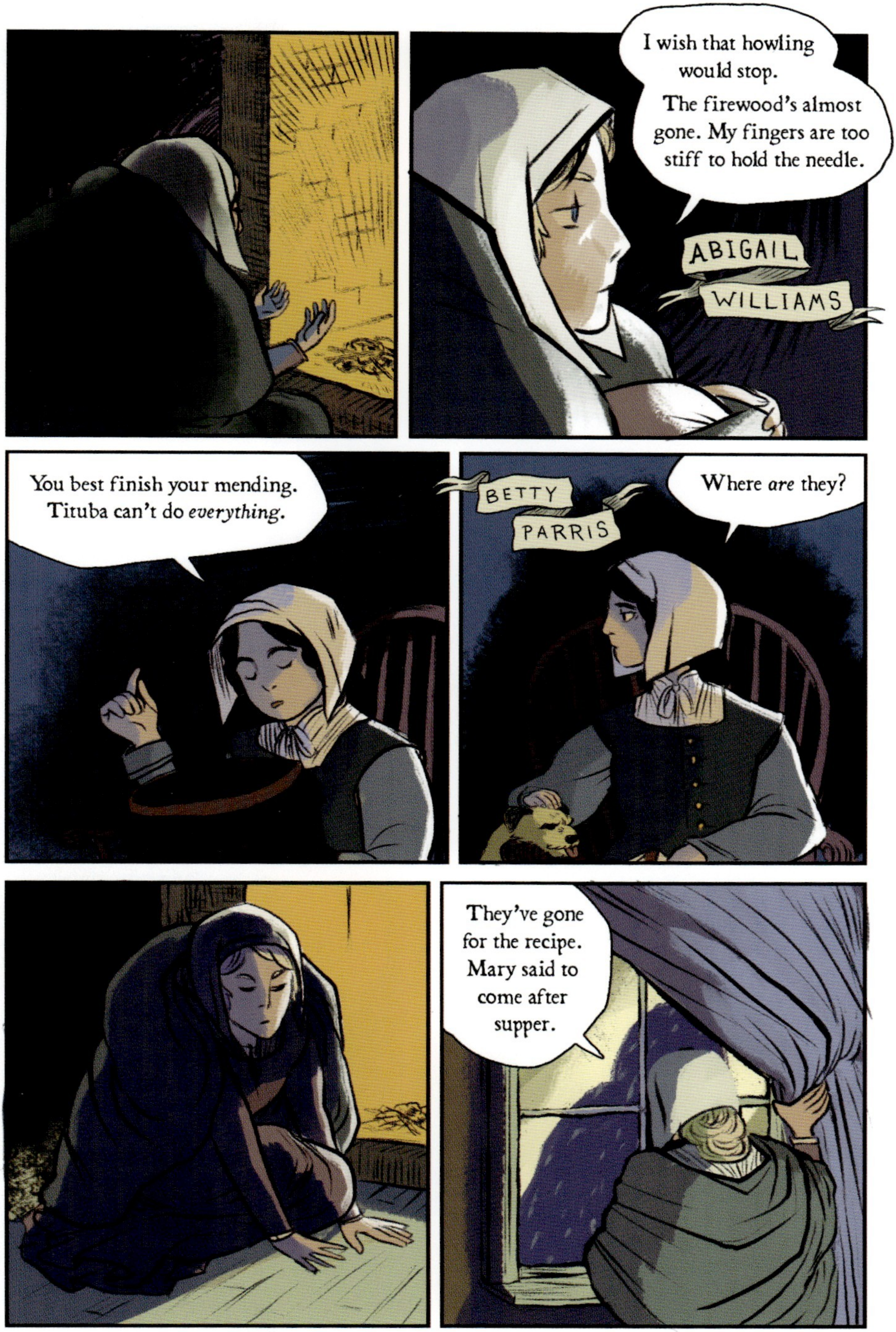
I wish that howling would stop.
The firewood's almost gone. My fingers are too stiff to hold the needle.
ABIGAIL WILLIAMS
You best finish your mending. Tituba can't do *everything*.
BETTY PARRIS
Where *are* they?
They've gone for the recipe. Mary said to come after supper.

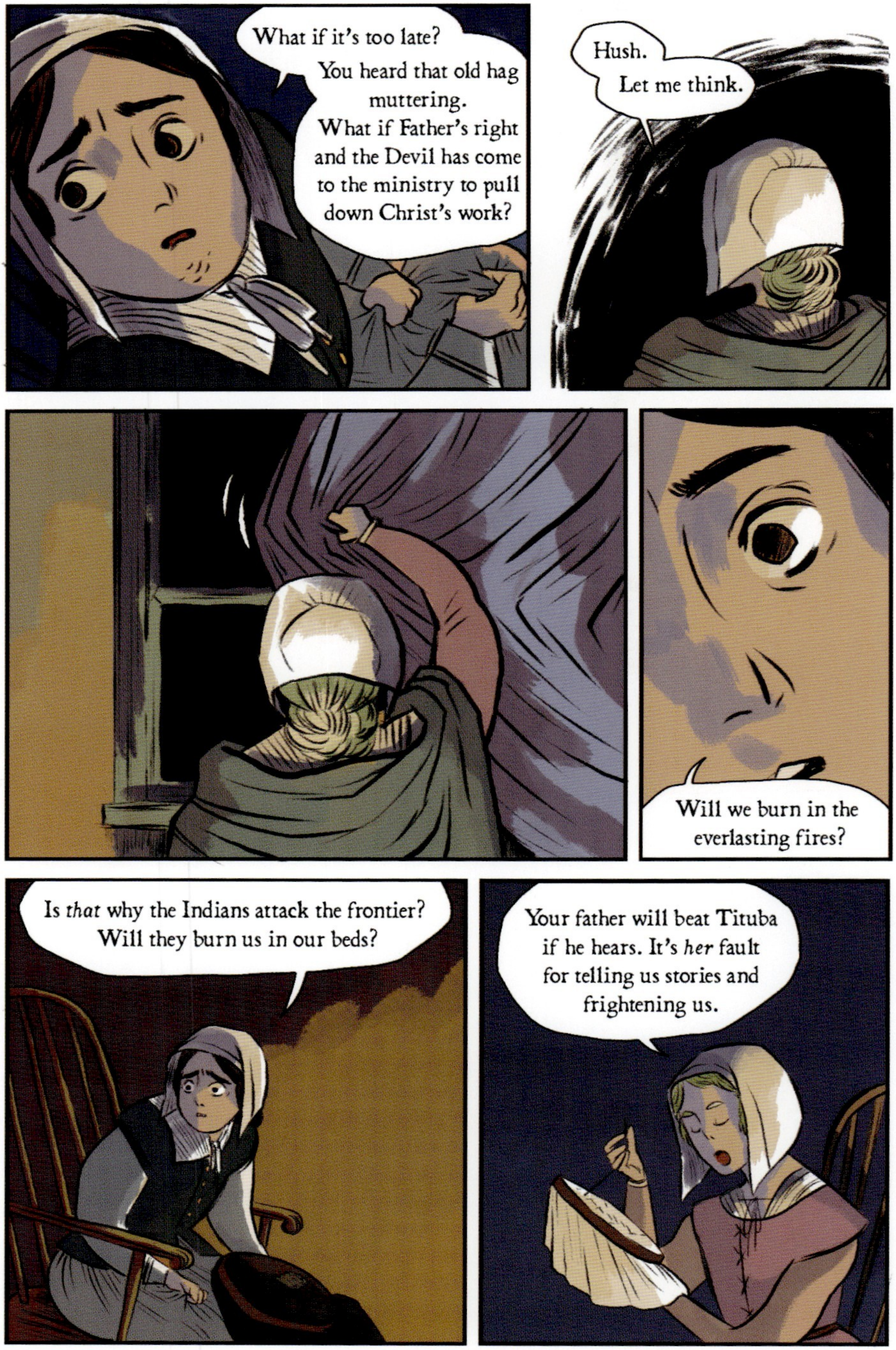
What if it's too late? You heard that old hag muttering. What if Father's right and the Devil has come to the ministry to pull down Christ's work?
Hush. Let me think.
Will we burn in the everlasting fires?
Is *that* why the Indians attack the frontier? Will they burn us in our beds?
Your father will beat Tituba if he hears. It's *her* fault for telling us stories and frightening us.

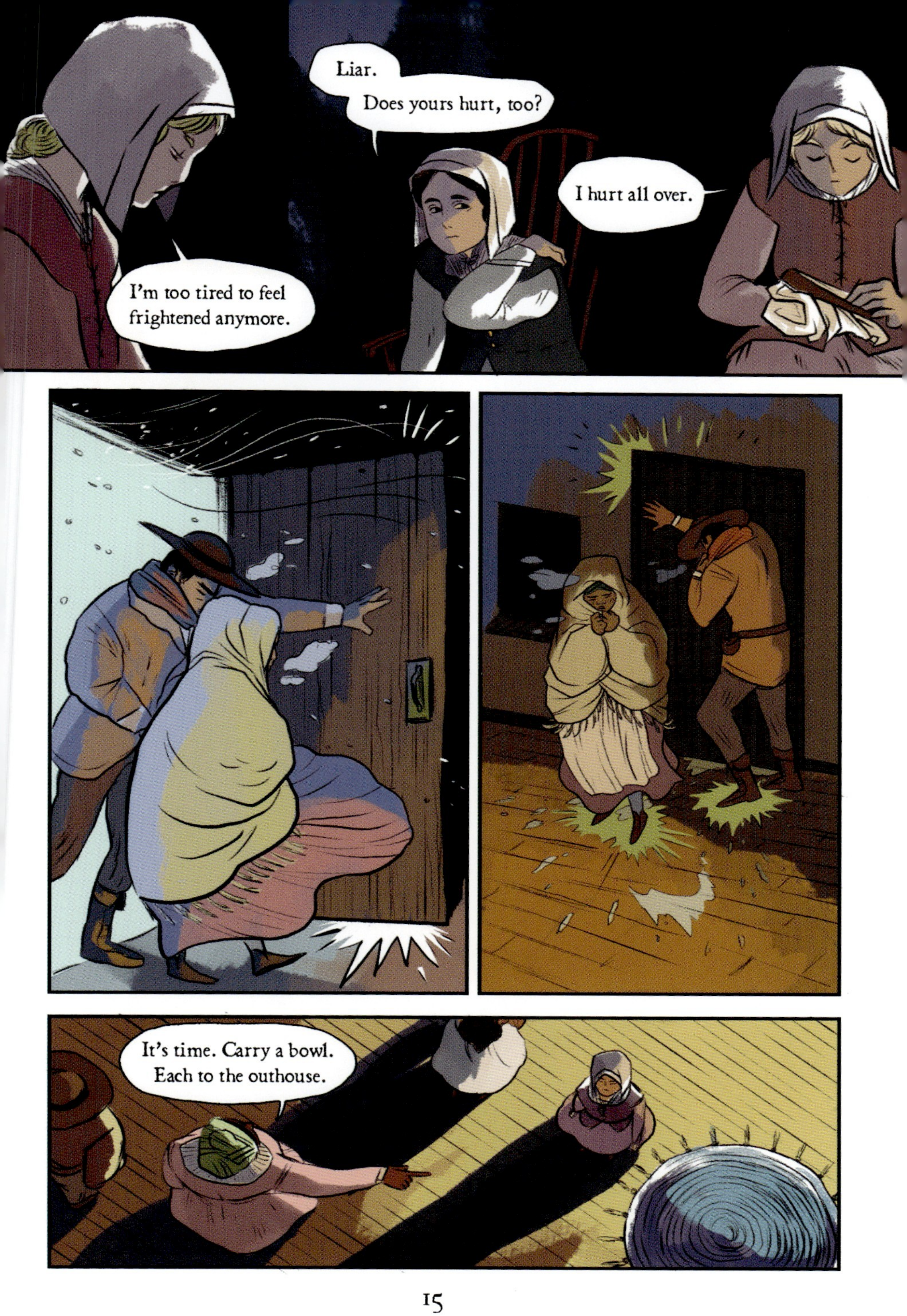
I'm too tired to feel frightened anymore.
Liar.
Does yours hurt, too?
I hurt all over.
It's time. Carry a bowl.
Each to the outhouse.

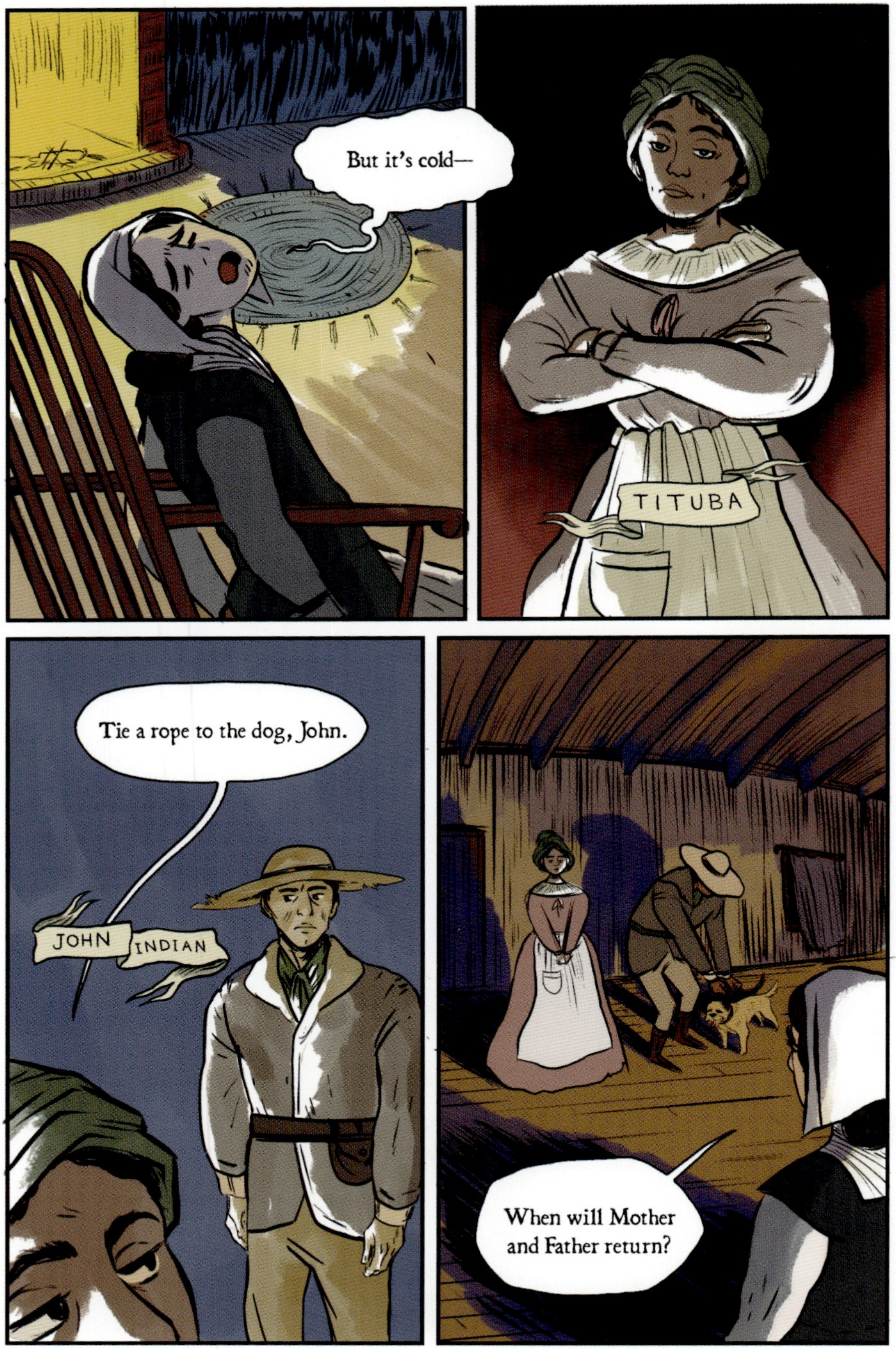
But it's cold—
TITUBA
Tie a rope to the dog, John.
JOHN INDIAN
When will Mother and Father return?

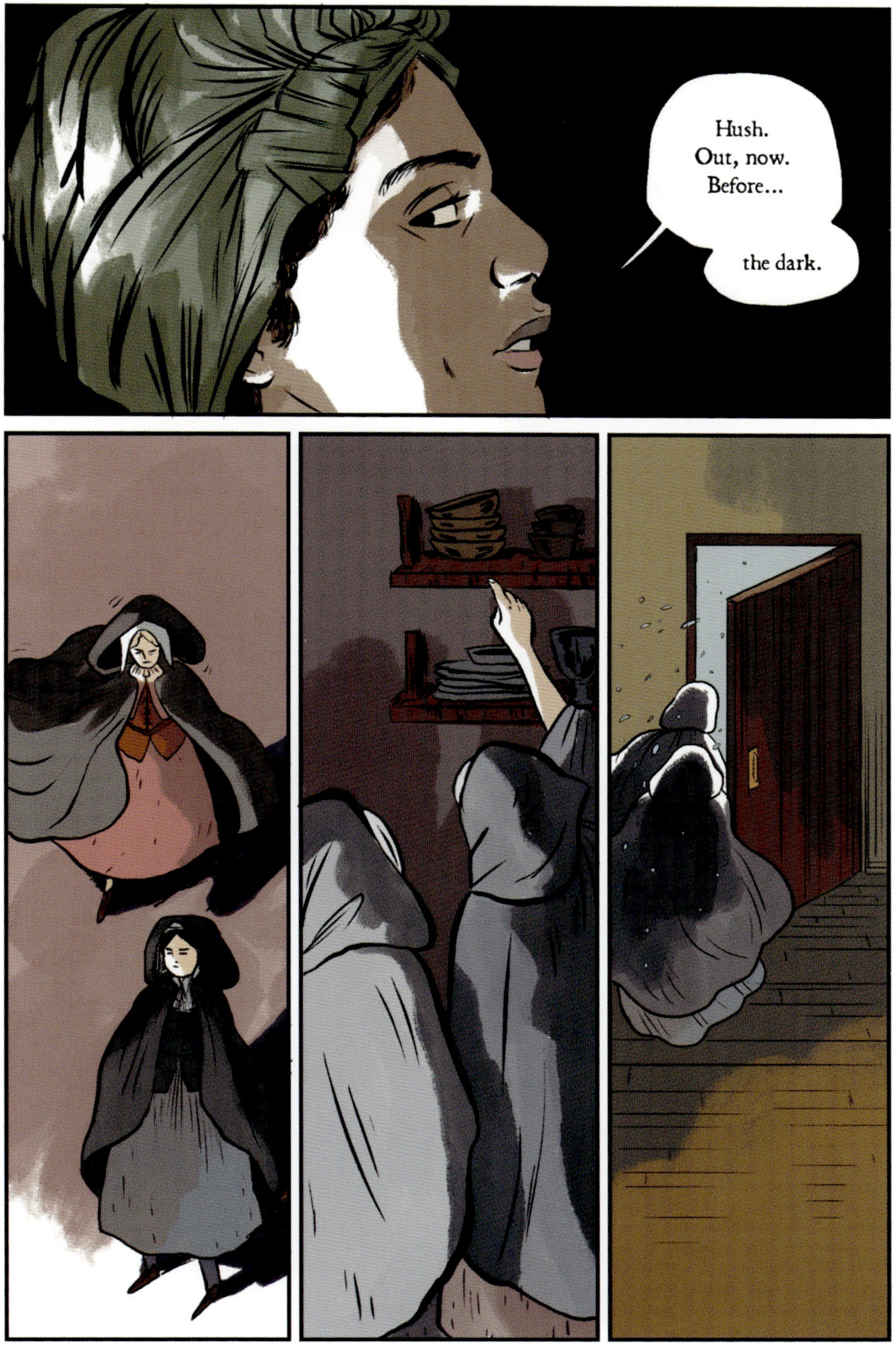
Hush.
Out, now.
Before...
the dark.

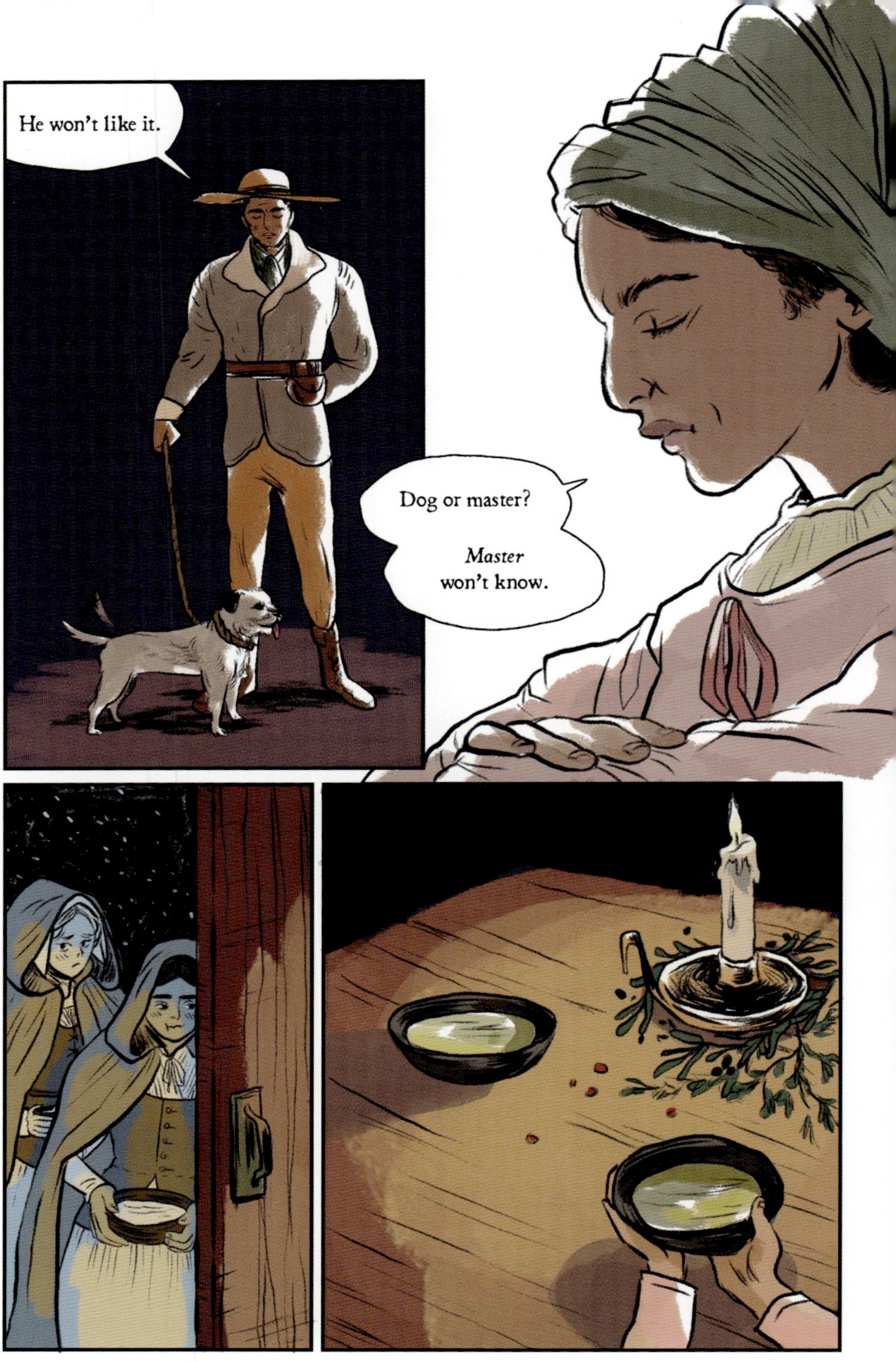
He won't like it.
Dog or master?
Master won't know.

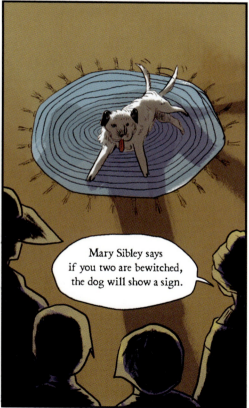

Mary Sibley says if you two are bewitched, the dog will show a sign.

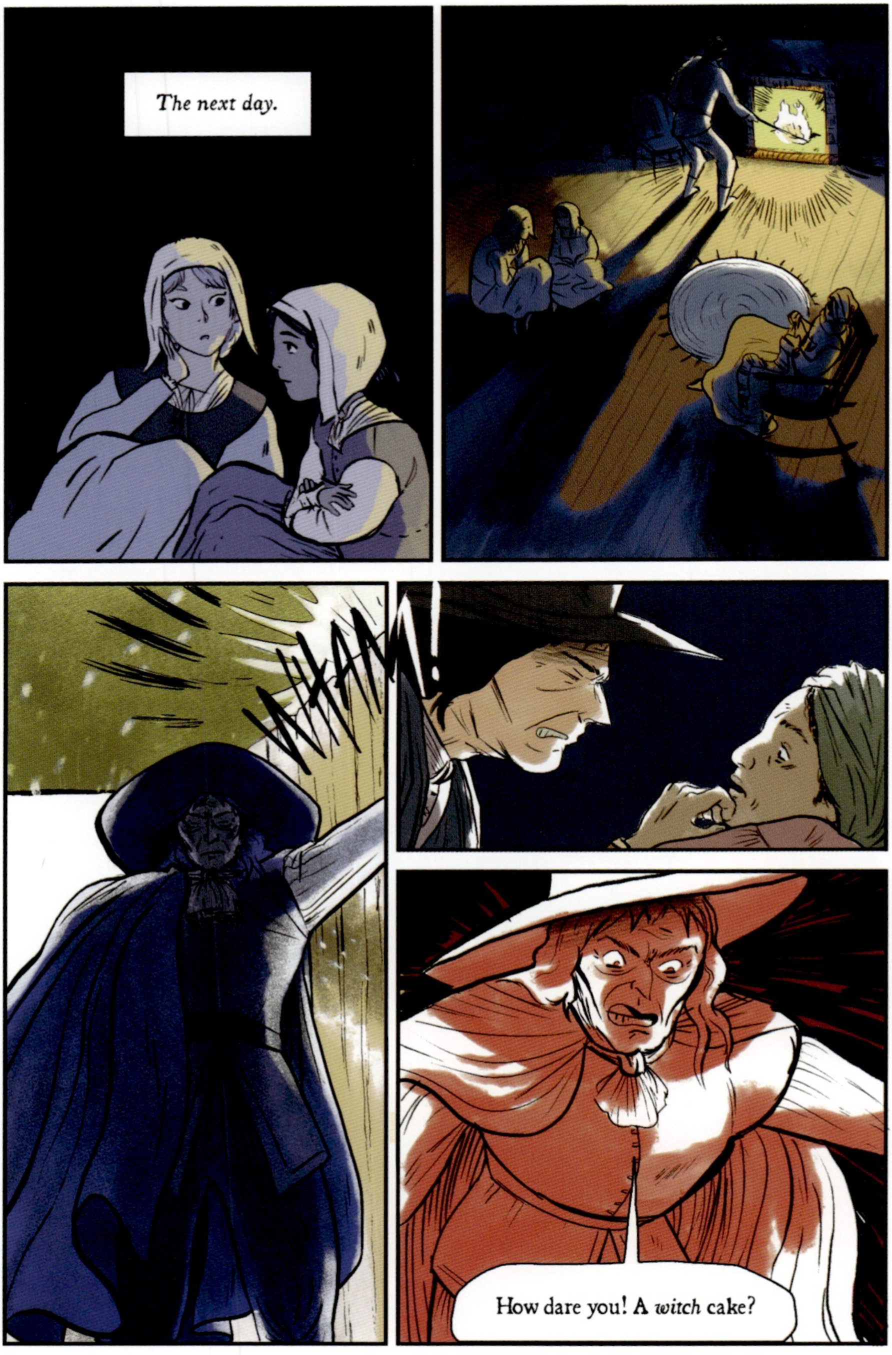
The next day.
WHAM!
How dare you! A witch cake?

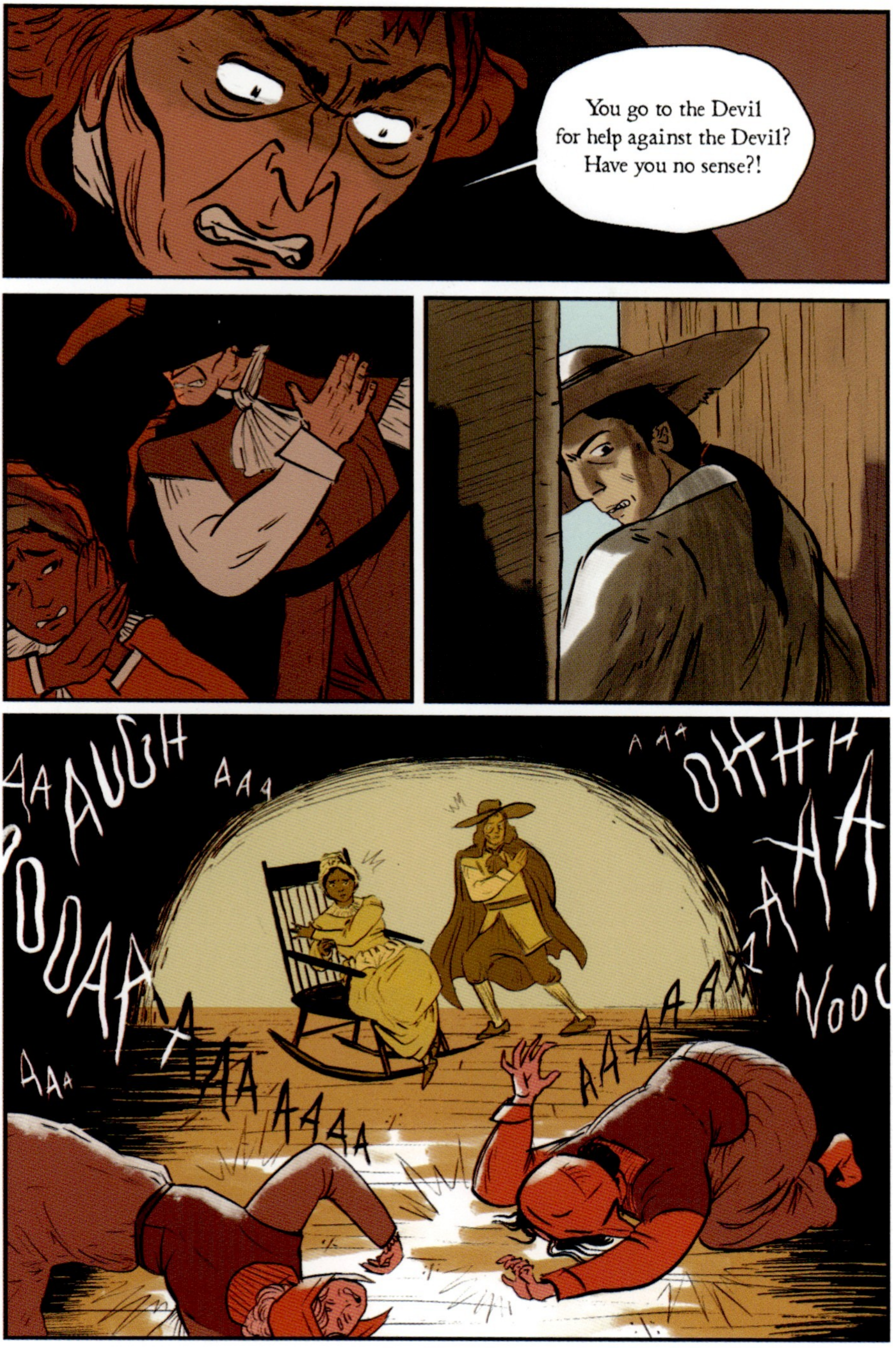
You go to the Devil
for help against the Devil?
Have you no sense?!

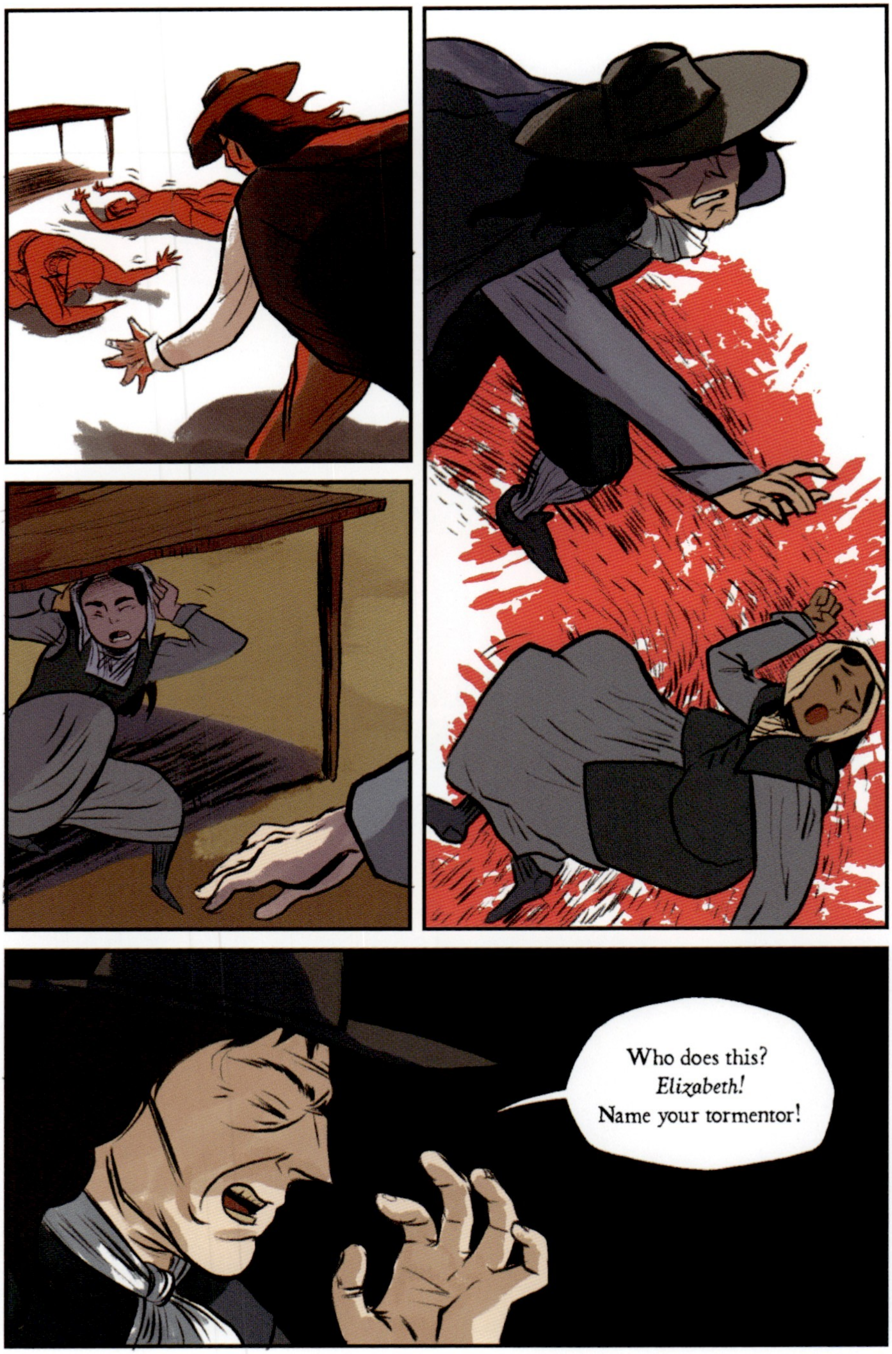
Who does this?
Elizabeth!
Name your tormentor!

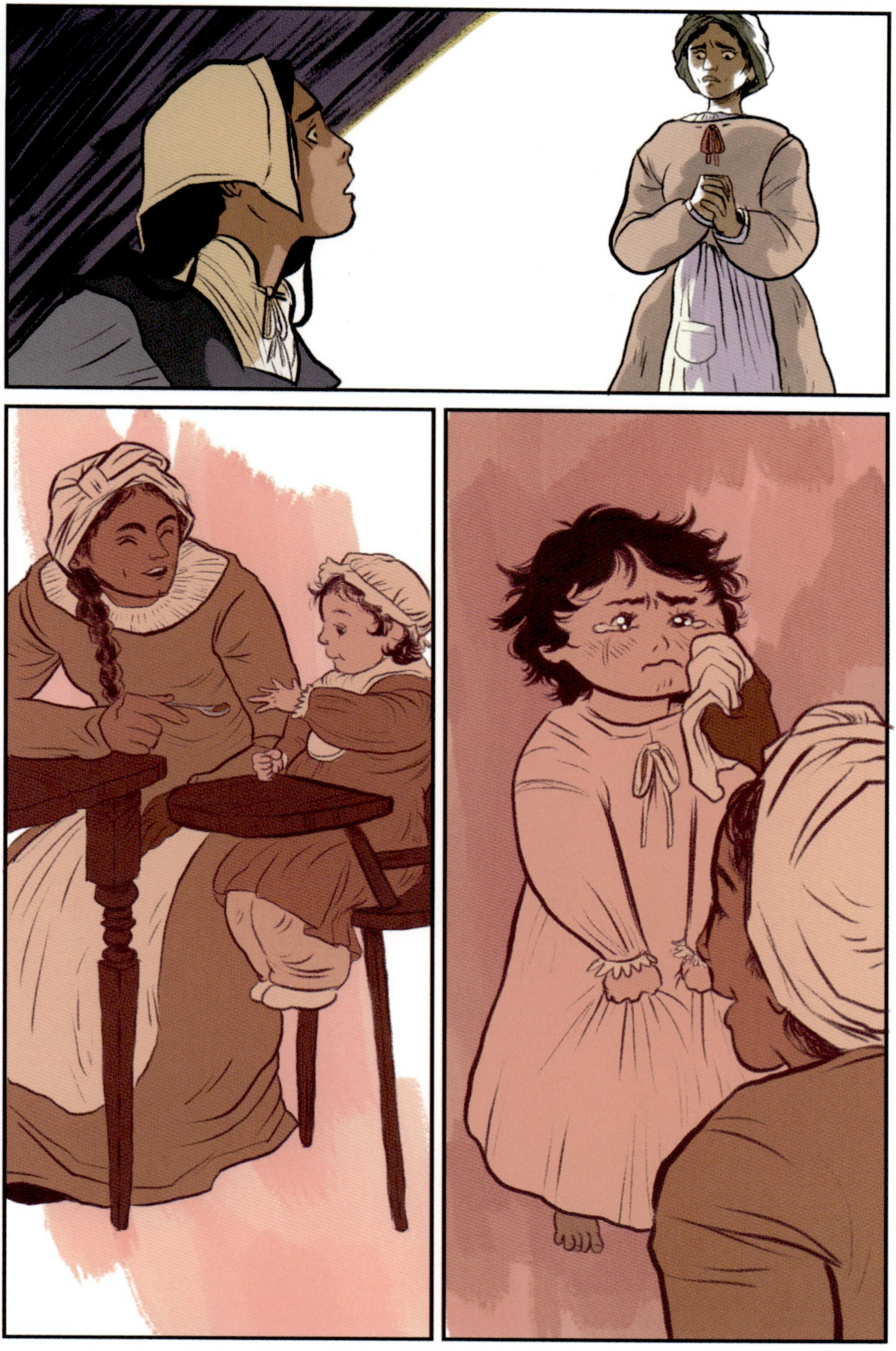

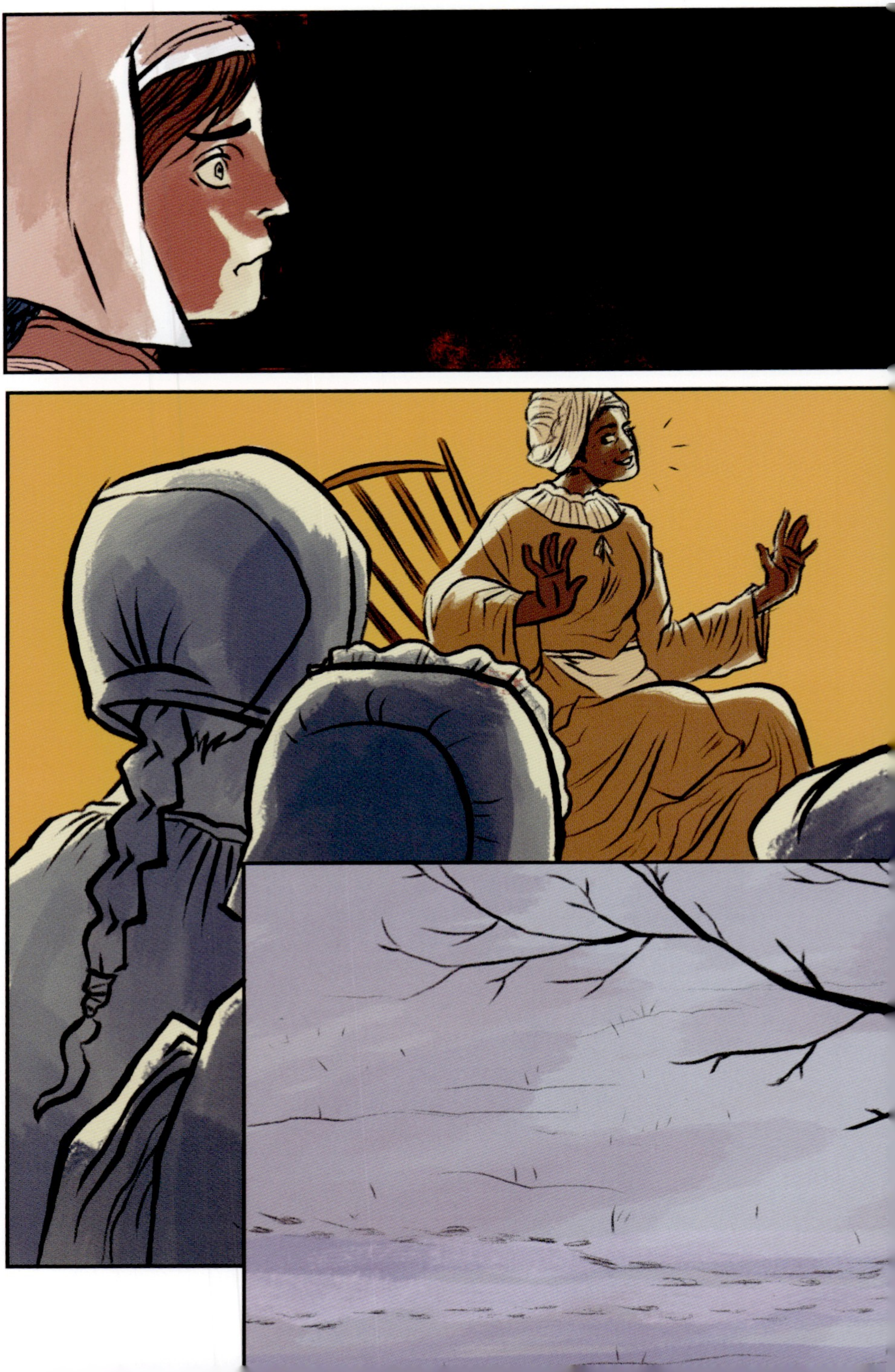

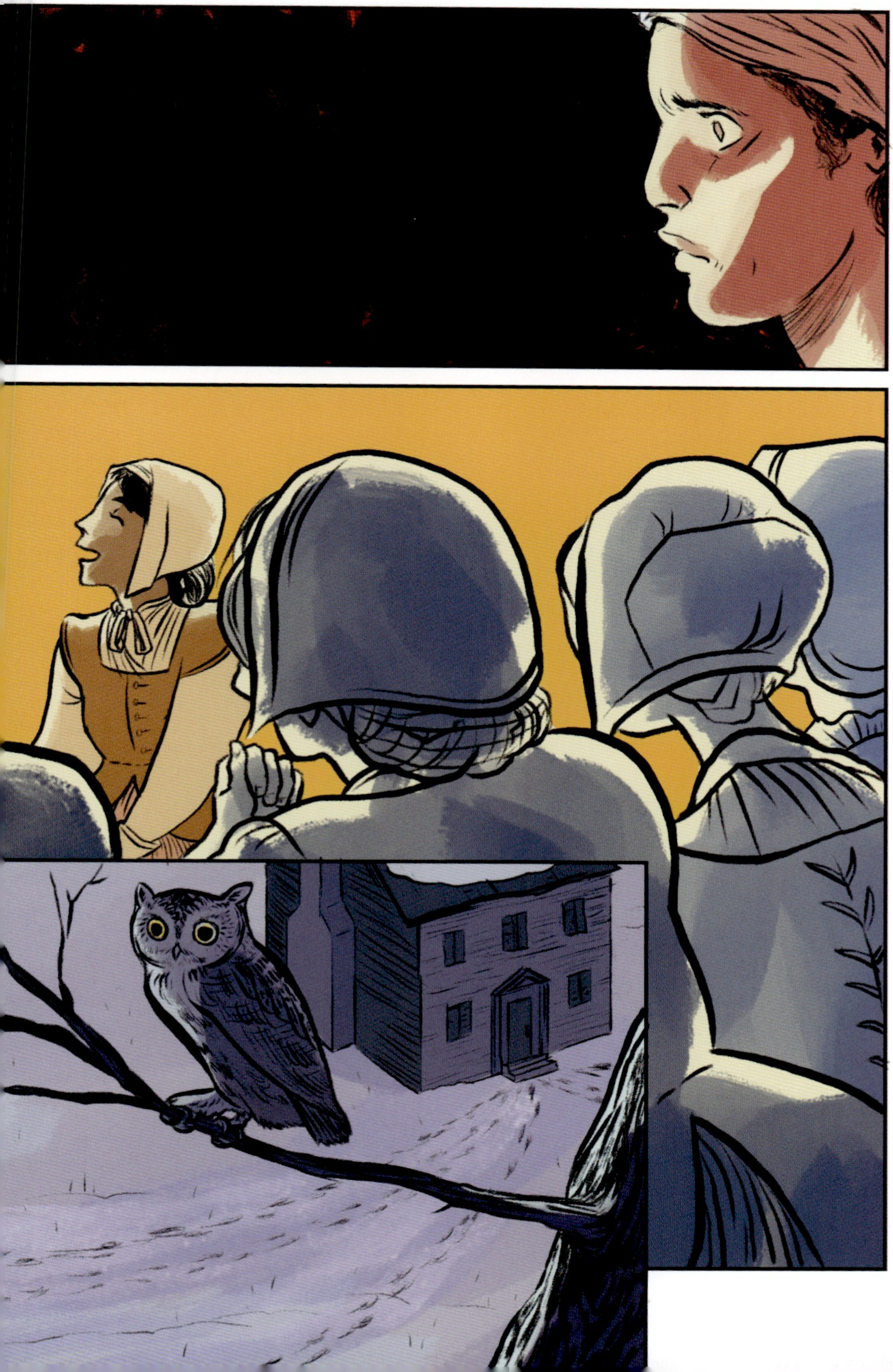

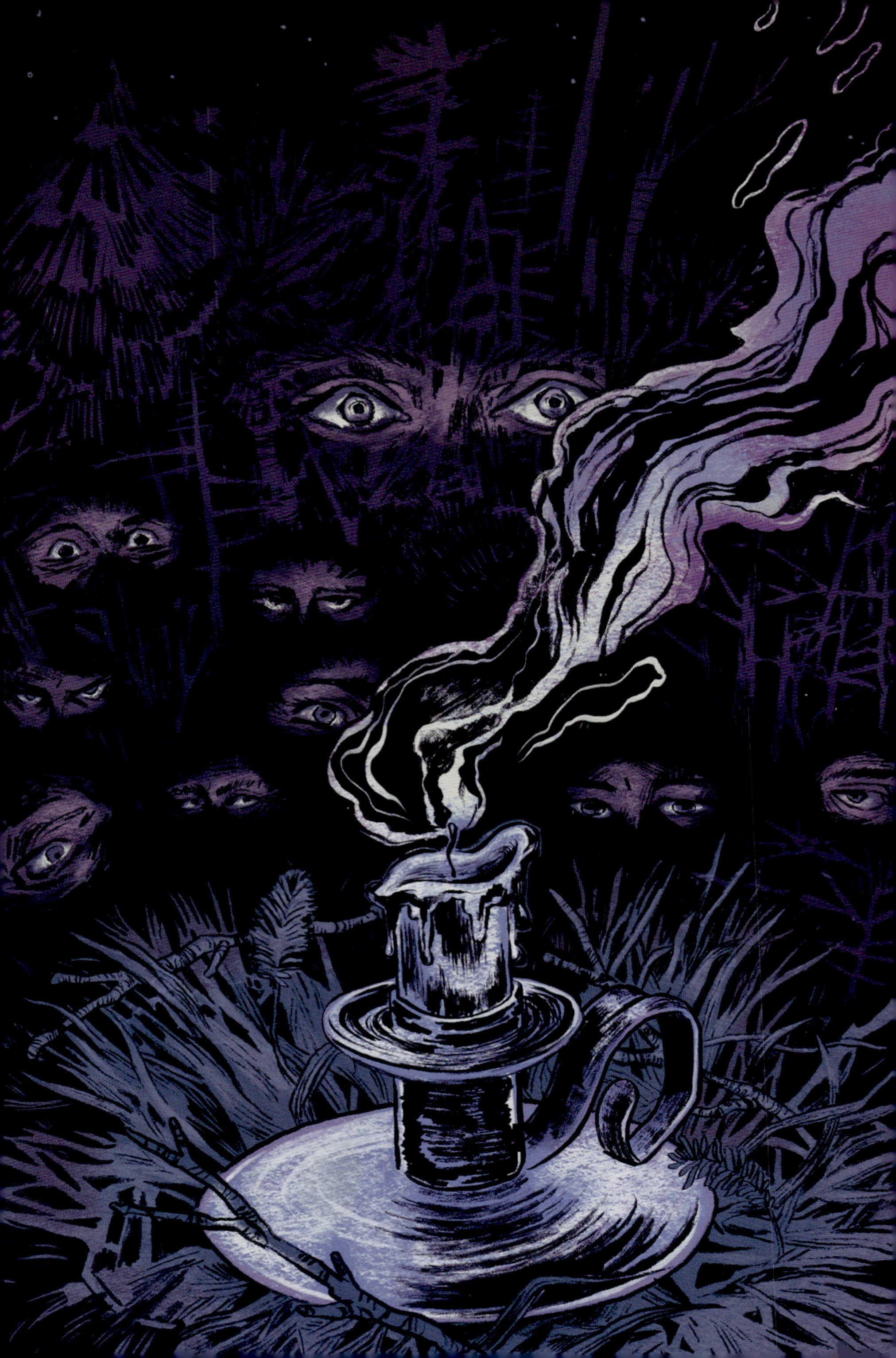

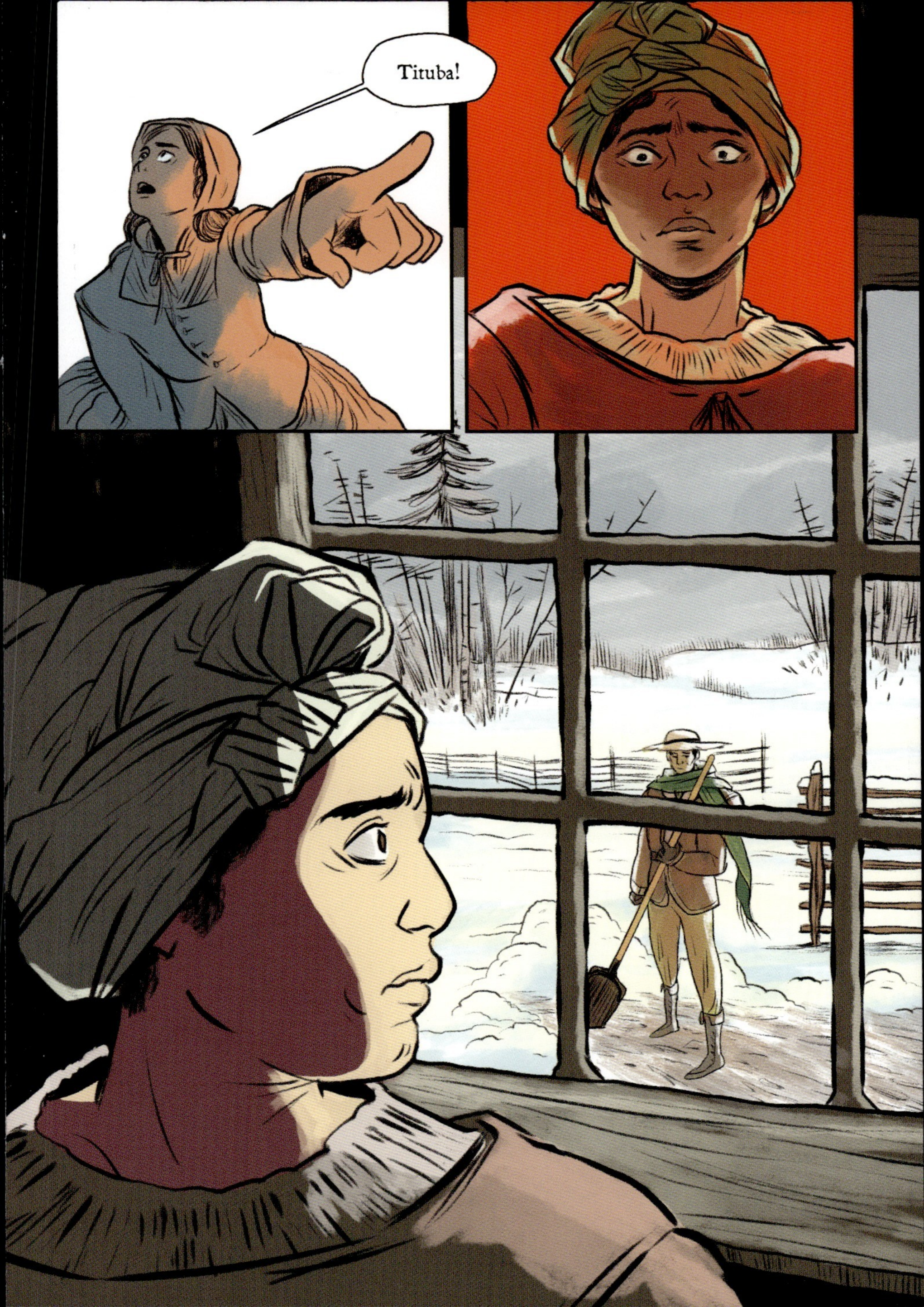
Tituba!

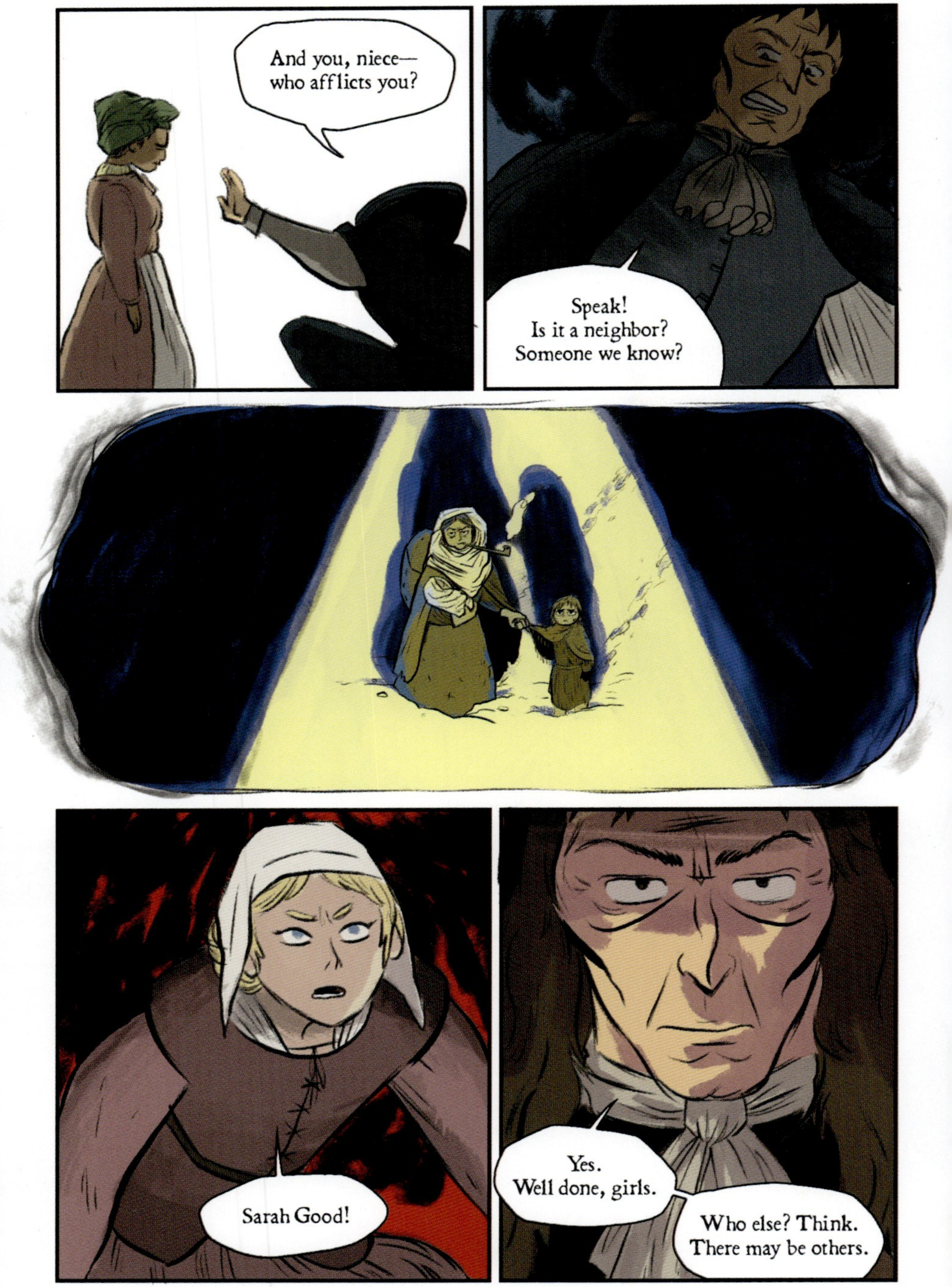
And you, niece—
who afflicts you?
Speak!
Is it a neighbor?
Someone we know?
Sarah Good!
Yes.
Well done, girls.
Who else? Think.
There may be others.

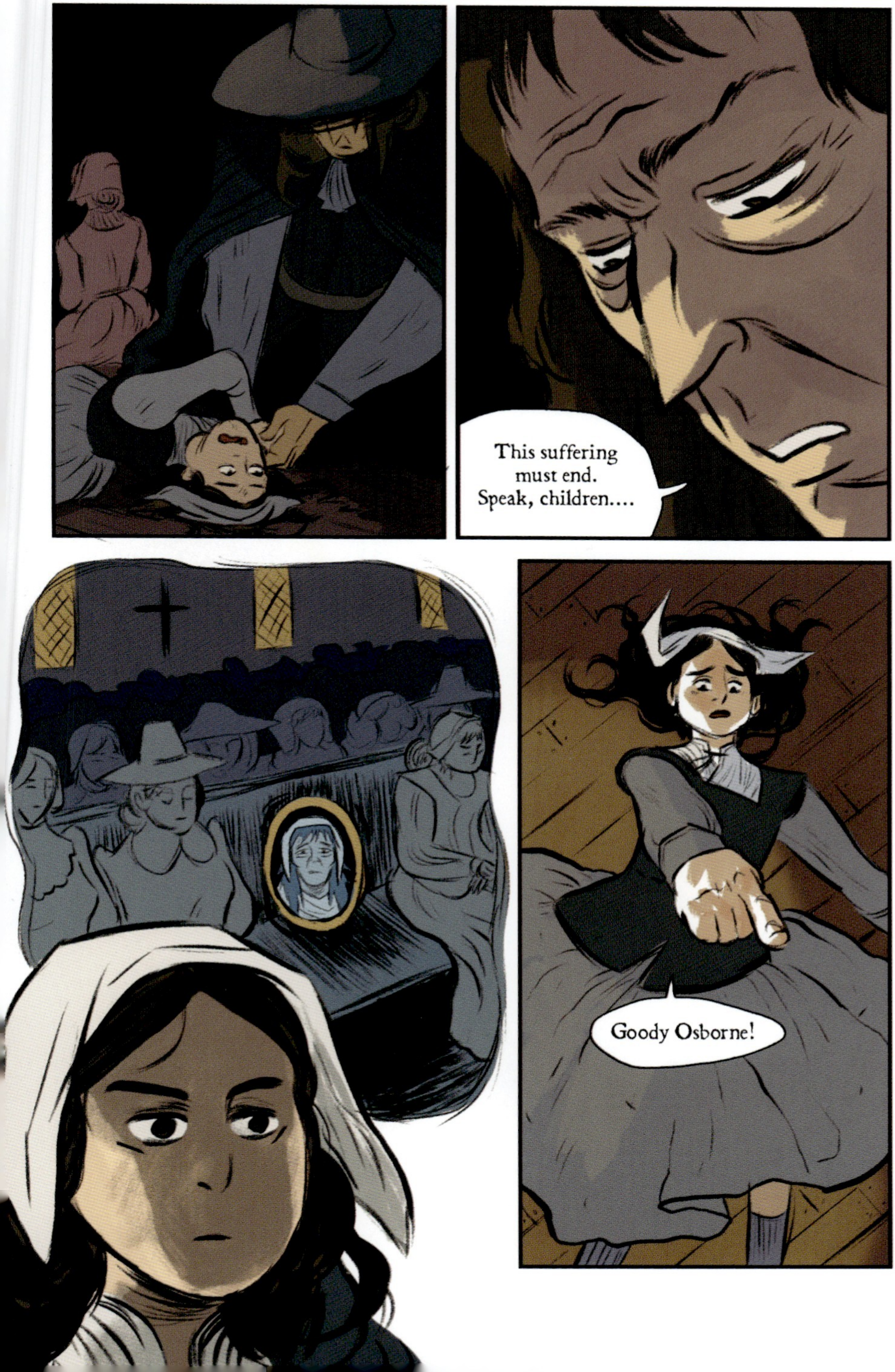
This suffering must end. Speak, children....
Goody Osborne!

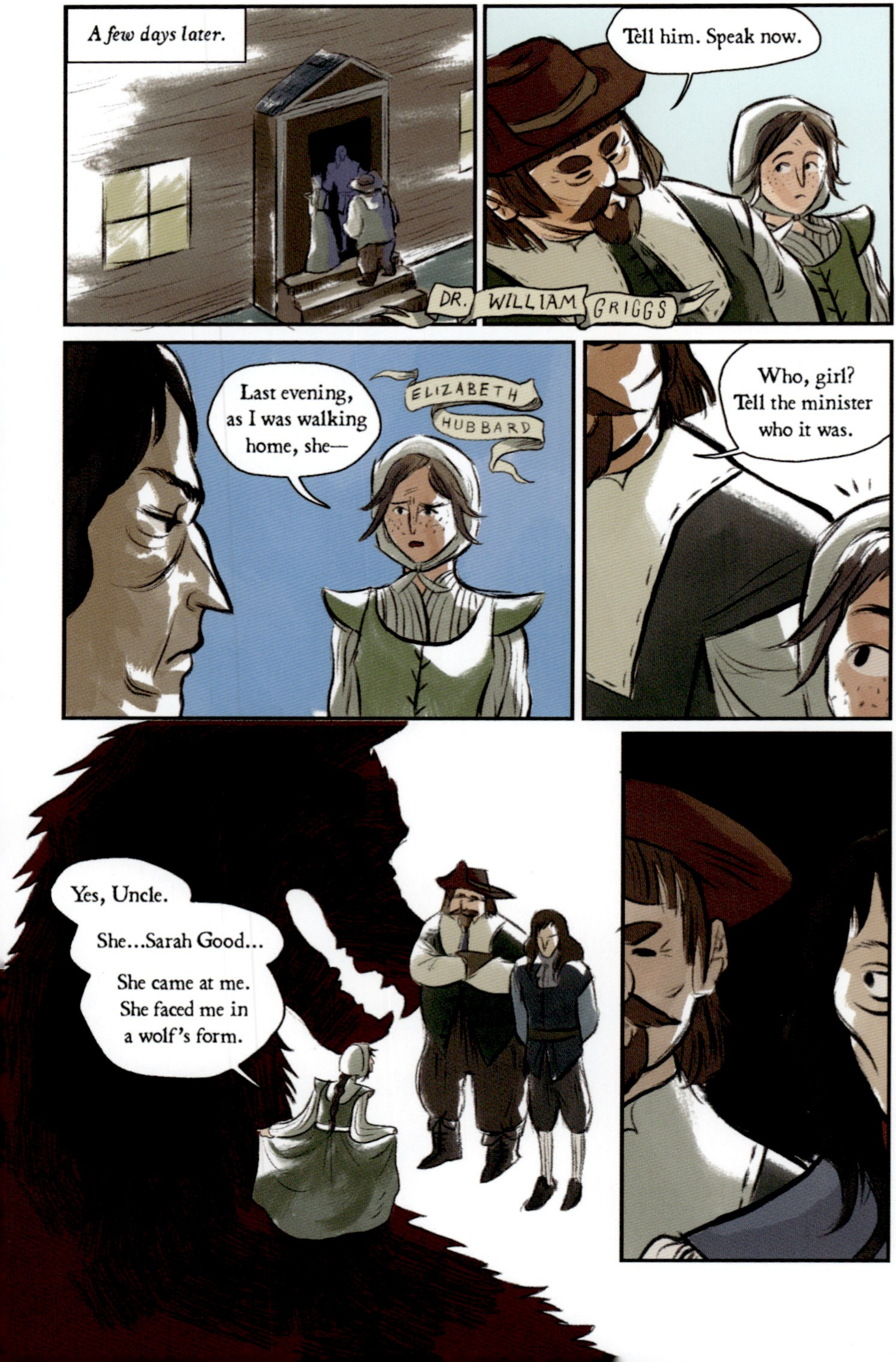
A few days later.
Tell him. Speak now.
DR. WILLIAM GRIGGS
Last evening, as I was walking home, she—
ELIZABETH HUBBARD
Who, girl? Tell the minister who it was.
Yes, Uncle.
She...Sarah Good...
She came at me. She faced me in a wolf's form.

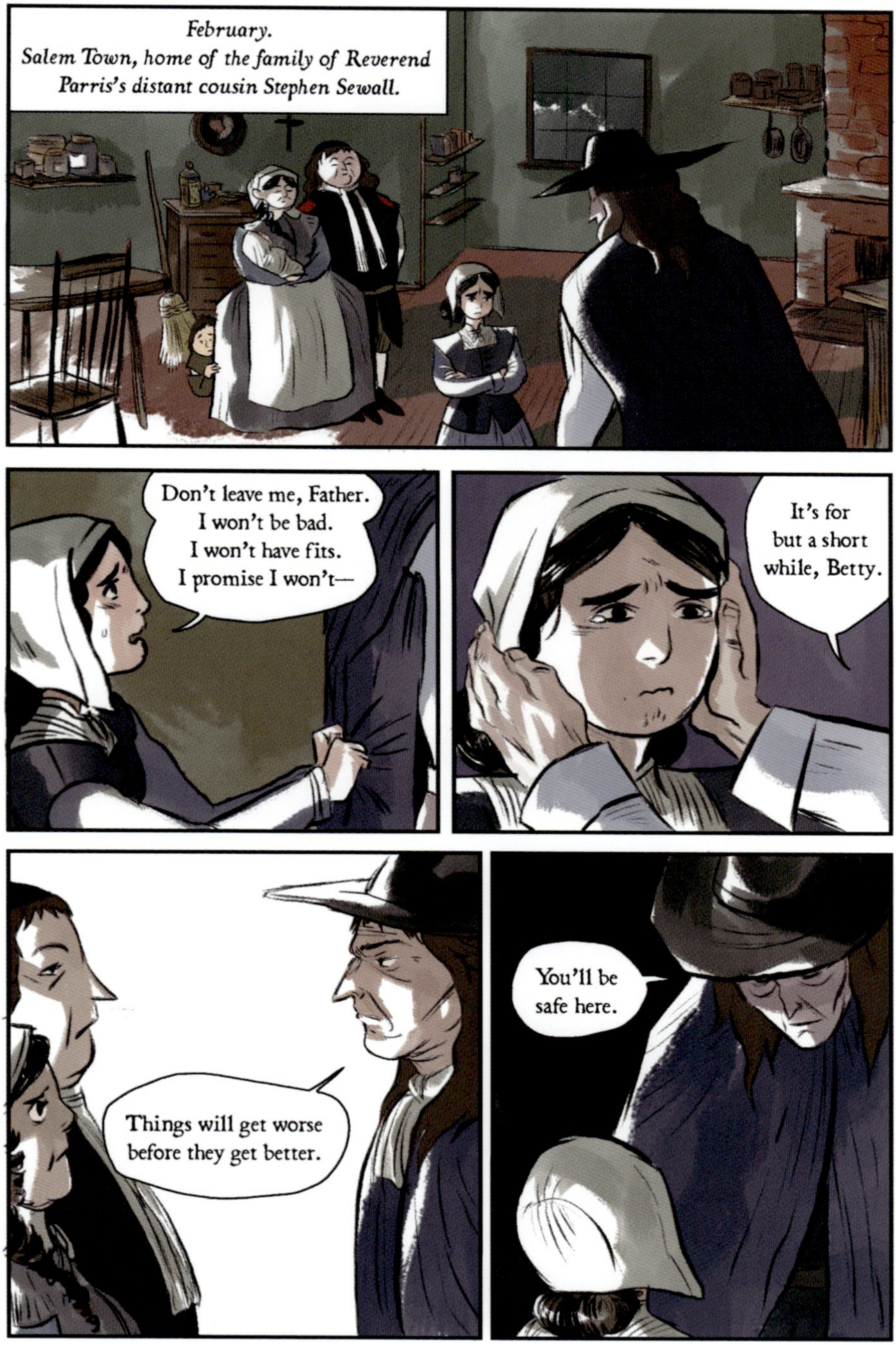
February.
Salem Town, home of the family of Reverend Parris's distant cousin Stephen Sewall.
Don't leave me, Father. I won't be bad. I won't have fits. I promise I won't—
It's for but a short while, Betty.
Things will get worse before they get better.
You'll be safe here.

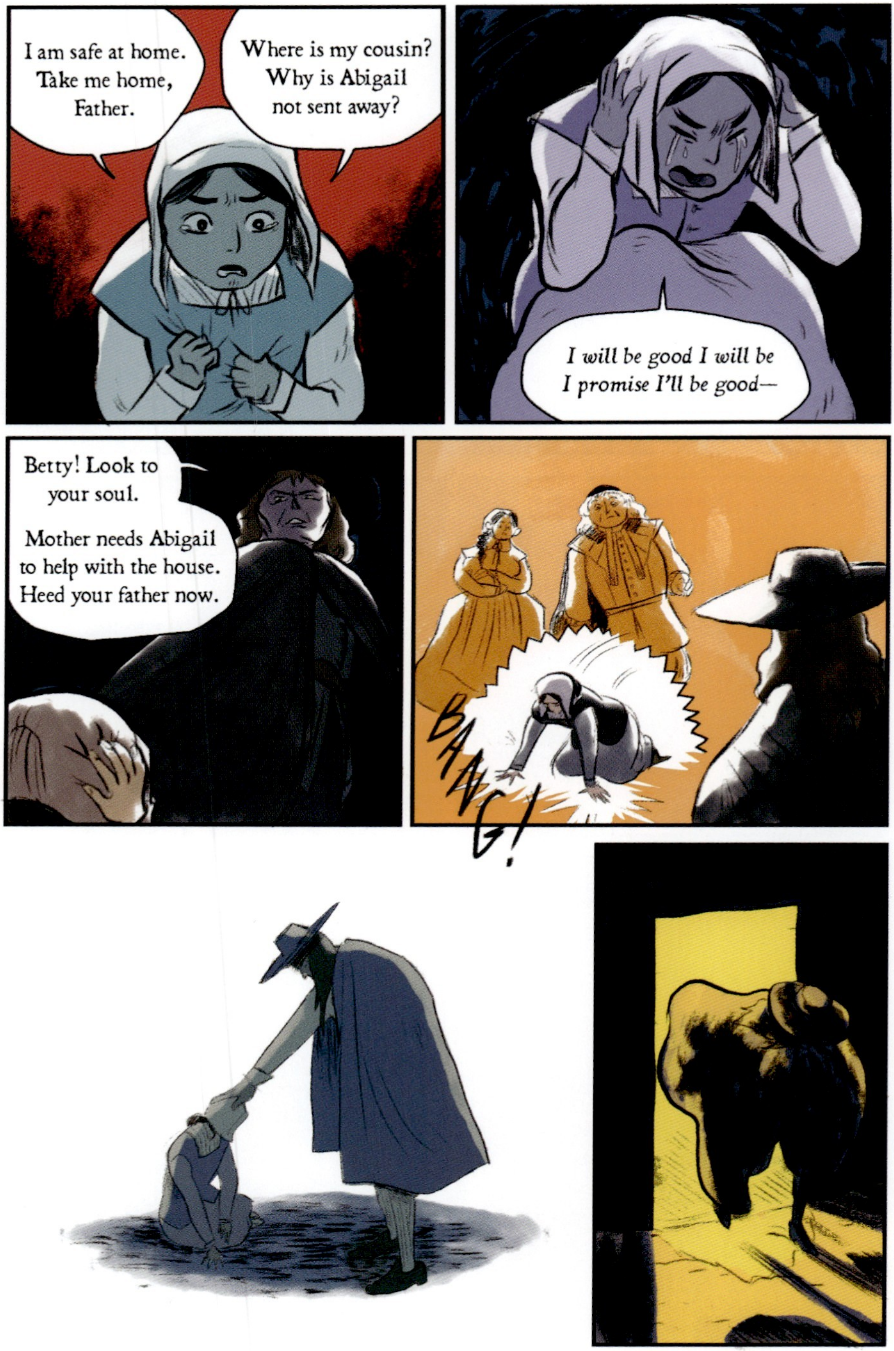
I am safe at home. Take me home, Father.
Where is my cousin? Why is Abigail not sent away?
I will be good I will be I promise I'll be good—
Betty! Look to your soul.
Mother needs Abigail to help with the house. Heed your father now.
BANG!

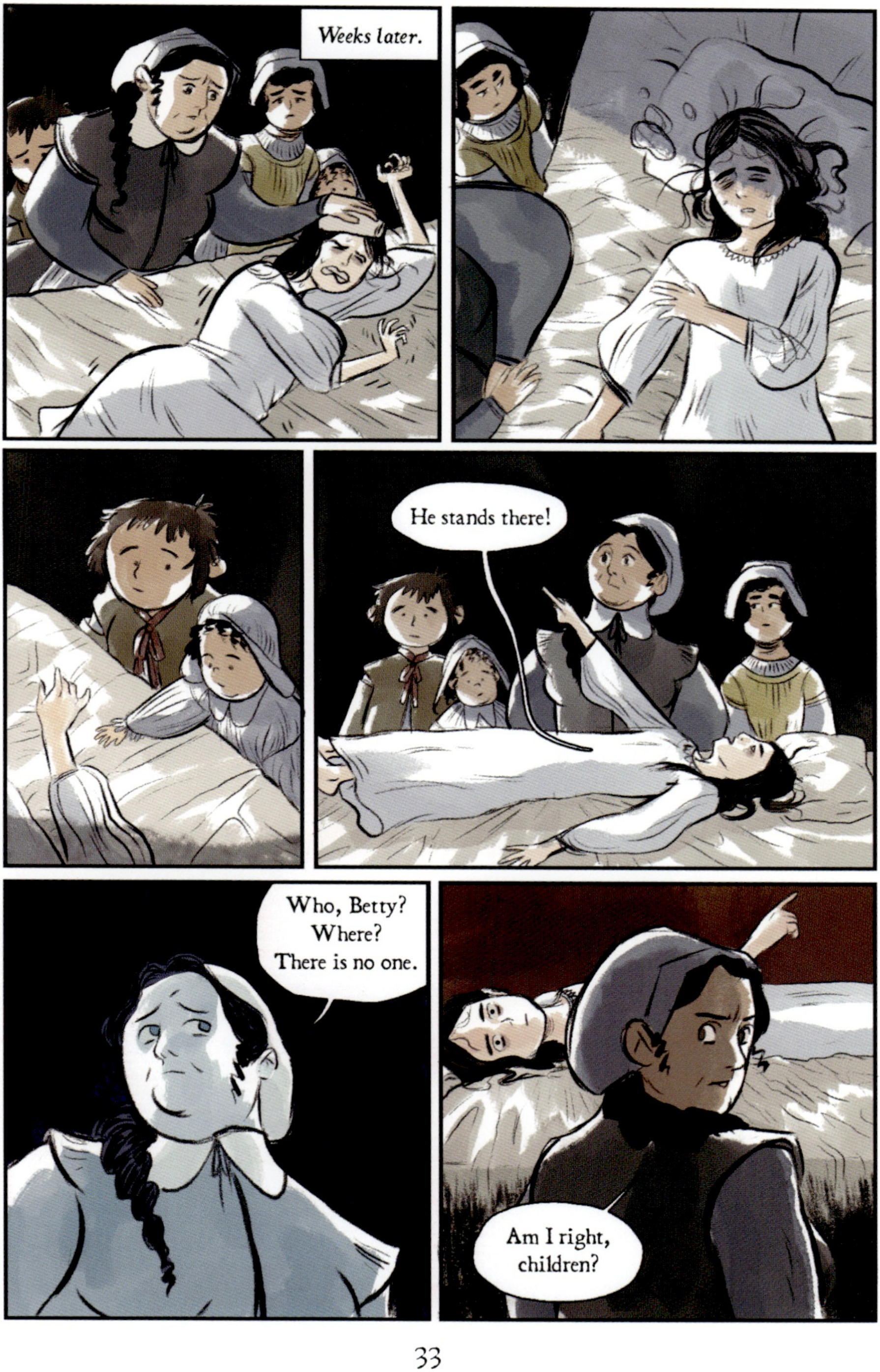
Weeks later.
He stands there!
Who, Betty? Where? There is no one.
Am I right, children?

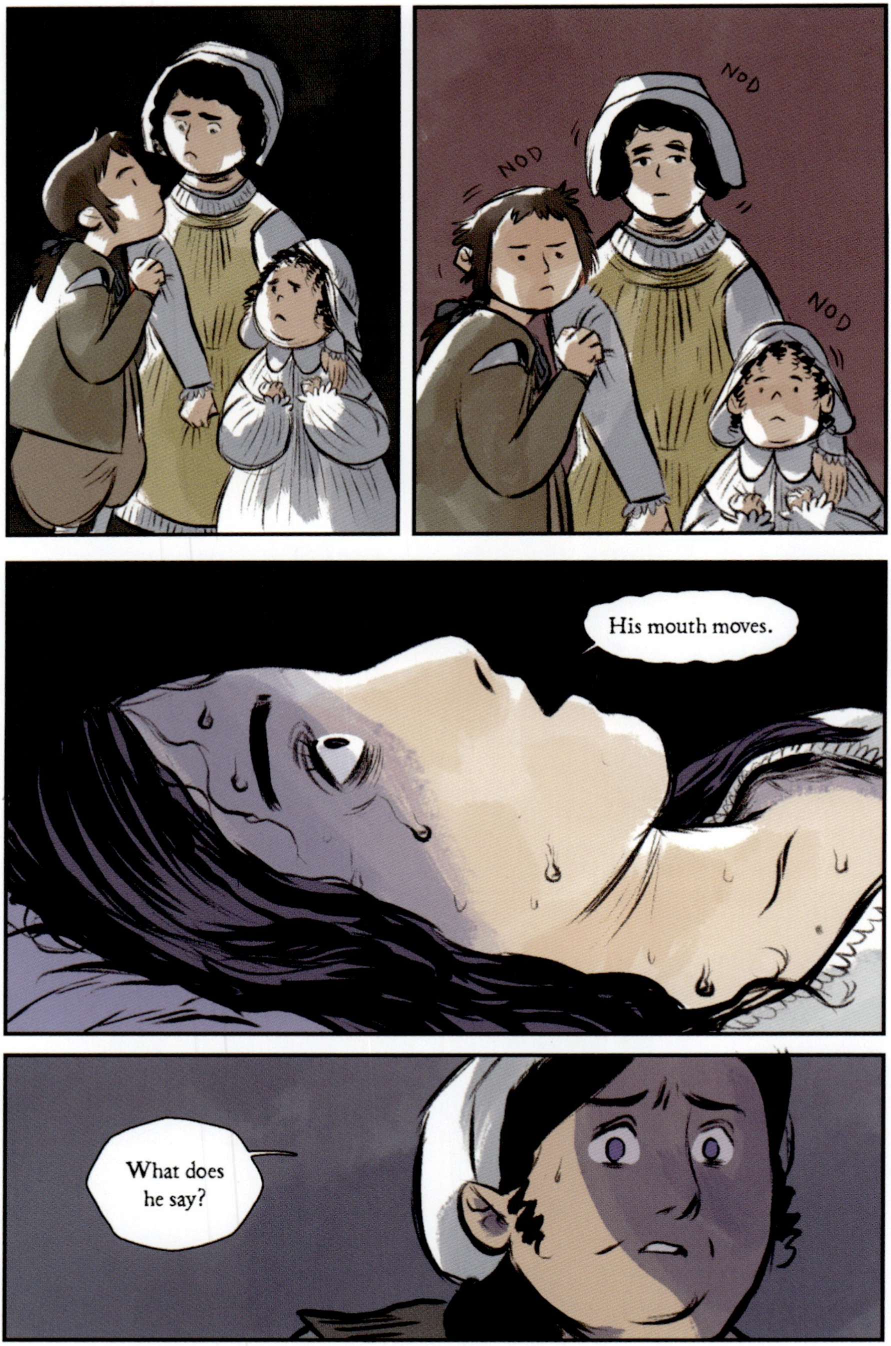
NOD
NOD
NOD
His mouth moves.
What does he say?

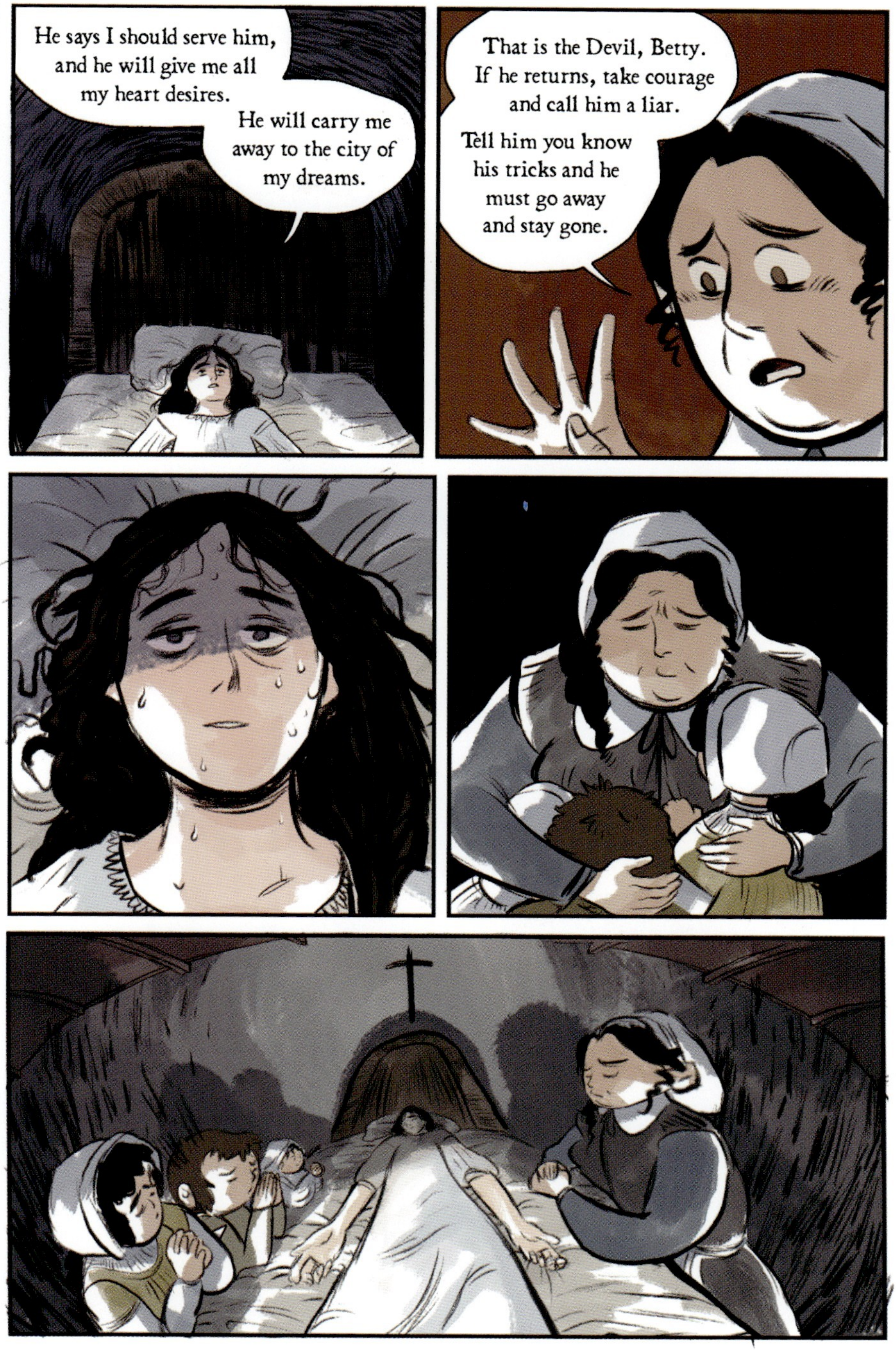
He says I should serve him, and he will give me all my heart desires.
He will carry me away to the city of my dreams.
That is the Devil, Betty. If he returns, take courage and call him a liar.
Tell him you know his tricks and he must go away and stay gone.

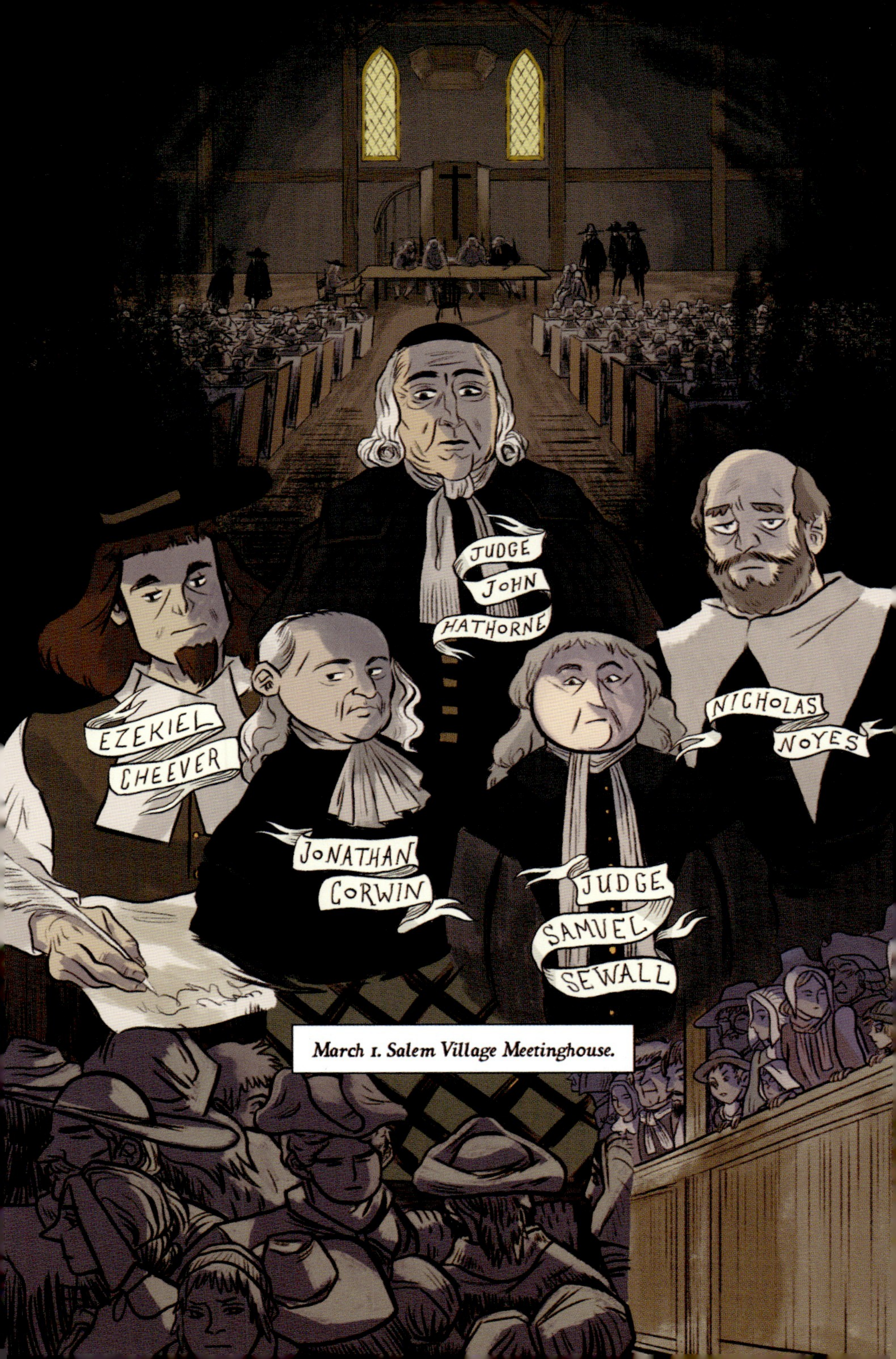
JUDGE JOHN HATHORNE
EZEKIEL CHEEVER
JONATHAN CORWIN
JUDGE SAMUEL SEWALL
NICHOLAS NOYES
March 1. Salem Village Meetinghouse.

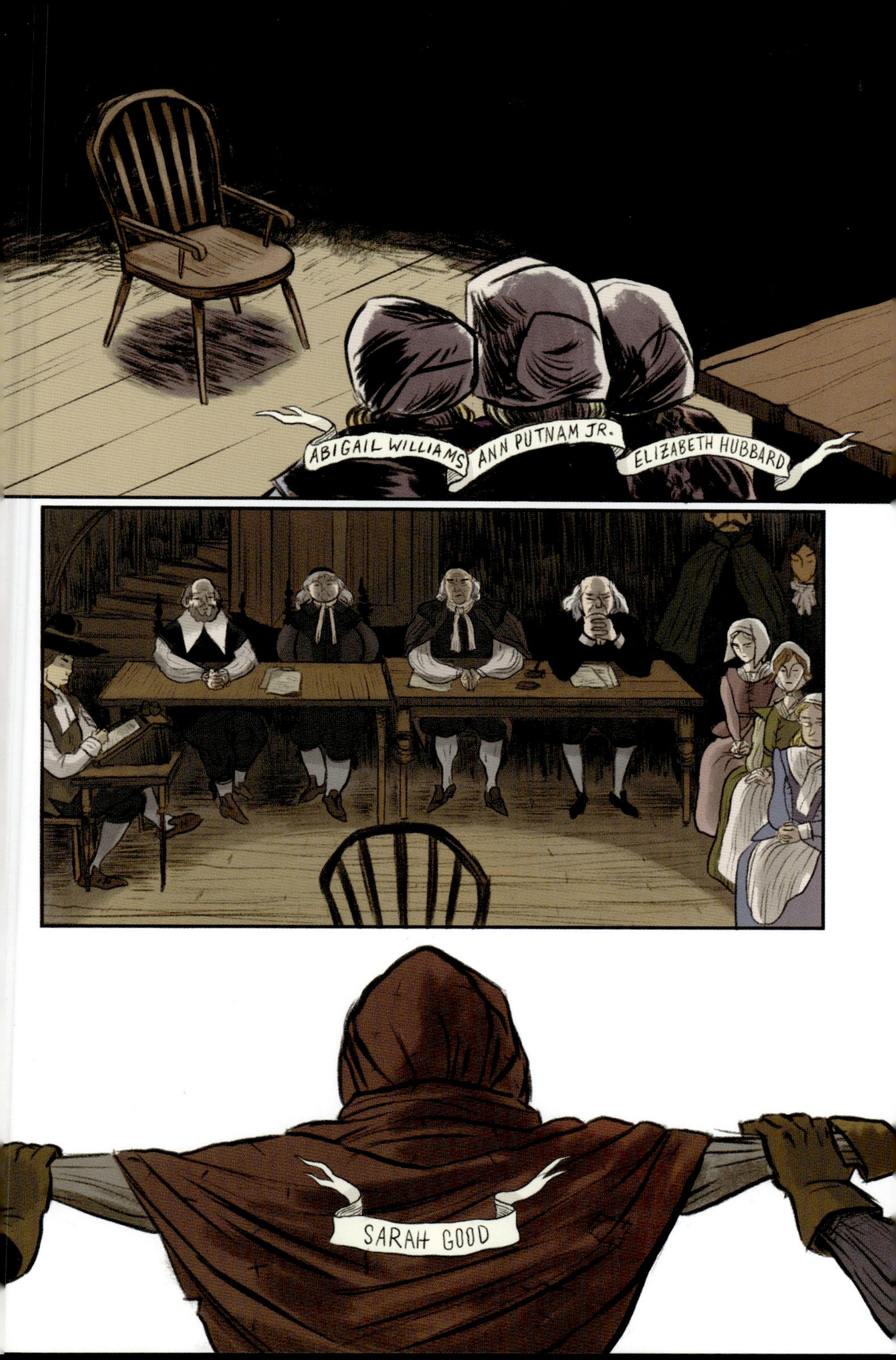
ABIGAIL WILLIAMS
ANN PUTNAM JR.
ELIZABETH HUBBARD
SARAH GOOD

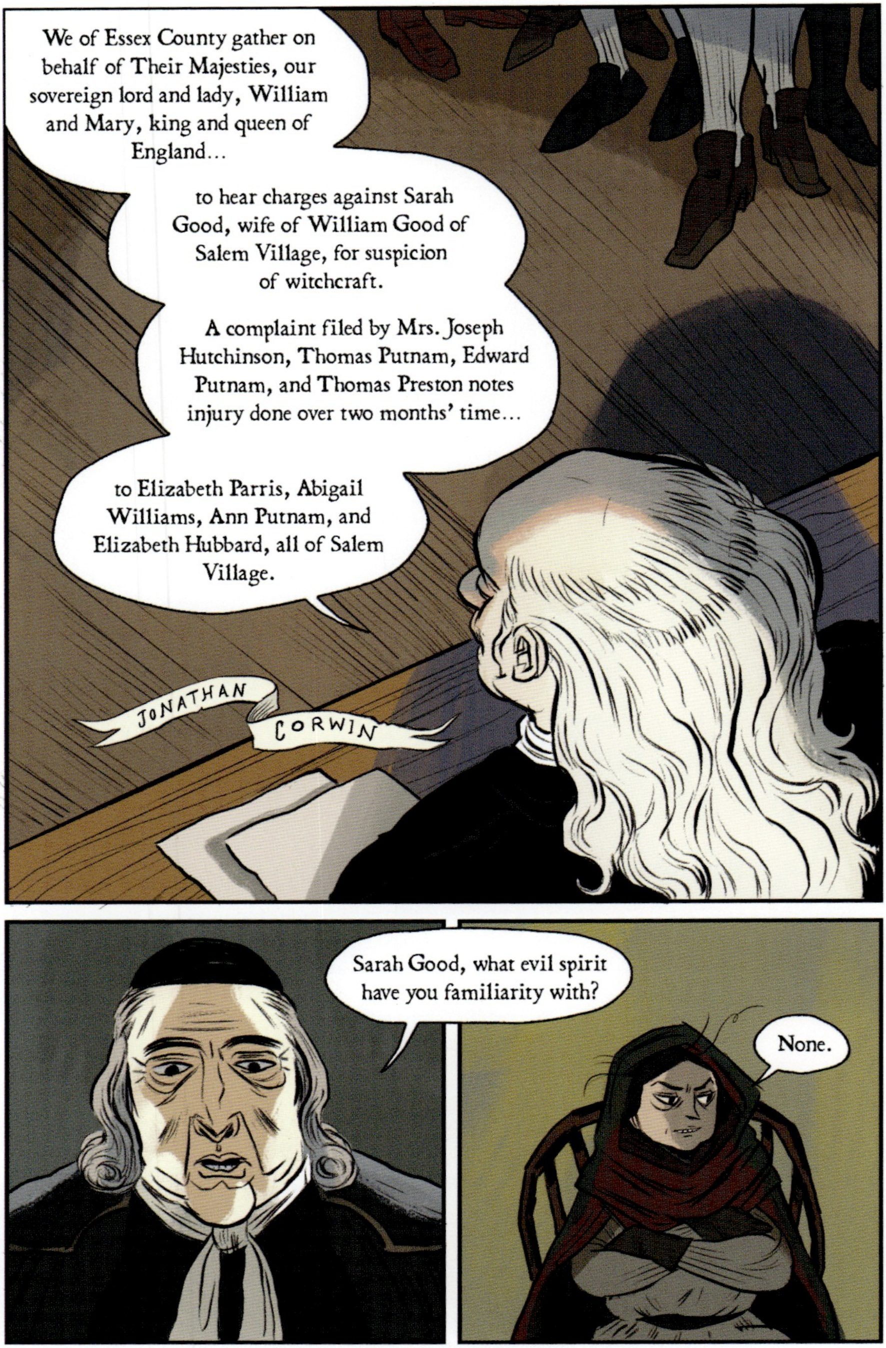
We of Essex County gather on behalf of Their Majesties, our sovereign lord and lady, William and Mary, king and queen of England...
to hear charges against Sarah Good, wife of William Good of Salem Village, for suspicion of witchcraft.
A complaint filed by Mrs. Joseph Hutchinson, Thomas Putnam, Edward Putnam, and Thomas Preston notes injury done over two months' time...
to Elizabeth Parris, Abigail Williams, Ann Putnam, and Elizabeth Hubbard, all of Salem Village.
JONATHAN CORWIN
Sarah Good, what evil spirit have you familiarity with?
None.

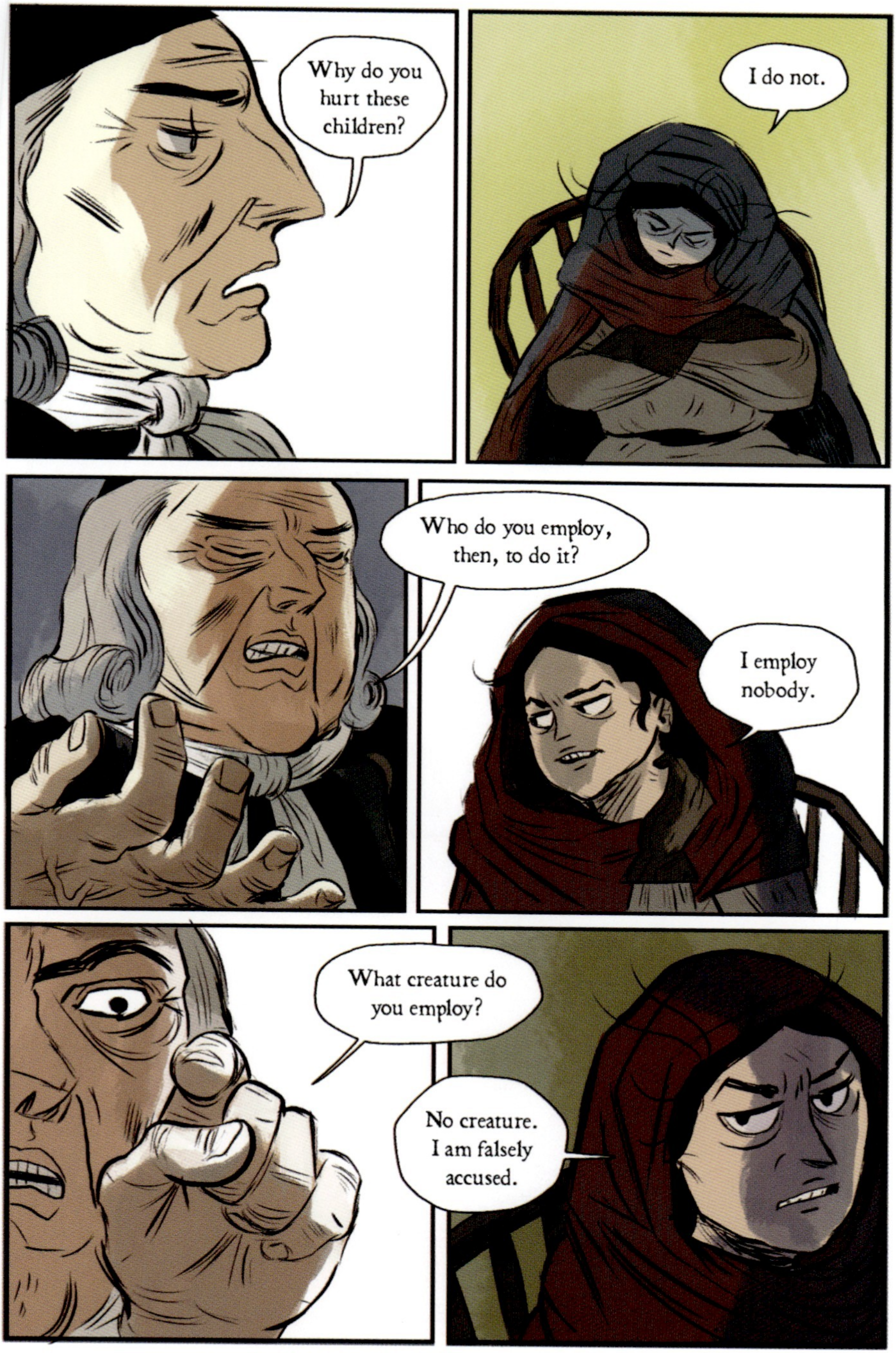
Why do you hurt these children?
I do not.
Who do you employ, then, to do it?
I employ nobody.
What creature do you employ?
No creature. I am falsely accused.

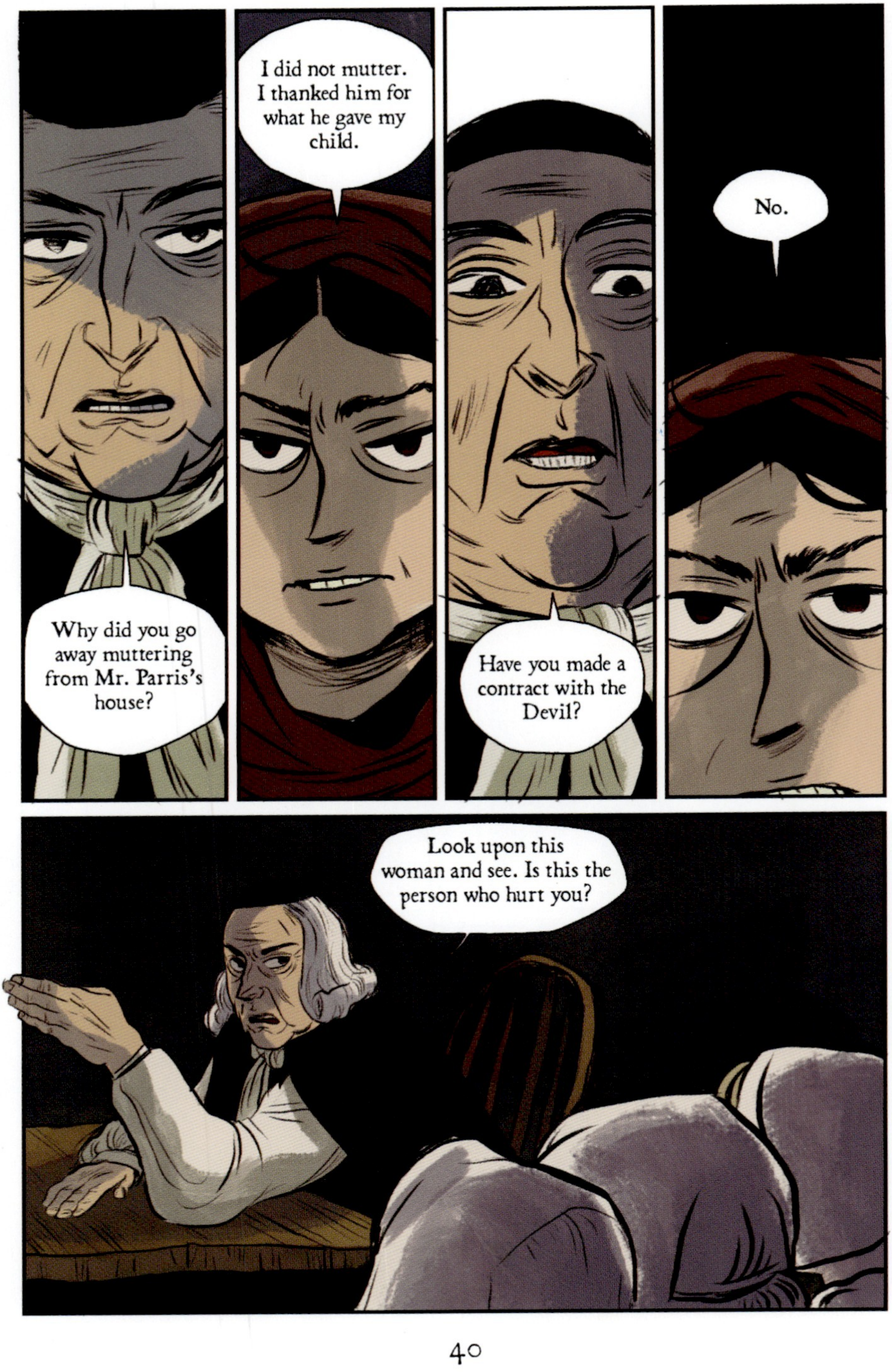
Why did you go away muttering from Mr. Parris's house?
I did not mutter. I thanked him for what he gave my child.
Have you made a contract with the Devil?
No.
Look upon this woman and see. Is this the person who hurt you?

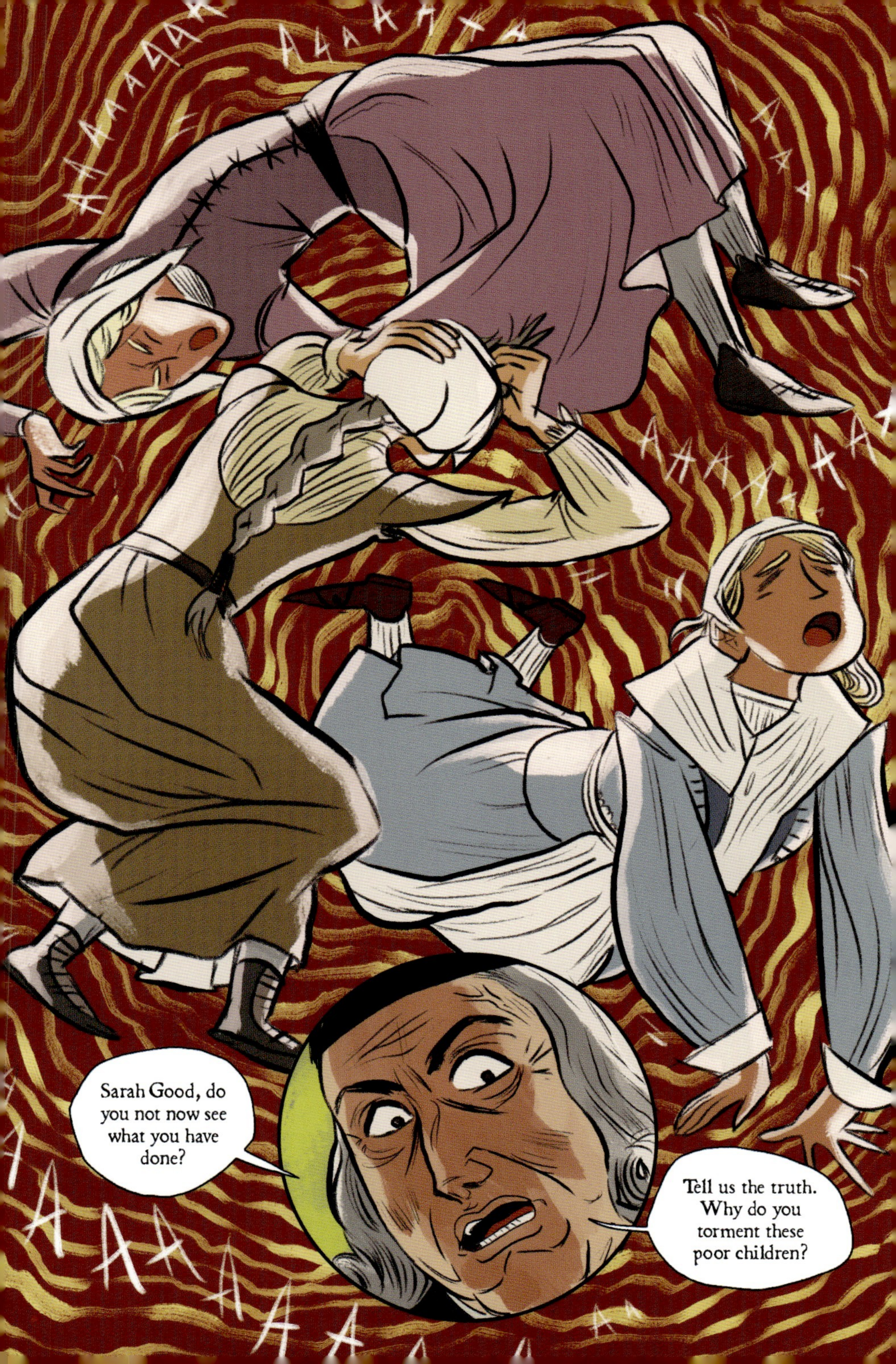
Sarah Good, do you not now see what you have done?
Tell us the truth. Why do you torment these poor children?

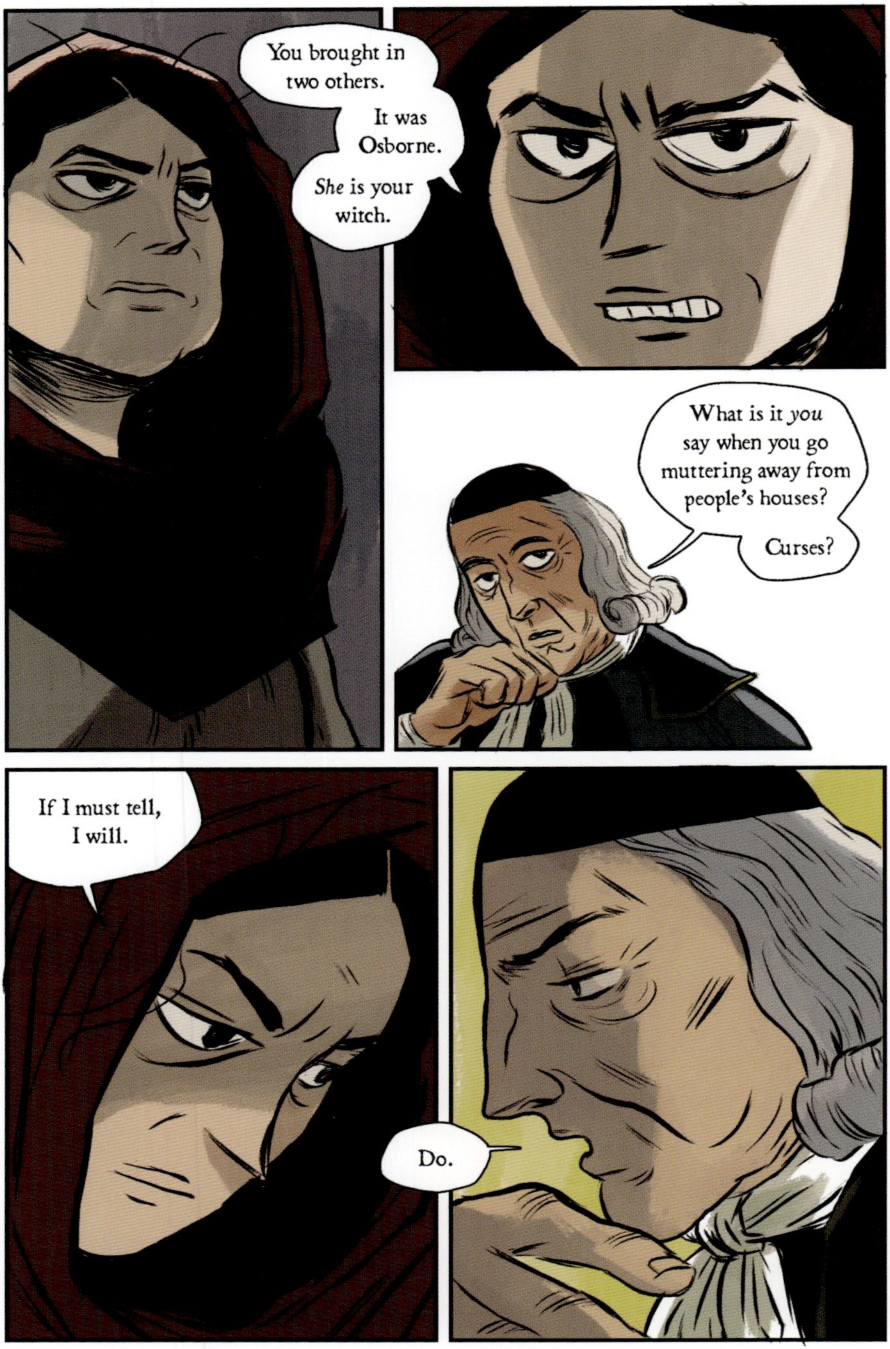
You brought in two others.
It was Osborne.
She is your witch.
What is it *you* say when you go muttering away from people's houses?
Curses?
If I must tell, I will.
Do.

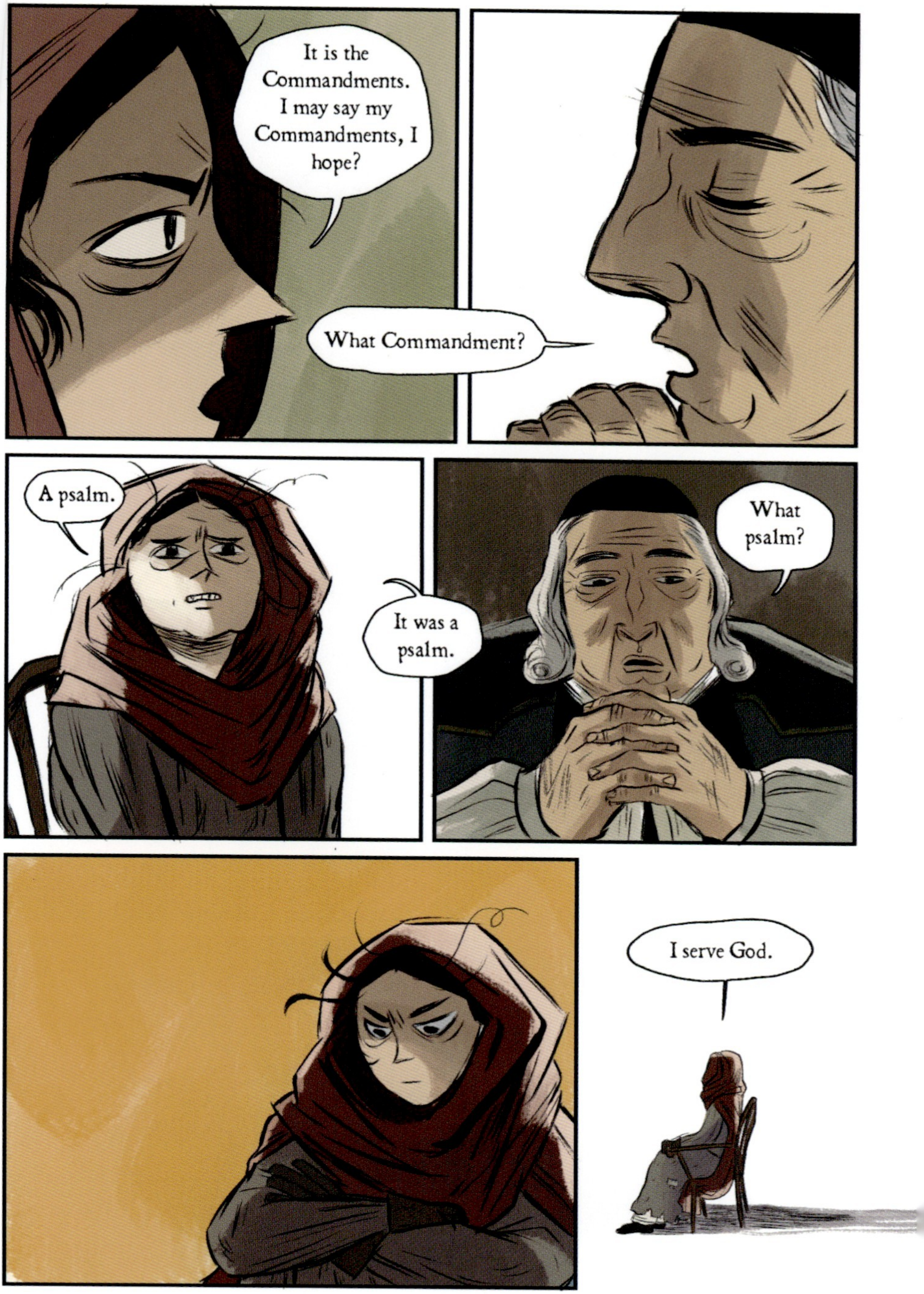
It is the Commandments. I may say my Commandments, I hope?
What Commandment?
A psalm.
It was a psalm.
What psalm?
I serve God.

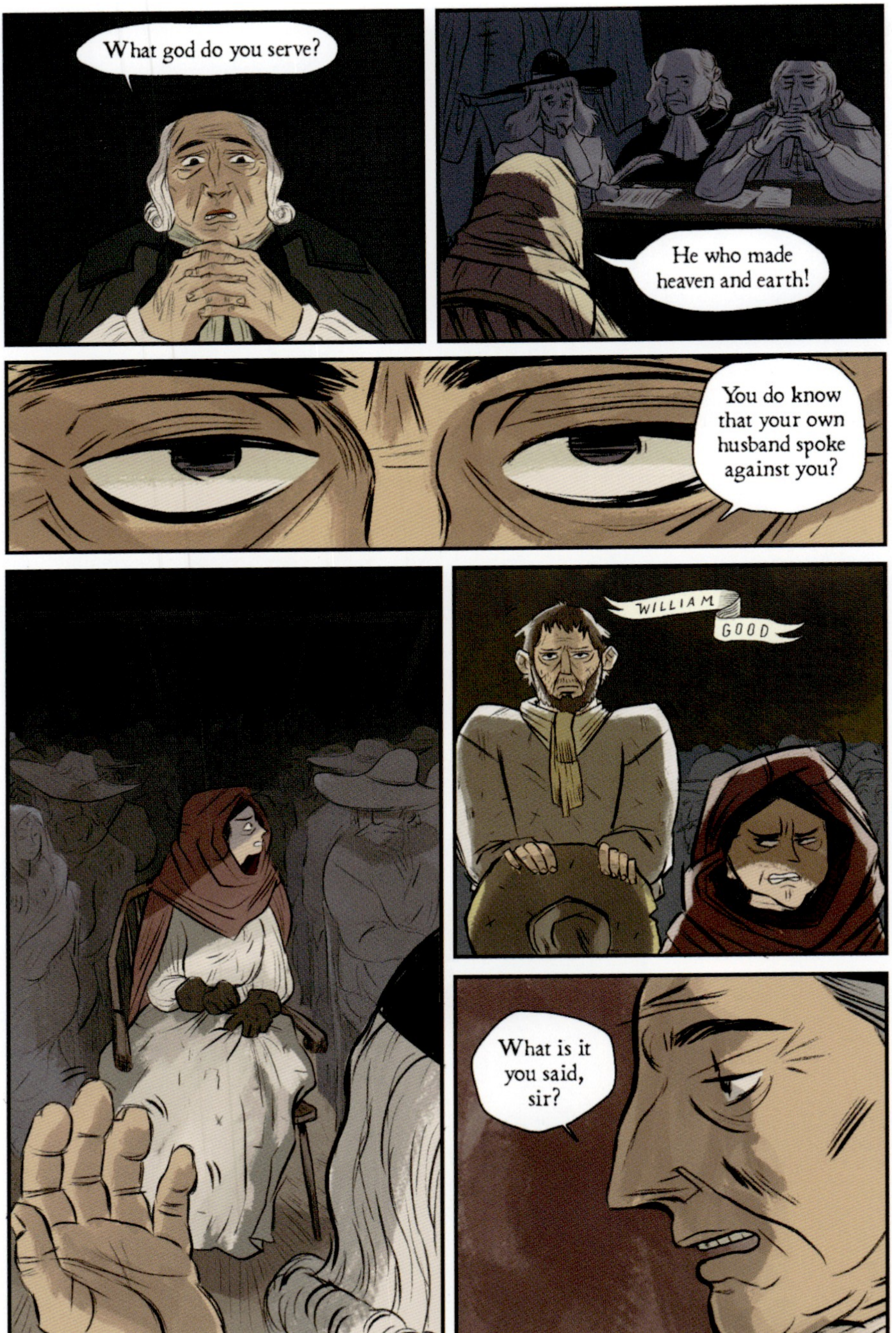
What god do you serve?
He who made heaven and earth!
You do know that your own husband spoke against you?
WILLIAM GOOD
What is it you said, sir?

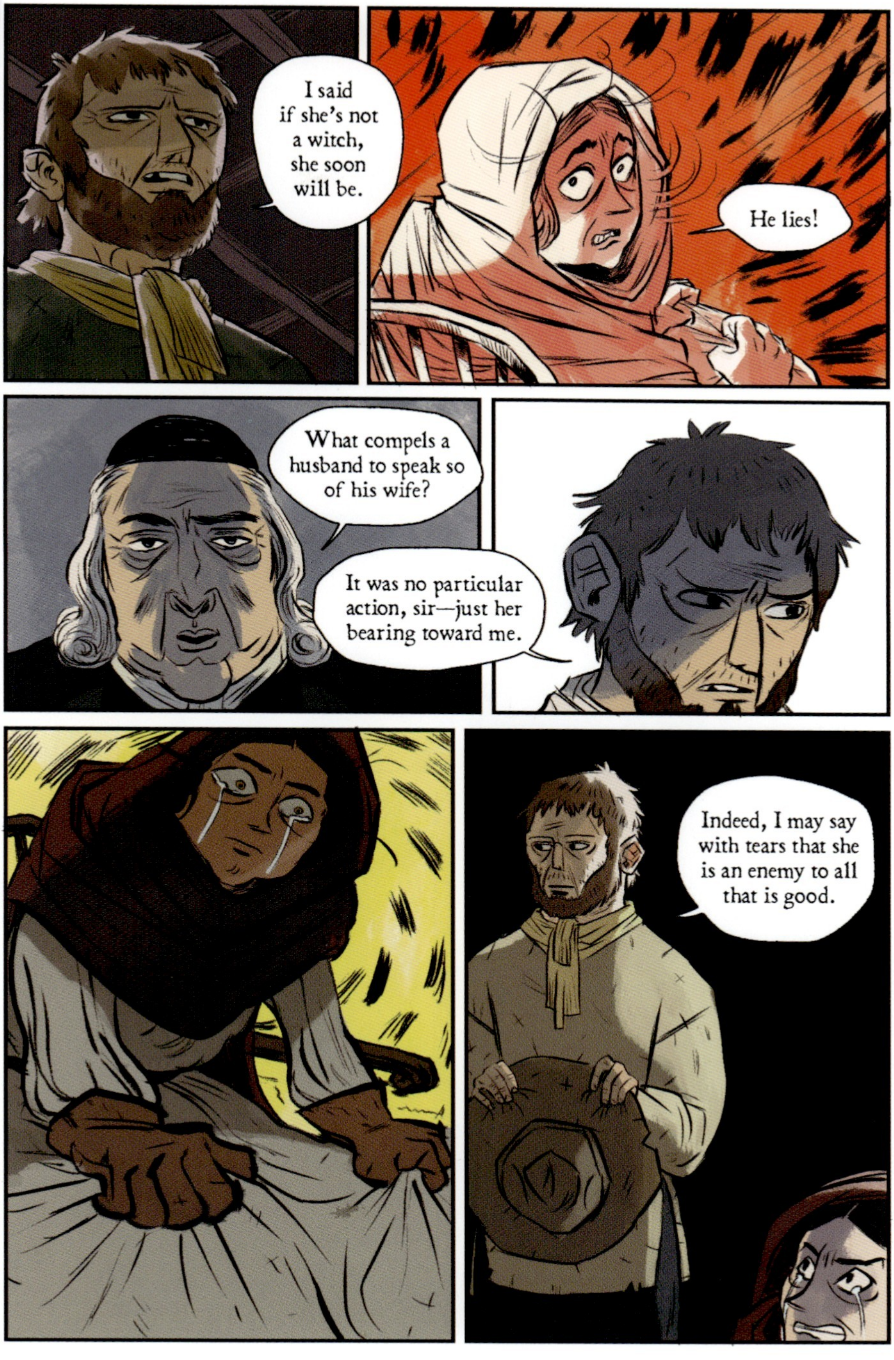
I said if she's not a witch, she soon will be.
He lies!
What compels a husband to speak so of his wife?
It was no particular action, sir—just her bearing toward me.
Indeed, I may say with tears that she is an enemy to all that is good.

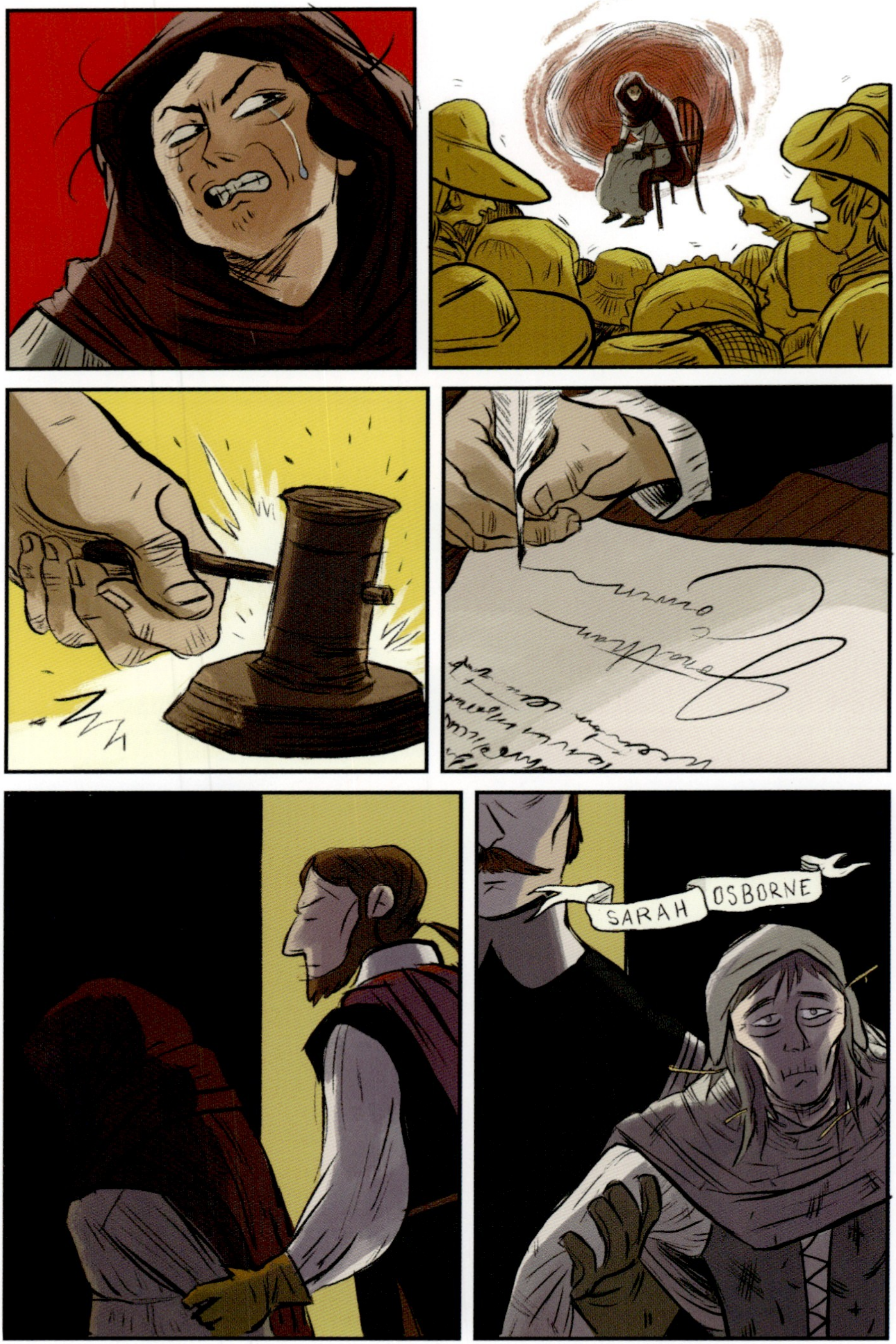
SARAH OSBORNE

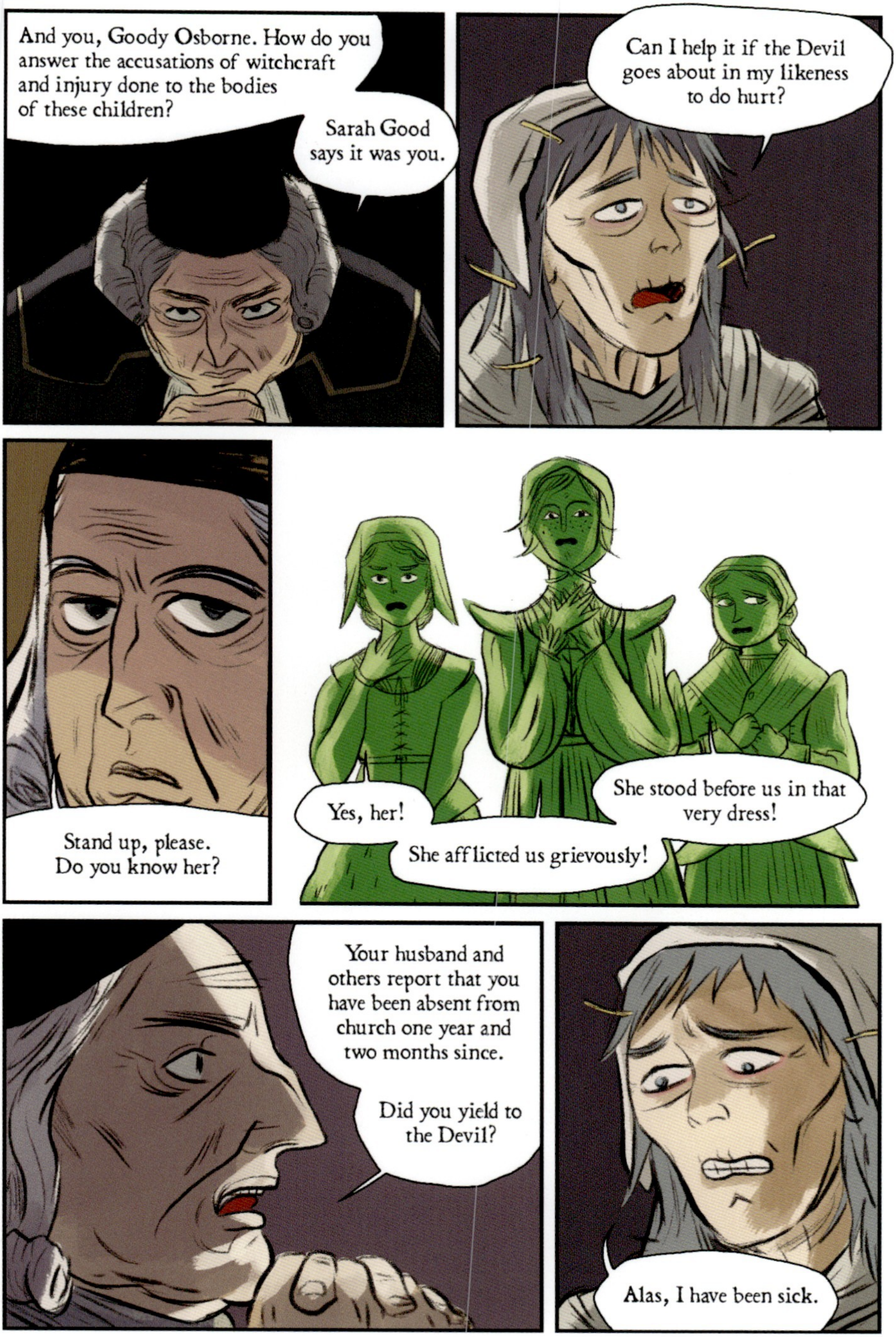
And you, Goody Osborne. How do you answer the accusations of witchcraft and injury done to the bodies of these children?
Sarah Good says it was you.
Can I help it if the Devil goes about in my likeness to do hurt?
Stand up, please. Do you know her?
Yes, her!
She afflicted us grievously!
She stood before us in that very dress!
Your husband and others report that you have been absent from church one year and two months since.
Did you yield to the Devil?
Alas, I have been sick.

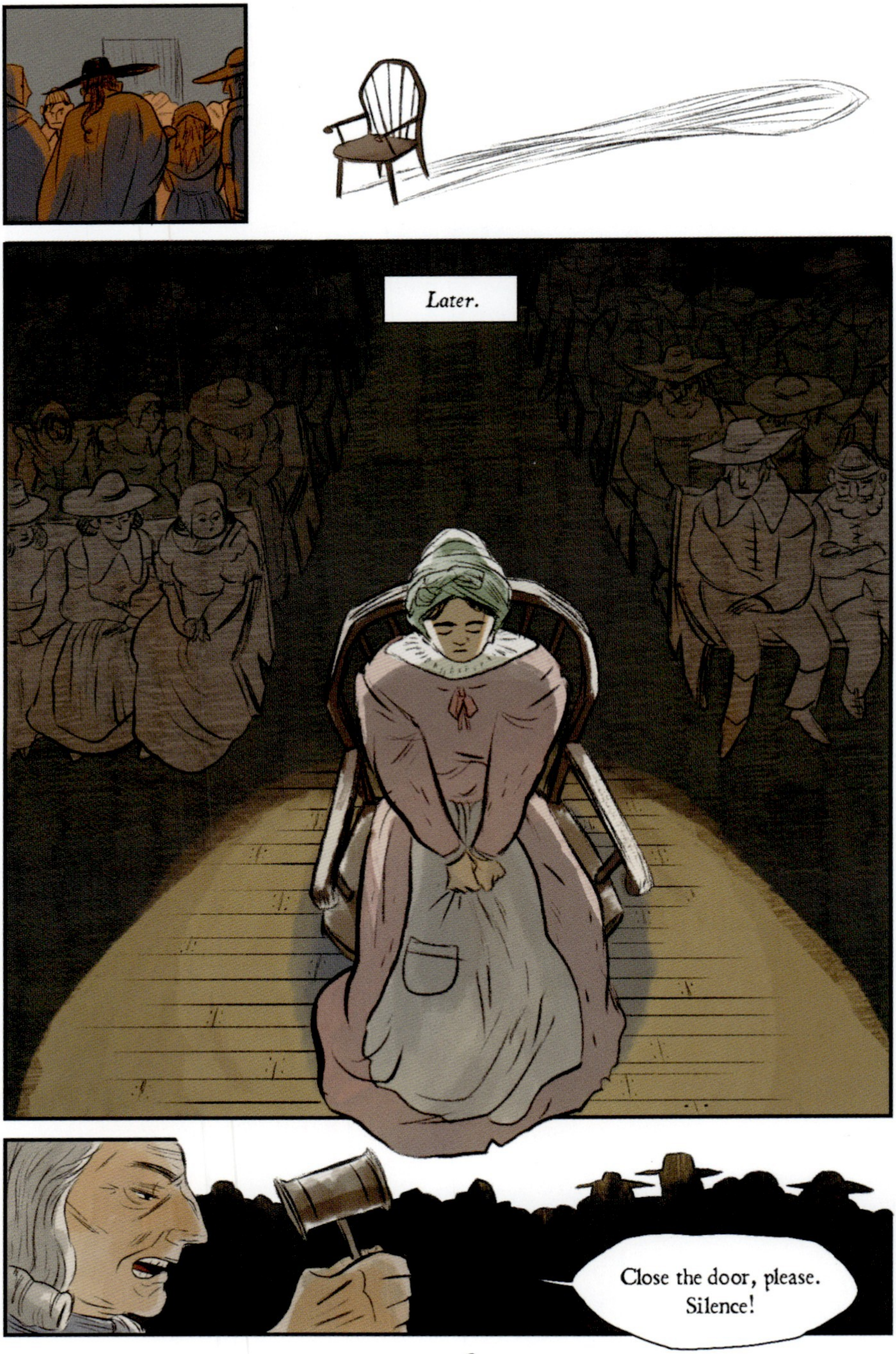
Later.
Close the door, please. Silence!

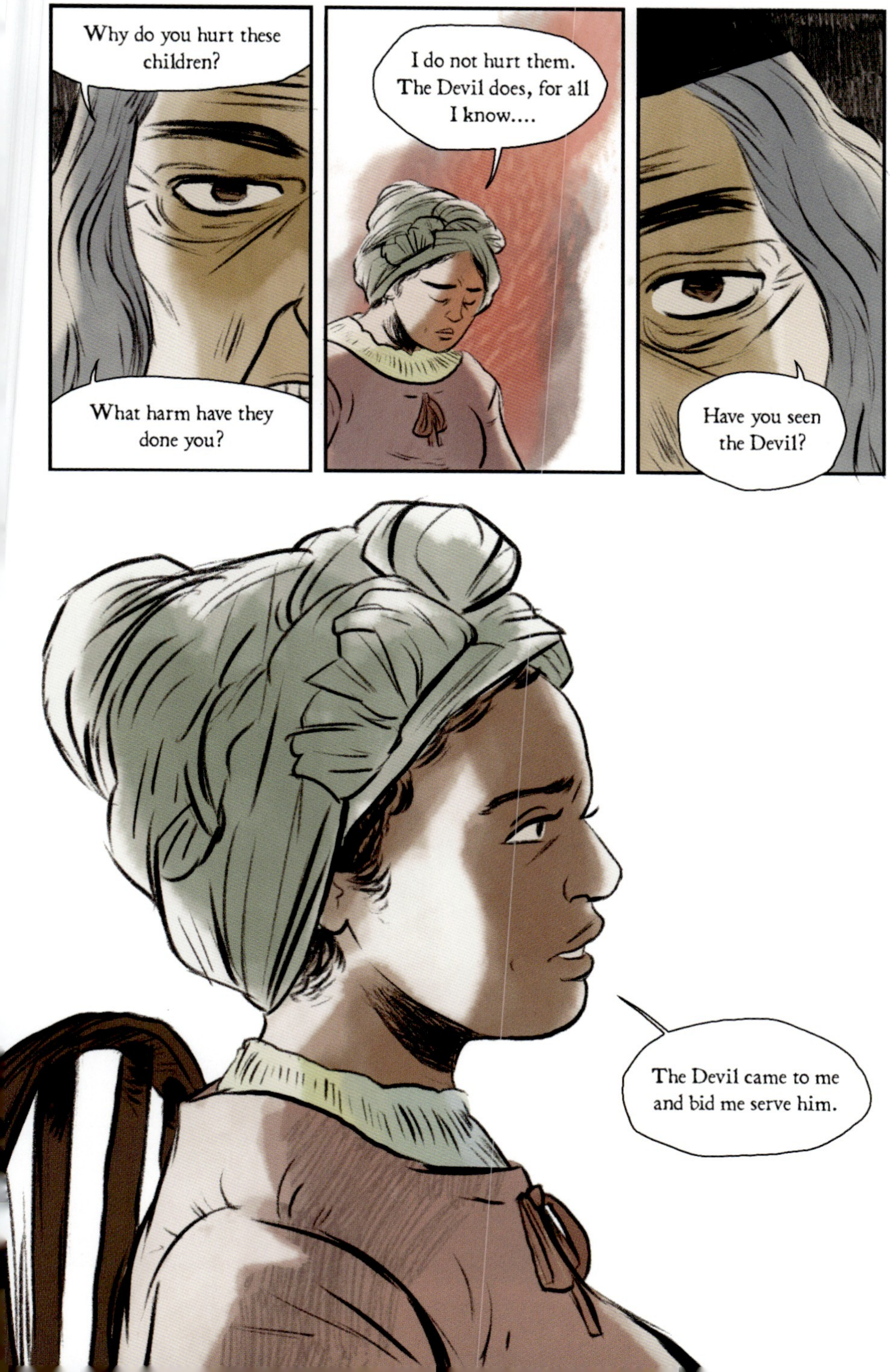
Why do you hurt these children?
What harm have they done you?
I do not hurt them. The Devil does, for all I know....
Have you seen the Devil?
The Devil came to me and bid me serve him.

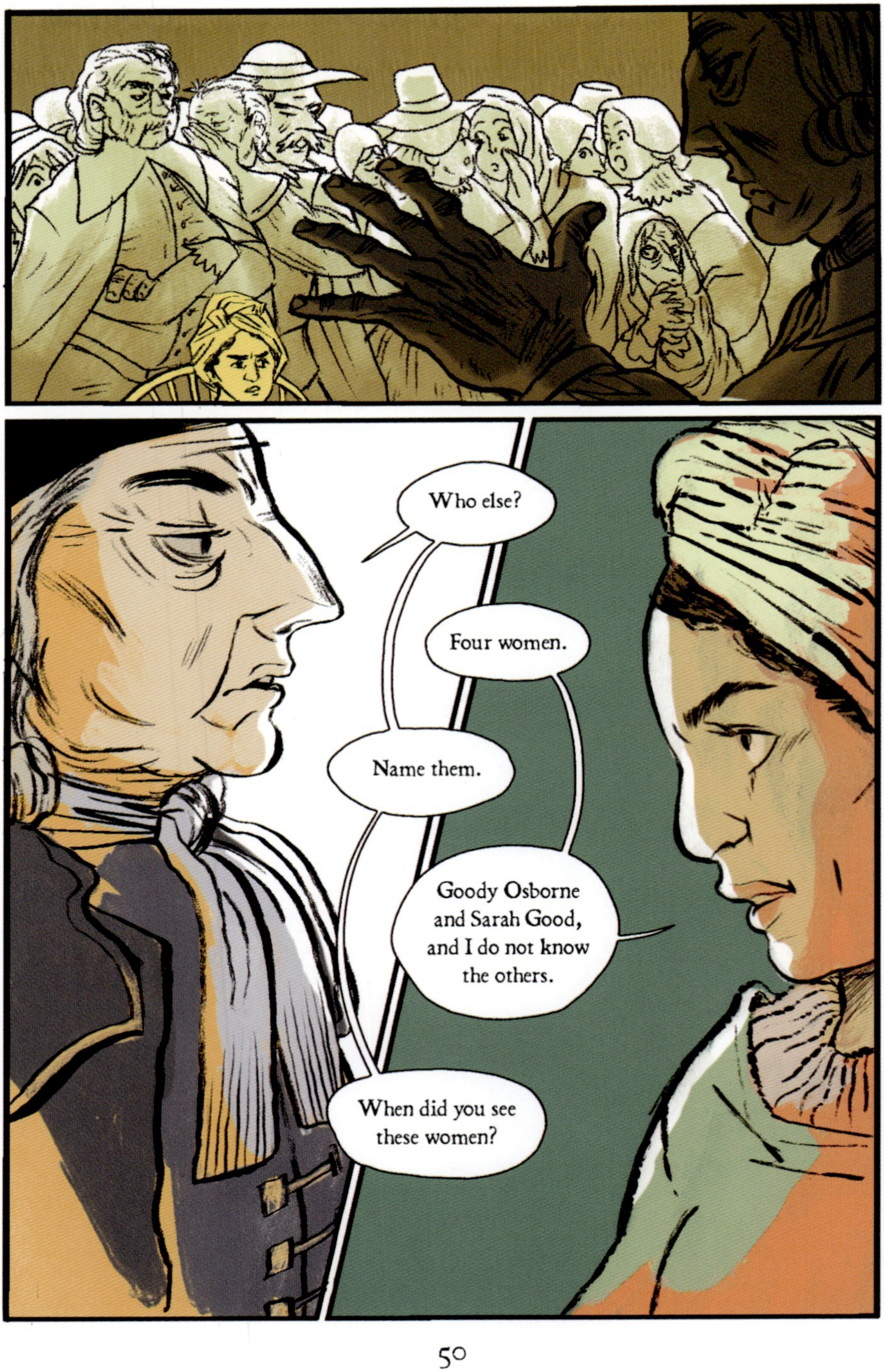
Who else?
Four women.
Name them.
Goody Osborne and Sarah Good, and I do not know the others.
When did you see these women?

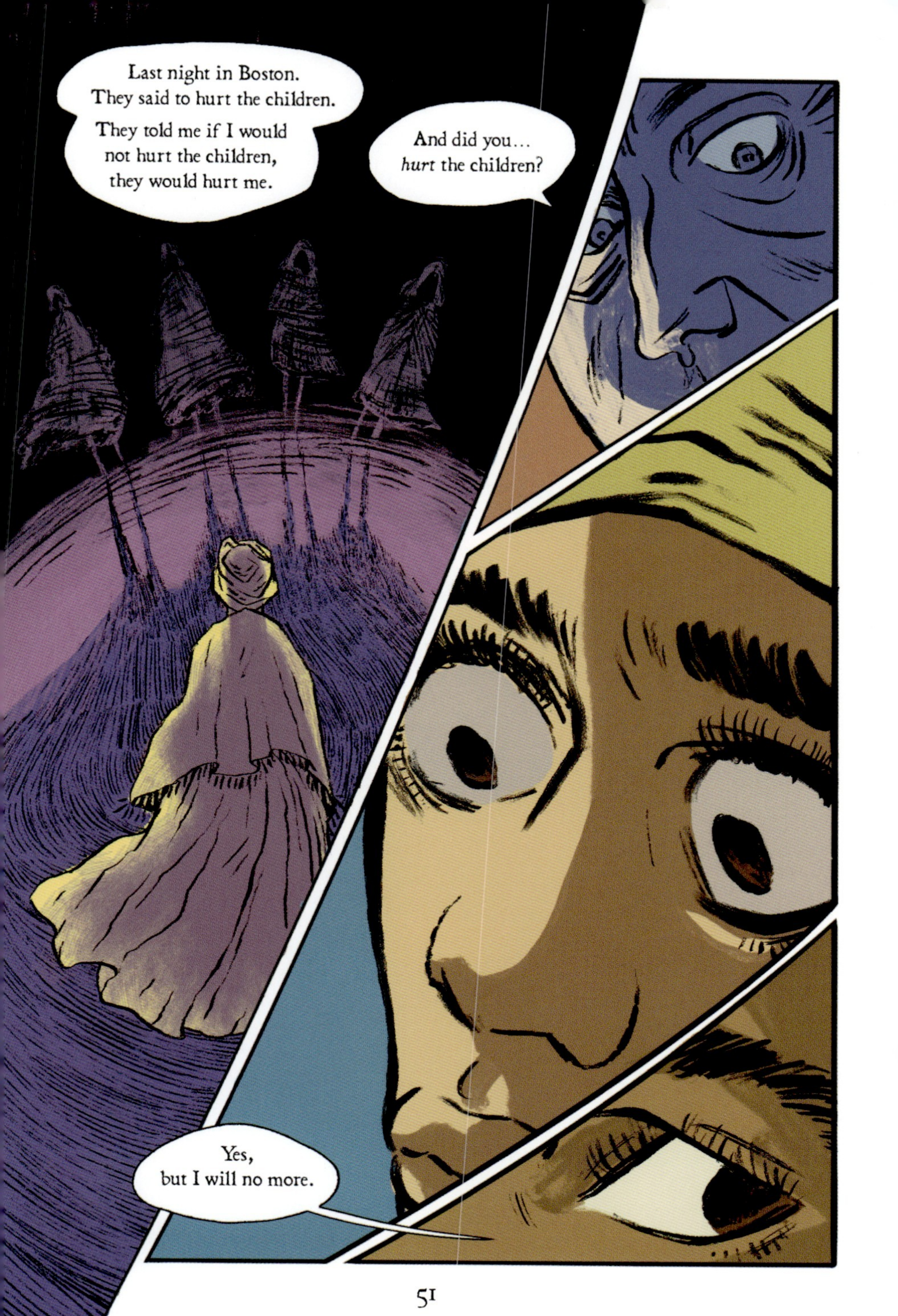
Last night in Boston. They said to hurt the children.
They told me if I would not hurt the children, they would hurt me.
And did you… *hurt* the children?
Yes, but I will no more.

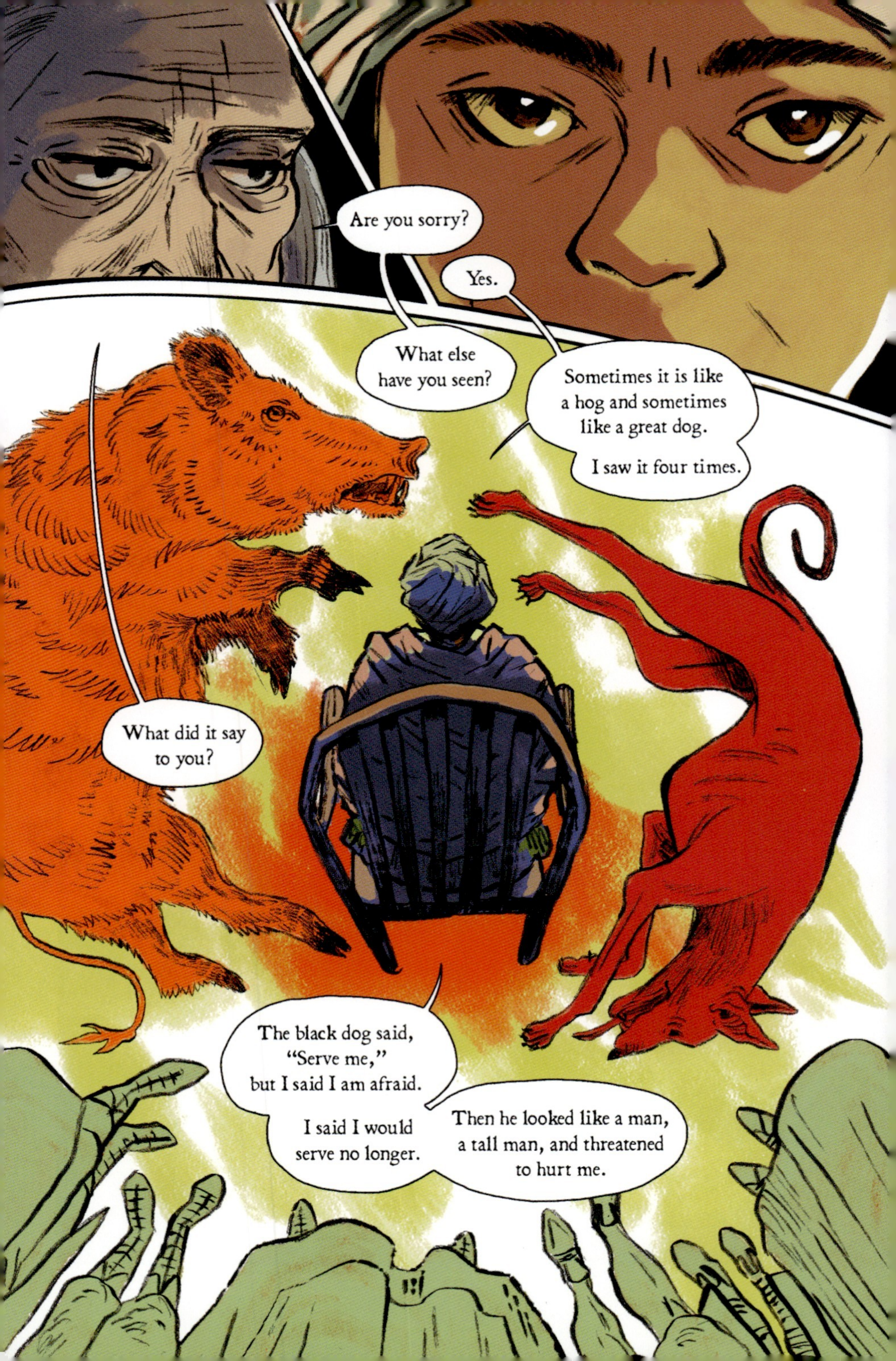
Are you sorry?
Yes.
What else have you seen?
Sometimes it is like a hog and sometimes like a great dog.
I saw it four times.
What did it say to you?
The black dog said, "Serve me," but I said I am afraid.
I said I would serve no longer.
Then he looked like a man, a tall man, and threatened to hurt me.

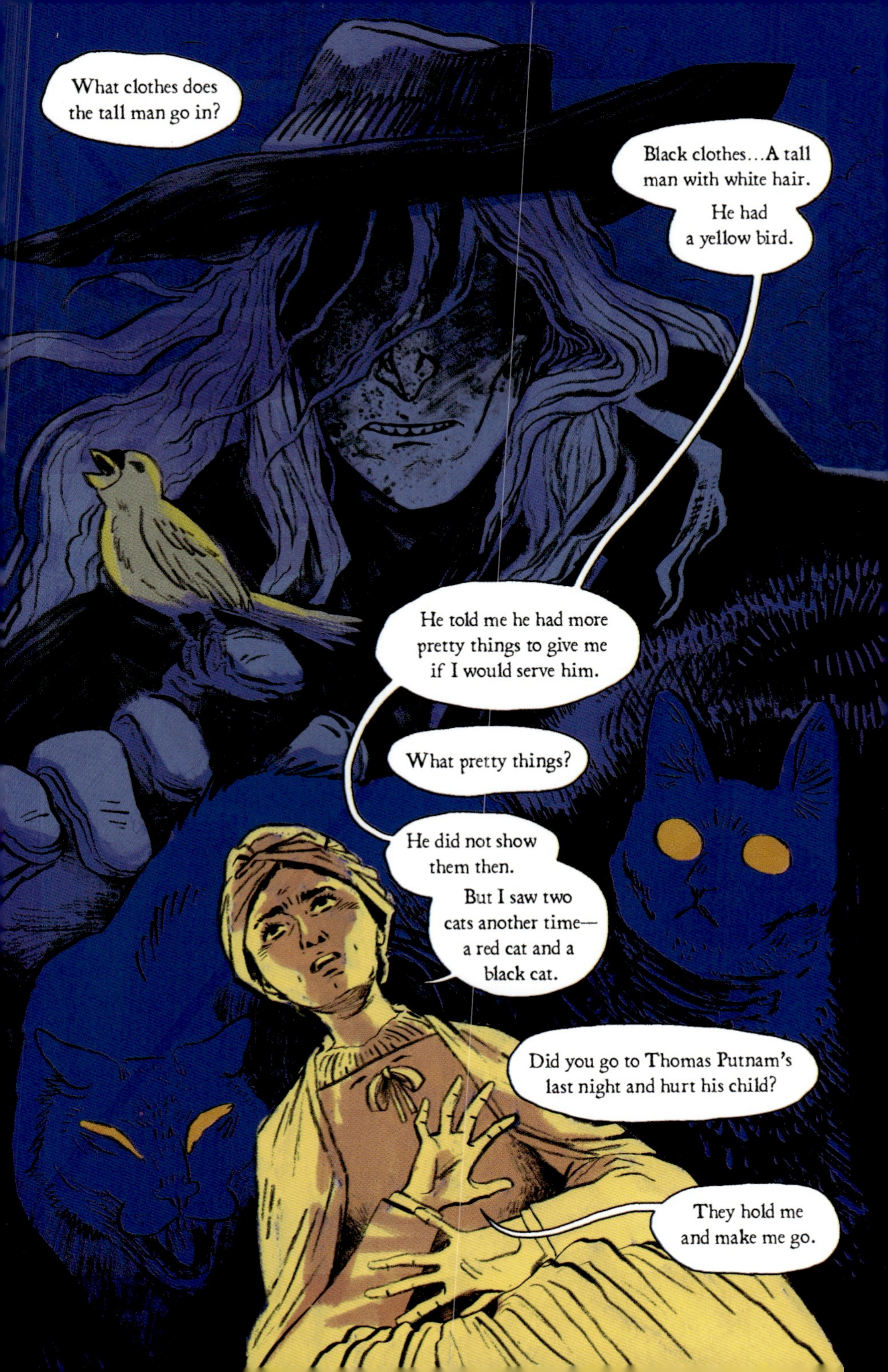
What clothes does the tall man go in?
Black clothes...A tall man with white hair.
He had a yellow bird.
He told me he had more pretty things to give me if I would serve him.
What pretty things?
He did not show them then.
But I saw two cats another time—a red cat and a black cat.
Did you go to Thomas Putnam's last night and hurt his child?
They hold me and make me go.

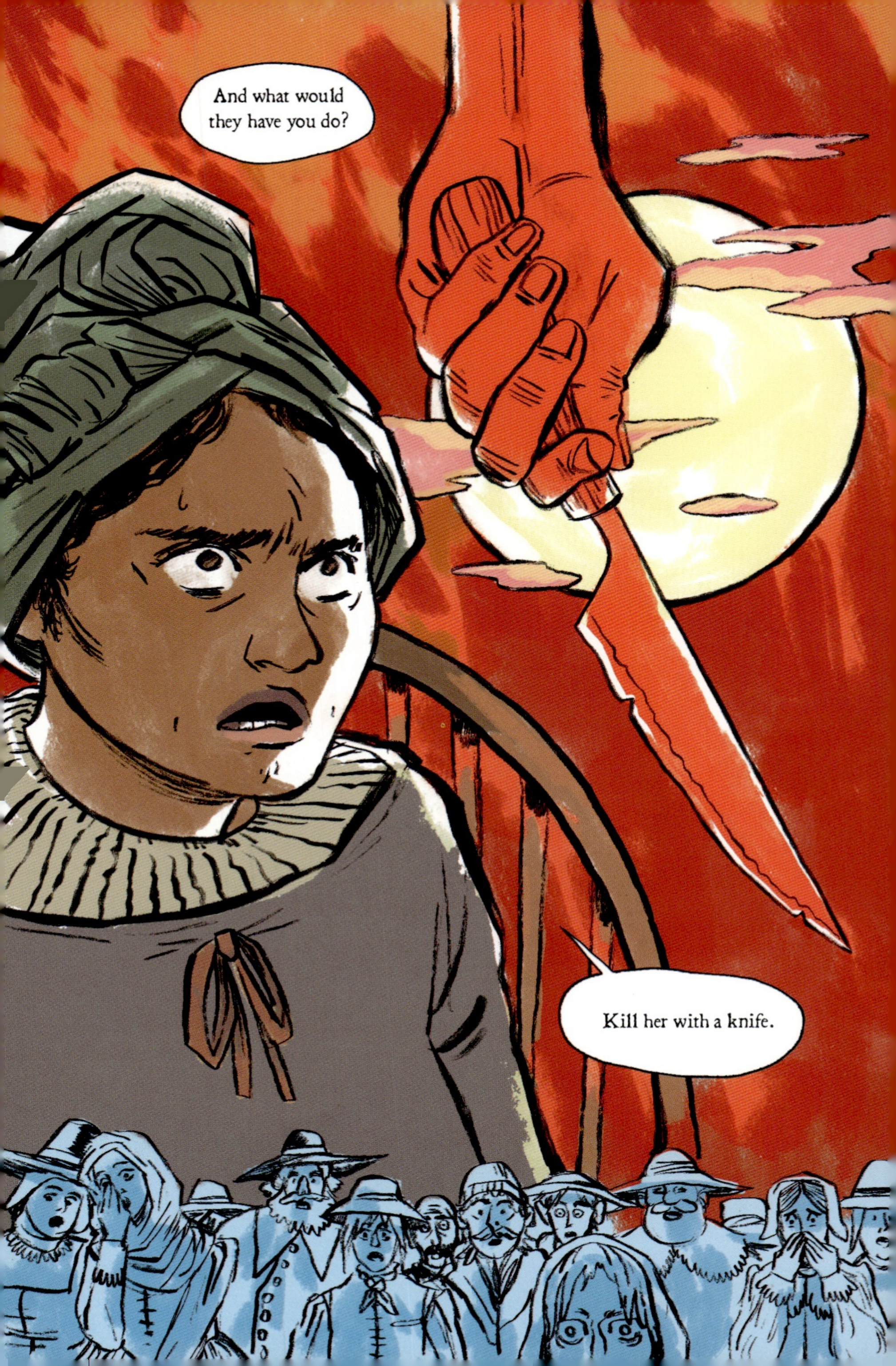
And what would they have you do?
Kill her with a knife.

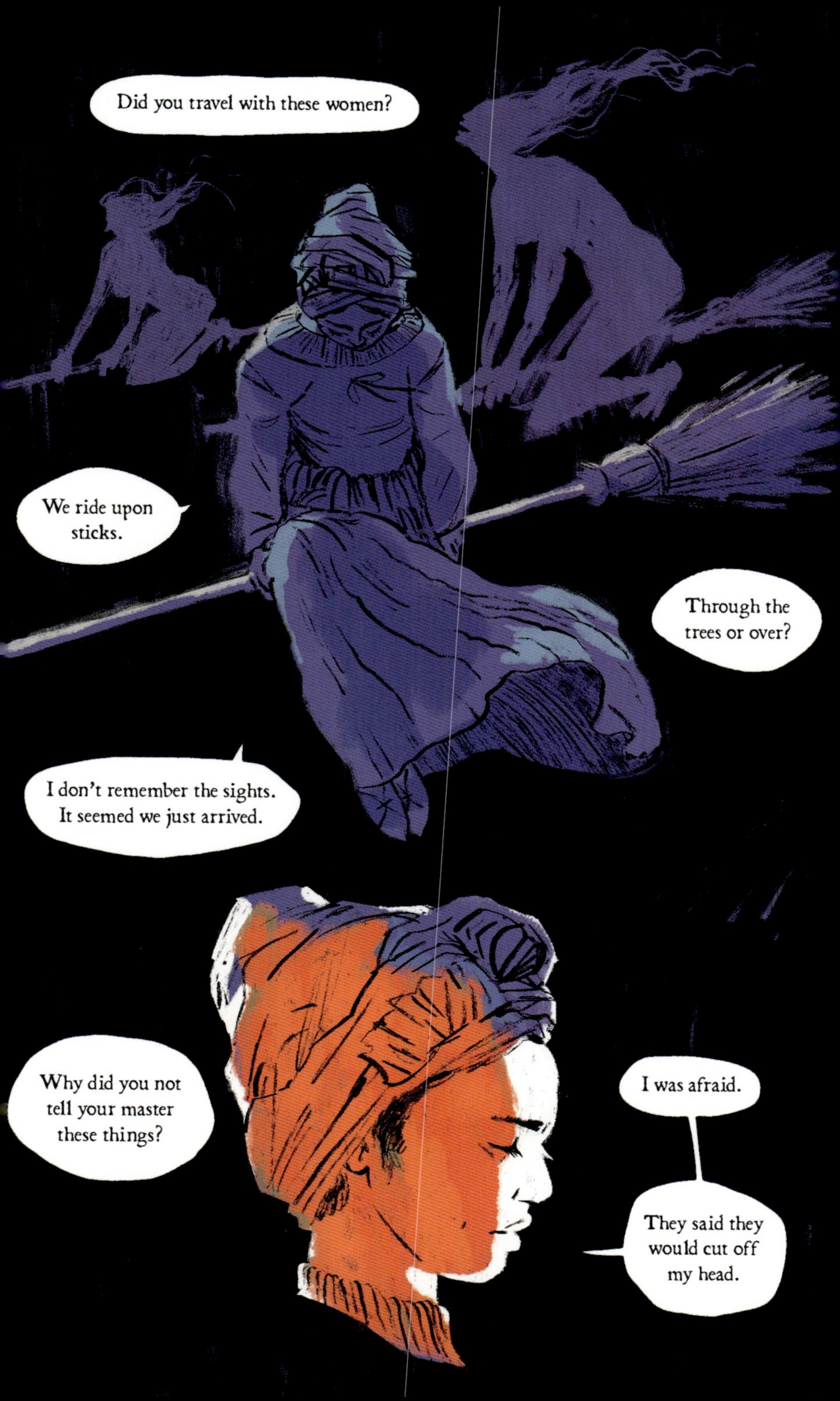
Did you travel with these women?
We ride upon sticks.
Through the trees or over?
I don't remember the sights. It seemed we just arrived.
Why did you not tell your master these things?
I was afraid.
They said they would cut off my head.

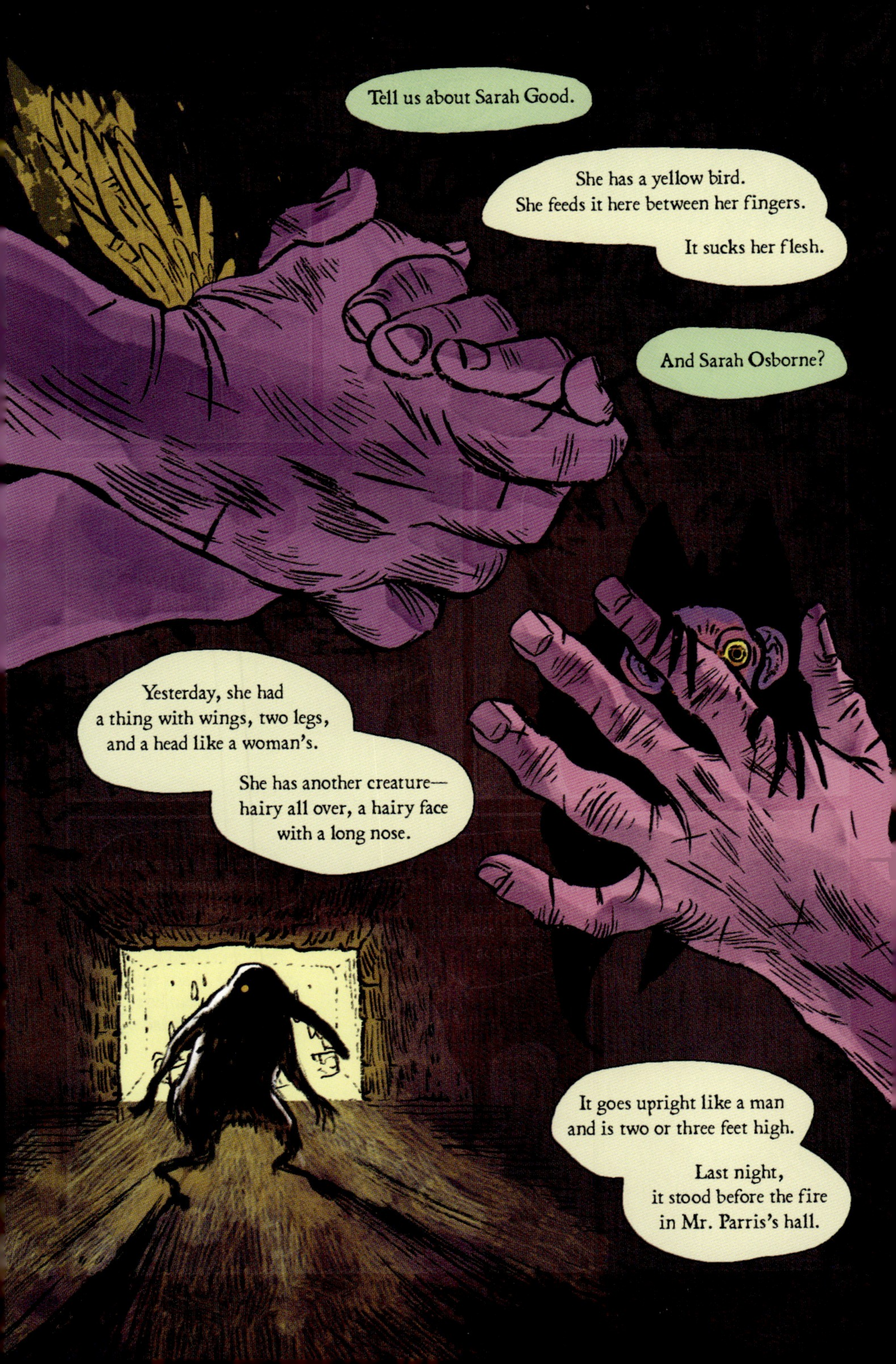
Tell us about Sarah Good.
She has a yellow bird. She feeds it here between her fingers.
It sucks her flesh.
And Sarah Osborne?
Yesterday, she had a thing with wings, two legs, and a head like a woman's.
She has another creature— hairy all over, a hairy face with a long nose.
It goes upright like a man and is two or three feet high.
Last night, it stood before the fire in Mr. Parris's hall.

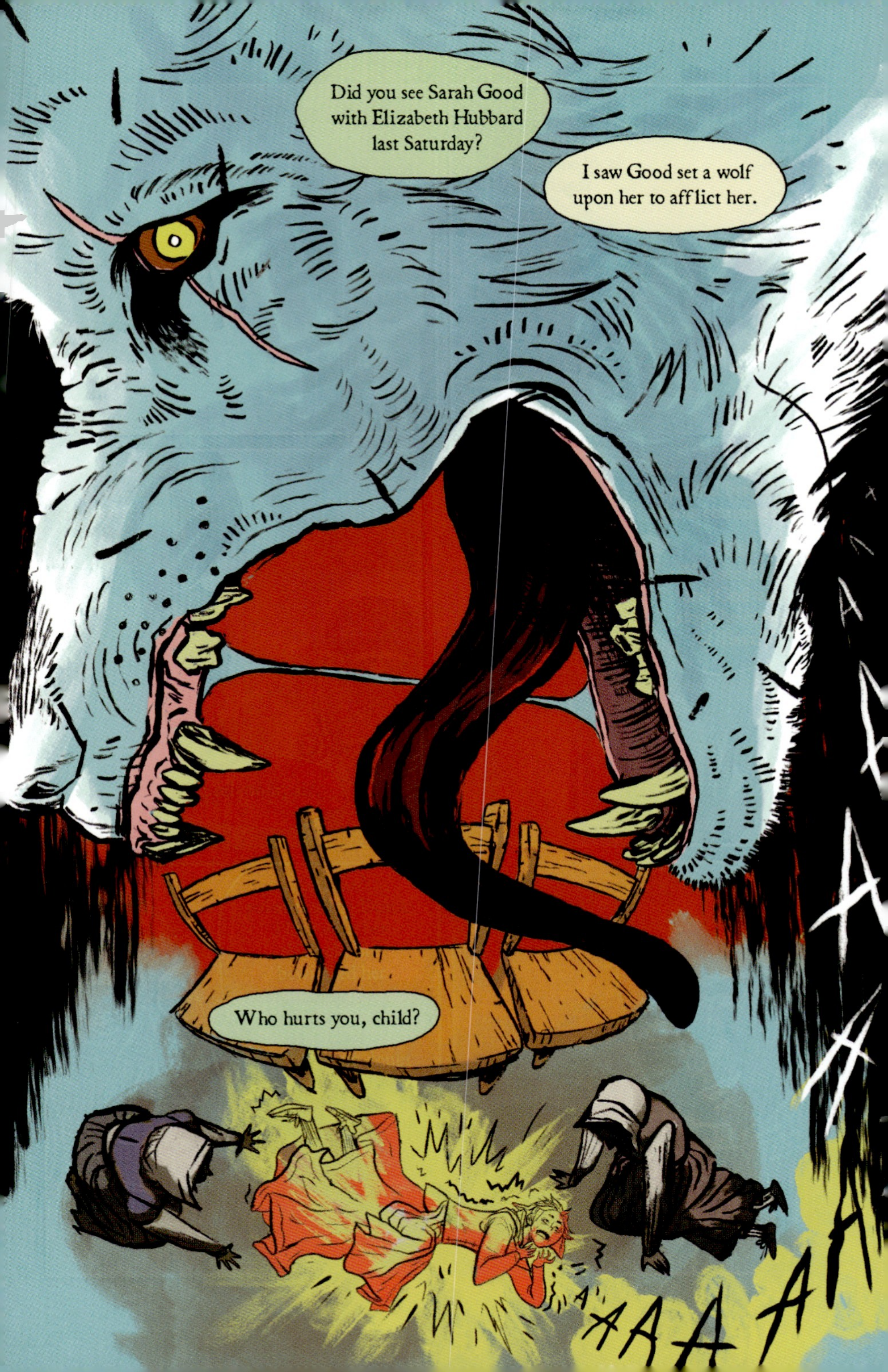
Did you see Sarah Good with Elizabeth Hubbard last Saturday?
I saw Good set a wolf upon her to afflict her.
Who hurts you, child?
AAAAAAAAA

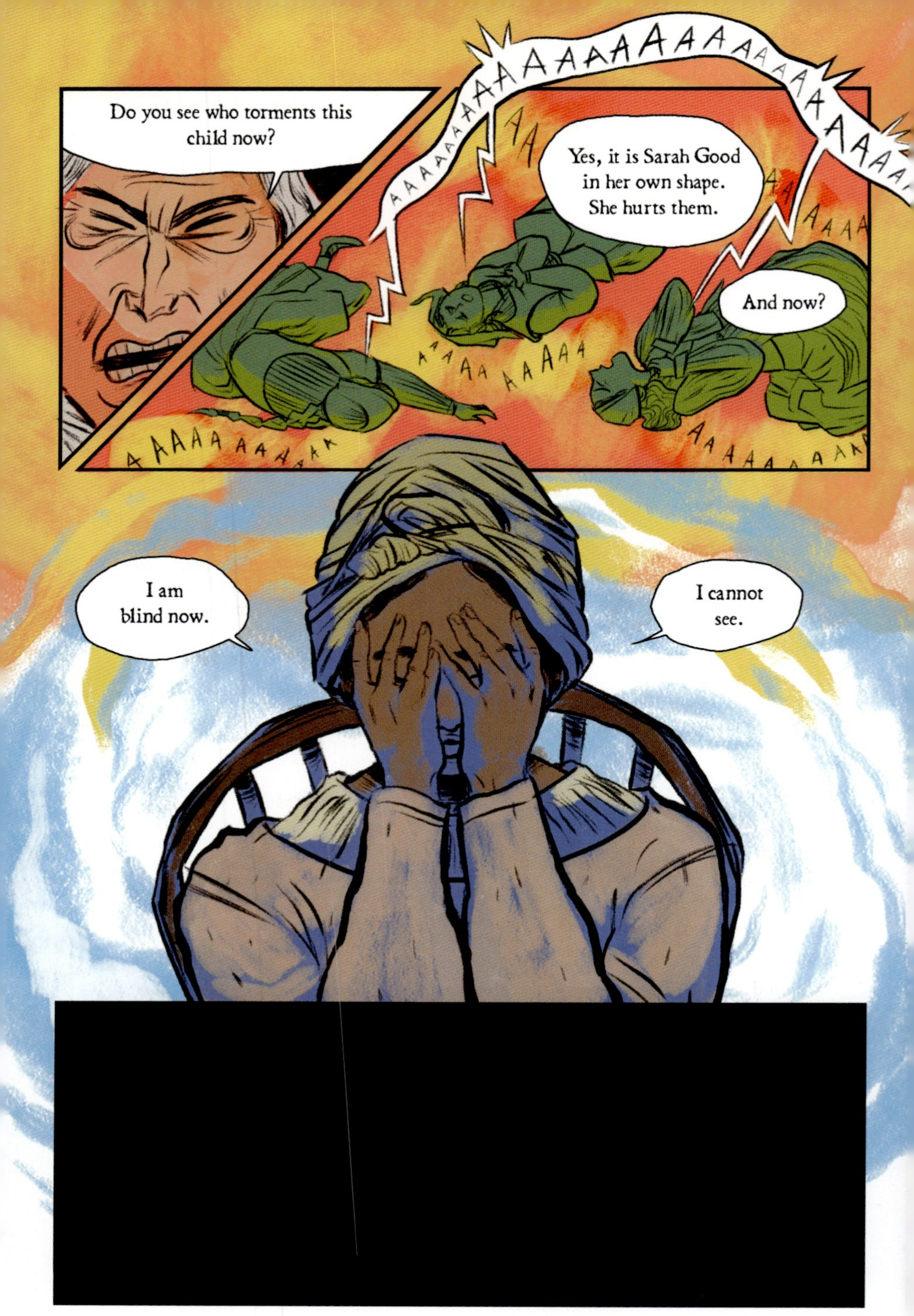
Do you see who torments this child now?
Yes, it is Sarah Good in her own shape. She hurts them.
And now?
I am blind now.
I cannot see.

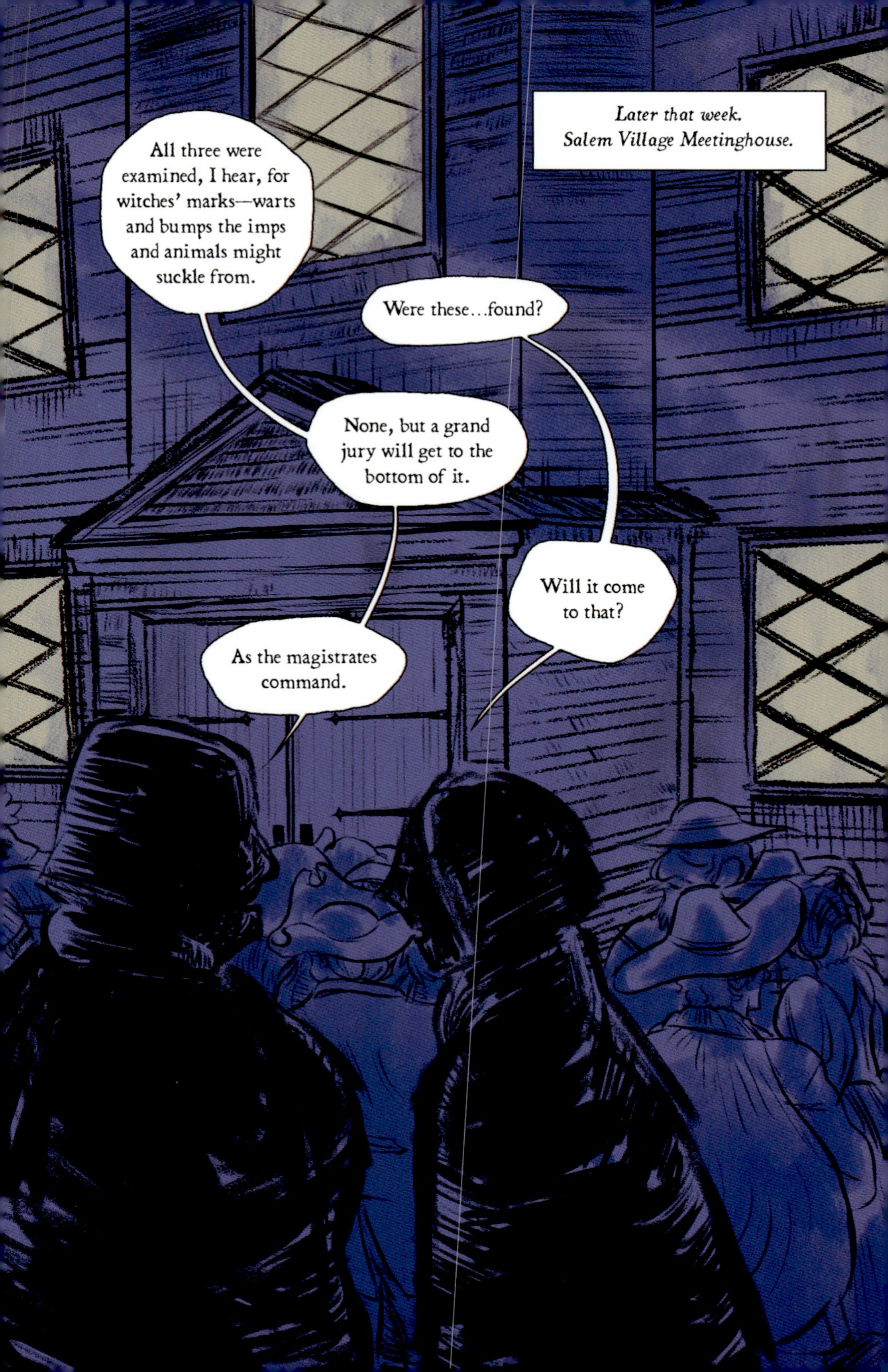
Later that week.
Salem Village Meetinghouse.
All three were examined, I hear, for witches' marks—warts and bumps the imps and animals might suckle from.
Were these...found?
None, but a grand jury will get to the bottom of it.
Will it come to that?
As the magistrates command.

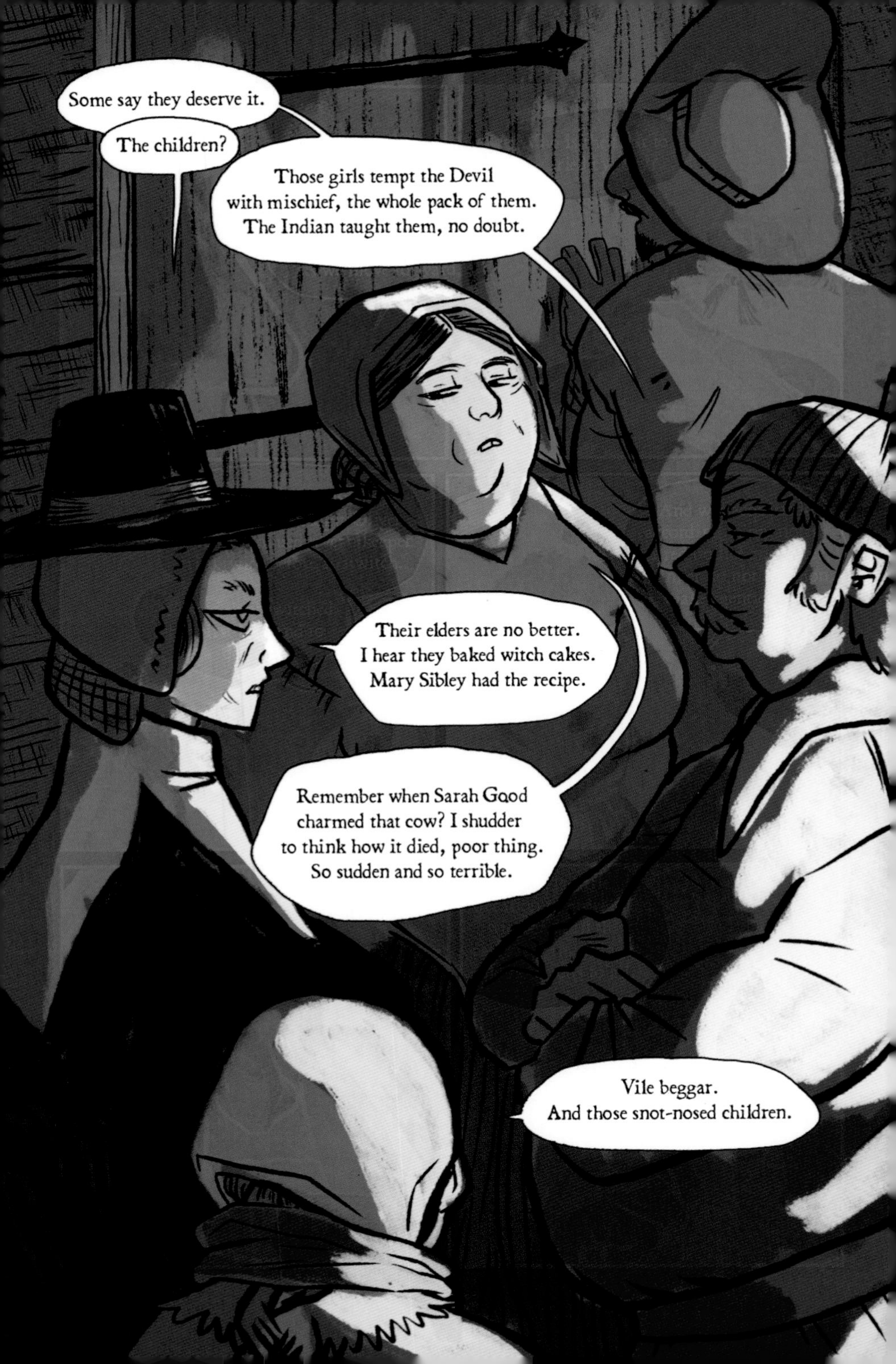
Some say they deserve it.
The children?
Those girls tempt the Devil with mischief, the whole pack of them. The Indian taught them, no doubt.
Their elders are no better. I hear they baked witch cakes. Mary Sibley had the recipe.
Remember when Sarah Good charmed that cow? I shudder to think how it died, poor thing. So sudden and so terrible.
Vile beggar. And those snot-nosed children.

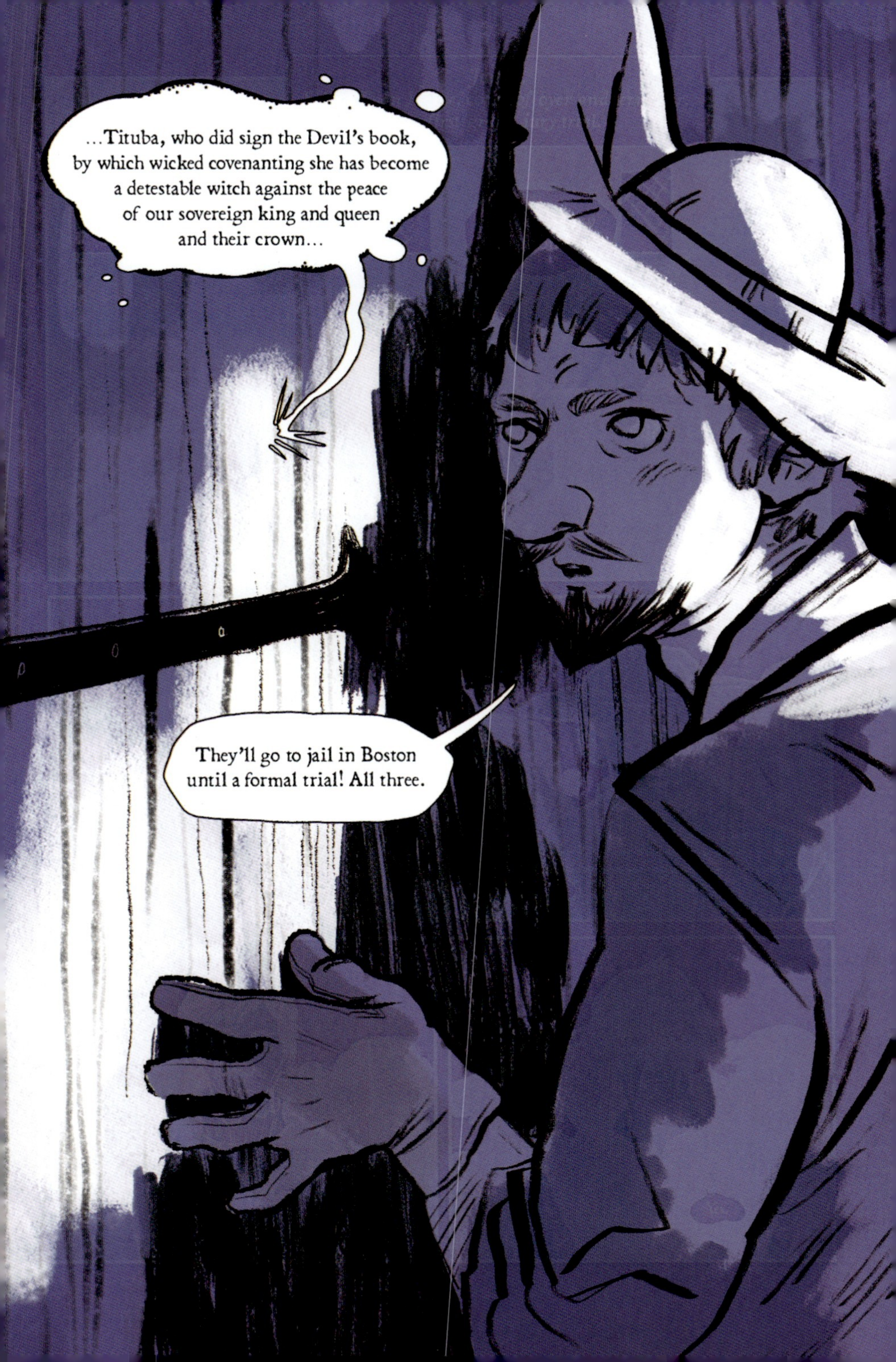
...Tituba, who did sign the Devil's book, by which wicked covenanting she has become a detestable witch against the peace of our sovereign king and queen and their crown...
They'll go to jail in Boston until a formal trial! All three.

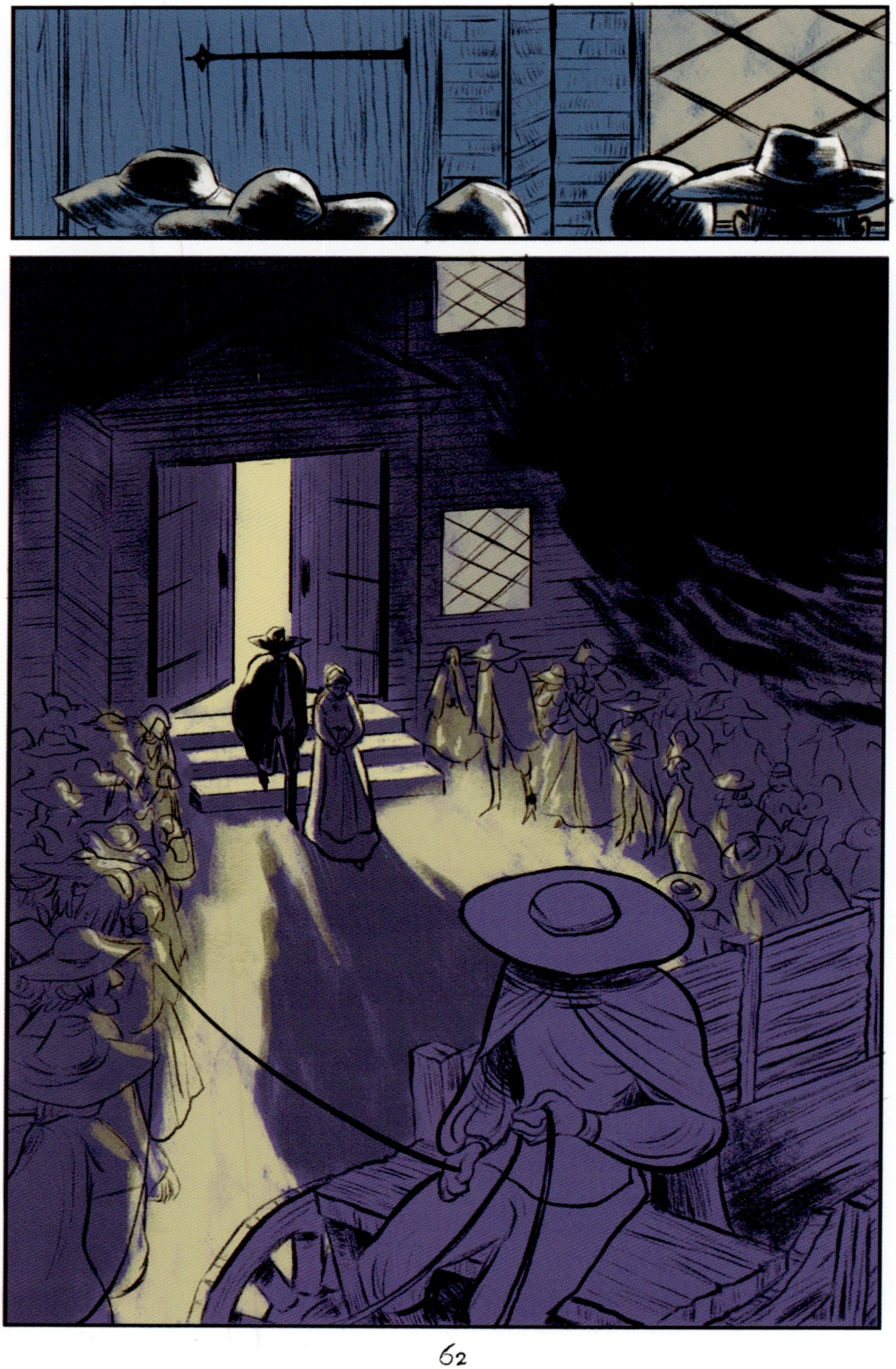

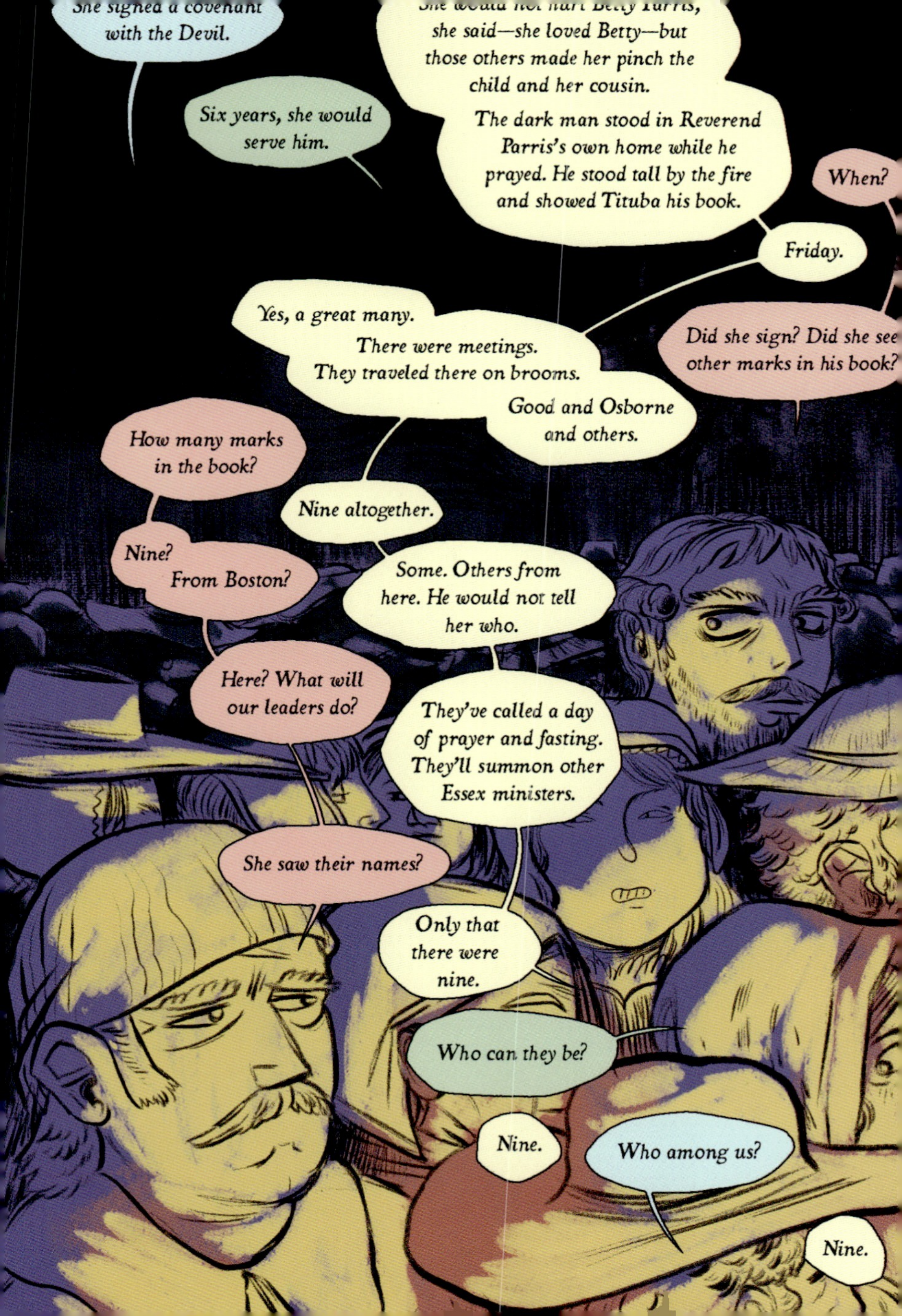
She signed a covenant with the Devil.
She would not hurt Betty Parris, she said—she loved Betty—but those others made her pinch the child and her cousin.
The dark man stood in Reverend Parris's own home while he prayed. He stood tall by the fire and showed Tituba his book.
Six years, she would serve him.
When?
Friday.
Did she sign? Did she see other marks in his book?
Yes, a great many.
There were meetings. They traveled there on brooms.
Good and Osborne and others.
How many marks in the book?
Nine altogether.
Nine? From Boston?
Some. Others from here. He would not tell her who.
Here? What will our leaders do?
They've called a day of prayer and fasting. They'll summon other Essex ministers.
She saw their names?
Only that there were nine.
Who can they be?
Nine.
Who among us?
Nine.

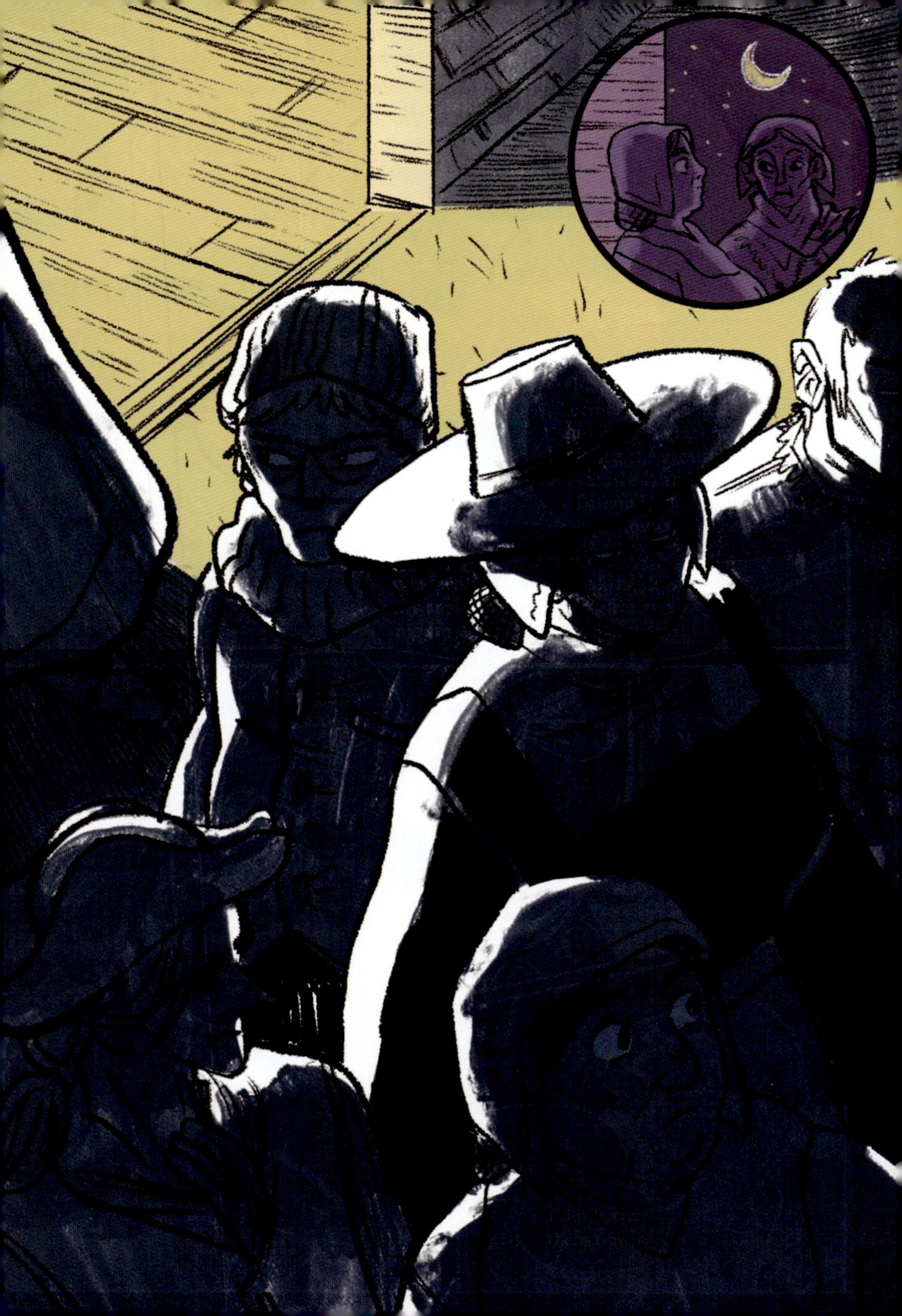

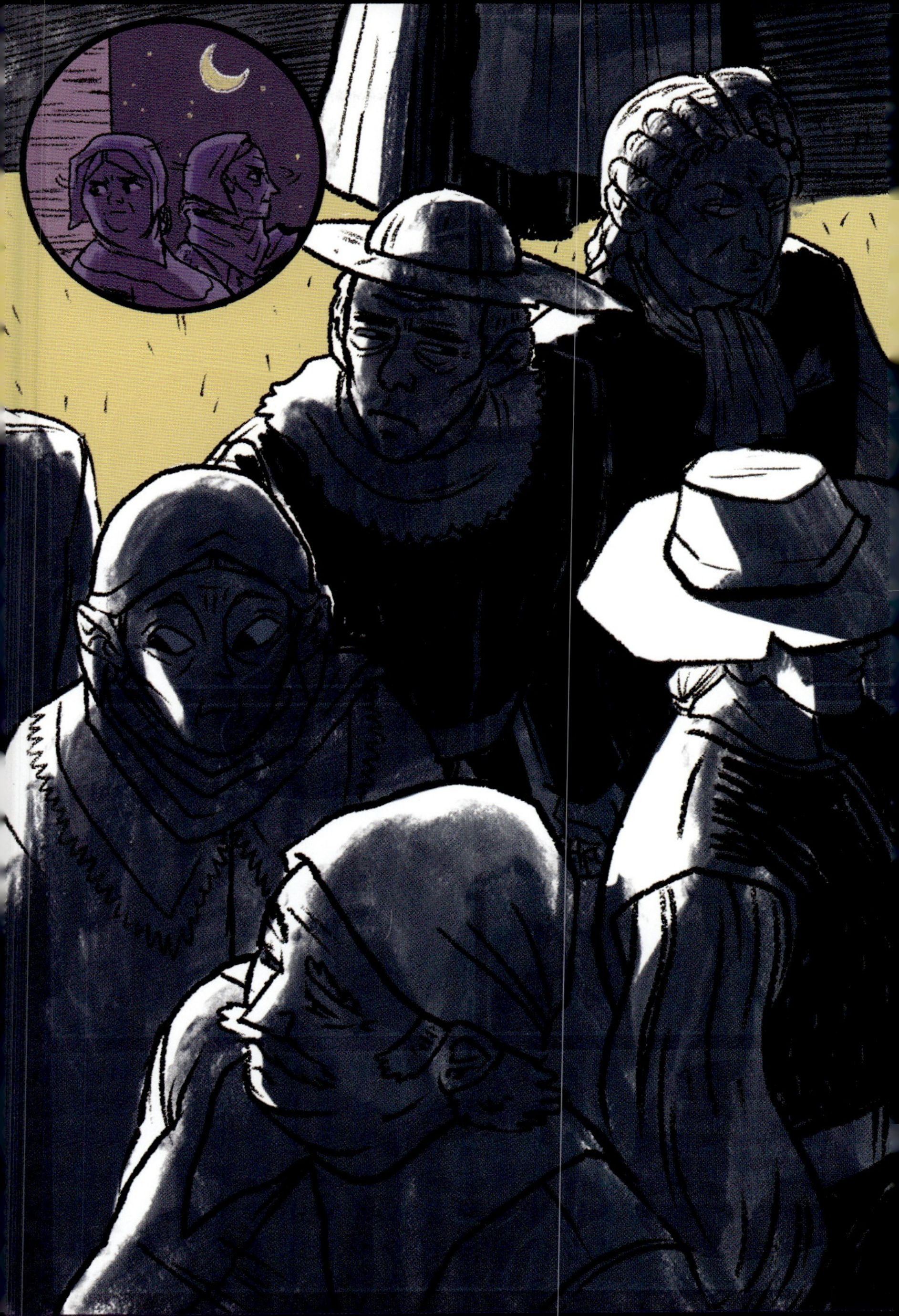

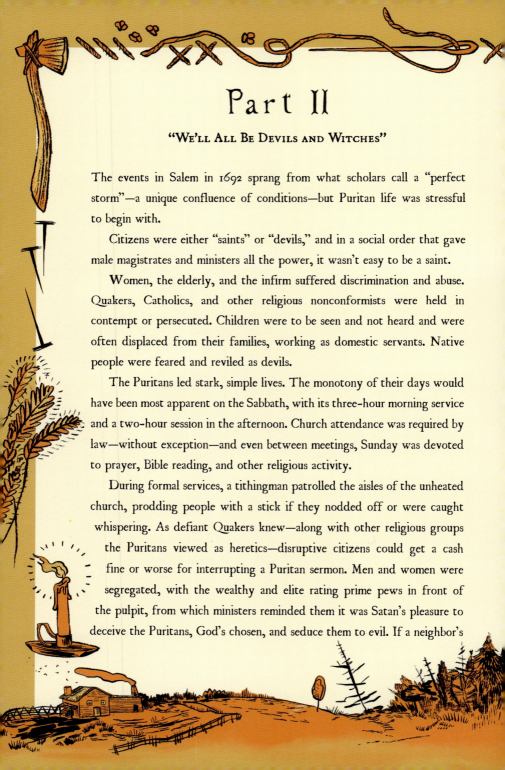

Part II

"We'll All Be Devils and Witches"

The events in Salem in 1692 sprang from what scholars call a "perfect storm"—a unique confluence of conditions—but Puritan life was stressful to begin with.

Citizens were either "saints" or "devils," and in a social order that gave male magistrates and ministers all the power, it wasn't easy to be a saint.

Women, the elderly, and the infirm suffered discrimination and abuse. Quakers, Catholics, and other religious nonconformists were held in contempt or persecuted. Children were to be seen and not heard and were often displaced from their families, working as domestic servants. Native people were feared and reviled as devils.

The Puritans led stark, simple lives. The monotony of their days would have been most apparent on the Sabbath, with its three-hour morning service and a two-hour session in the afternoon. Church attendance was required by law—without exception—and even between meetings, Sunday was devoted to prayer, Bible reading, and other religious activity.

During formal services, a tithingman patrolled the aisles of the unheated church, prodding people with a stick if they nodded off or were caught whispering. As defiant Quakers knew—along with other religious groups the Puritans viewed as heretics—disruptive citizens could get a cash fine or worse for interrupting a Puritan sermon. Men and women were segregated, with the wealthy and elite rating prime pews in front of the pulpit, from which ministers reminded them it was Satan's pleasure to deceive the Puritans, God's chosen, and seduce them to evil. If a neighbor's

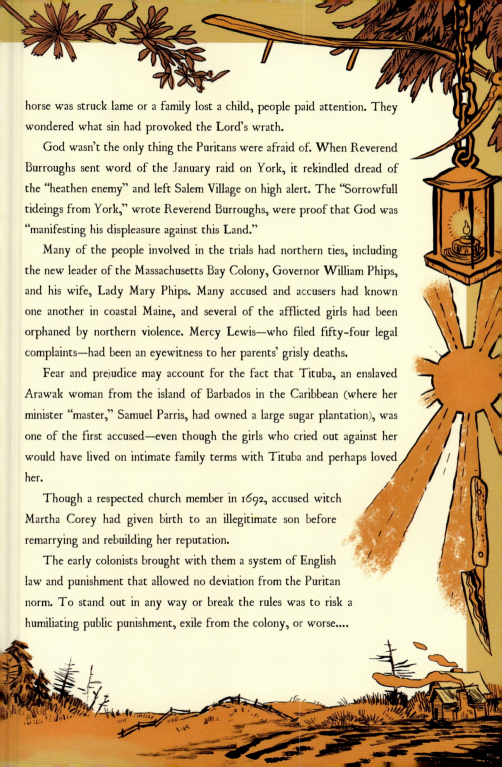

horse was struck lame or a family lost a child, people paid attention. They wondered what sin had provoked the Lord's wrath.

God wasn't the only thing the Puritans were afraid of. When Reverend Burroughs sent word of the January raid on York, it rekindled dread of the "heathen enemy" and left Salem Village on high alert. The "Sorrowfull tideings from York," wrote Reverend Burroughs, were proof that God was "manifesting his displeasure against this Land."

Many of the people involved in the trials had northern ties, including the new leader of the Massachusetts Bay Colony, Governor William Phips, and his wife, Lady Mary Phips. Many accused and accusers had known one another in coastal Maine, and several of the afflicted girls had been orphaned by northern violence. Mercy Lewis—who filed fifty-four legal complaints—had been an eyewitness to her parents' grisly deaths.

Fear and prejudice may account for the fact that Tituba, an enslaved Arawak woman from the island of Barbados in the Caribbean (where her minister "master," Samuel Parris, had owned a large sugar plantation), was one of the first accused—even though the girls who cried out against her would have lived on intimate family terms with Tituba and perhaps loved her.

Though a respected church member in 1692, accused witch Martha Corey had given birth to an illegitimate son before remarrying and rebuilding her reputation.

The early colonists brought with them a system of English law and punishment that allowed no deviation from the Puritan norm. To stand out in any way or break the rules was to risk a humiliating public punishment, exile from the colony, or worse....

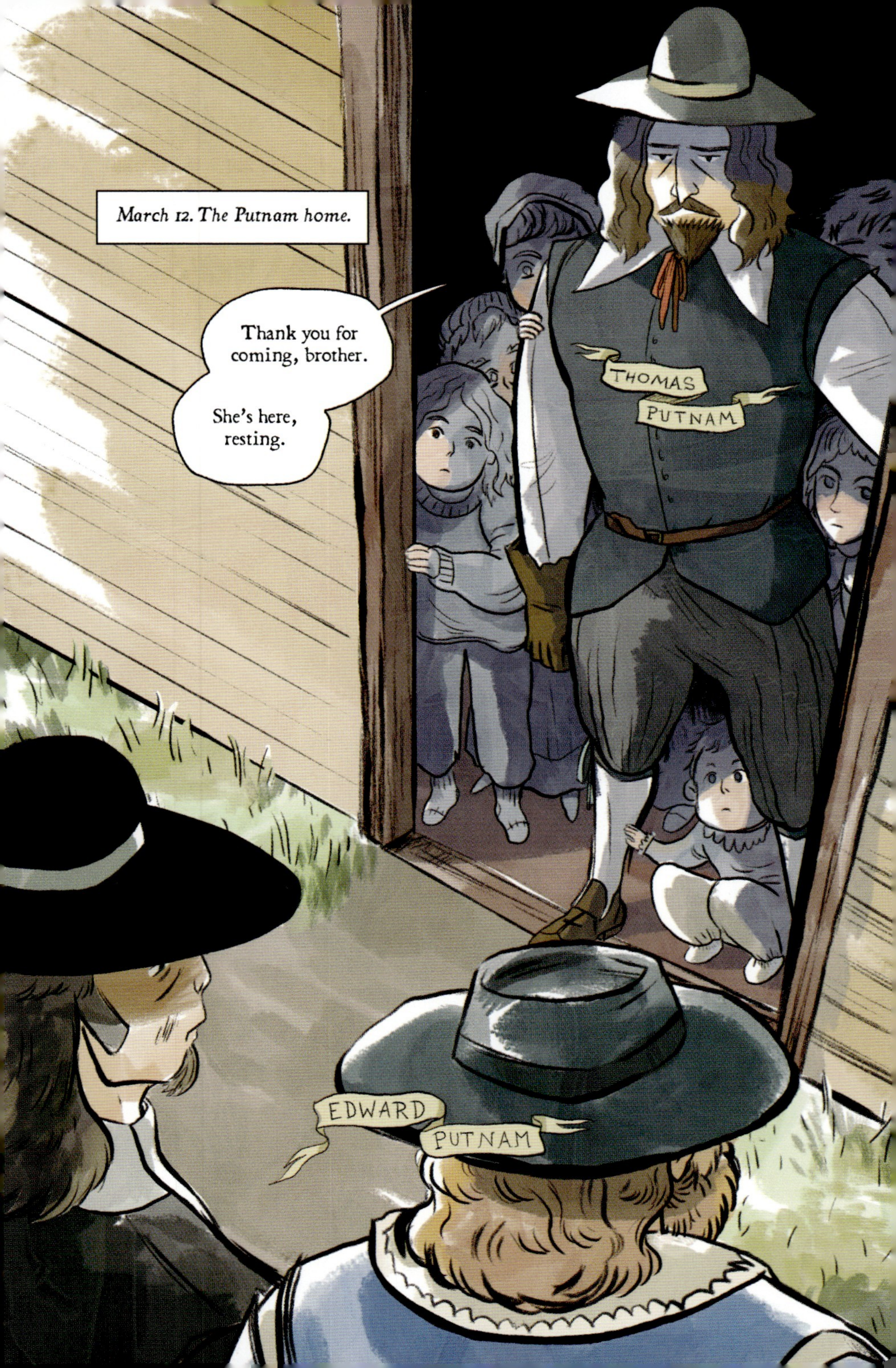
March 12. The Putnam home.
Thank you for coming, brother.
She's here, resting.
THOMAS PUTNAM
EDWARD PUTNAM

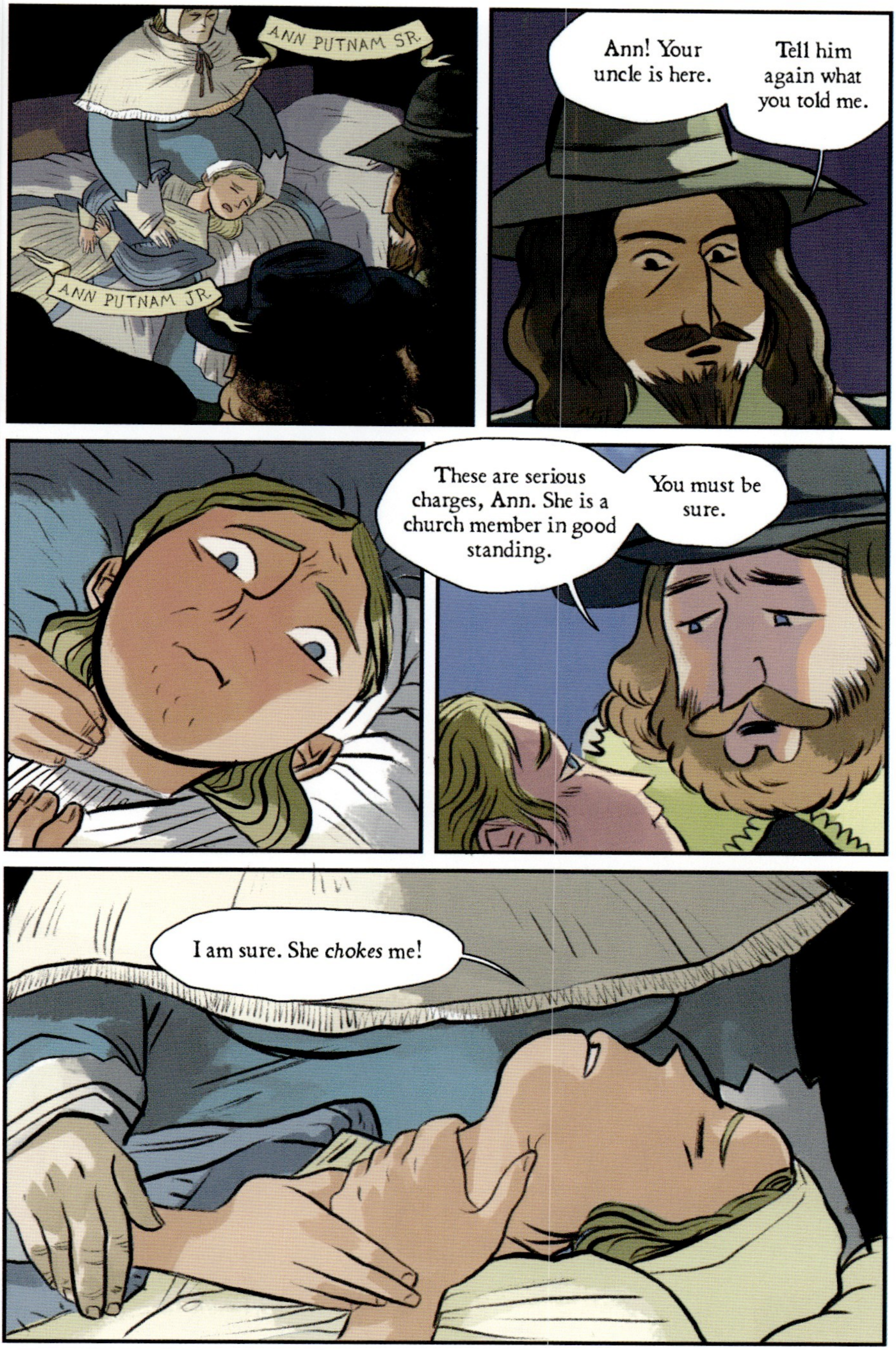
ANN PUTNAM SR.
ANN PUTNAM JR.
Ann! Your uncle is here.
Tell him again what you told me.
These are serious charges, Ann. She is a church member in good standing.
You must be sure.
I am sure. She *chokes* me!

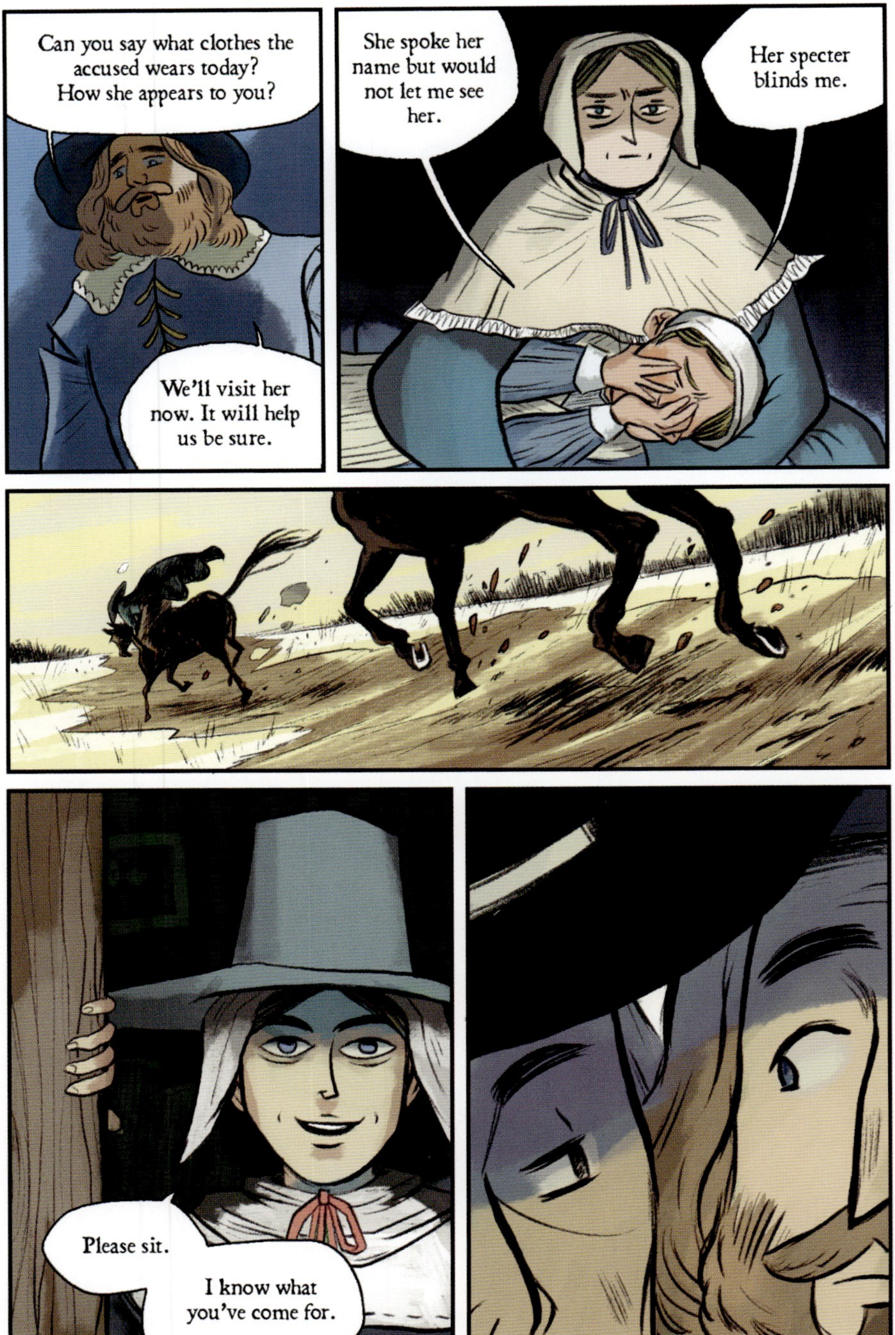

Can you say what clothes the accused wears today? How she appears to you?
We'll visit her now. It will help us be sure.
She spoke her name but would not let me see her.
Her specter blinds me.
Please sit.
I know what you've come for.

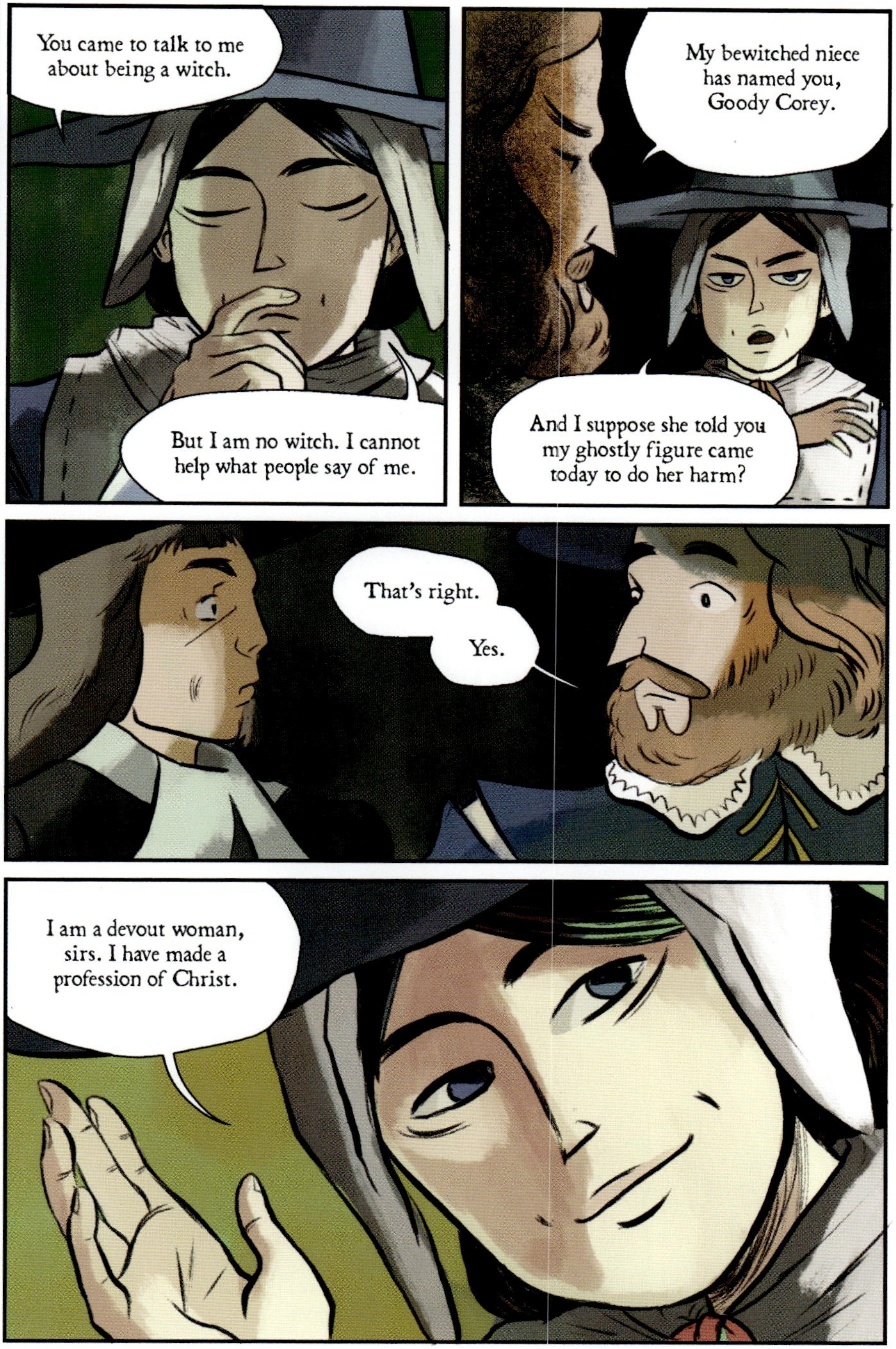
You came to talk to me about being a witch.
But I am no witch. I cannot help what people say of me.
My bewitched niece has named you, Goody Corey.
And I suppose she told you my ghostly figure came today to do her harm?
That's right.
Yes.
I am a devout woman, sirs. I have made a profession of Christ.

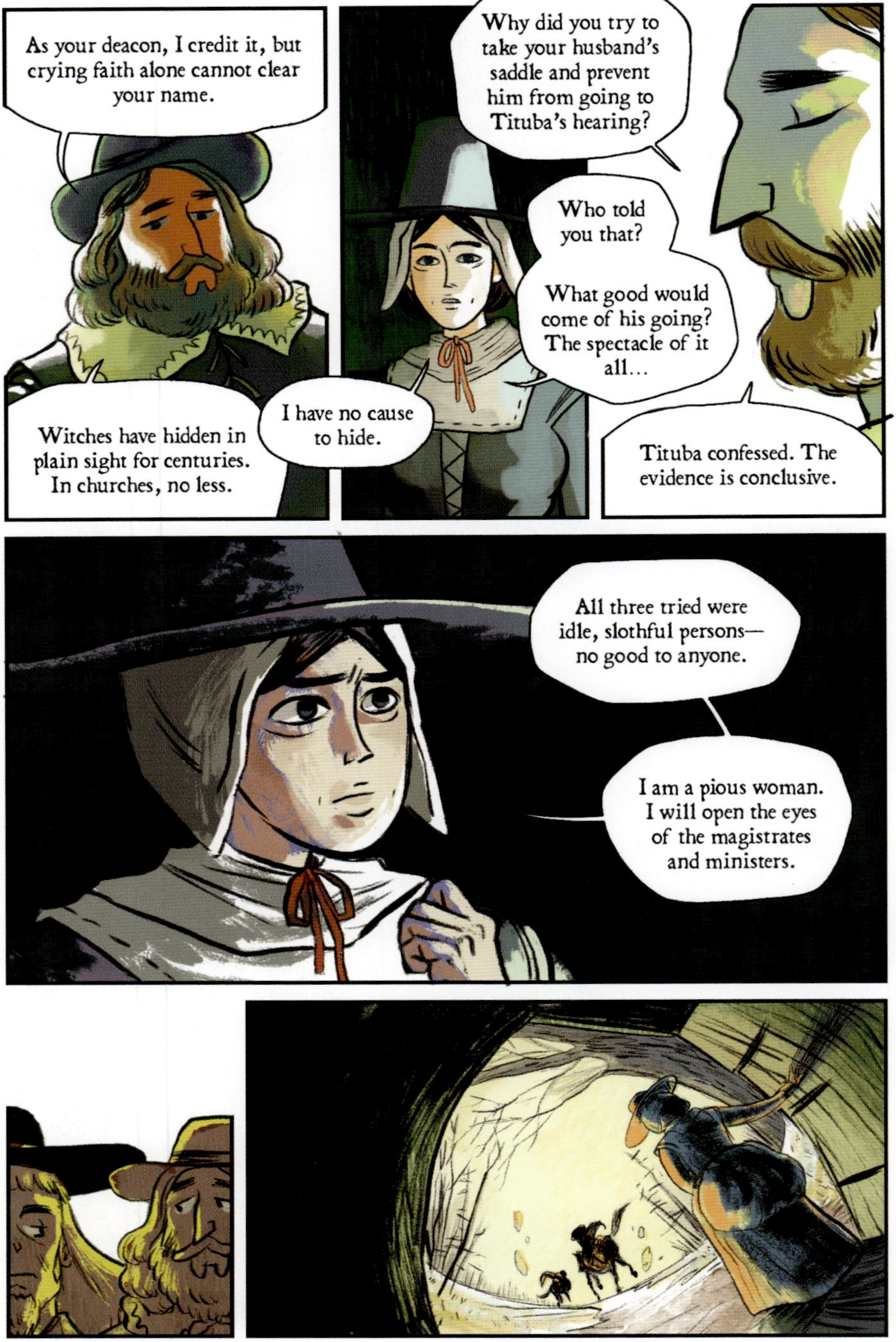

As your deacon, I credit it, but crying faith alone cannot clear your name.
Witches have hidden in plain sight for centuries. In churches, no less.
I have no cause to hide.
Why did you try to take your husband's saddle and prevent him from going to Tituba's hearing?
Who told you that?
What good would come of his going? The spectacle of it all...
Tituba confessed. The evidence is conclusive.
All three tried were idle, slothful persons— no good to anyone.
I am a pious woman. I will open the eyes of the magistrates and ministers.

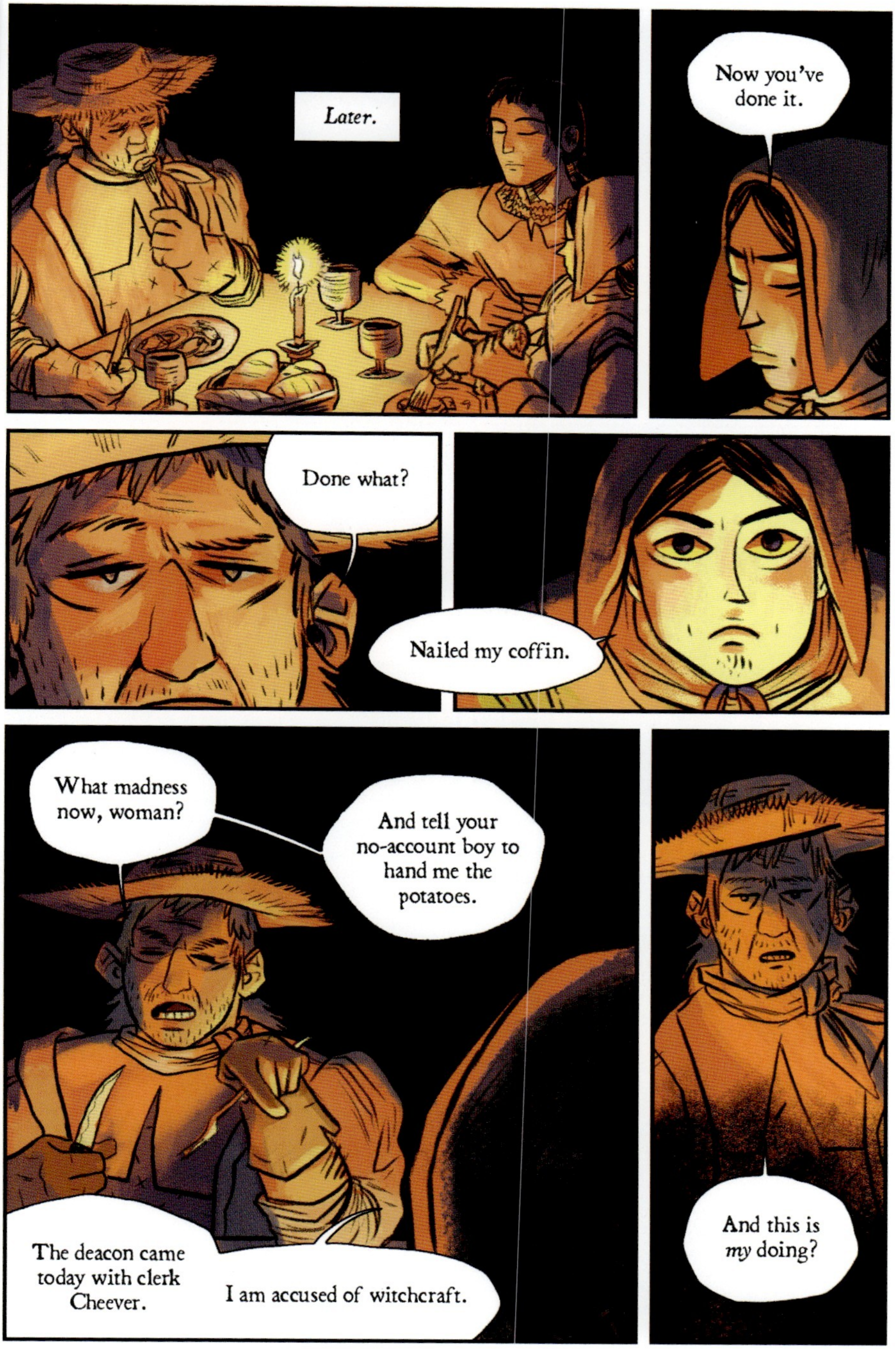
Later.
Now you've done it.
Done what?
Nailed my coffin.
What madness now, woman?
And tell your no-account boy to hand me the potatoes.
The deacon came today with clerk Cheever.
I am accused of witchcraft.
And this is *my* doing?

You went to court against my will...

then came here and filled my head with mischief.

The mischief in your head, wife, is your own.

I have done all I could to live a blameless life for your sake.

But now they will add the old blame to the new.

Thomas Putnam's messenger has since summoned me.

To his home? What does he want?

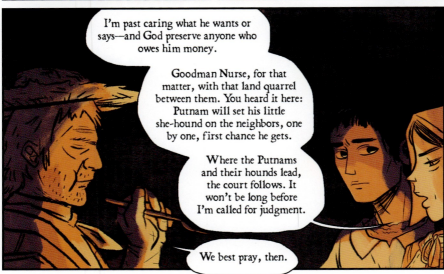

I'm past caring what he wants or says—and God preserve anyone who owes him money.

Goodman Nurse, for that matter, with that land quarrel between them. You heard it here: Putnam will set his little she-hound on the neighbors, one by one, first chance he gets.

Where the Putnams and their hounds lead, the court follows. It won't be long before I'm called for judgment.

We best pray, then.

74

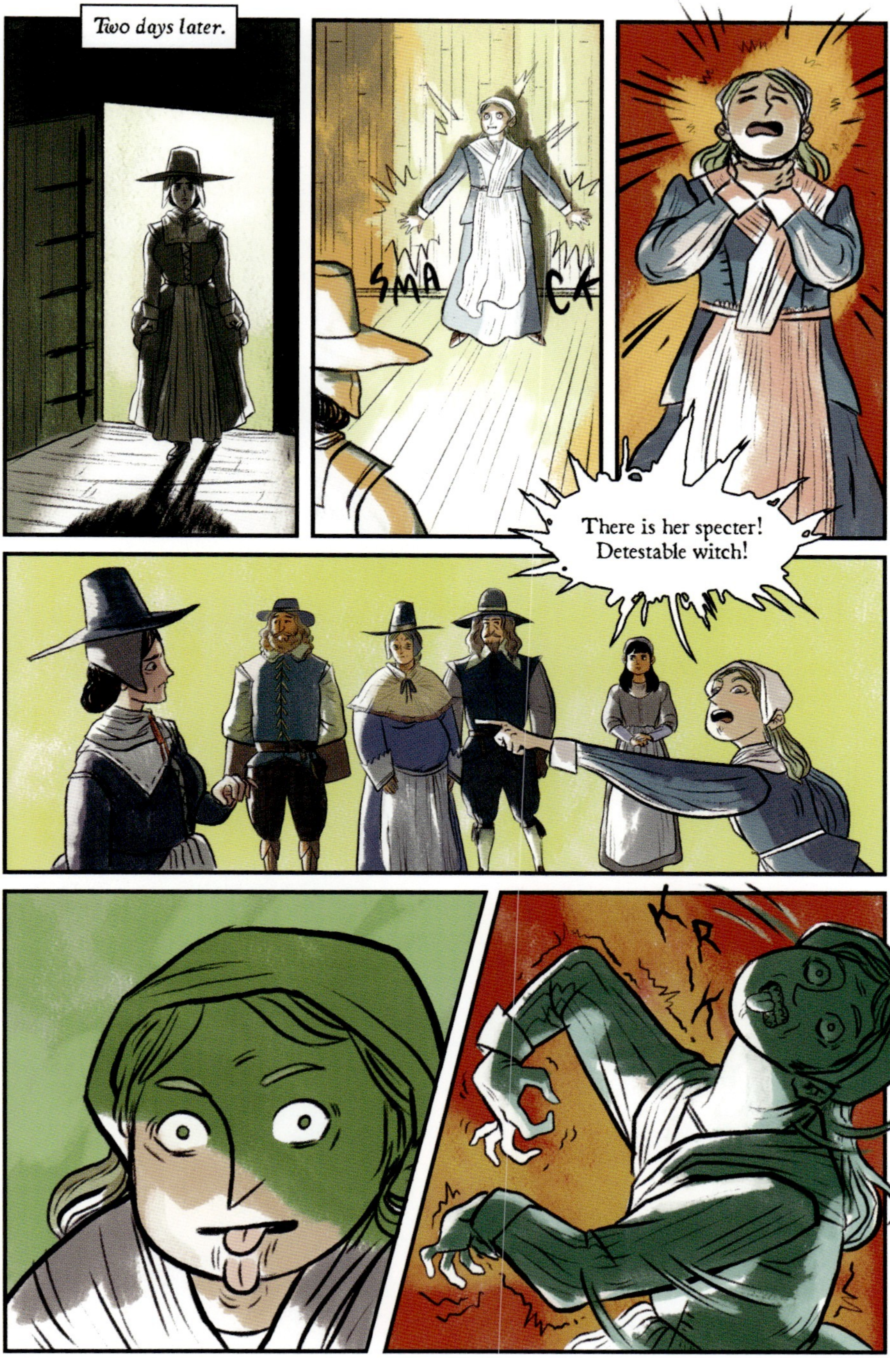

Two days later.
SMACK
There is her specter! Detestable witch!
KRIK

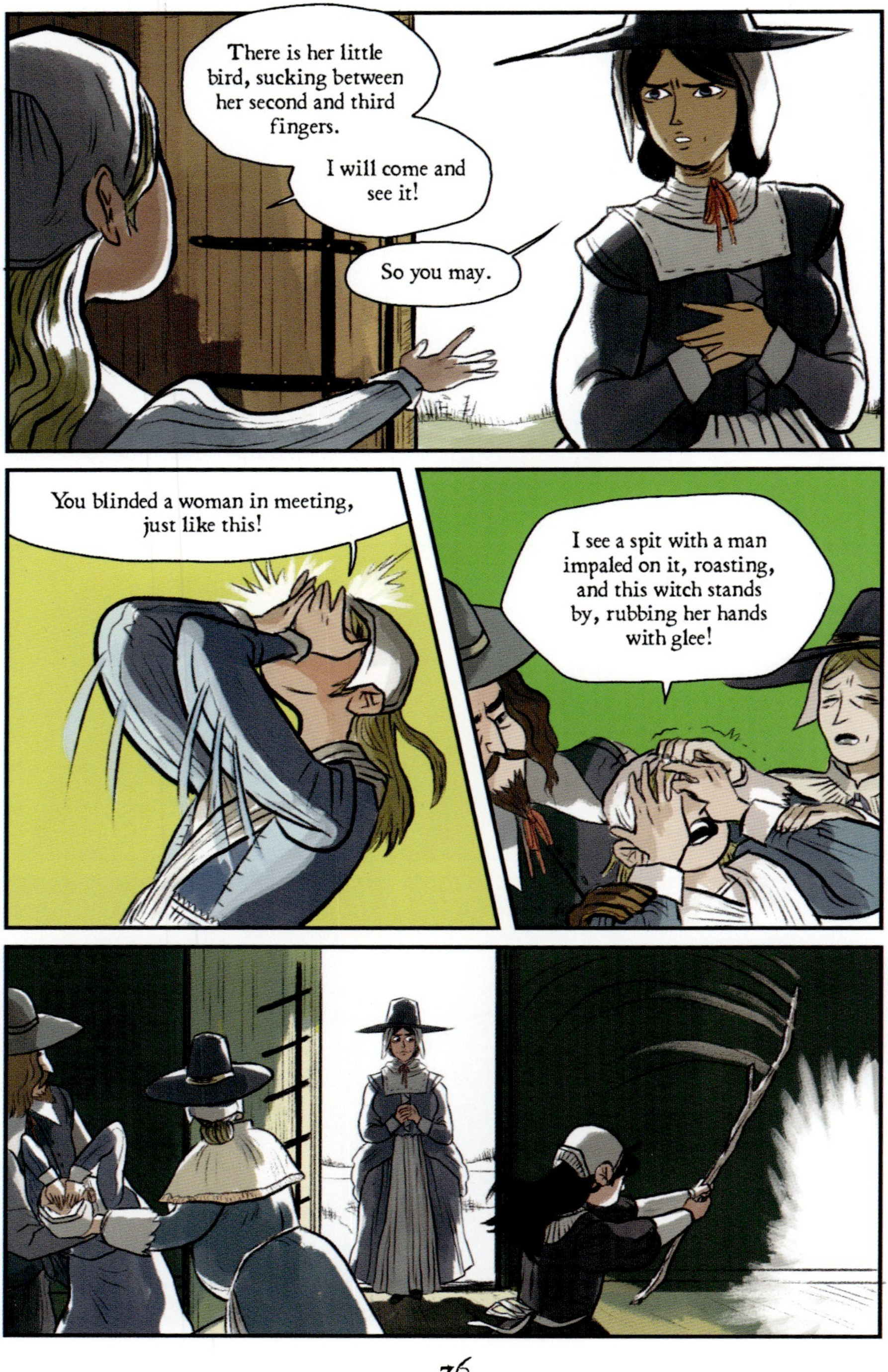
There is her little bird, sucking between her second and third fingers.
I will come and see it!
So you may.
You blinded a woman in meeting, just like this!
I see a spit with a man impaled on it, roasting, and this witch stands by, rubbing her hands with glee!

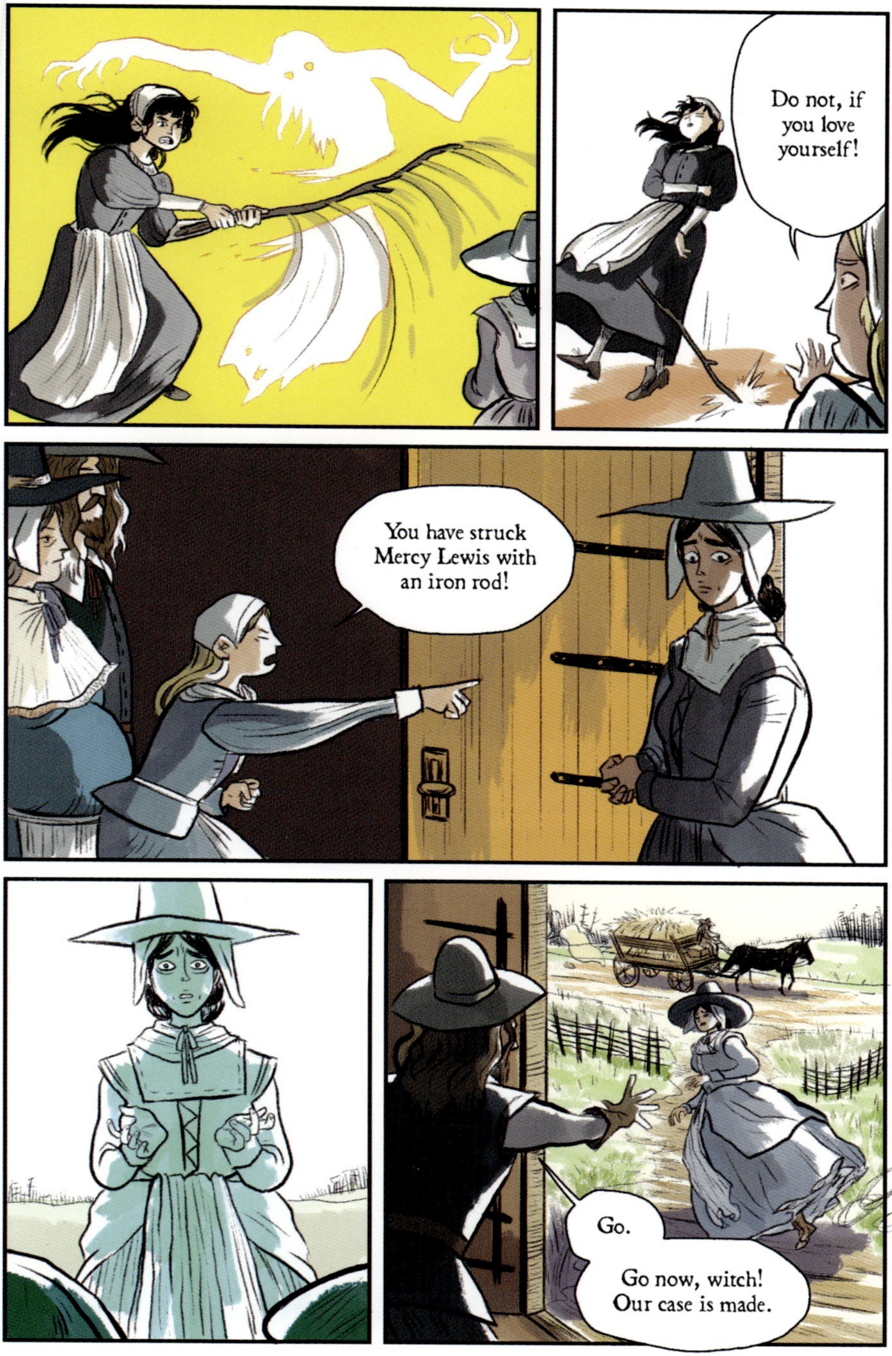
Do not, if you love yourself!
You have struck Mercy Lewis with an iron rod!
Go.
Go now, witch! Our case is made.

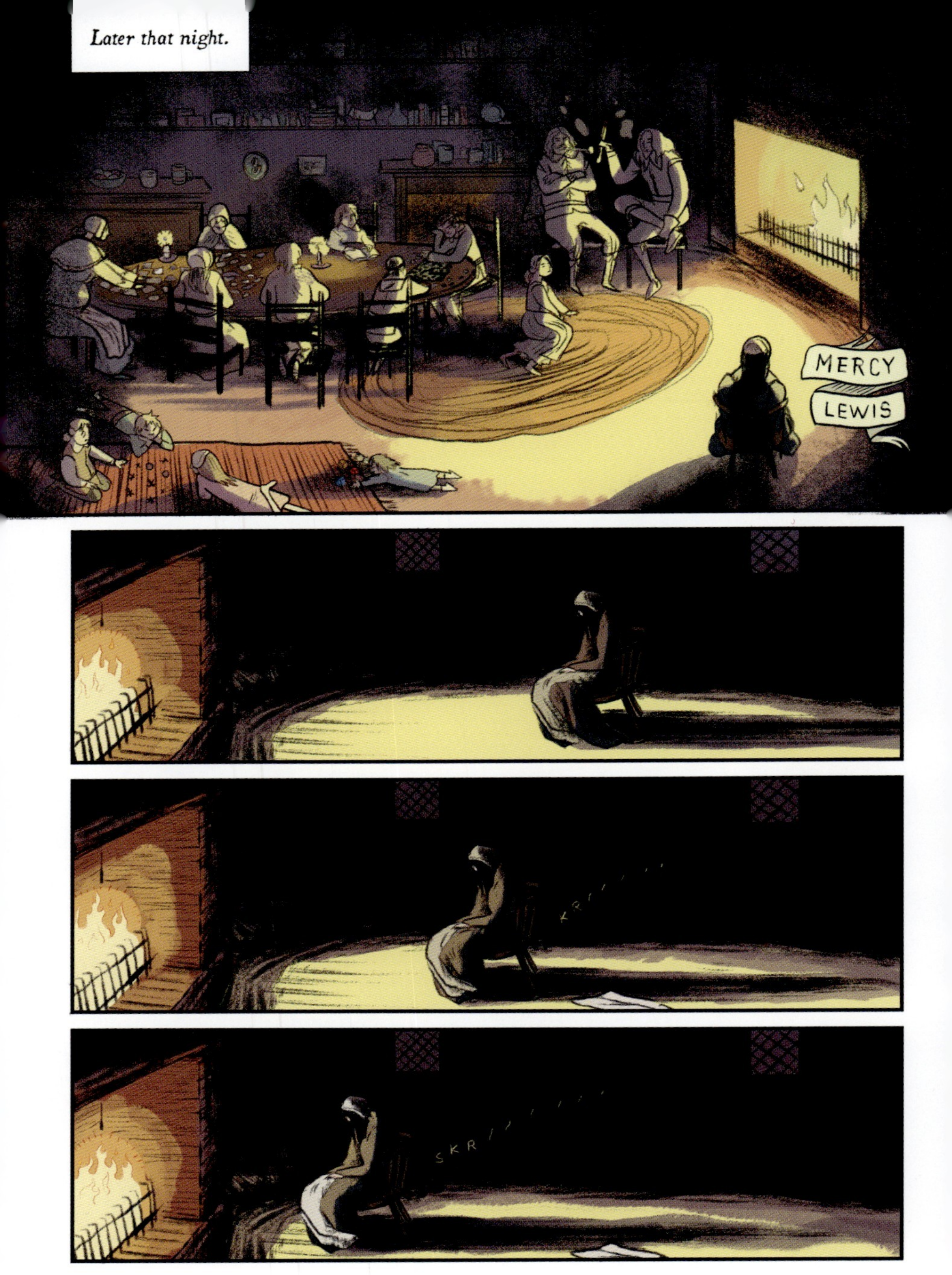
Later that night.
MERCY
LEWIS
KR
SKR

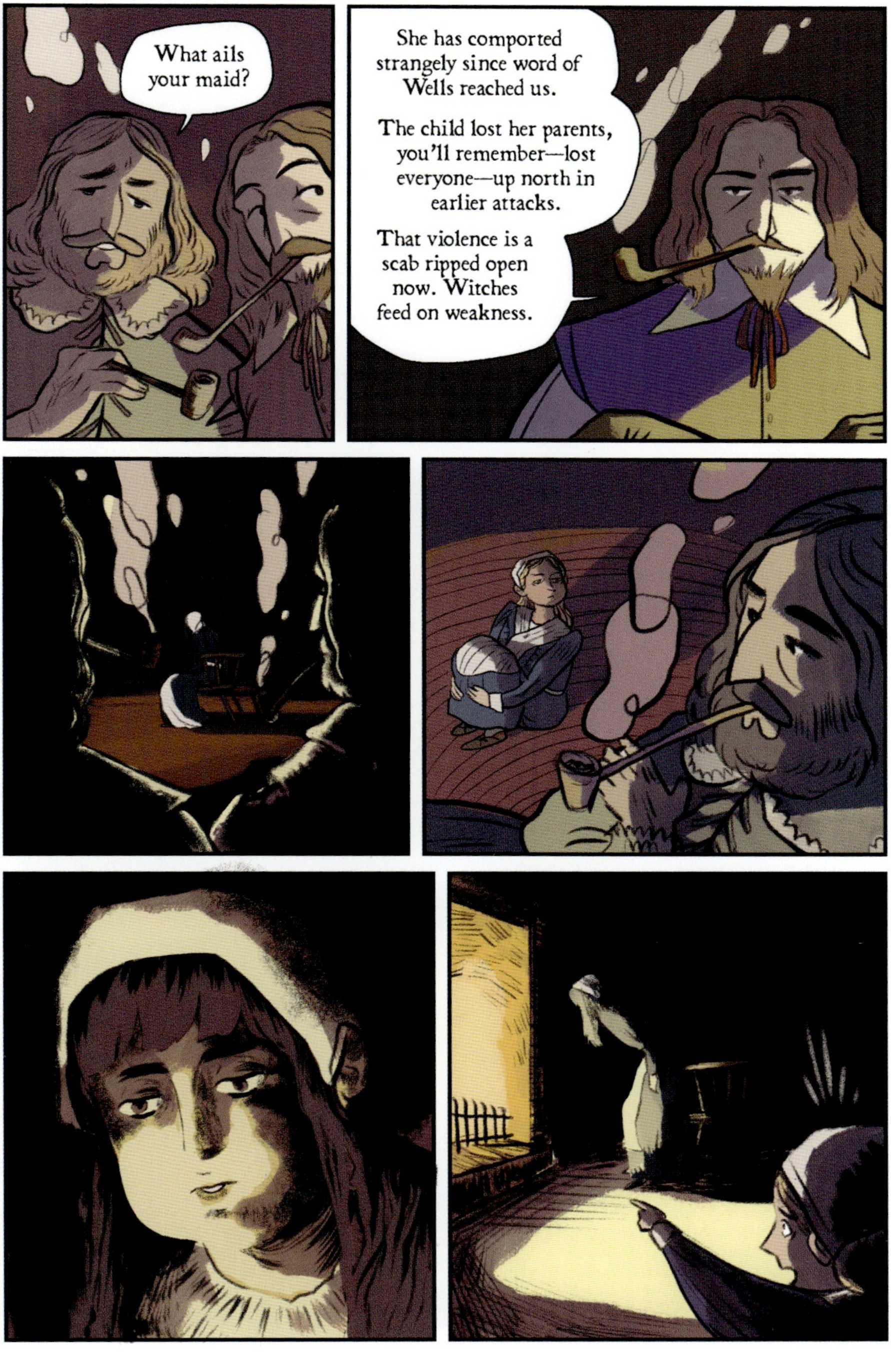
What ails your maid?
She has comported strangely since word of Wells reached us.
The child lost her parents, you'll remember—lost everyone—up north in earlier attacks.
That violence is a scab ripped open now. Witches feed on weakness.

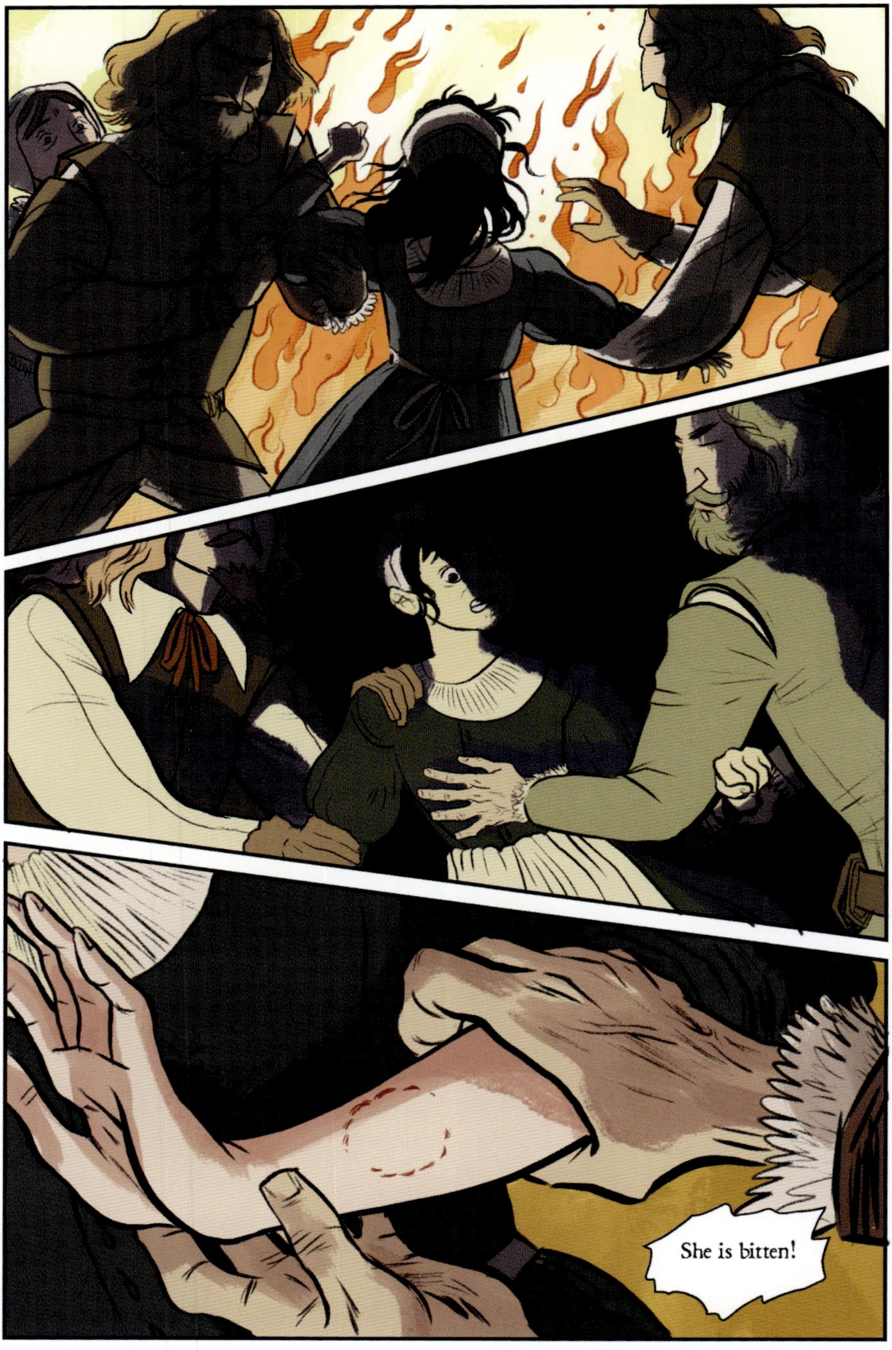
She is bitten!

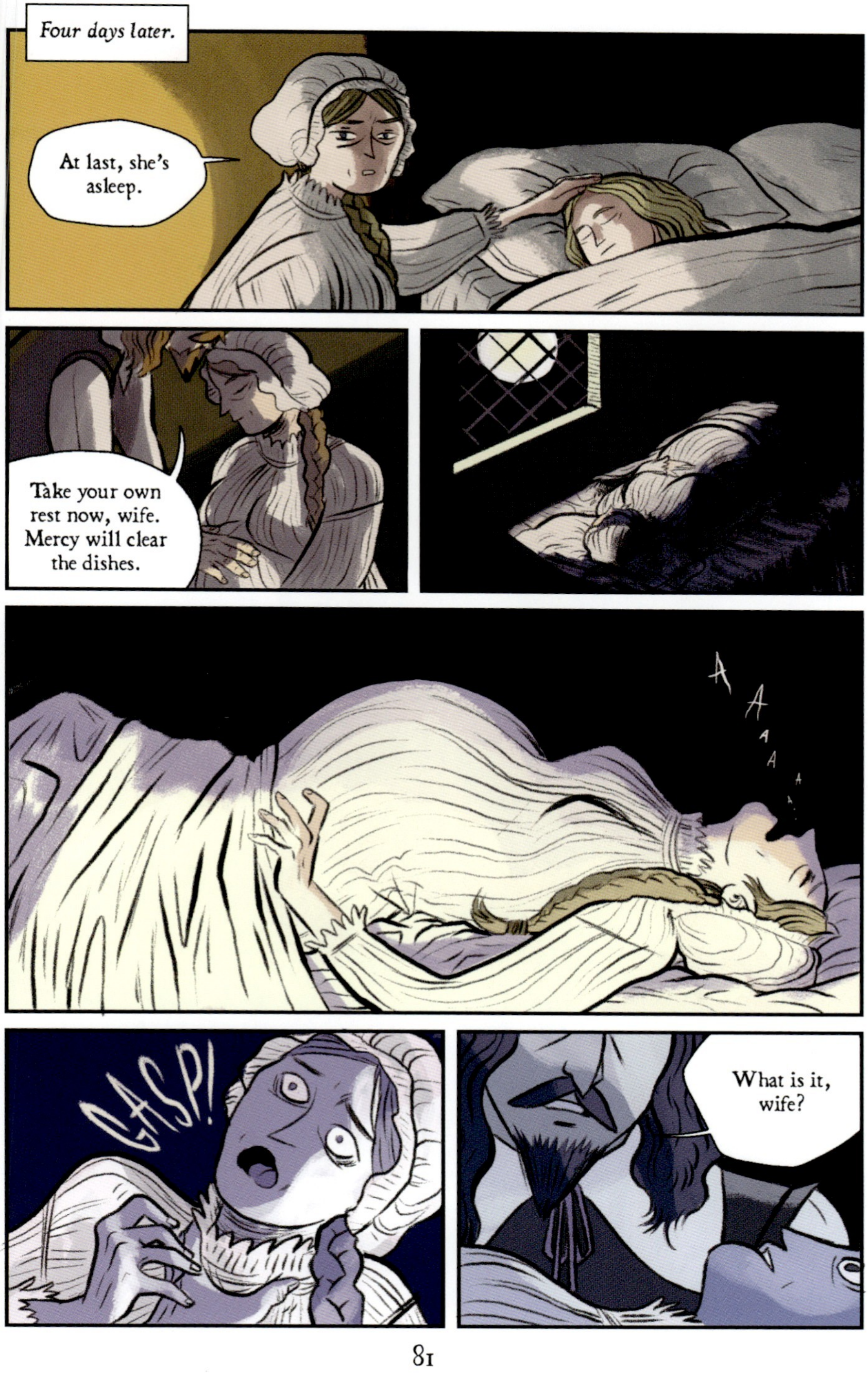
Four days later.
At last, she's asleep.
Take your own rest now, wife. Mercy will clear the dishes.
A A A A A A
GASP!
What is it, wife?

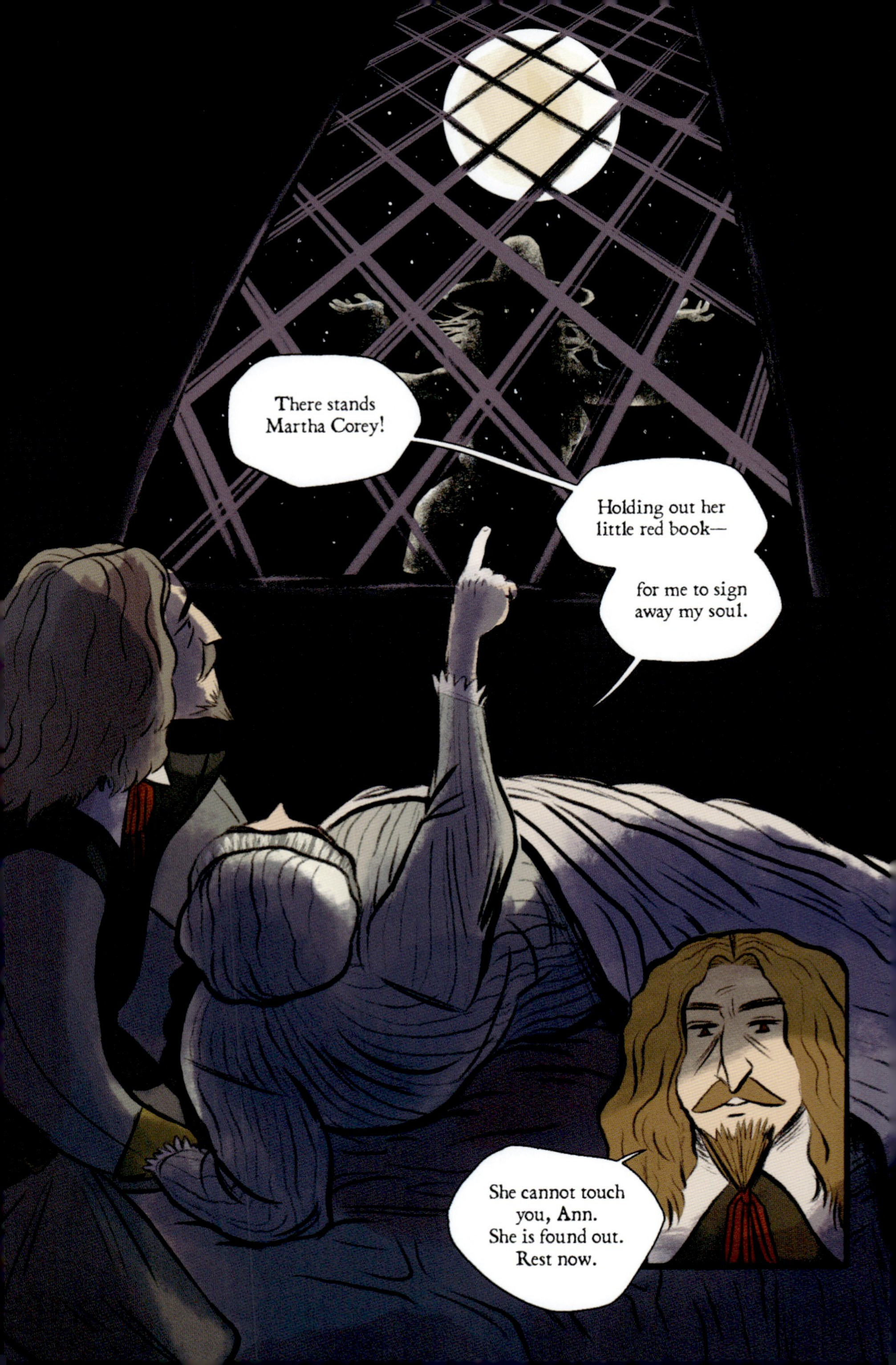
There stands Martha Corey!
Holding out her little red book—
for me to sign away my soul.
She cannot touch you, Ann. She is found out. Rest now.

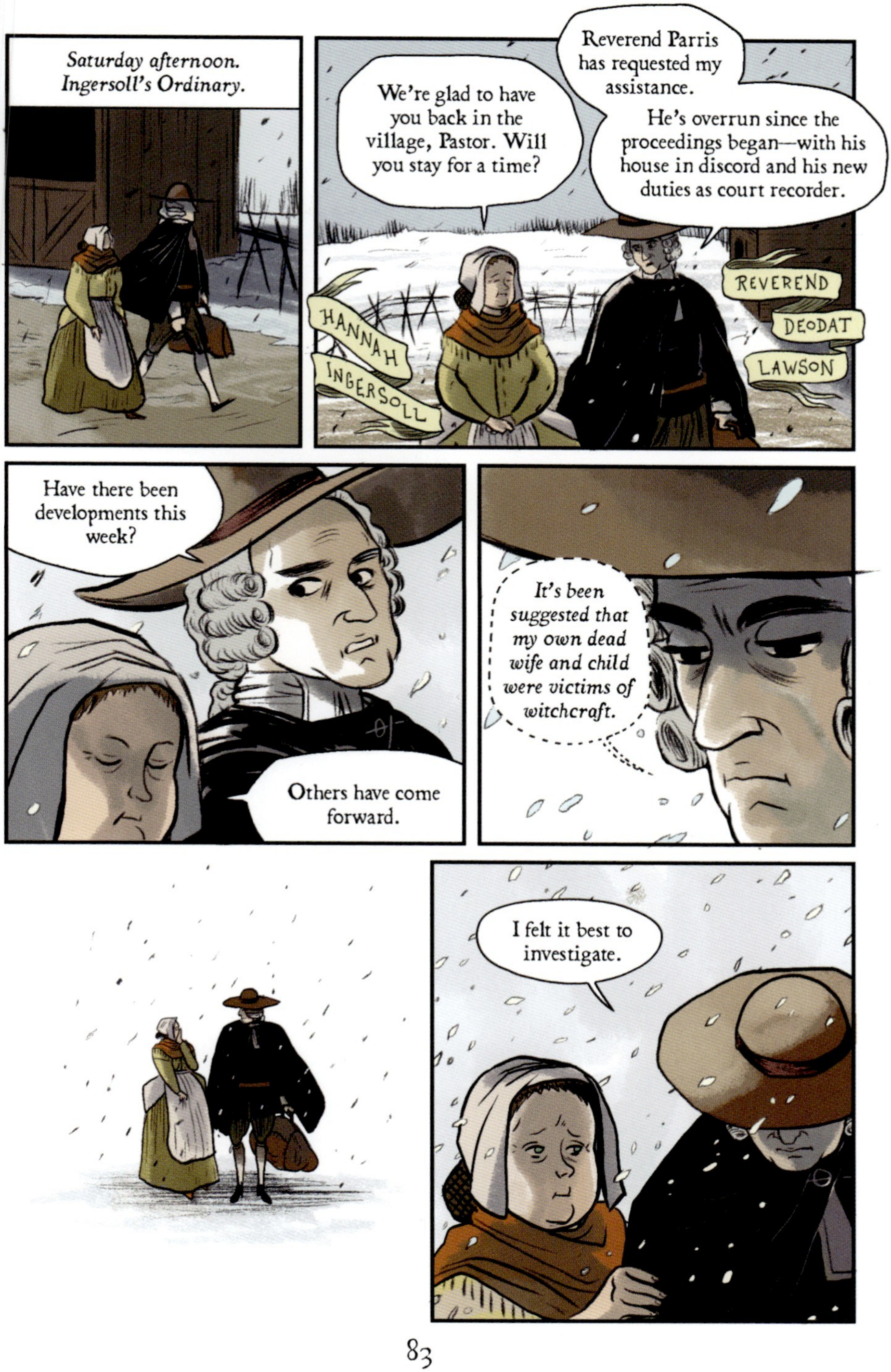
Saturday afternoon. Ingersoll's Ordinary.
We're glad to have you back in the village, Pastor. Will you stay for a time?
Reverend Parris has requested my assistance.
He's overrun since the proceedings began—with his house in discord and his new duties as court recorder.
HANNAH INGERSOLL
REVEREND DEODAT LAWSON
Have there been developments this week?
Others have come forward.
It's been suggested that my own dead wife and child were victims of witchcraft.
I felt it best to investigate.

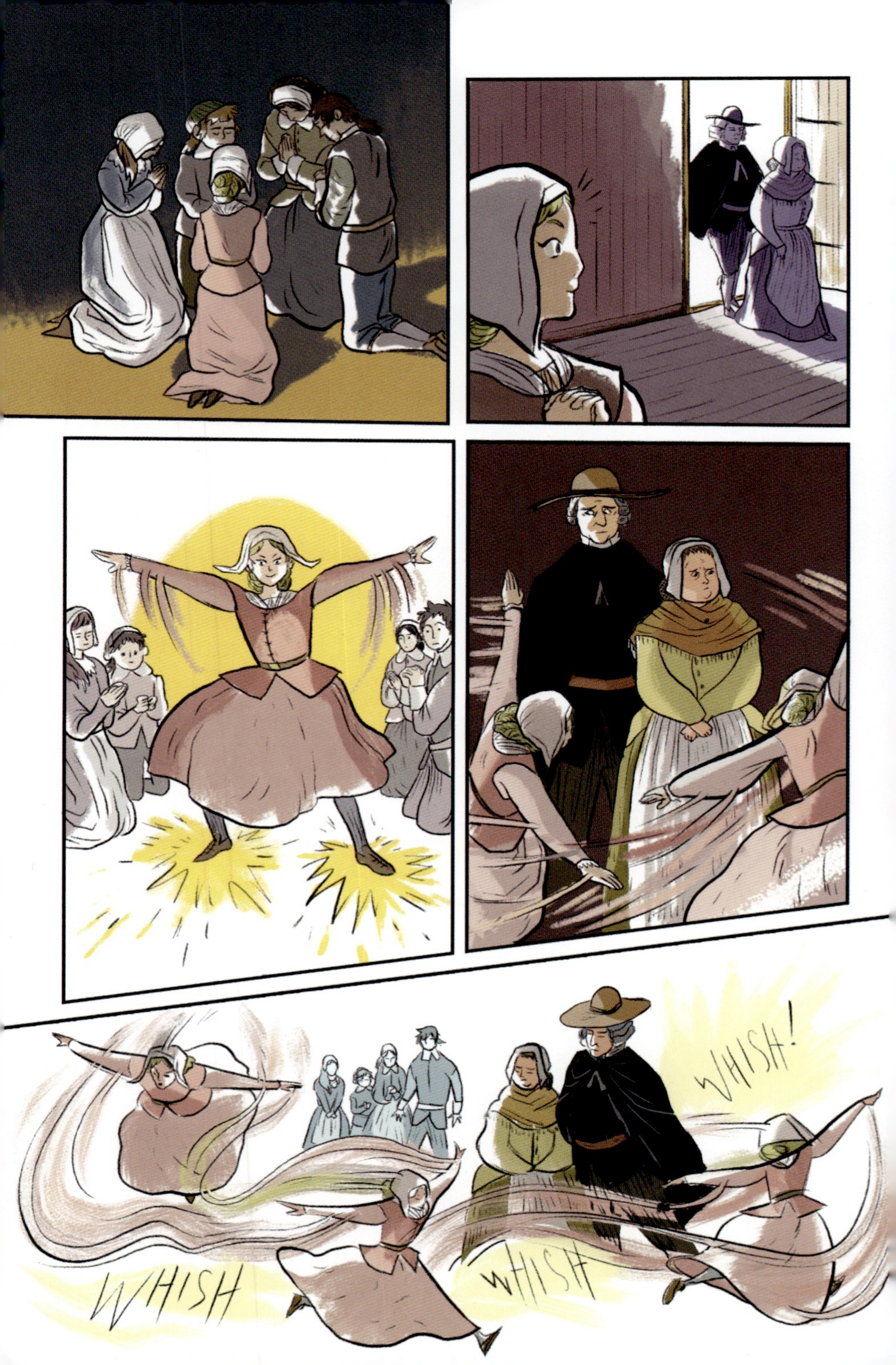

WHISH!
WHISH
WHISH

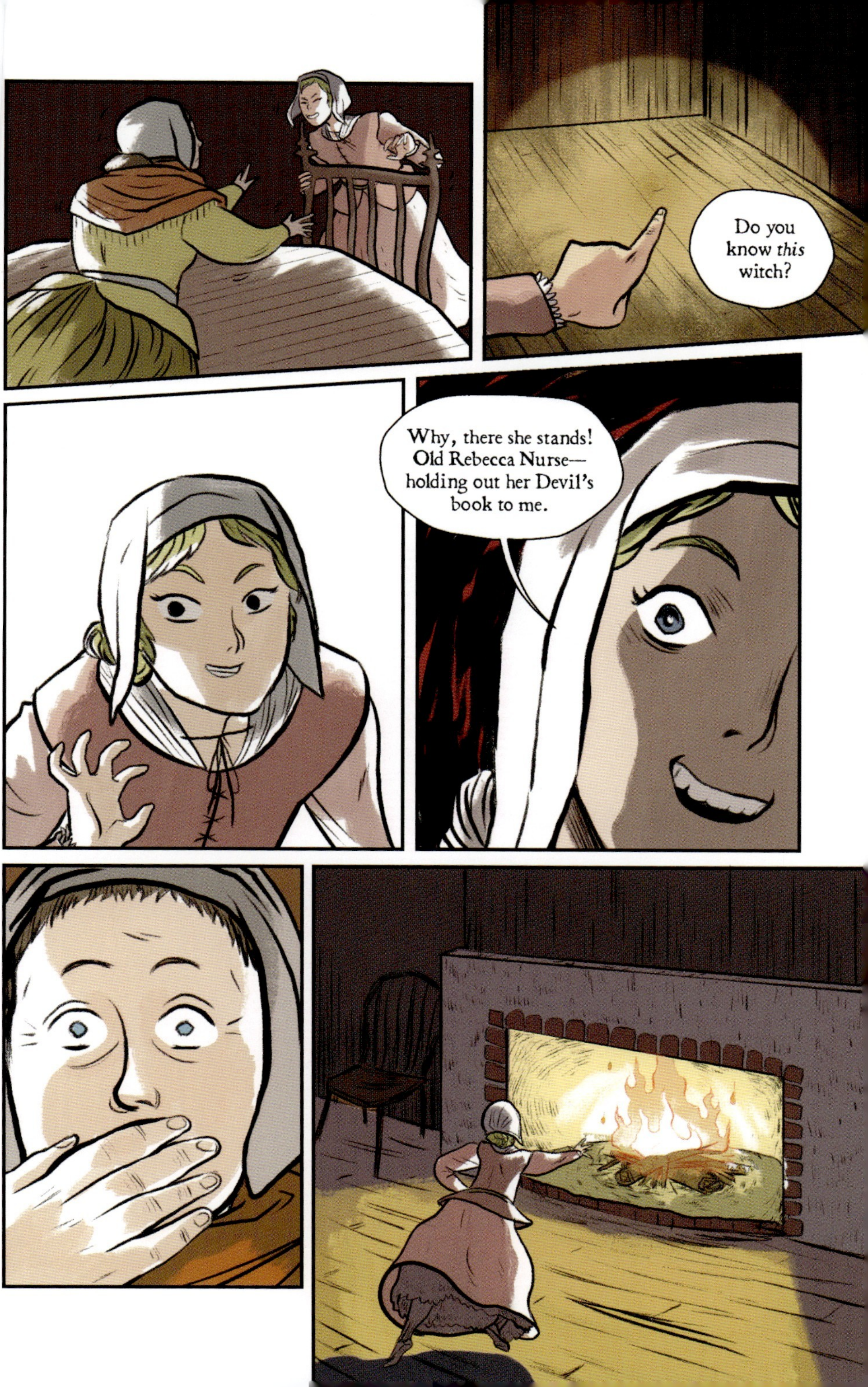
Do you know *this* witch?
Why, there she stands! Old Rebecca Nurse—holding out her Devil's book to me.

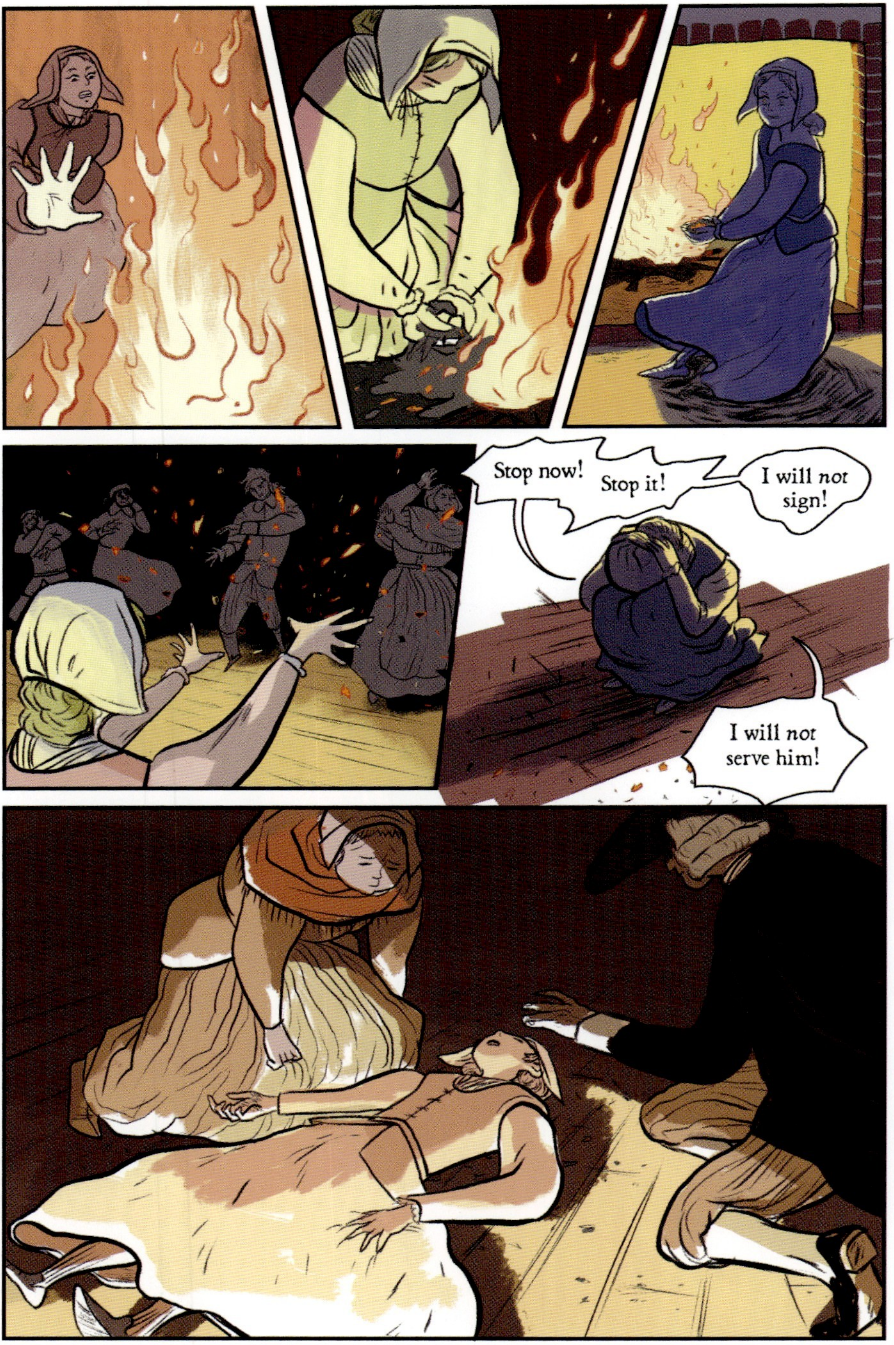
Stop now!
Stop it!
I will *not* sign!
I will *not* serve him!

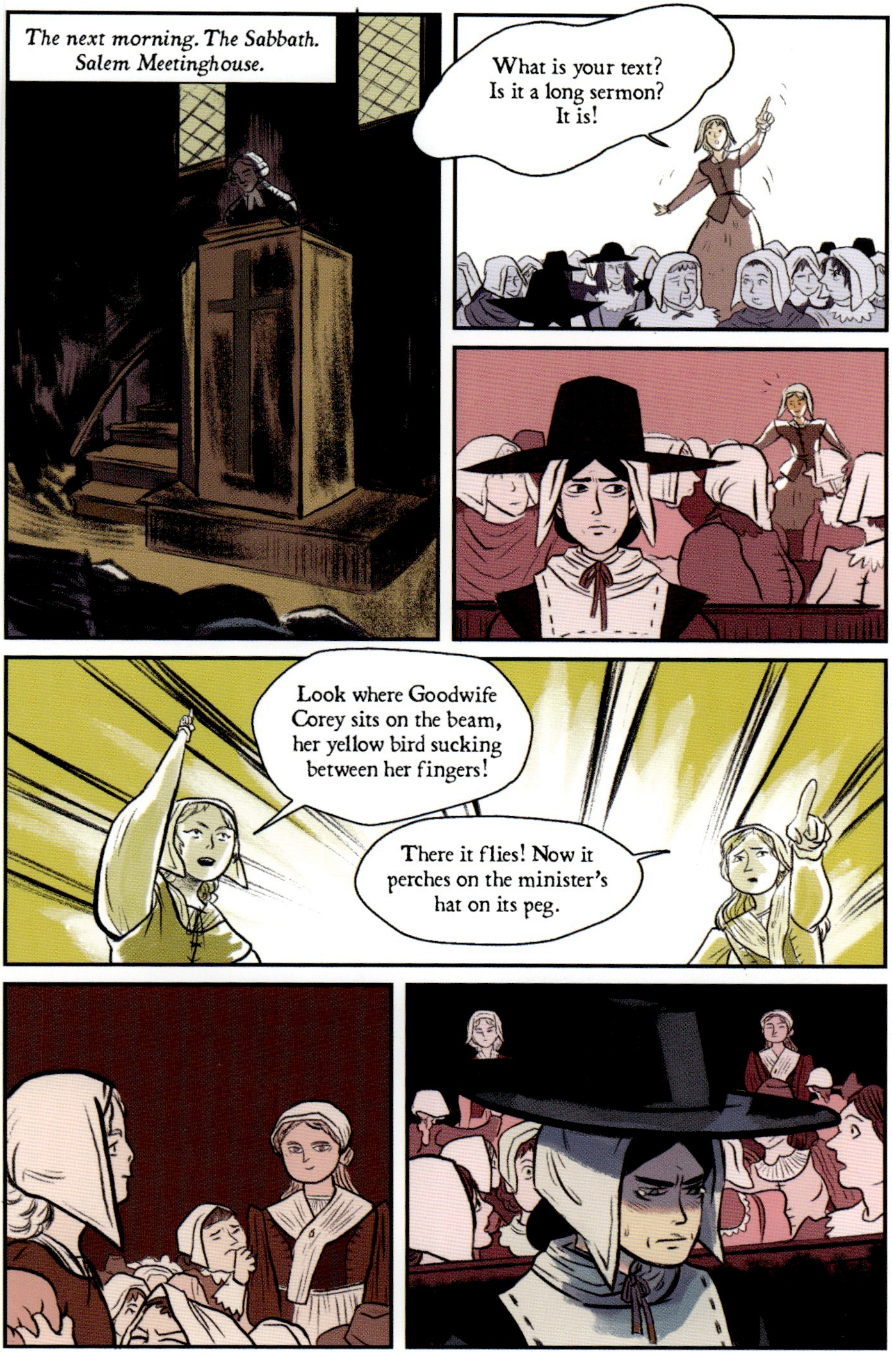
The next morning. The Sabbath. Salem Meetinghouse.
What is your text? Is it a long sermon? It is!
Look where Goodwife Corey sits on the beam, her yellow bird sucking between her fingers!
There it flies! Now it perches on the minister's hat on its peg.

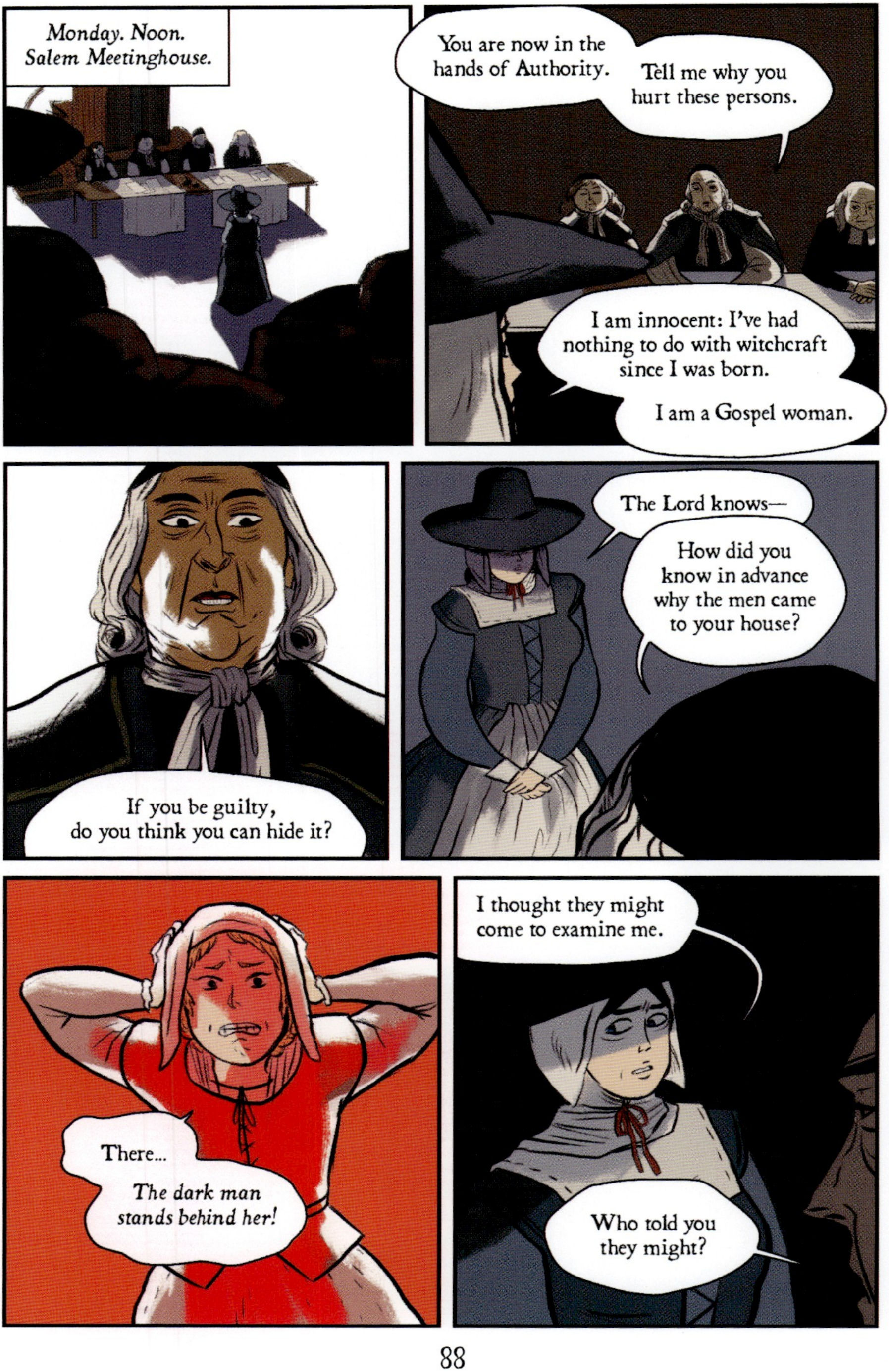
Monday. Noon.
Salem Meetinghouse.
You are now in the hands of Authority.
Tell me why you hurt these persons.
I am innocent: I've had nothing to do with witchcraft since I was born.
I am a Gospel woman.
If you be guilty, do you think you can hide it?
The Lord knows—
How did you know in advance why the men came to your house?
There...
The dark man stands behind her!
I thought they might come to examine me.
Who told you they might?

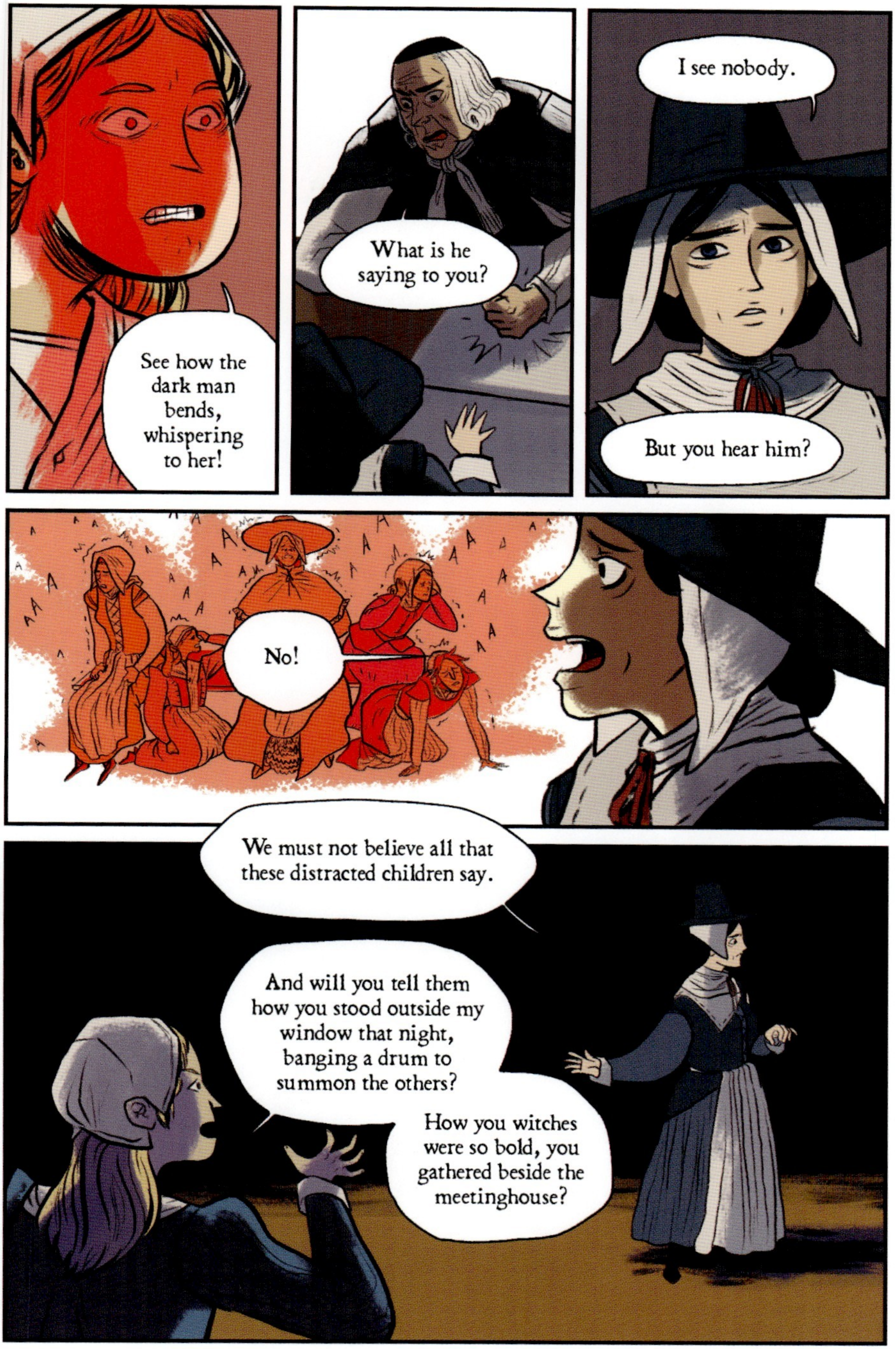
See how the dark man bends, whispering to her!
What is he saying to you?
I see nobody.
But you hear him?
No!
We must not believe all that these distracted children say.
And will you tell them how you stood outside my window that night, banging a drum to summon the others?
How you witches were so bold, you gathered beside the meetinghouse?

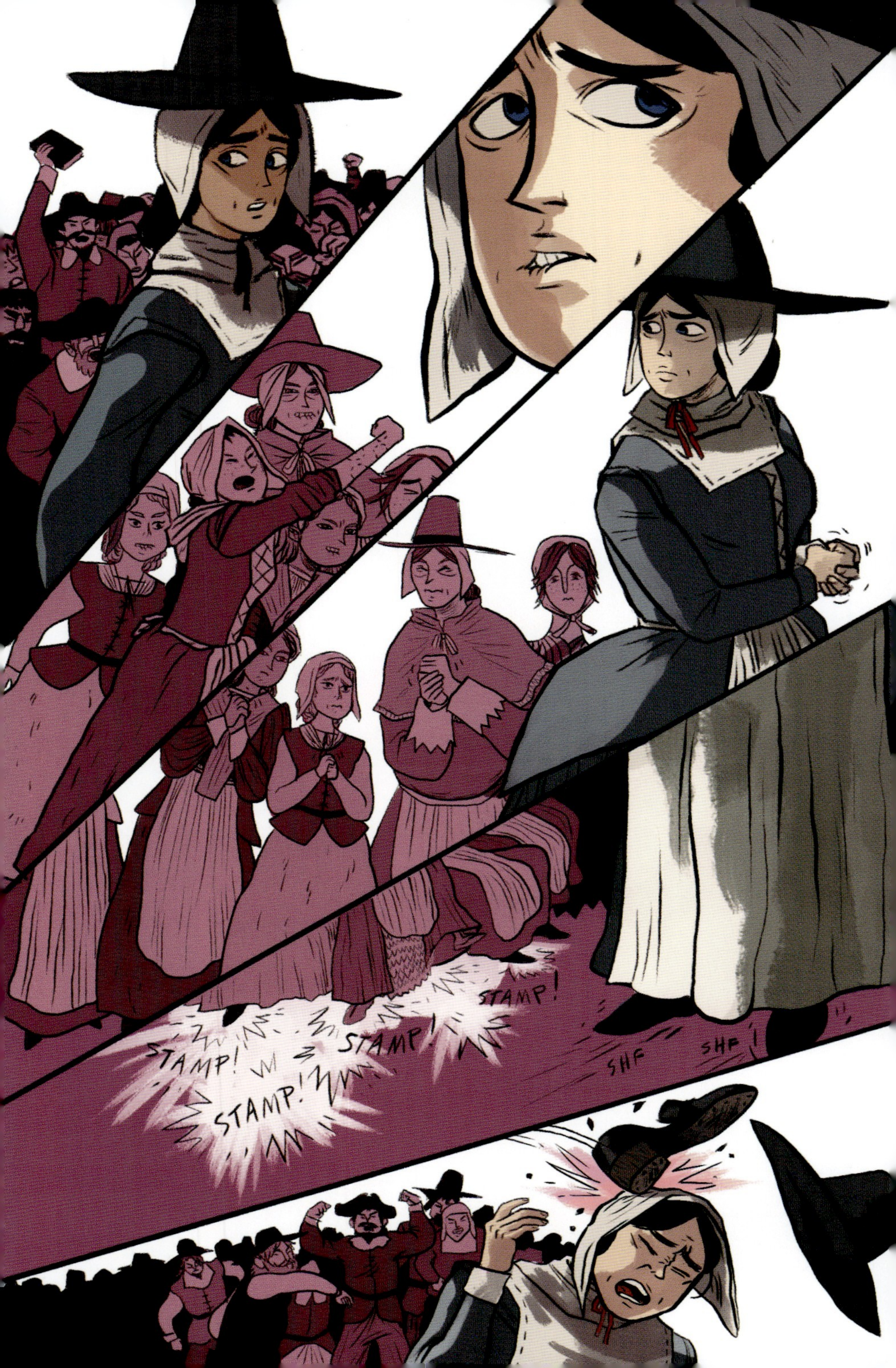
STAMP!
STAMP!
STAMP!
STAMP!
SHF SHF

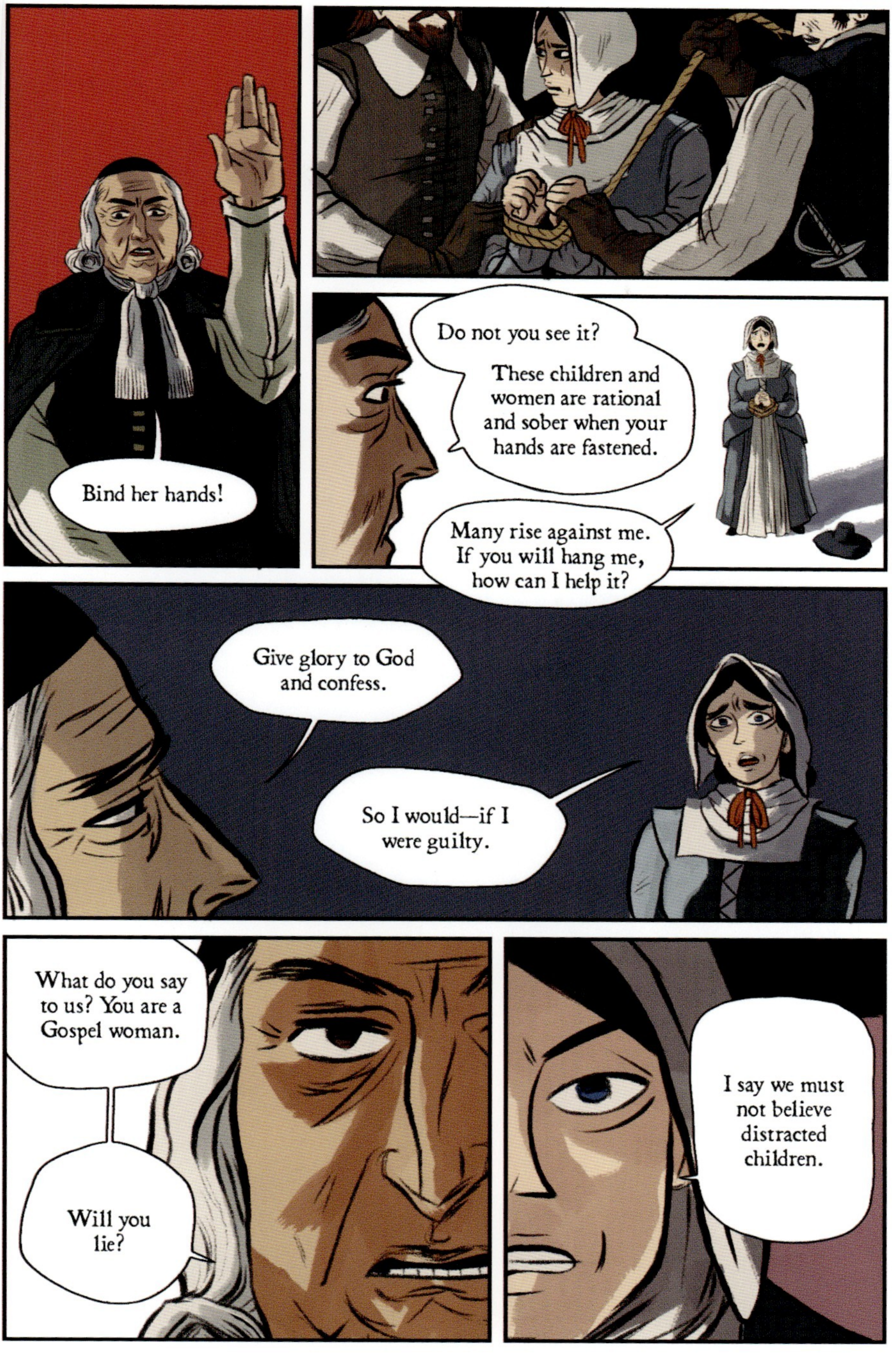
Bind her hands!
Do not you see it?
These children and women are rational and sober when your hands are fastened.
Many rise against me. If you will hang me, how can I help it?
Give glory to God and confess.
So I would—if I were guilty.
What do you say to us? You are a Gospel woman.
Will you lie?
I say we must not believe distracted children.

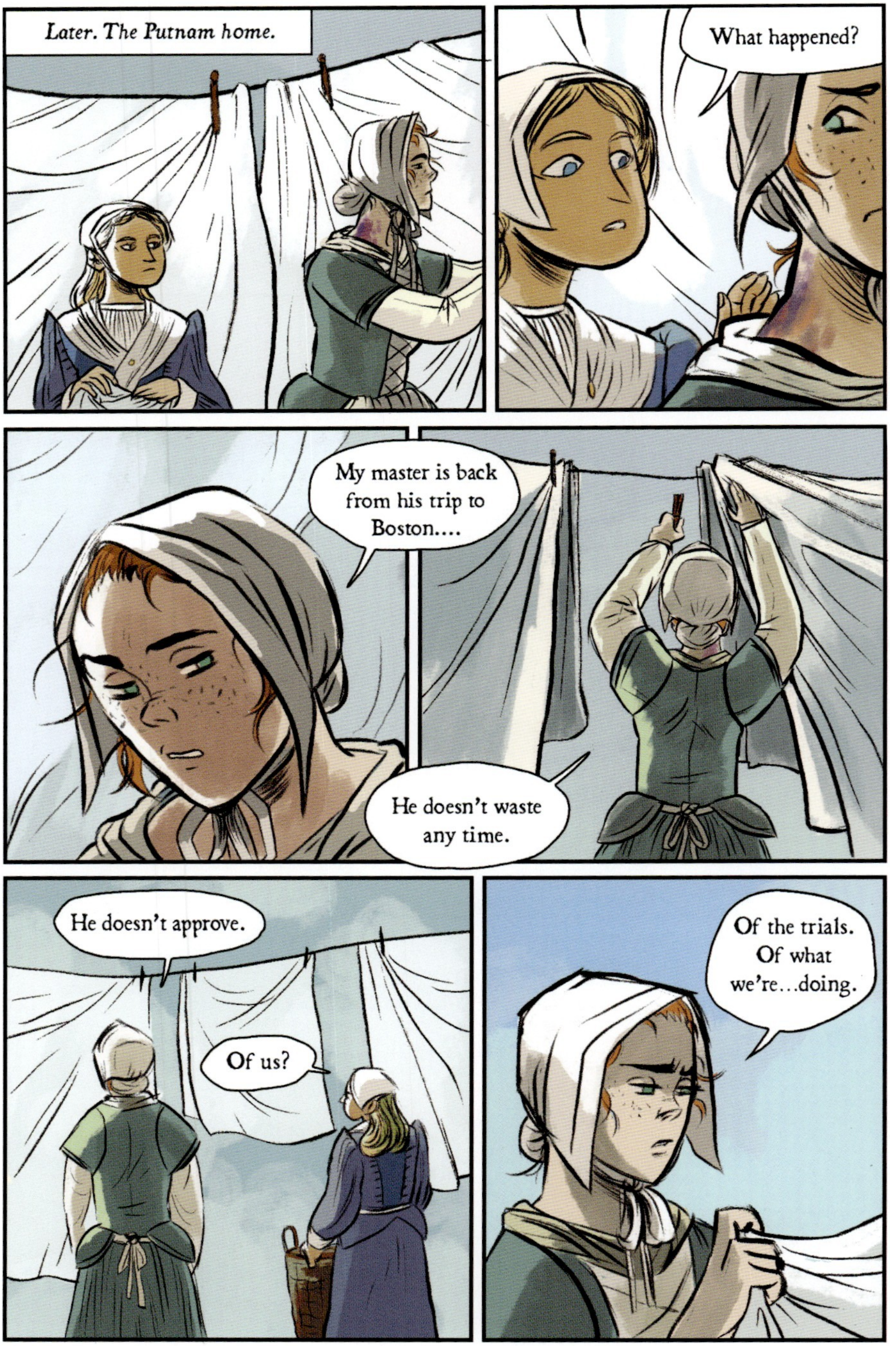
Later. The Putnam home.
What happened?
My master is back from his trip to Boston....
He doesn't waste any time.
He doesn't approve.
Of us?
Of the trials. Of what we're...doing.

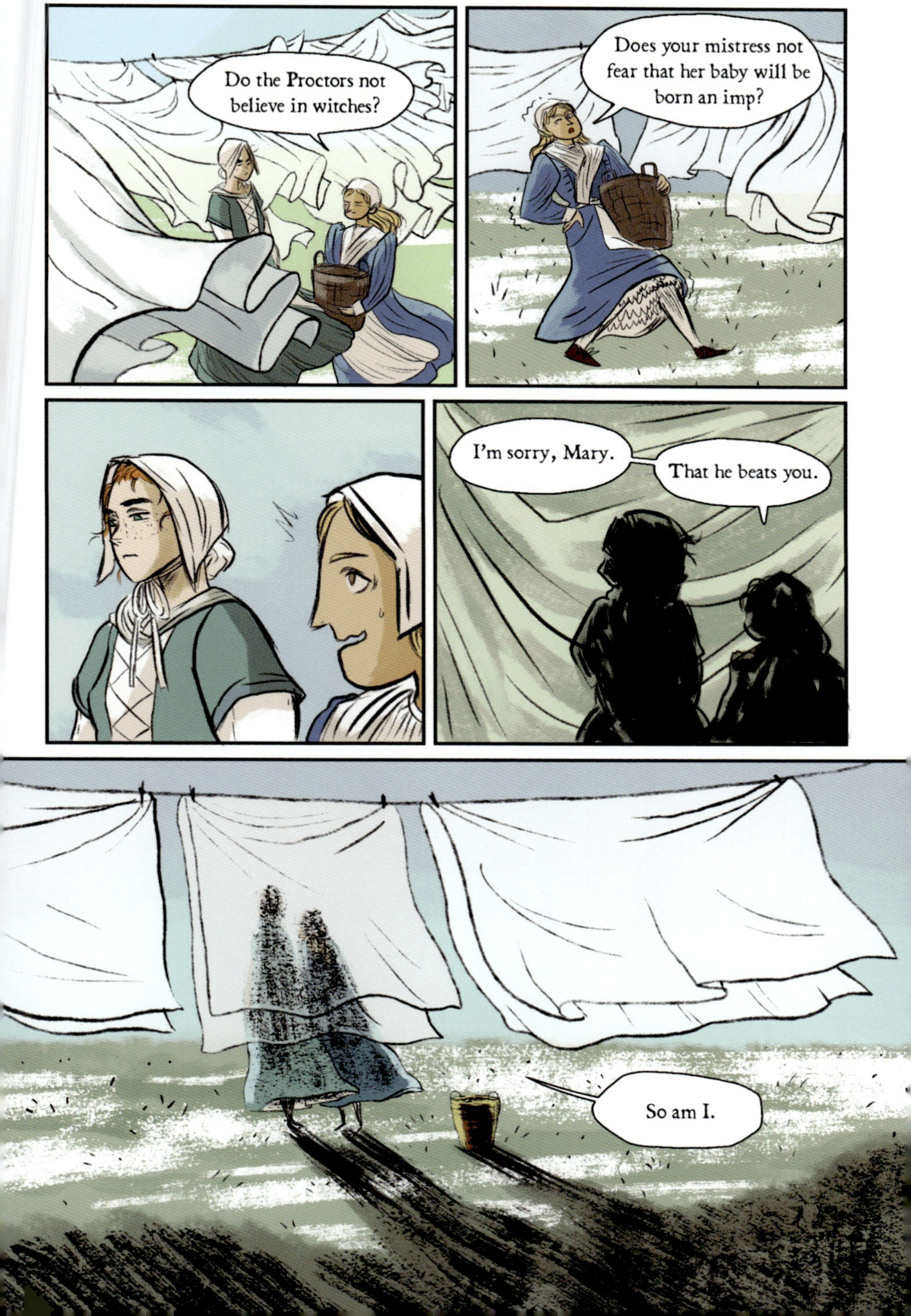
Do the Proctors not believe in witches?
Does your mistress not fear that her baby will be born an imp?
I'm sorry, Mary.
That he beats you.
So am I.

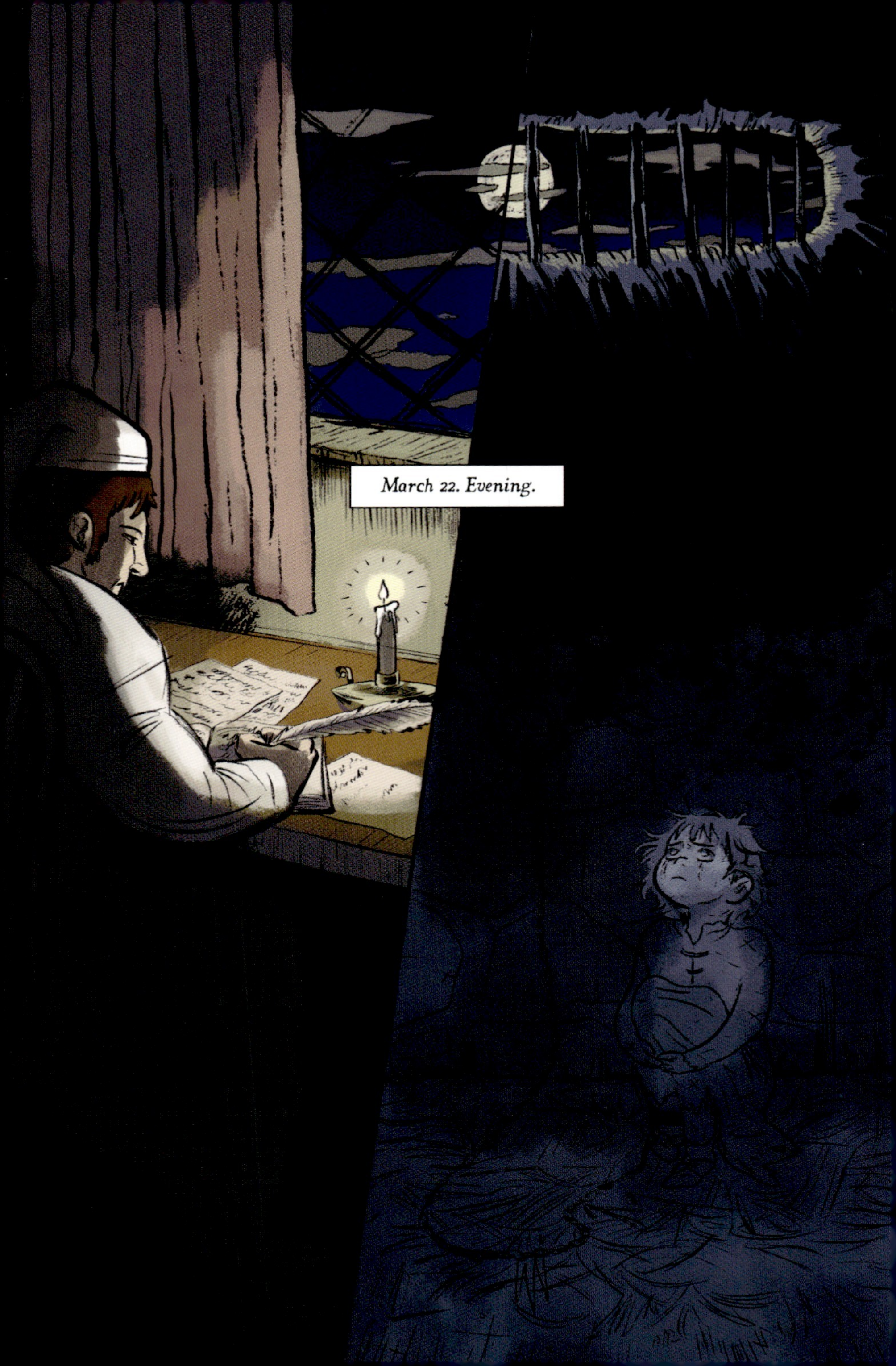
March 22. Evening.

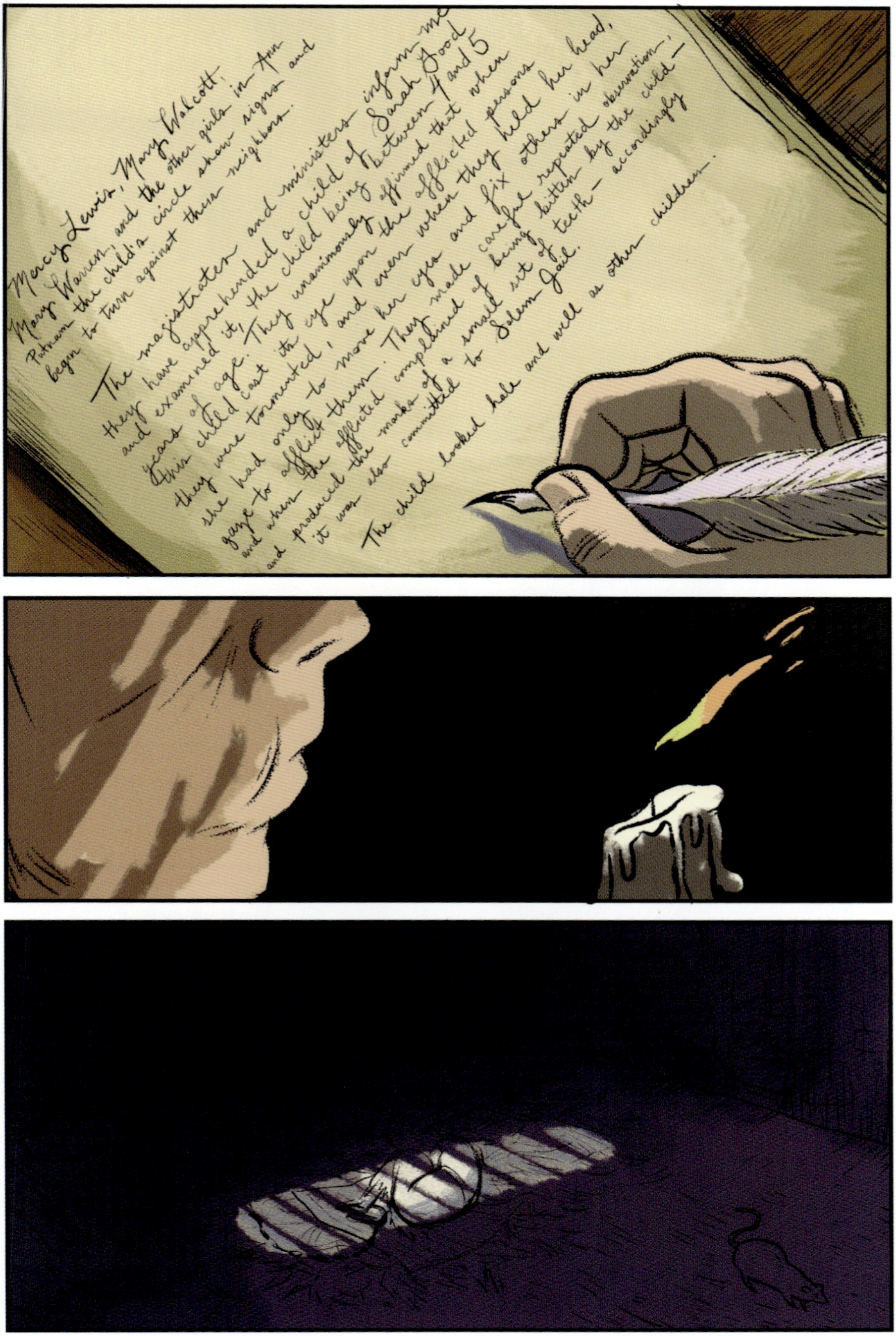
Mercy Lewis, Mary Walcott,
Mary Warren, and the other girls in Ann
Putnam the child's circle show signs and
begin to turn against their neighbors.
The magistrates and ministers inform me
they have apprehended a child of Sarah Good
and examined it, the child being between 4 and 5
years of age. They unanimously affirmed that when
this child cast its eye upon the afflicted persons
they were tormented, and even when they held her head,
she had only to move her eyes and fix others in her
gaze to afflict them. They made careful repeated observation—
and when the afflicted complained of being bitten by the child—
and produced the marks of a small set of teeth— accordingly
it was also committed to Salem Jail.
The child looked hale and well as other children.

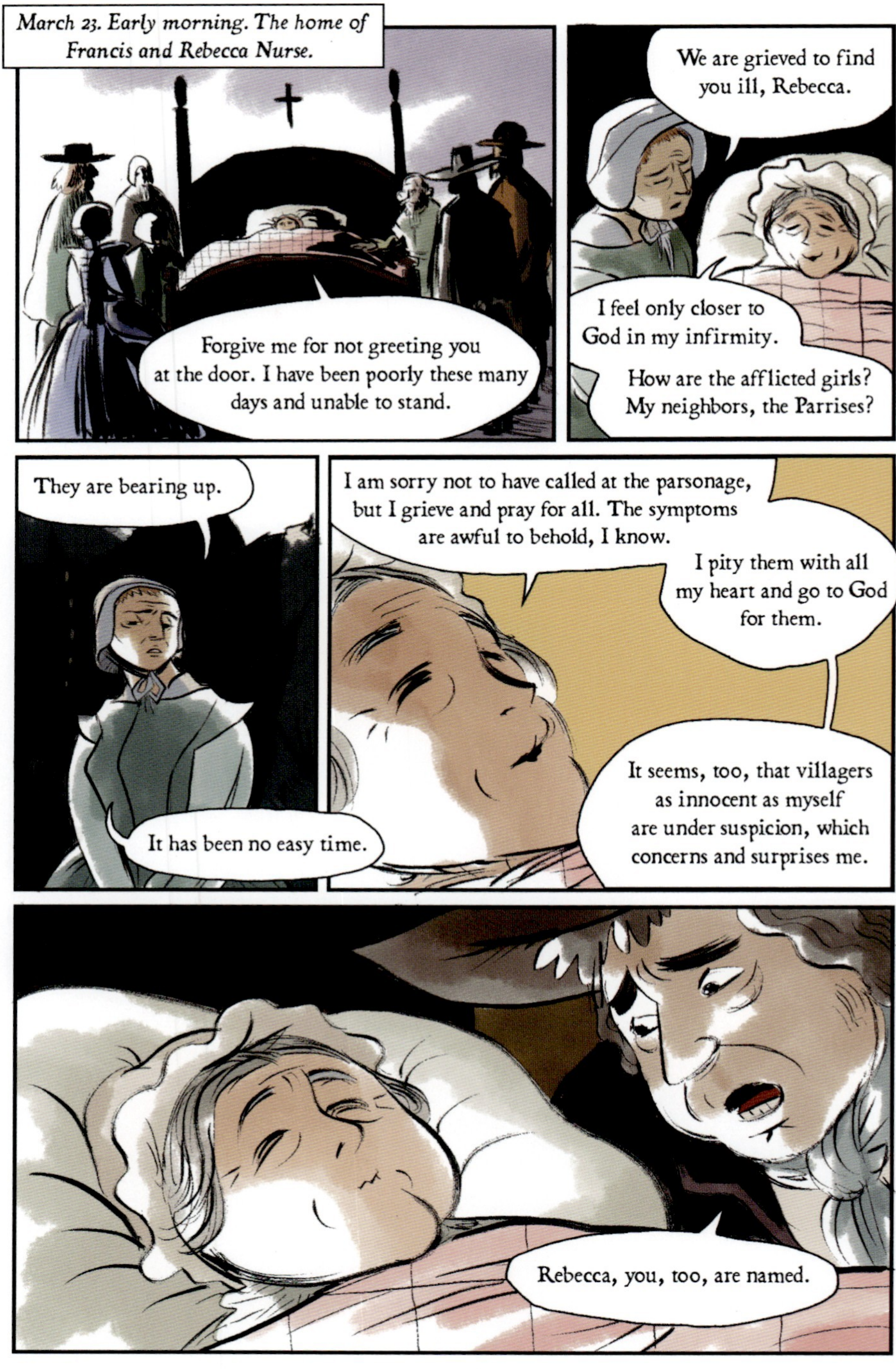
March 23. Early morning. The home of Francis and Rebecca Nurse.
Forgive me for not greeting you at the door. I have been poorly these many days and unable to stand.
We are grieved to find you ill, Rebecca.
I feel only closer to God in my infirmity.
How are the afflicted girls? My neighbors, the Parrises?
They are bearing up.
It has been no easy time.
I am sorry not to have called at the parsonage, but I grieve and pray for all. The symptoms are awful to behold, I know.
I pity them with all my heart and go to God for them.
It seems, too, that villagers as innocent as myself are under suspicion, which concerns and surprises me.
Rebecca, you, too, are named.

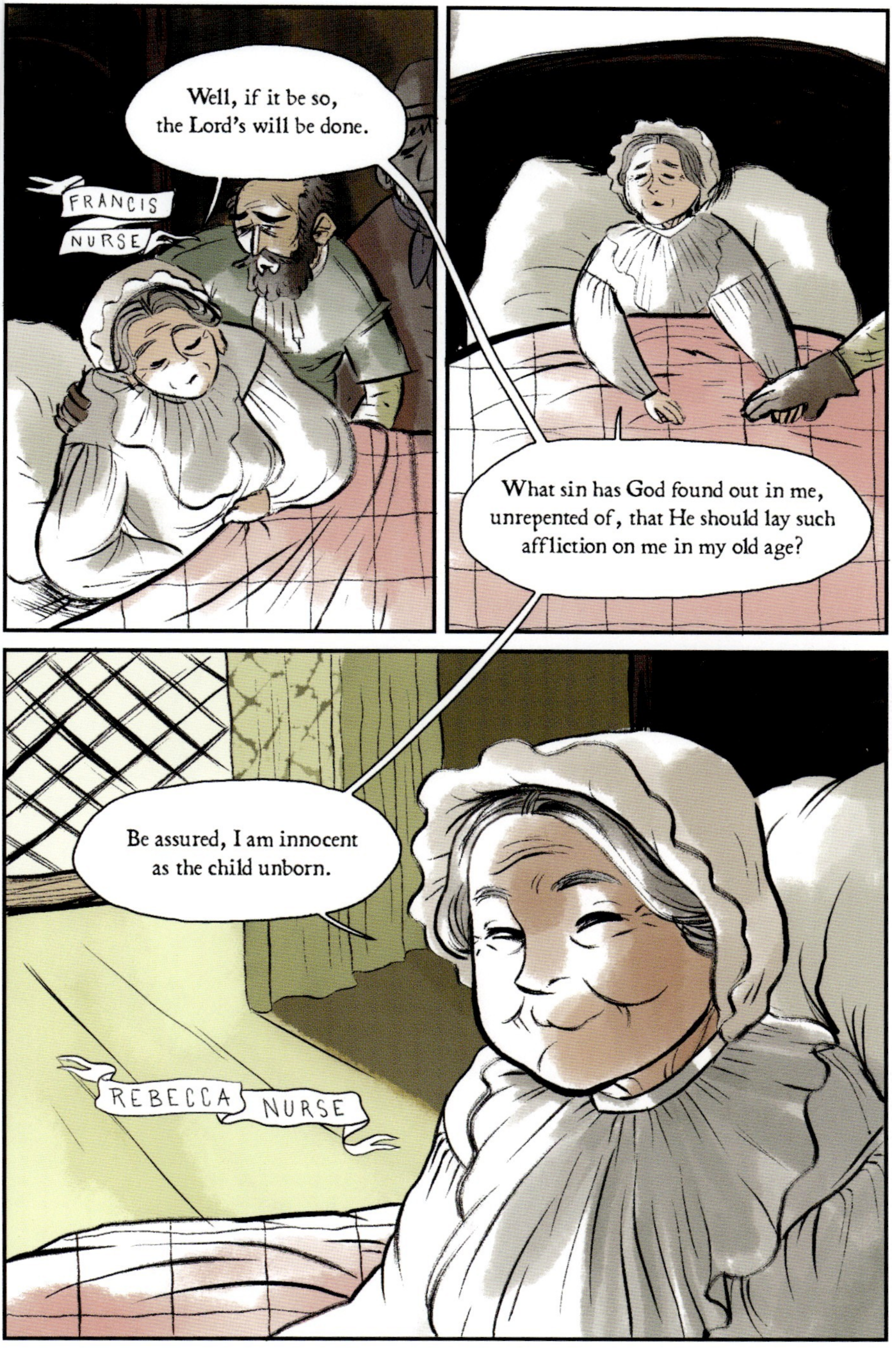
Well, if it be so, the Lord's will be done.
FRANCIS NURSE
What sin has God found out in me, unrepented of, that He should lay such affliction on me in my old age?
Be assured, I am innocent as the child unborn.
REBECCA NURSE

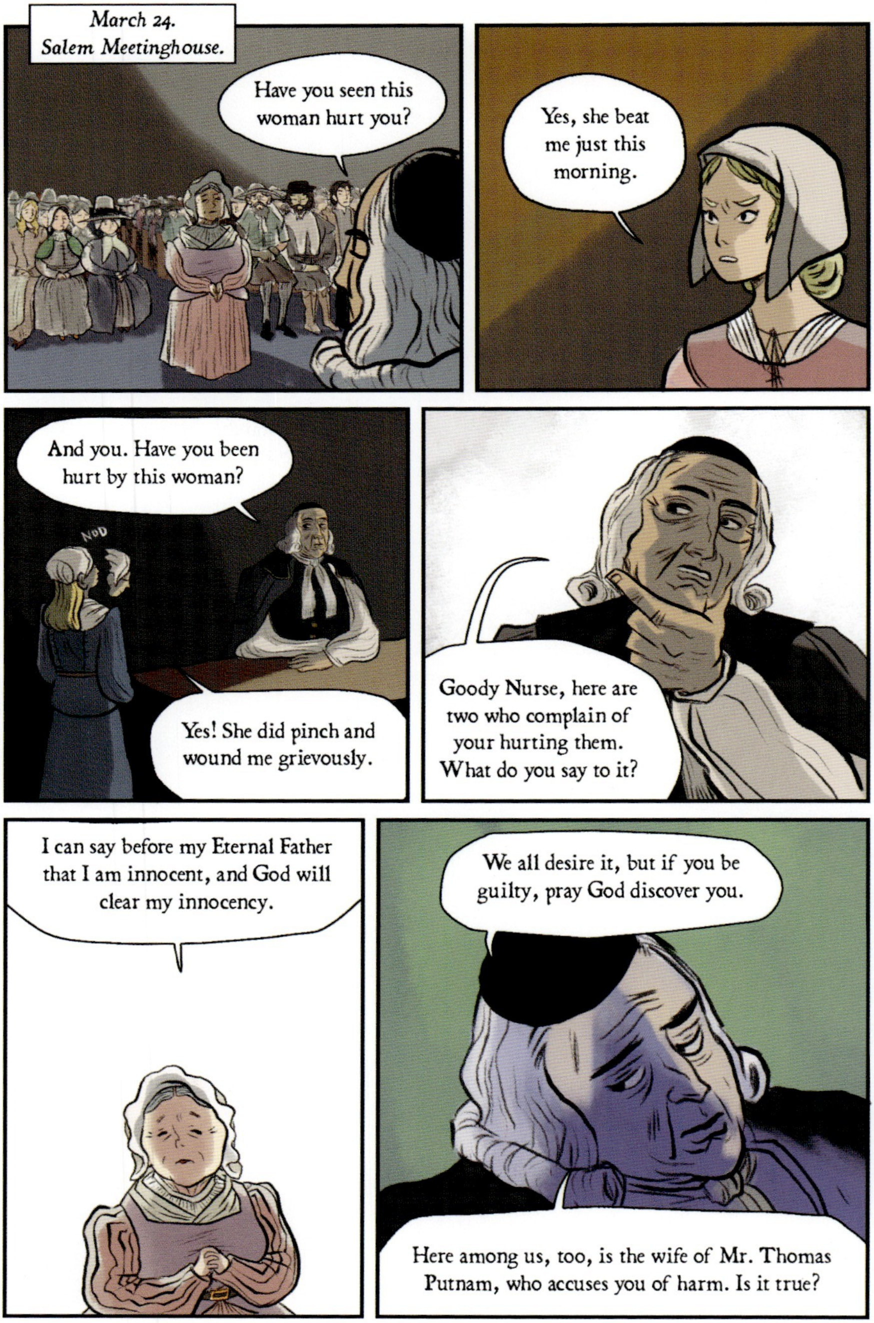
March 24.
Salem Meetinghouse.
Have you seen this woman hurt you?
Yes, she beat me just this morning.
And you. Have you been hurt by this woman?
NOD
Yes! She did pinch and wound me grievously.
Goody Nurse, here are two who complain of your hurting them. What do you say to it?
I can say before my Eternal Father that I am innocent, and God will clear my innocency.
We all desire it, but if you be guilty, pray God discover you.
Here among us, too, is the wife of Mr. Thomas Putnam, who accuses you of harm. Is it true?

I am innocent and clear and have not even been able to get out of doors these last eight or nine days.

Did you not bring the Devil with you?! Did you not bid me tempt God and die?

How often have you eaten and drunk a demon sacrament? What do you say to them?

Oh, Lord, help me.

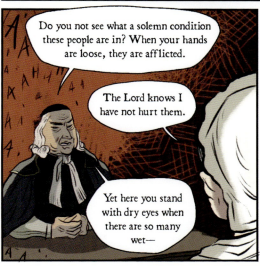

Do you not see what a solemn condition these people are in? When your hands are loose, they are afflicted.

The Lord knows I have not hurt them.

Yet here you stand with dry eyes when there are so many wet—

You do not know my heart.

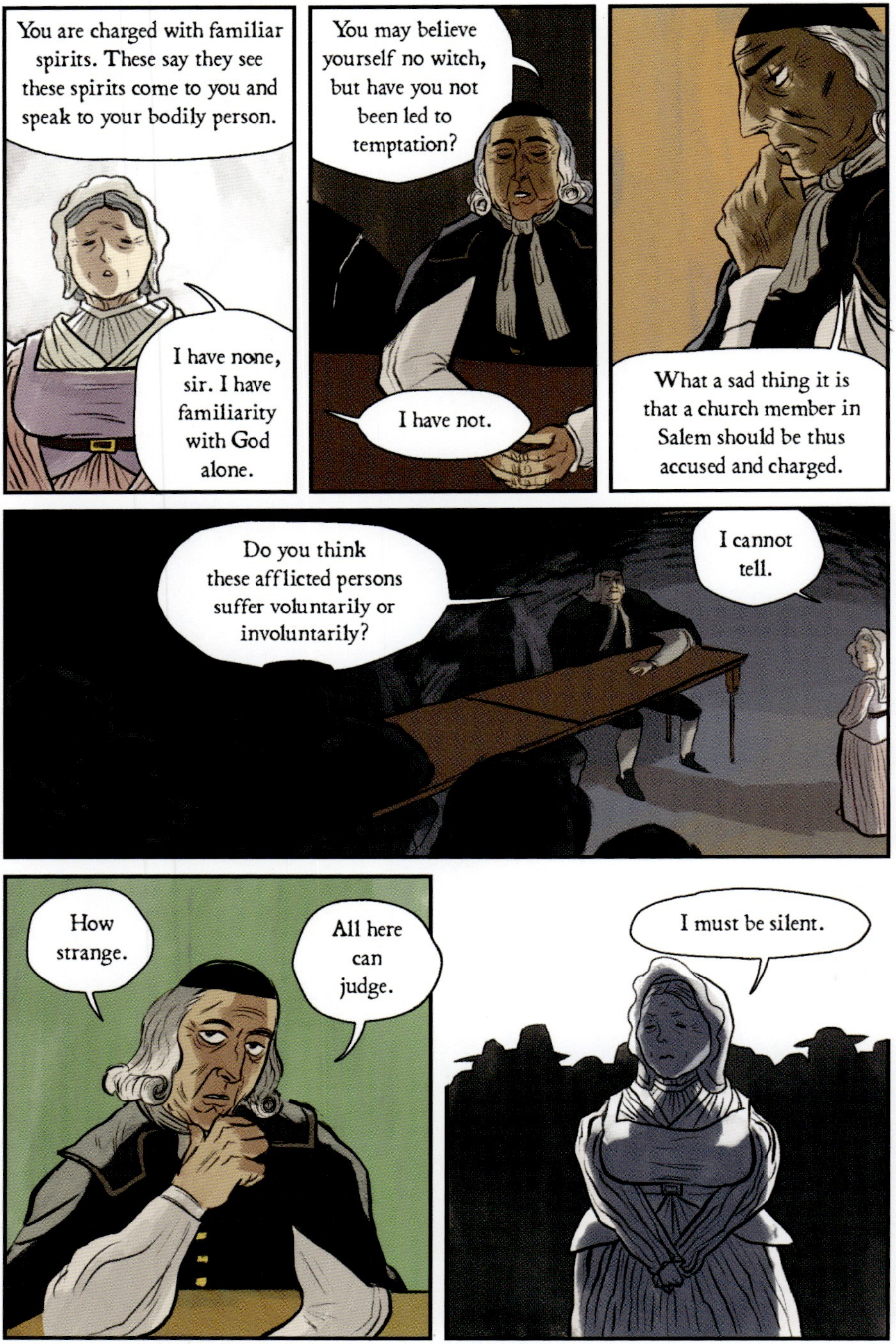

You are charged with familiar spirits. These say they see these spirits come to you and speak to your bodily person.
I have none, sir. I have familiarity with God alone.
You may believe yourself no witch, but have you not been led to temptation?
I have not.
What a sad thing it is that a church member in Salem should be thus accused and charged.
Do you think these afflicted persons suffer voluntarily or involuntarily?
I cannot tell.
How strange.
All here can judge.
I must be silent.

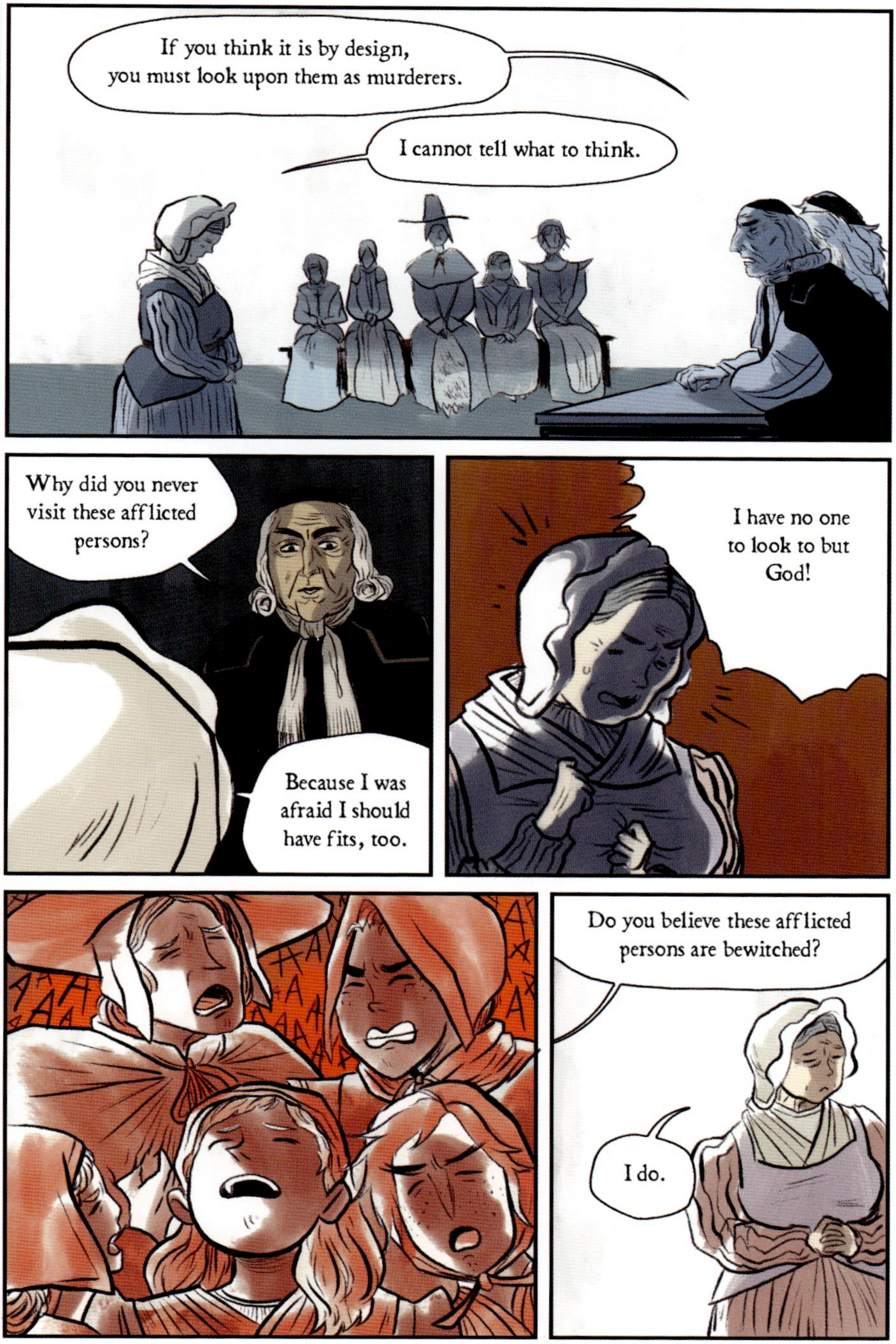
If you think it is by design, you must look upon them as murderers.
I cannot tell what to think.
Why did you never visit these afflicted persons?
Because I was afraid I should have fits, too.
I have no one to look to but God!
Do you believe these afflicted persons are bewitched?
I do.

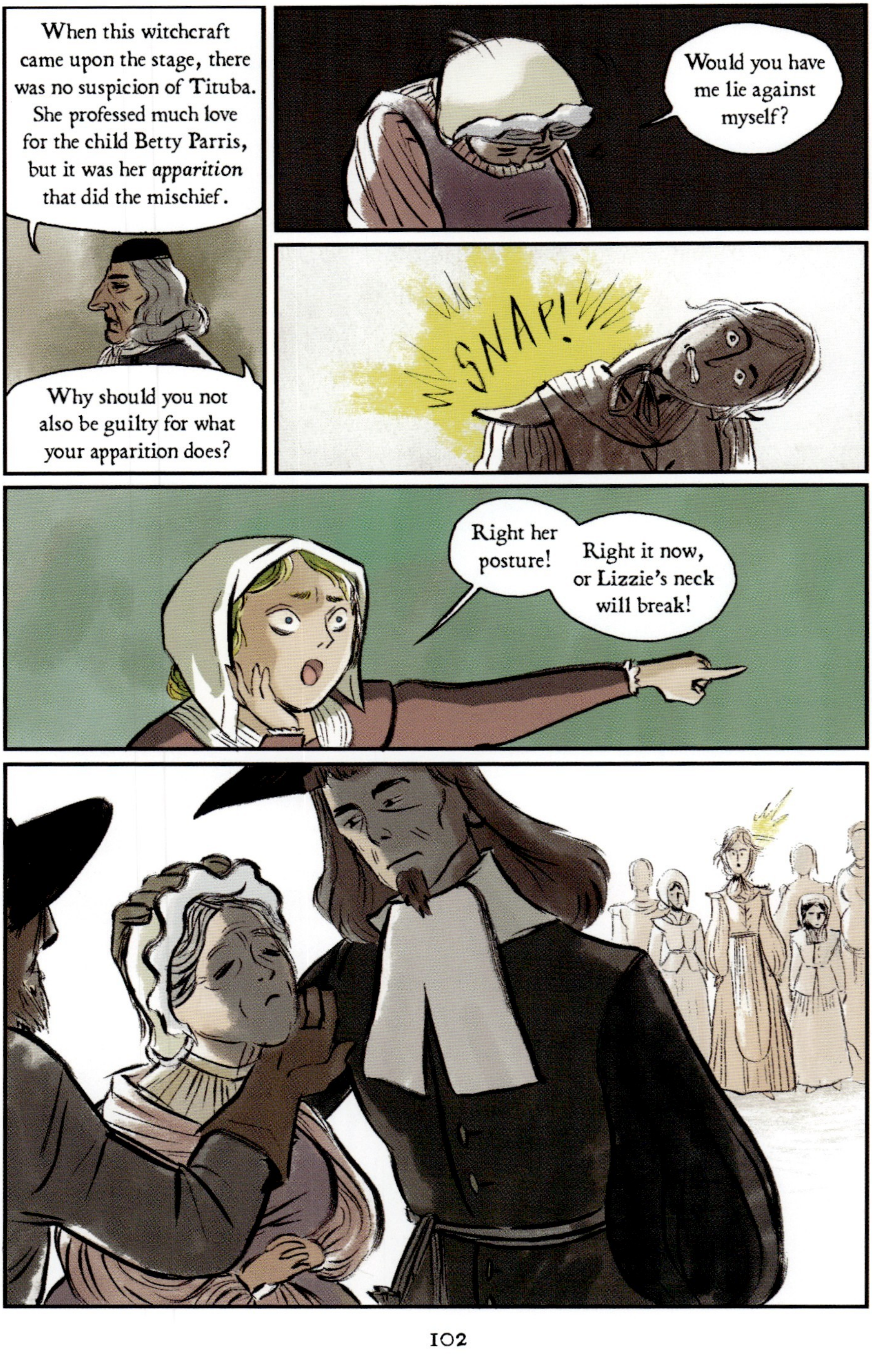
When this witchcraft came upon the stage, there was no suspicion of Tituba. She professed much love for the child Betty Parris, but it was her *apparition* that did the mischief.
Why should you not also be guilty for what your apparition does?
Would you have me lie against myself?
SNAP!
Right her posture!
Right it now, or Lizzie's neck will break!

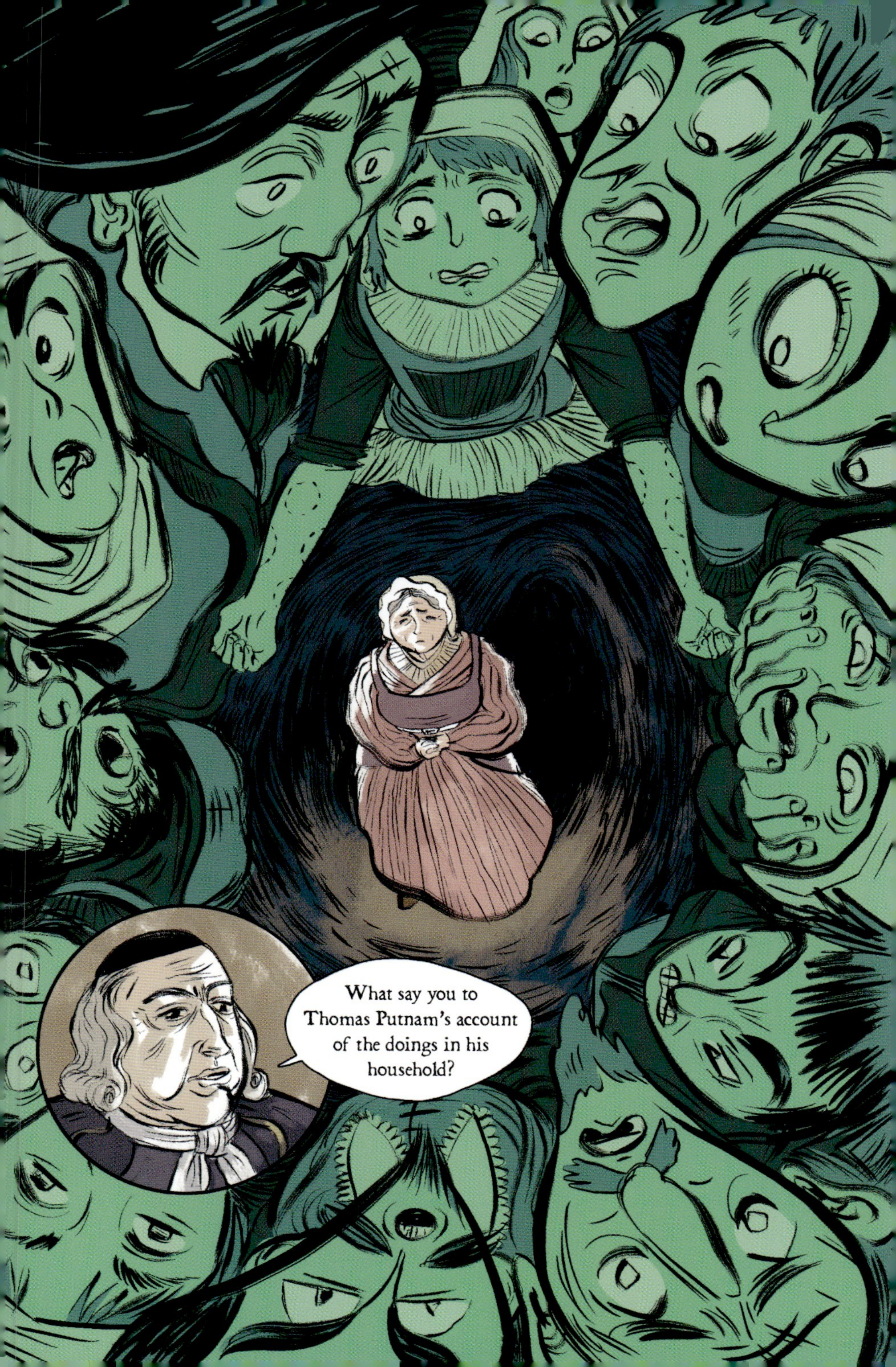
What say you to Thomas Putnam's account of the doings in his household?

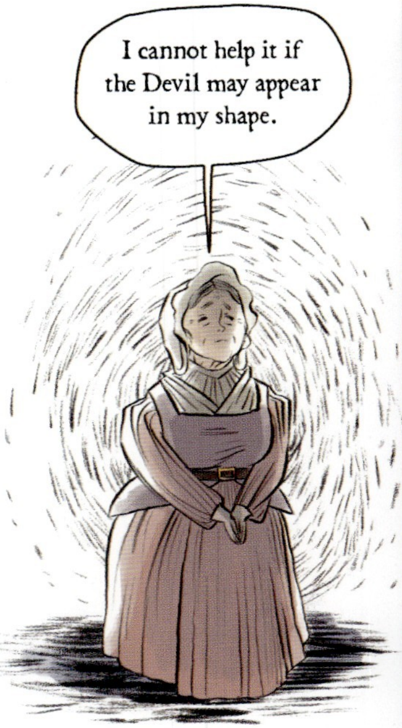
I cannot help it if the Devil may appear in my shape.

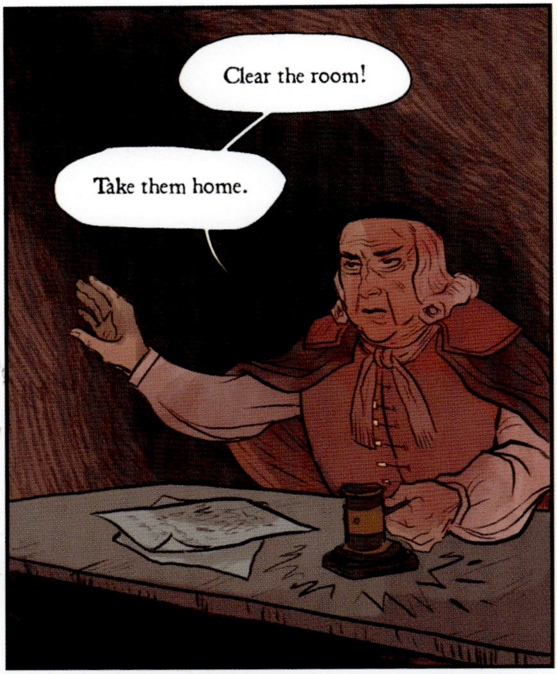
Clear the room!
Take them home.

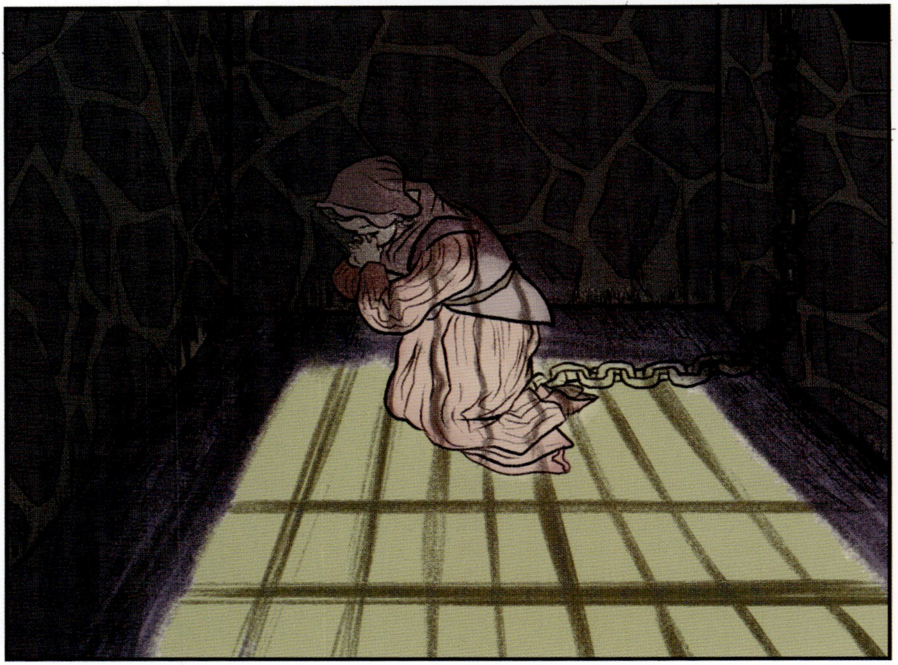

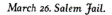
March 26. Salem Jail.

Take care. She seems able to cripple others with a glance, even with several men holding her head in place.

Perhaps without the afflicted girls here, the child will hold her peace?

Do you know why we have come, Dorothy?

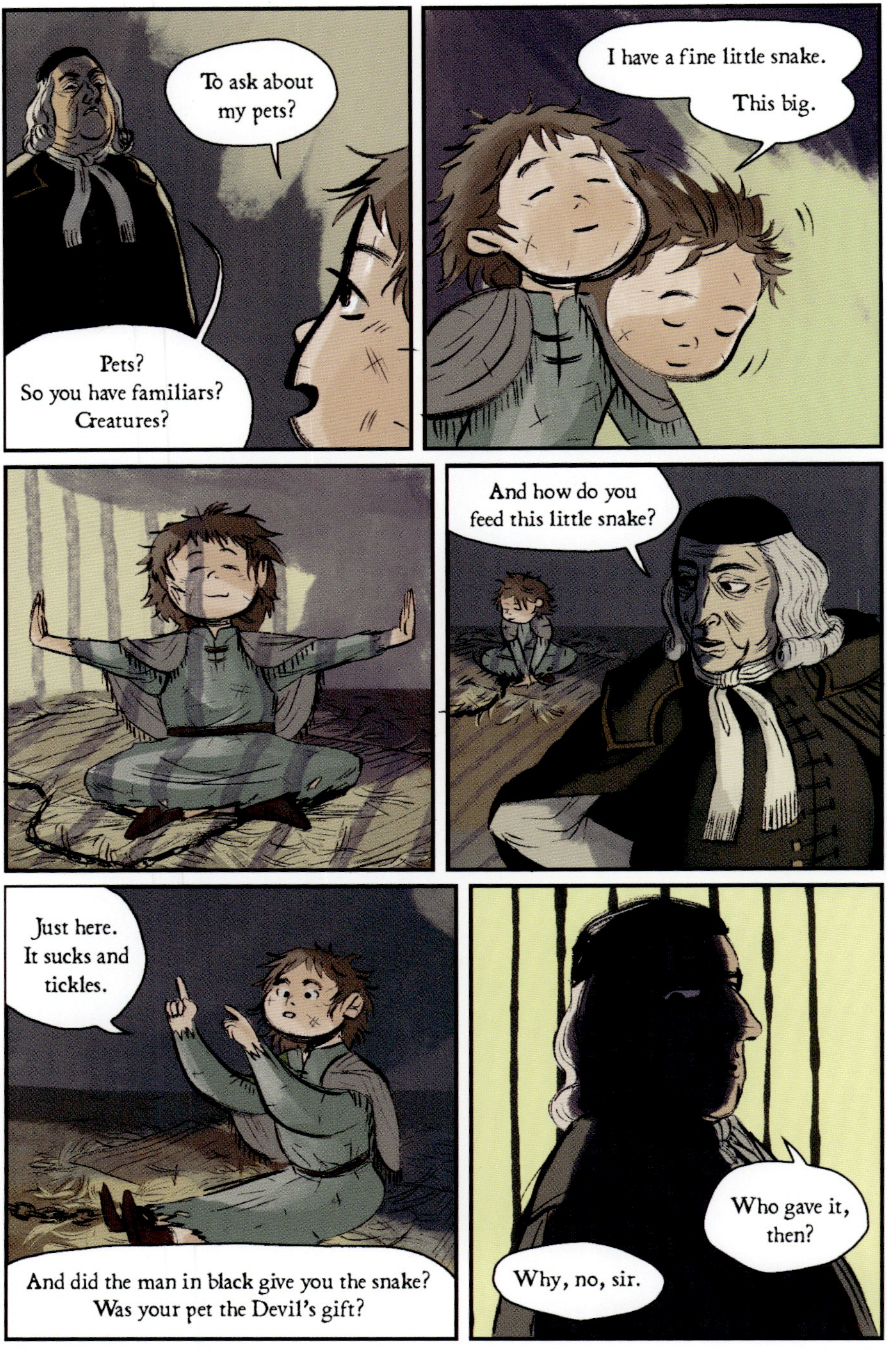
To ask about my pets?
Pets? So you have familiars? Creatures?
I have a fine little snake.
This big.
And how do you feed this little snake?
Just here. It sucks and tickles.
And did the man in black give you the snake? Was your pet the Devil's gift?
Why, no, sir.
Who gave it, then?

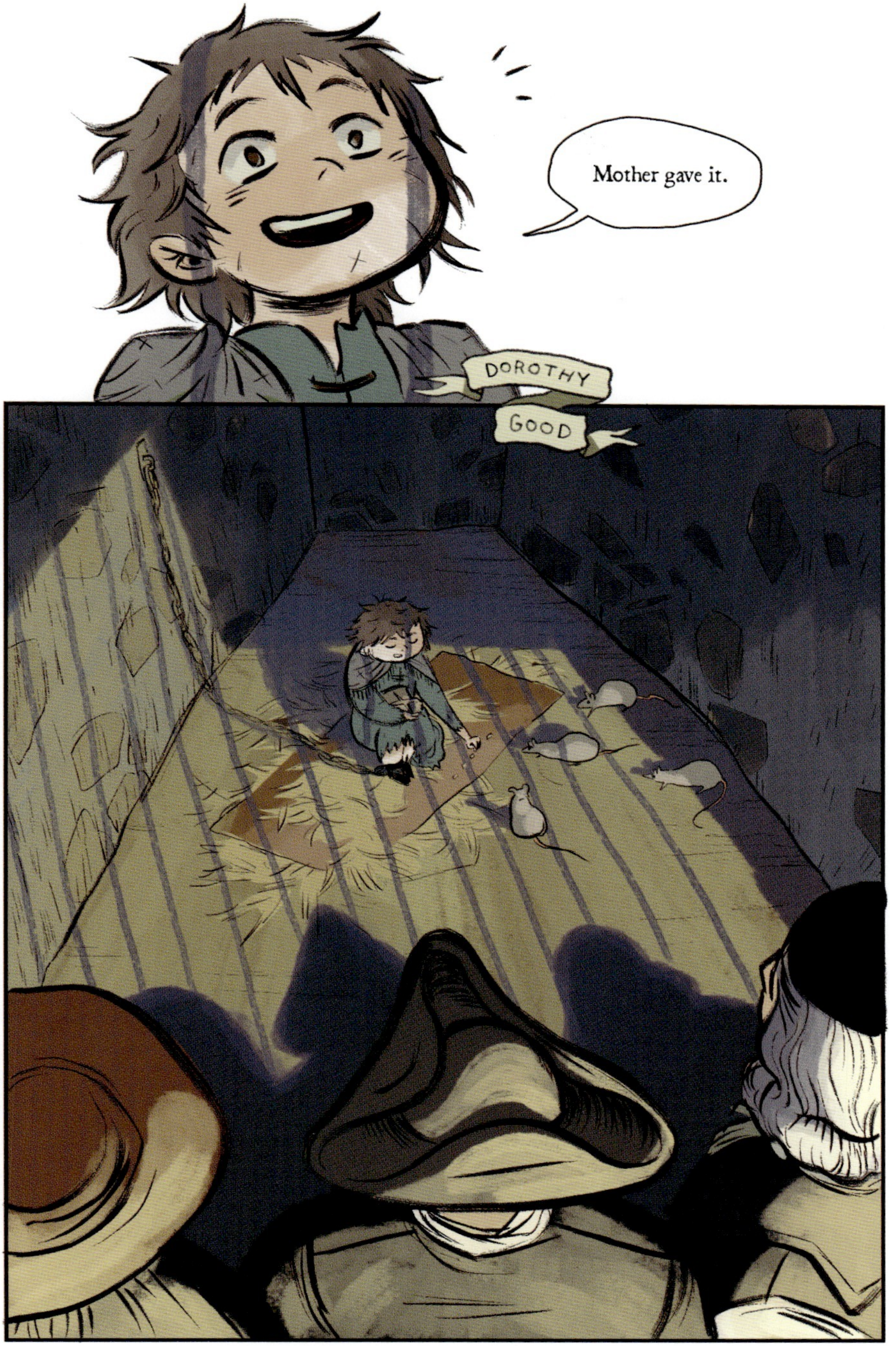
Mother gave it.
DOROTHY
GOOD

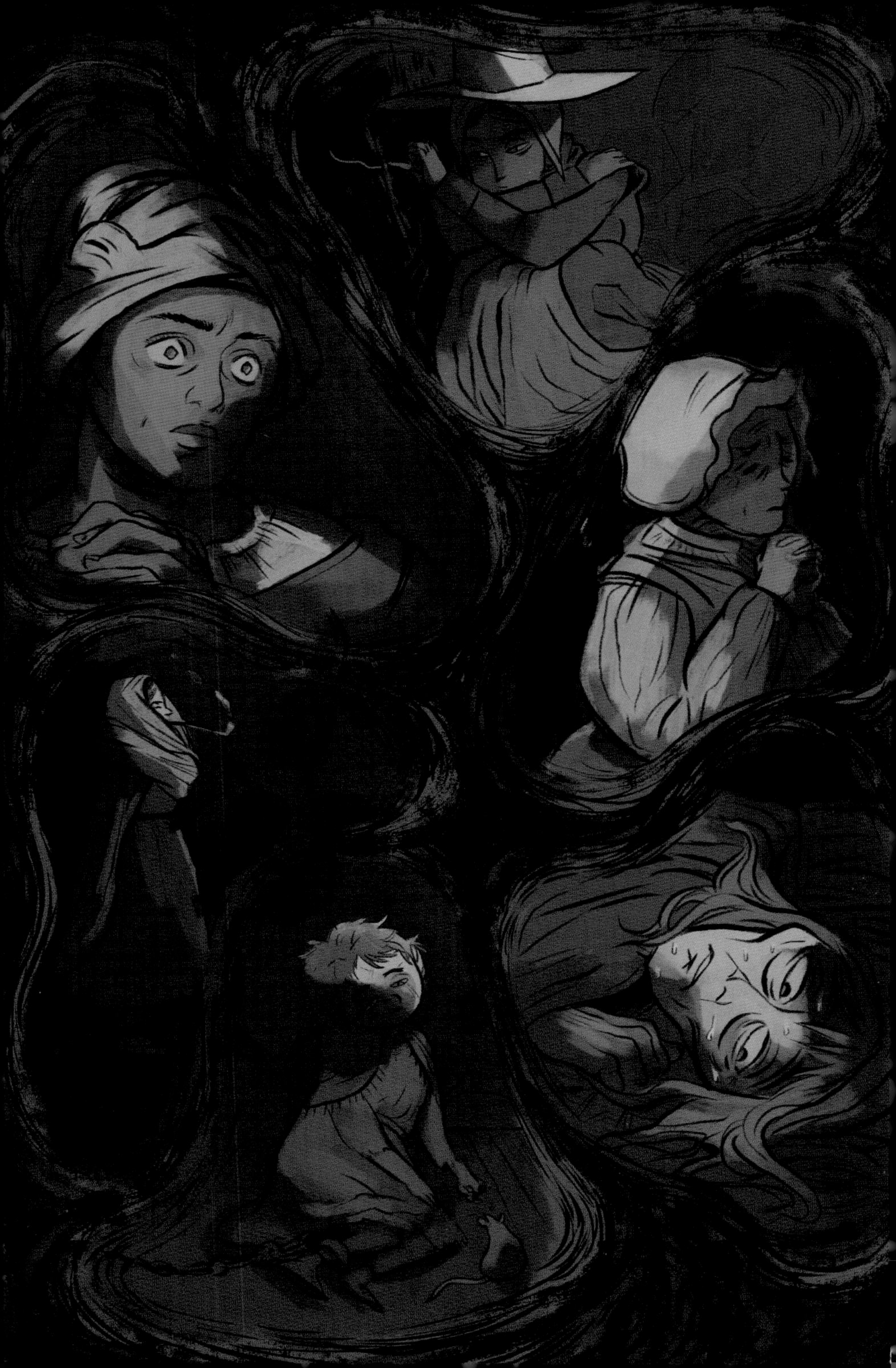

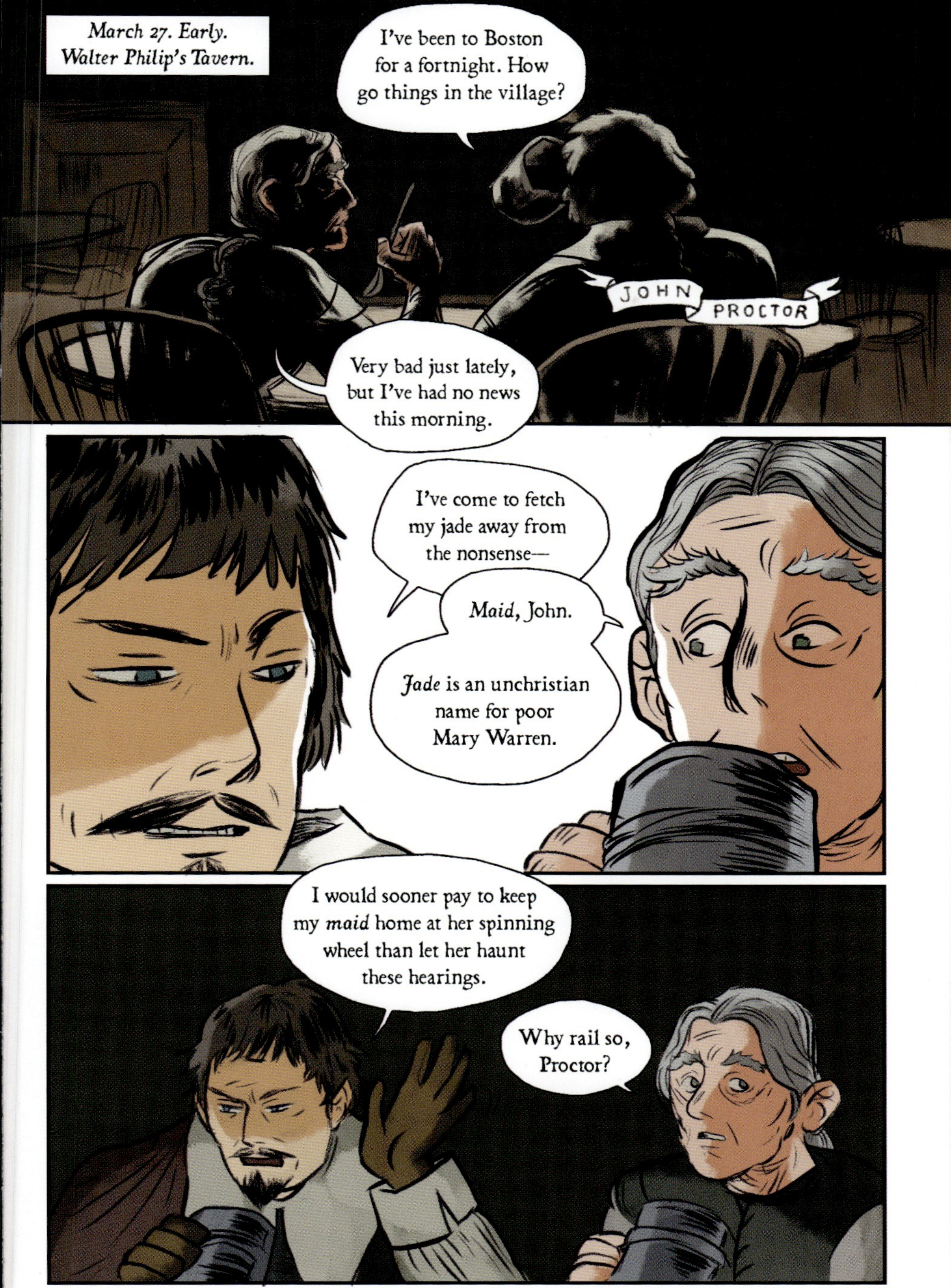
March 27. Early. Walter Philip's Tavern.
I've been to Boston for a fortnight. How go things in the village?
JOHN PROCTOR
Very bad just lately, but I've had no news this morning.
I've come to fetch my jade away from the nonsense—
Maid, John.
Jade is an unchristian name for poor Mary Warren.
I would sooner pay to keep my *maid* home at her spinning wheel than let her haunt these hearings.
Why rail so, Proctor?

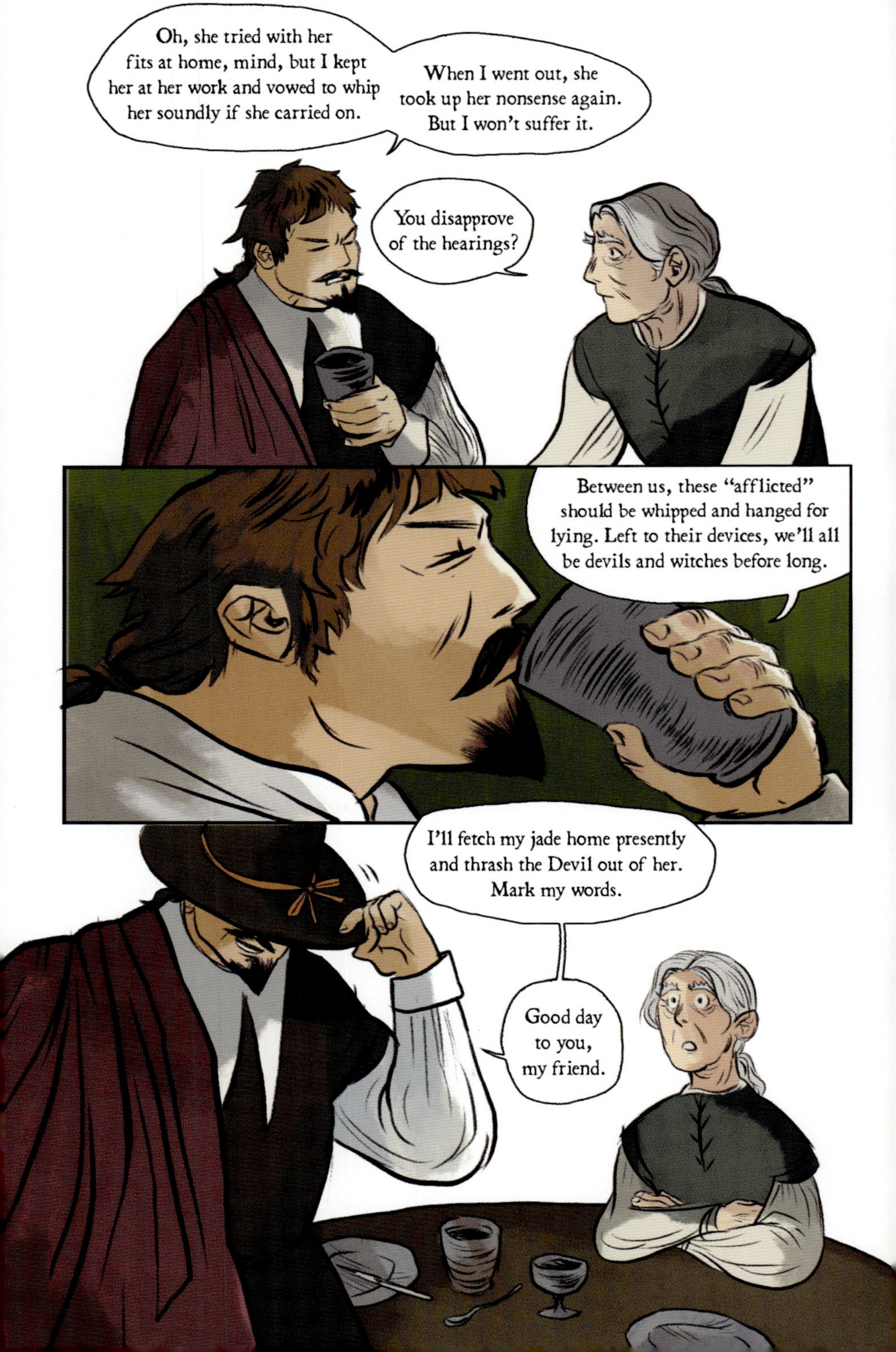
Oh, she tried with her fits at home, mind, but I kept her at her work and vowed to whip her soundly if she carried on.
When I went out, she took up her nonsense again. But I won't suffer it.
You disapprove of the hearings?
Between us, these "afflicted" should be whipped and hanged for lying. Left to their devices, we'll all be devils and witches before long.
I'll fetch my jade home presently and thrash the Devil out of her. Mark my words.
Good day to you, my friend.

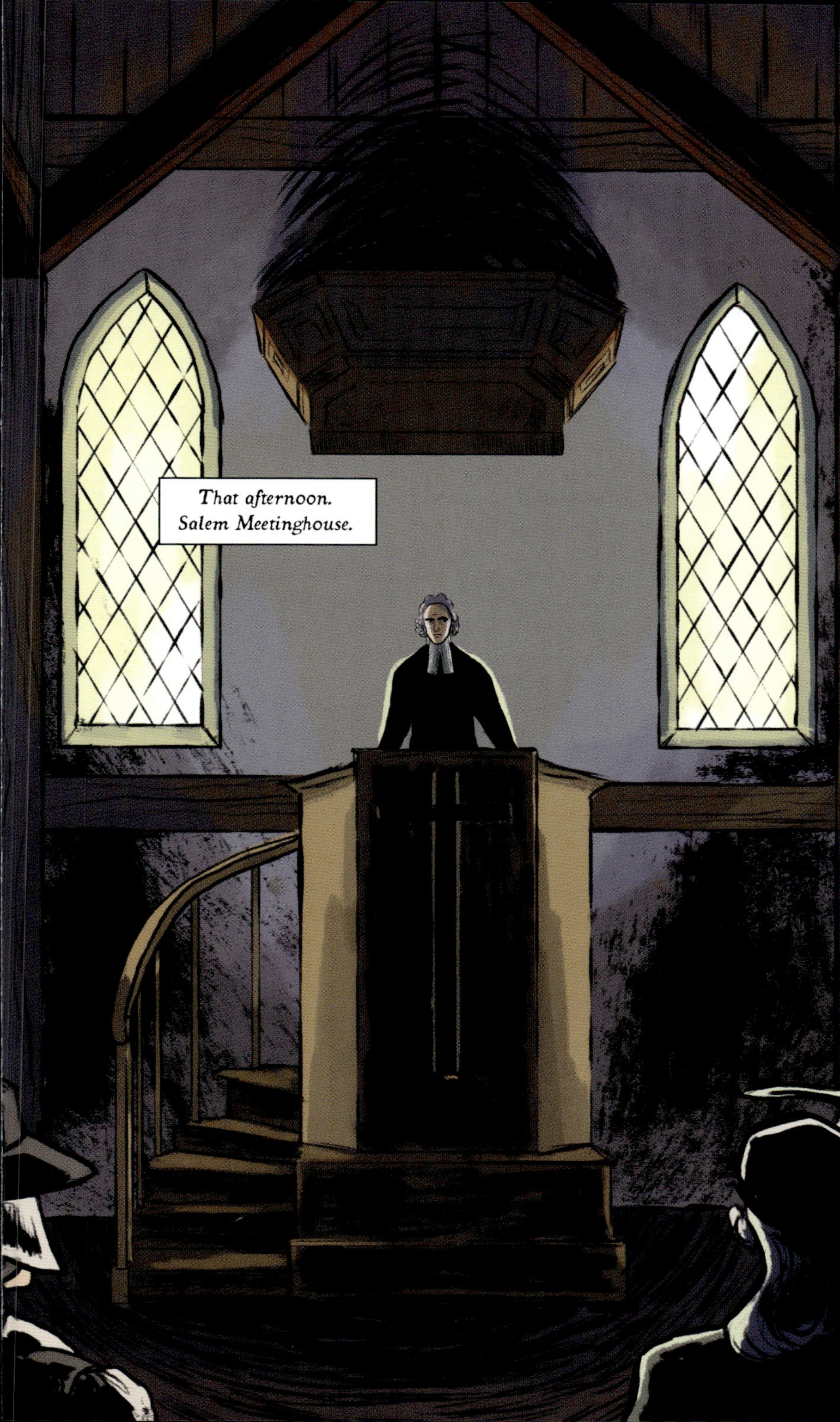
That afternoon.
Salem Meetinghouse.

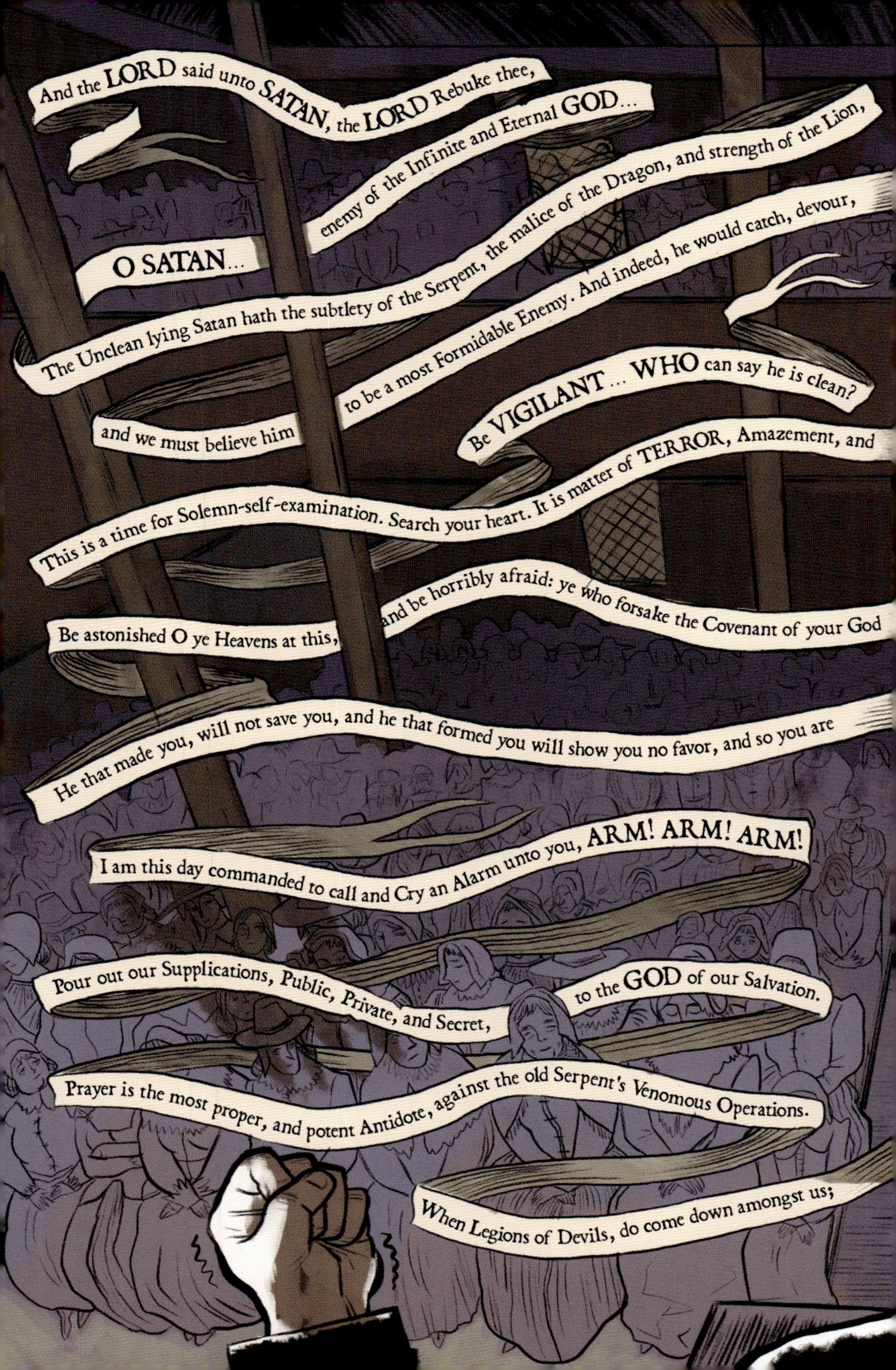

And the LORD said unto SATAN, the LORD Rebuke thee,
enemy of the Infinite and Eternal GOD...
O SATAN...
The Unclean lying Satan hath the subtlety of the Serpent, the malice of the Dragon, and strength of the Lion,
and we must believe him
to be a most Formidable Enemy. And indeed, he would catch, devour,
Be VIGILANT... WHO can say he is clean?
This is a time for Solemn-self-examination. Search your heart. It is matter of TERROR, Amazement, and
Be astonished O ye Heavens at this,
and be horribly afraid: ye who forsake the Covenant of your God
He that made you, will not save you, and he that formed you will show you no favor, and so you are
I am this day commanded to call and Cry an Alarm unto you, ARM! ARM! ARM!
Pour out our Supplications, Public, Private, and Secret,
to the GOD of our Salvation.
Prayer is the most proper, and potent Antidote, against the old Serpent's Venomous Operations.
When Legions of Devils, do come down amongst us;

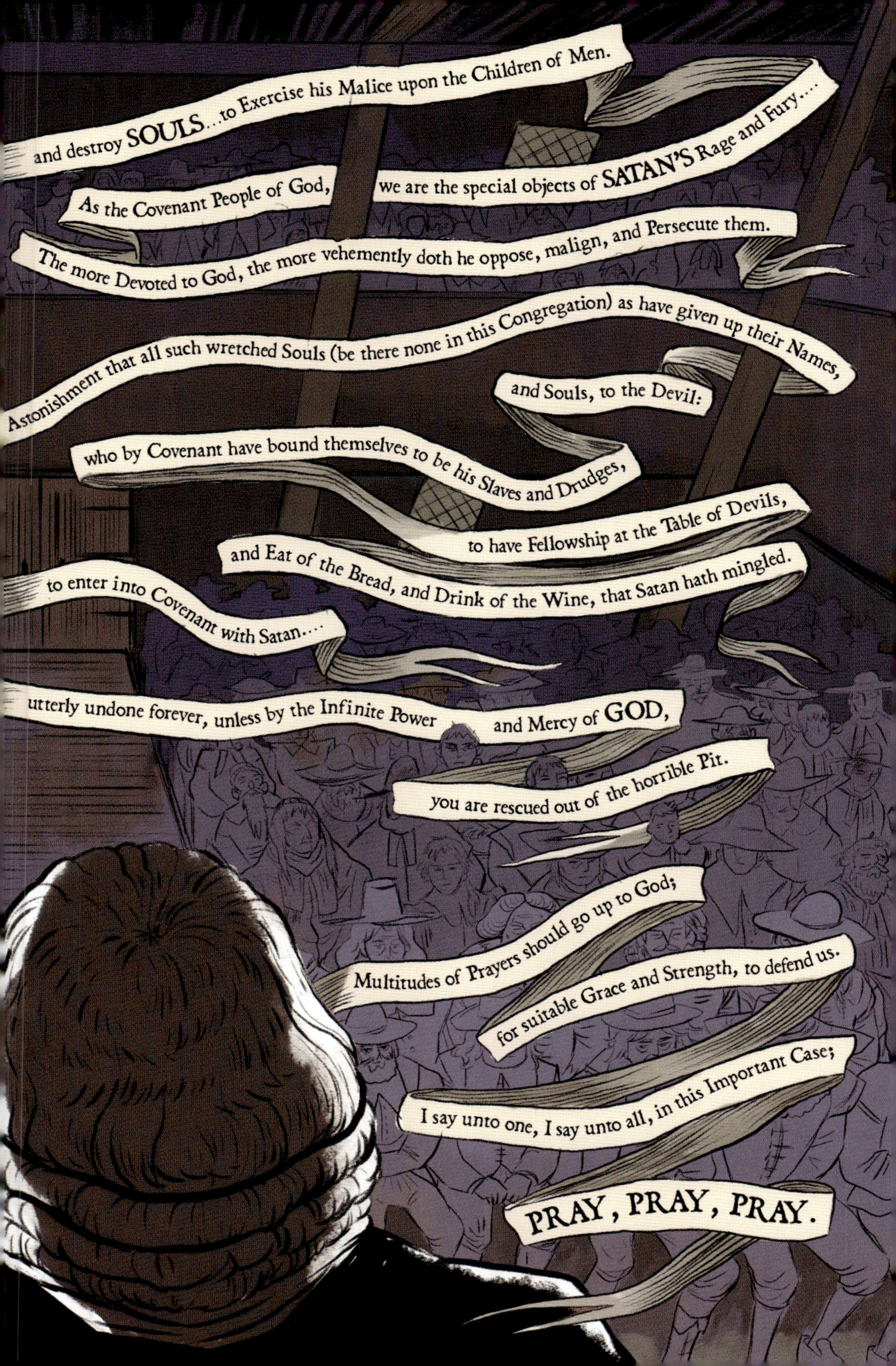
and destroy SOULS...to Exercise his Malice upon the Children of Men.
As the Covenant People of God, we are the special objects of SATAN'S Rage and Fury....
The more Devoted to God, the more vehemently doth he oppose, malign, and Persecute them.
Astonishment that all such wretched Souls (be there none in this Congregation) as have given up their Names,
and Souls, to the Devil:
who by Covenant have bound themselves to be his Slaves and Drudges,
to have Fellowship at the Table of Devils,
and Eat of the Bread, and Drink of the Wine, that Satan hath mingled.
to enter into Covenant with Satan....
utterly undone forever, unless by the Infinite Power and Mercy of GOD,
you are rescued out of the horrible Pit.
Multitudes of Prayers should go up to God;
for suitable Grace and Strength, to defend us.
I say unto one, I say unto all, in this Important Case;
PRAY, PRAY, PRAY.

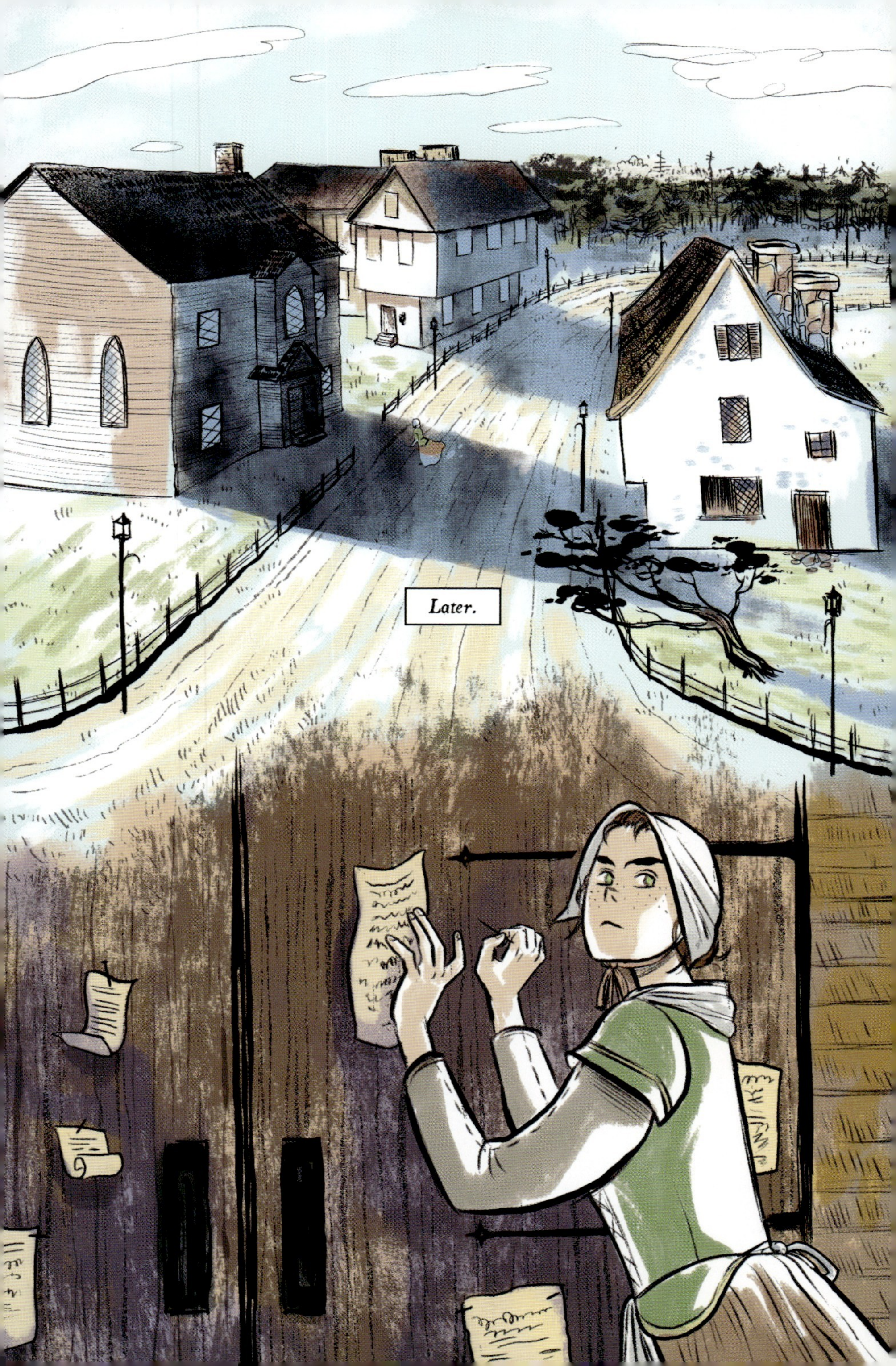
Later.

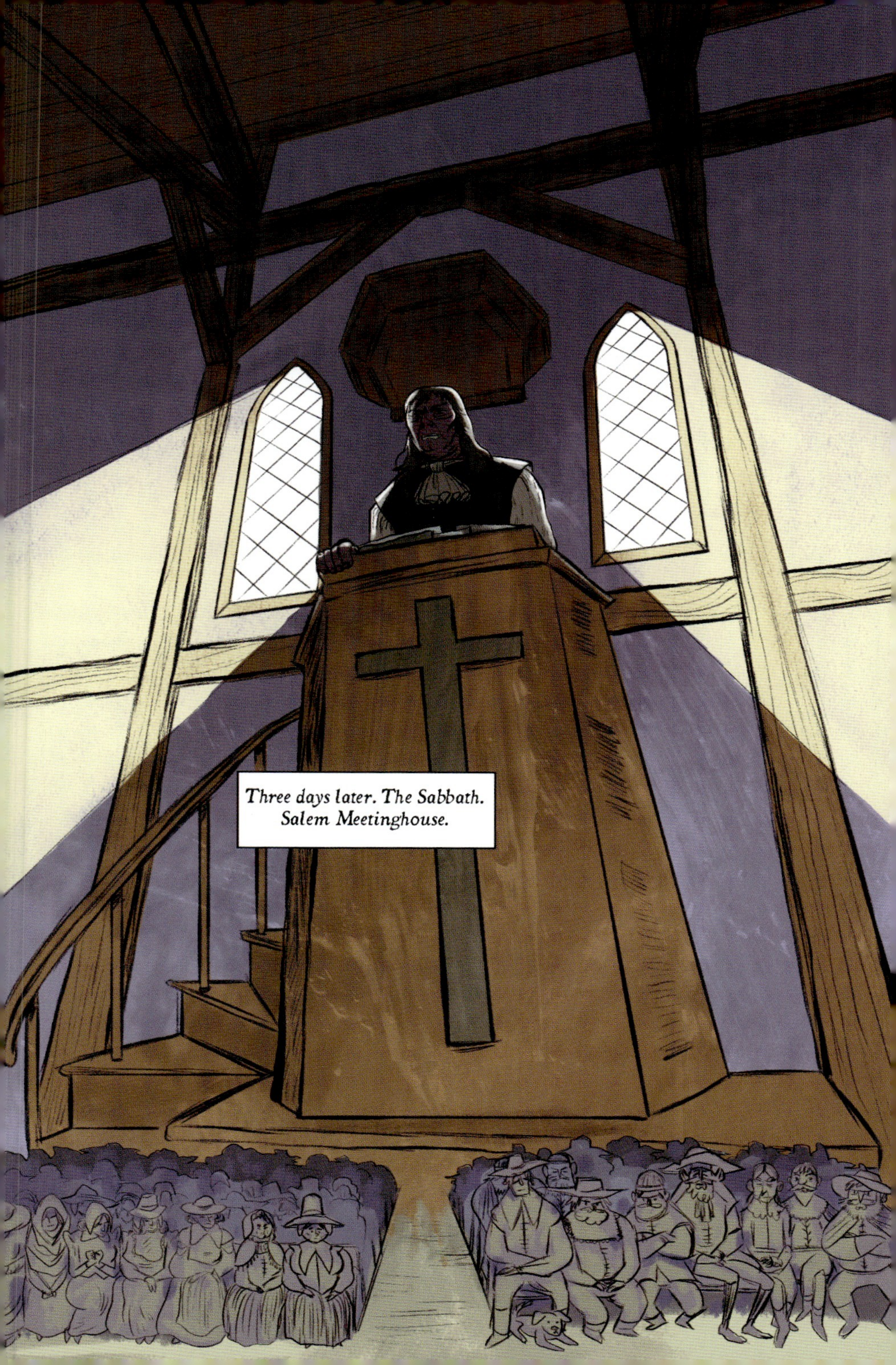
Three days later. The Sabbath.
Salem Meetinghouse.

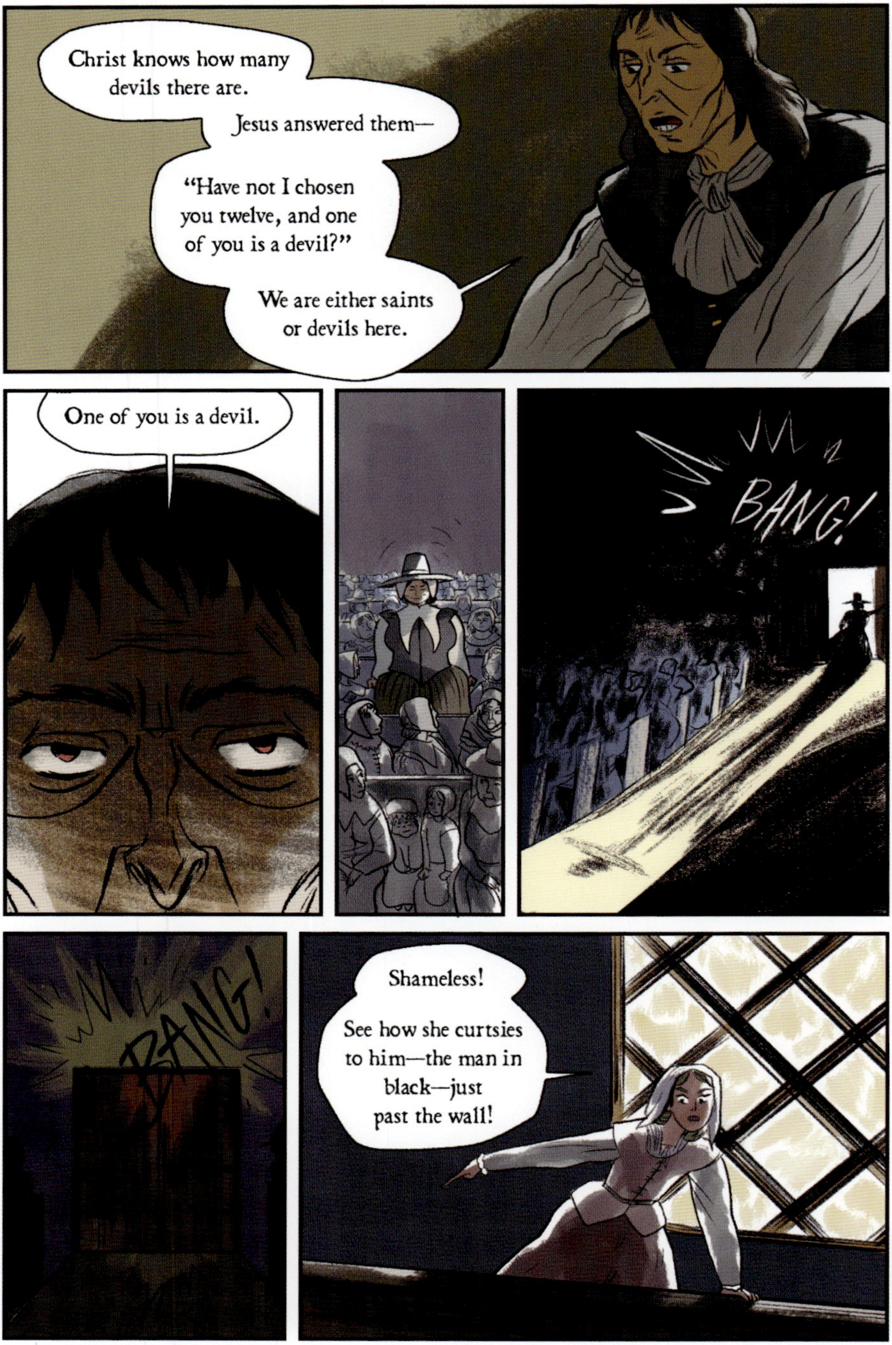
Christ knows how many devils there are.
Jesus answered them—
"Have not I chosen you twelve, and one of you is a devil?"
We are either saints or devils here.
One of you is a devil.
BANG!
BANG!
Shameless!
See how she curtsies to him—the man in black—just past the wall!

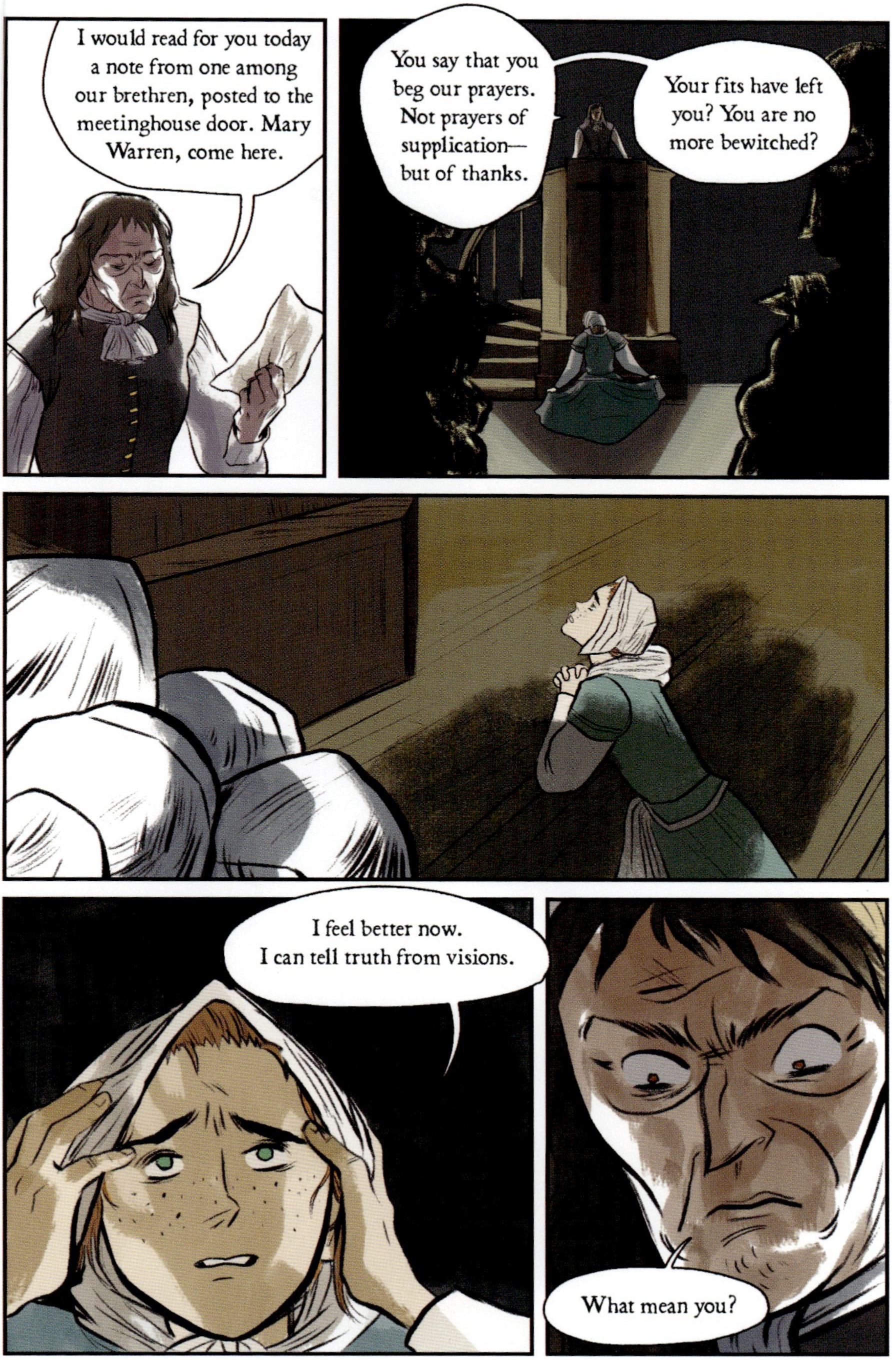
I would read for you today a note from one among our brethren, posted to the meetinghouse door. Mary Warren, come here.
You say that you beg our prayers. Not prayers of supplication— but of thanks.
Your fits have left you? You are no more bewitched?
I feel better now. I can tell truth from visions.
What mean you?

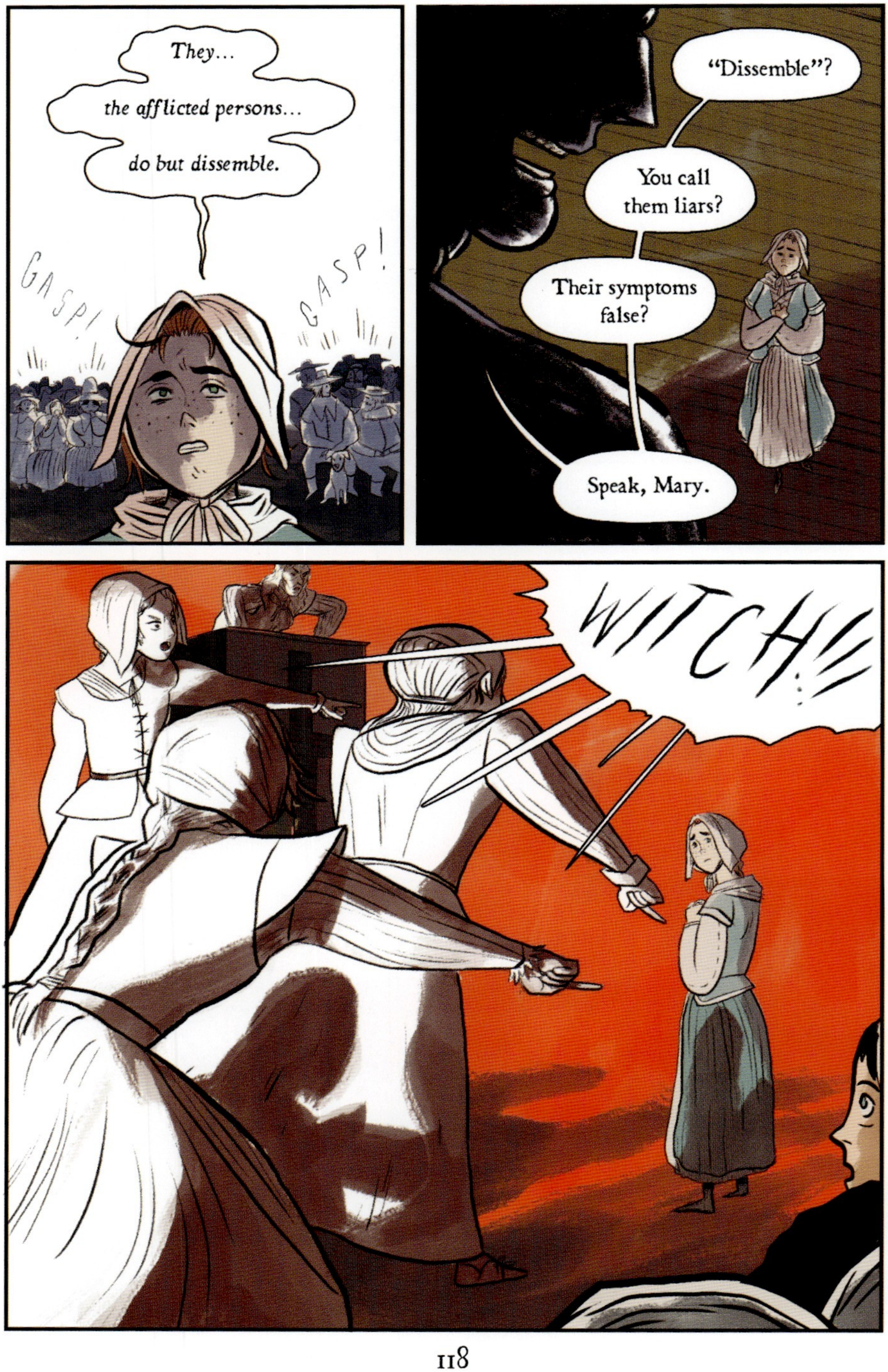
They...
the afflicted persons...
do but dissemble.
GASP!
GASP!
"Dissemble"?
You call them liars?
Their symptoms false?
Speak, Mary.
WITCH!!

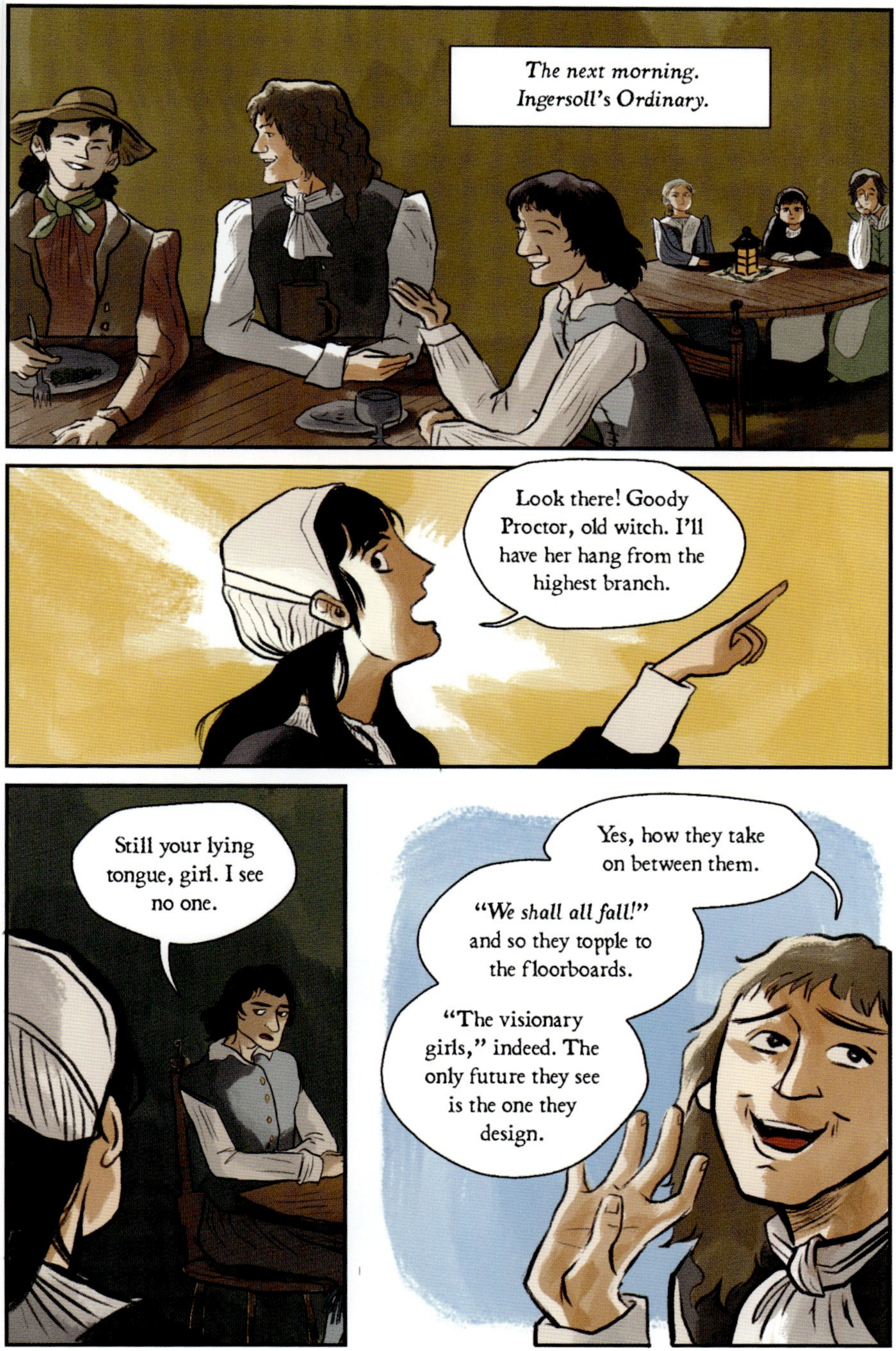
The next morning. Ingersoll's Ordinary.
Look there! Goody Proctor, old witch. I'll have her hang from the highest branch.
Still your lying tongue, girl. I see no one.
Yes, how they take on between them.
"*We shall all fall!*" and so they topple to the floorboards.
"The visionary girls," indeed. The only future they see is the one they design.

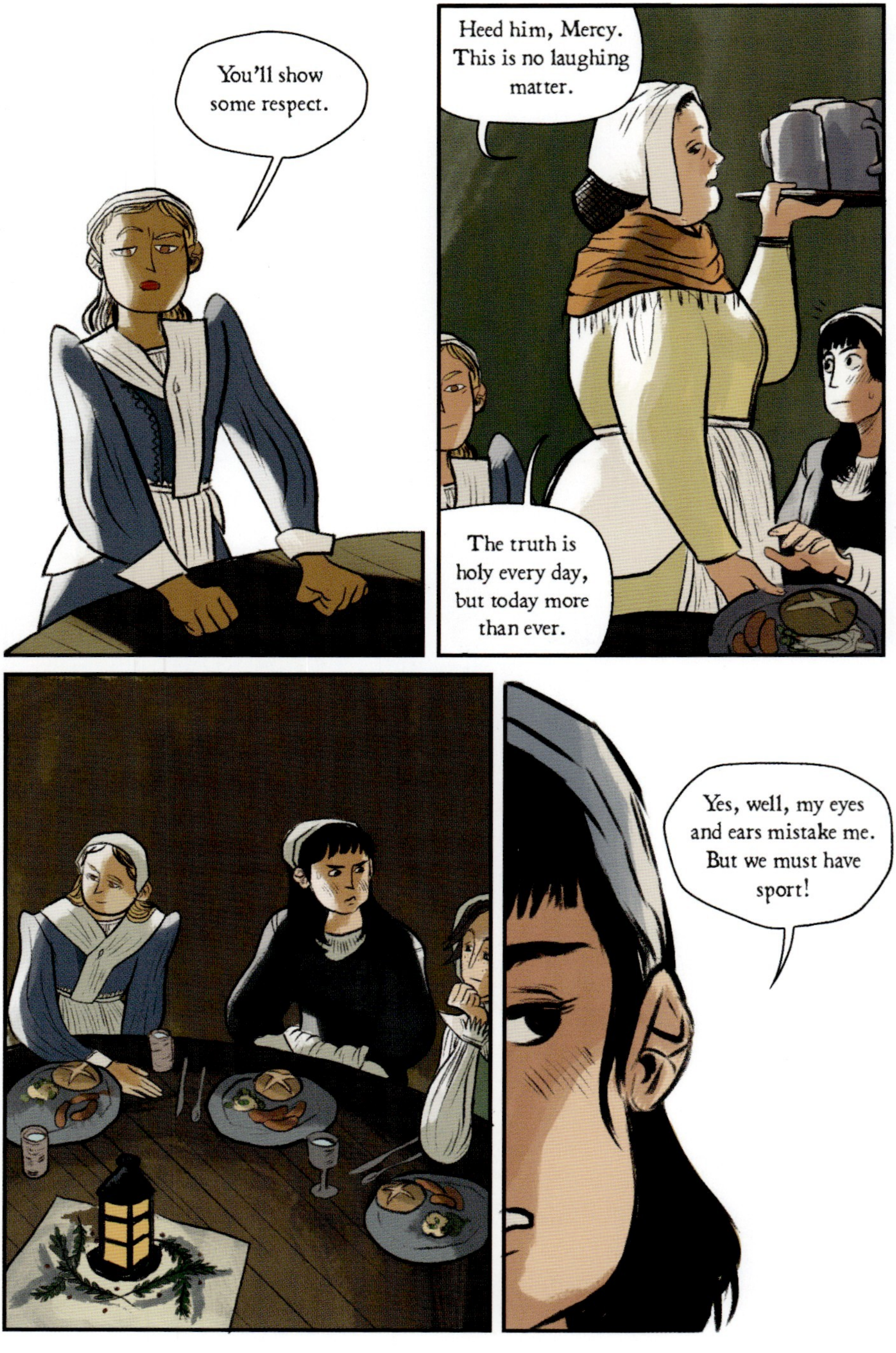
You'll show some respect.
Heed him, Mercy. This is no laughing matter.
The truth is holy every day, but today more than ever.
Yes, well, my eyes and ears mistake me. But we must have sport!

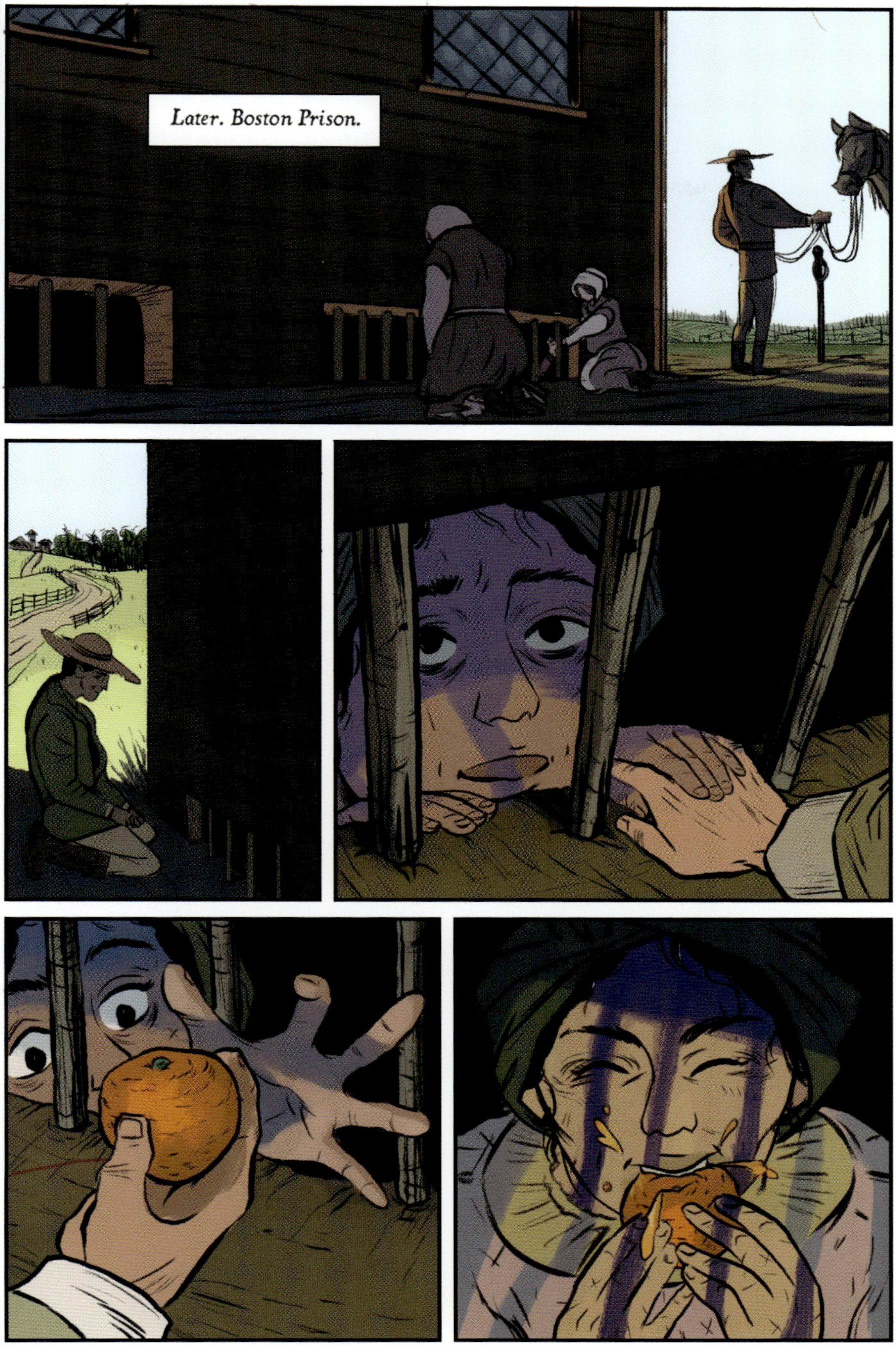
Later. Boston Prison.

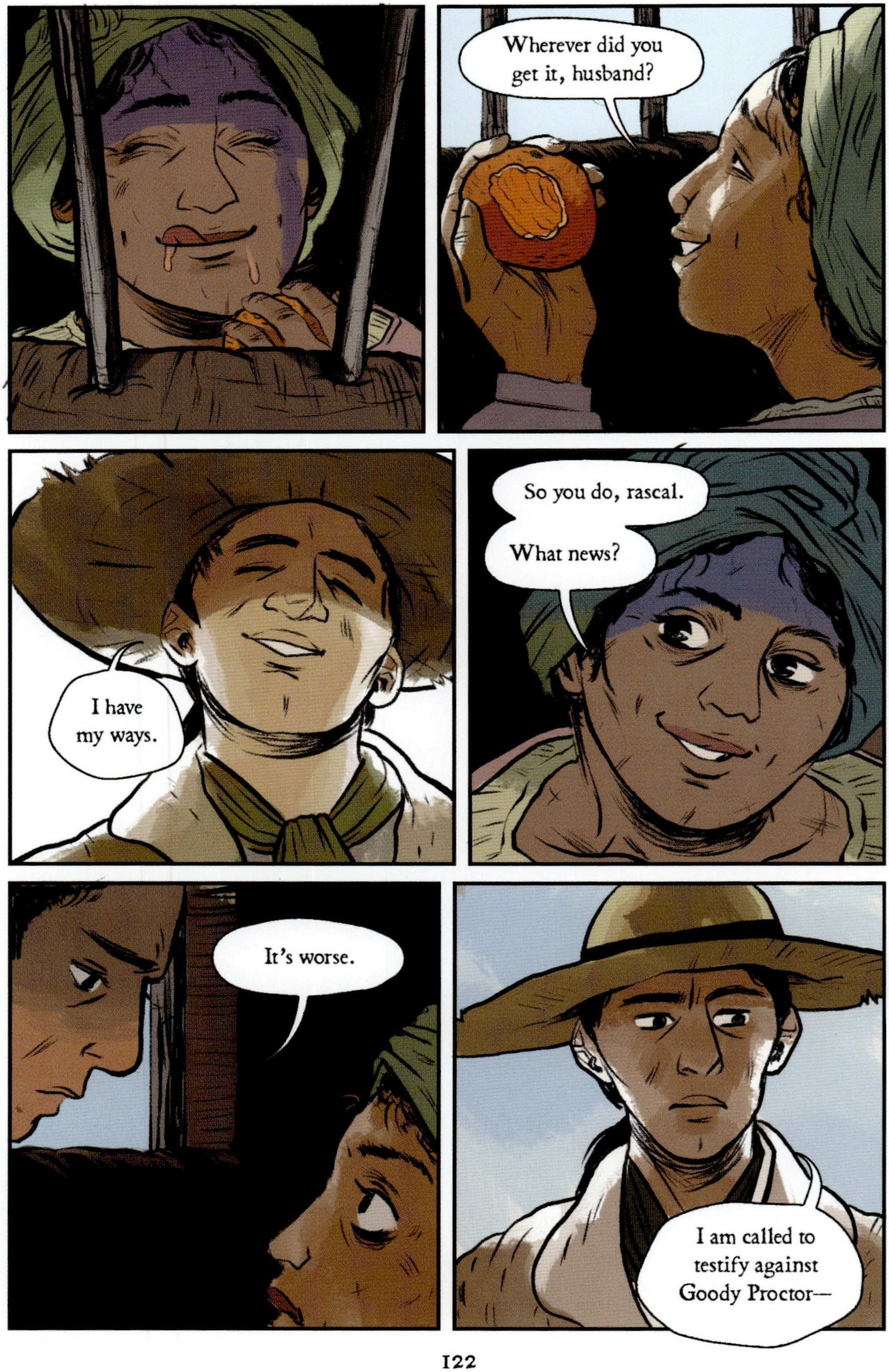

Wherever did you get it, husband?
I have my ways.
So you do, rascal.
What news?
It's worse.
I am called to testify against Goody Proctor—

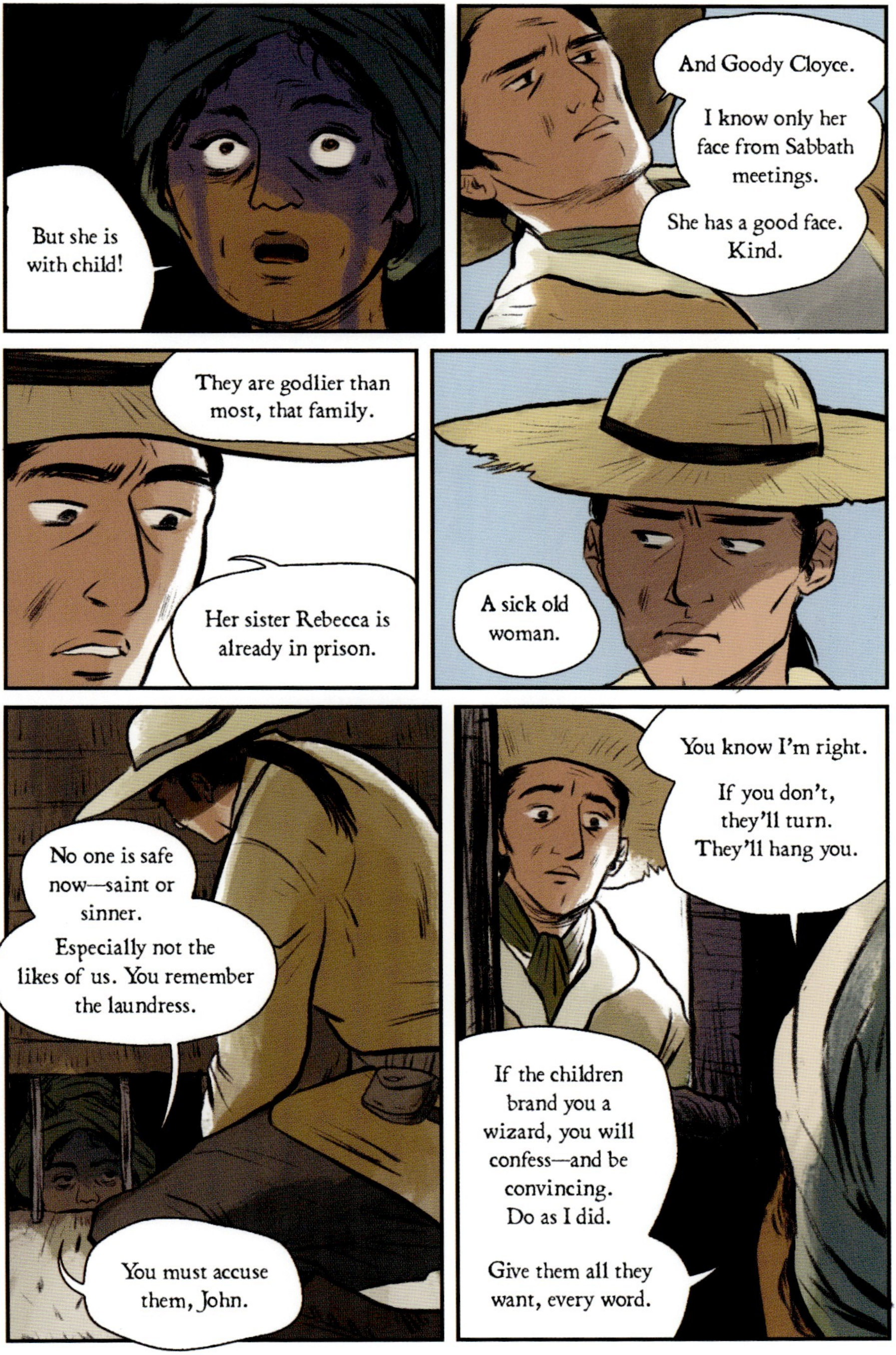
But she is with child!
And Goody Cloyce.
I know only her face from Sabbath meetings.
She has a good face. Kind.
They are godlier than most, that family.
Her sister Rebecca is already in prison.
A sick old woman.
No one is safe now—saint or sinner.
Especially not the likes of us. You remember the laundress.
You must accuse them, John.
You know I'm right.
If you don't, they'll turn. They'll hang you.
If the children brand you a wizard, you will confess—and be convincing. Do as I did.
Give them all they want, every word.

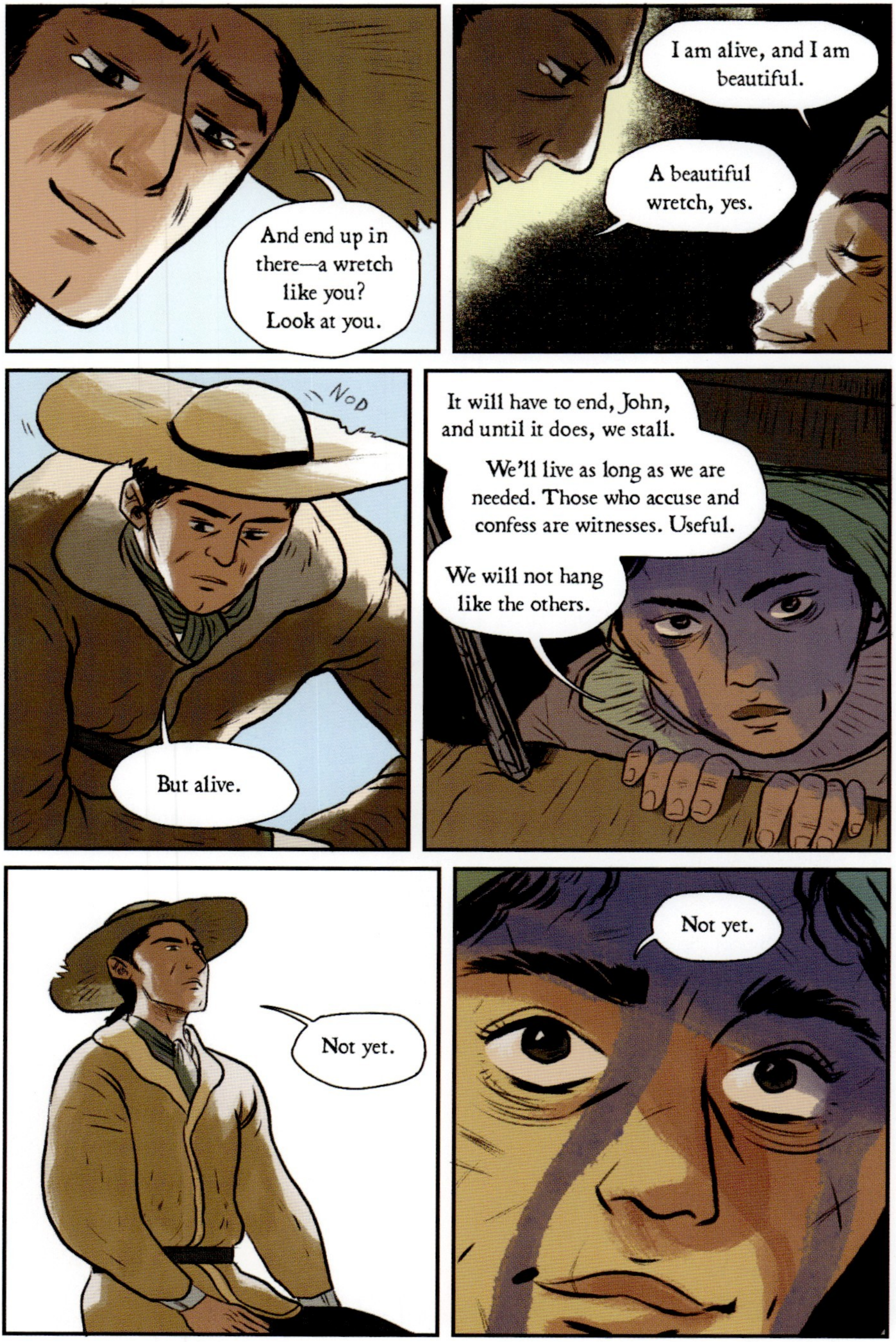
And end up in there—a wretch like you? Look at you.
I am alive, and I am beautiful.
A beautiful wretch, yes.
NOD
But alive.
It will have to end, John, and until it does, we stall.
We'll live as long as we are needed. Those who accuse and confess are witnesses. Useful.
We will not hang like the others.
Not yet.
Not yet.

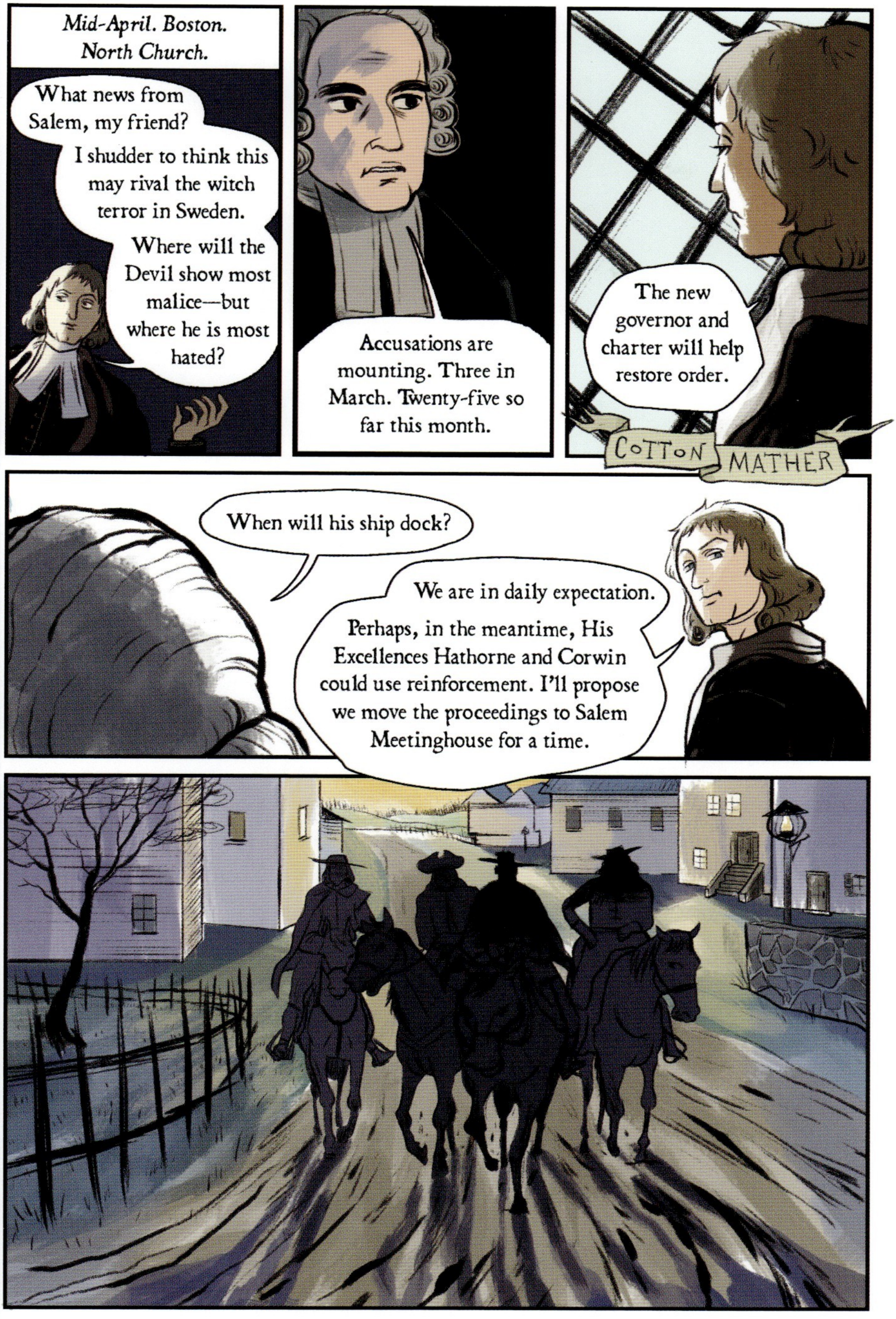
Mid-April. Boston. North Church.
What news from Salem, my friend?
I shudder to think this may rival the witch terror in Sweden.
Where will the Devil show most malice—but where he is most hated?
Accusations are mounting. Three in March. Twenty-five so far this month.
The new governor and charter will help restore order.
COTTON MATHER
When will his ship dock?
We are in daily expectation.
Perhaps, in the meantime, His Excellences Hathorne and Corwin could use reinforcement. I'll propose we move the proceedings to Salem Meetinghouse for a time.

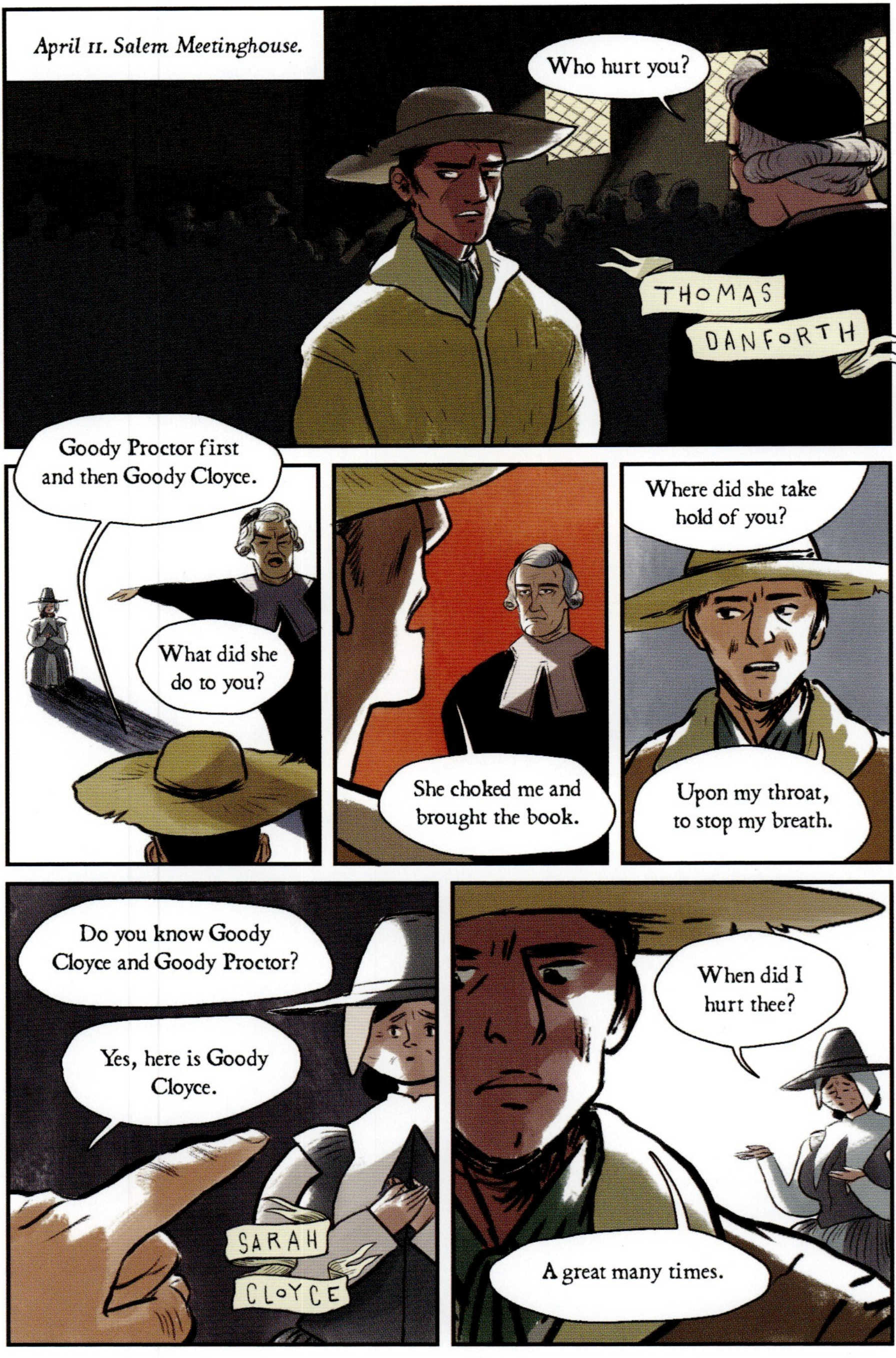
April 11. Salem Meetinghouse.
Who hurt you?
THOMAS DANFORTH
Goody Proctor first and then Goody Cloyce.
What did she do to you?
She choked me and brought the book.
Where did she take hold of you?
Upon my throat, to stop my breath.
Do you know Goody Cloyce and Goody Proctor?
Yes, here is Goody Cloyce.
SARAH CLOYCE
When did I hurt thee?
A great many times.

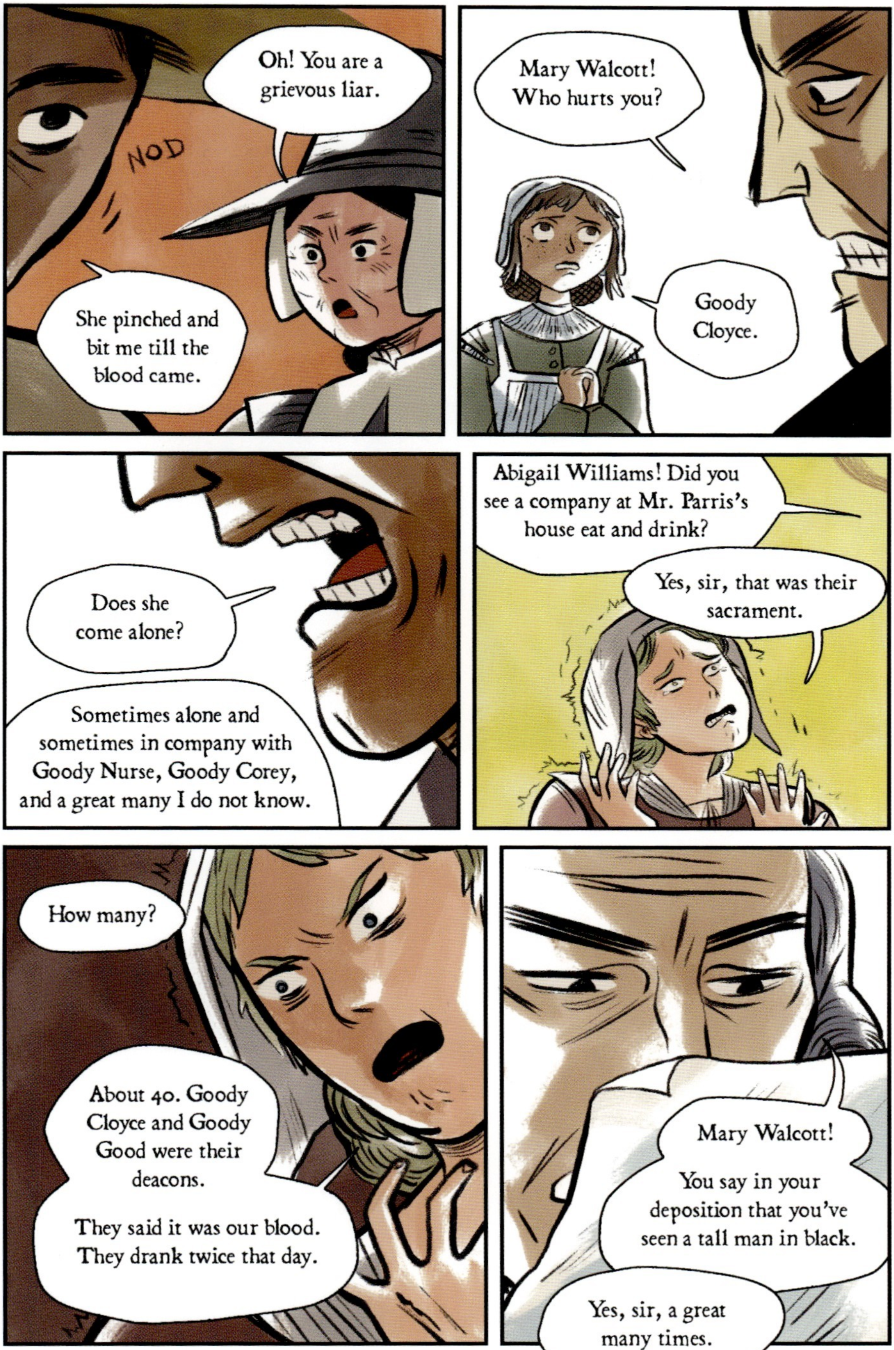

Oh! You are a grievous liar.
NOD
She pinched and bit me till the blood came.
Mary Walcott! Who hurts you?
Goody Cloyce.
Does she come alone?
Sometimes alone and sometimes in company with Goody Nurse, Goody Corey, and a great many I do not know.
Abigail Williams! Did you see a company at Mr. Parris's house eat and drink?
Yes, sir, that was their sacrament.
How many?
About 40. Goody Cloyce and Goody Good were their deacons.
They said it was our blood. They drank twice that day.
Mary Walcott!
You say in your deposition that you've seen a tall man in black.
Yes, sir, a great many times.

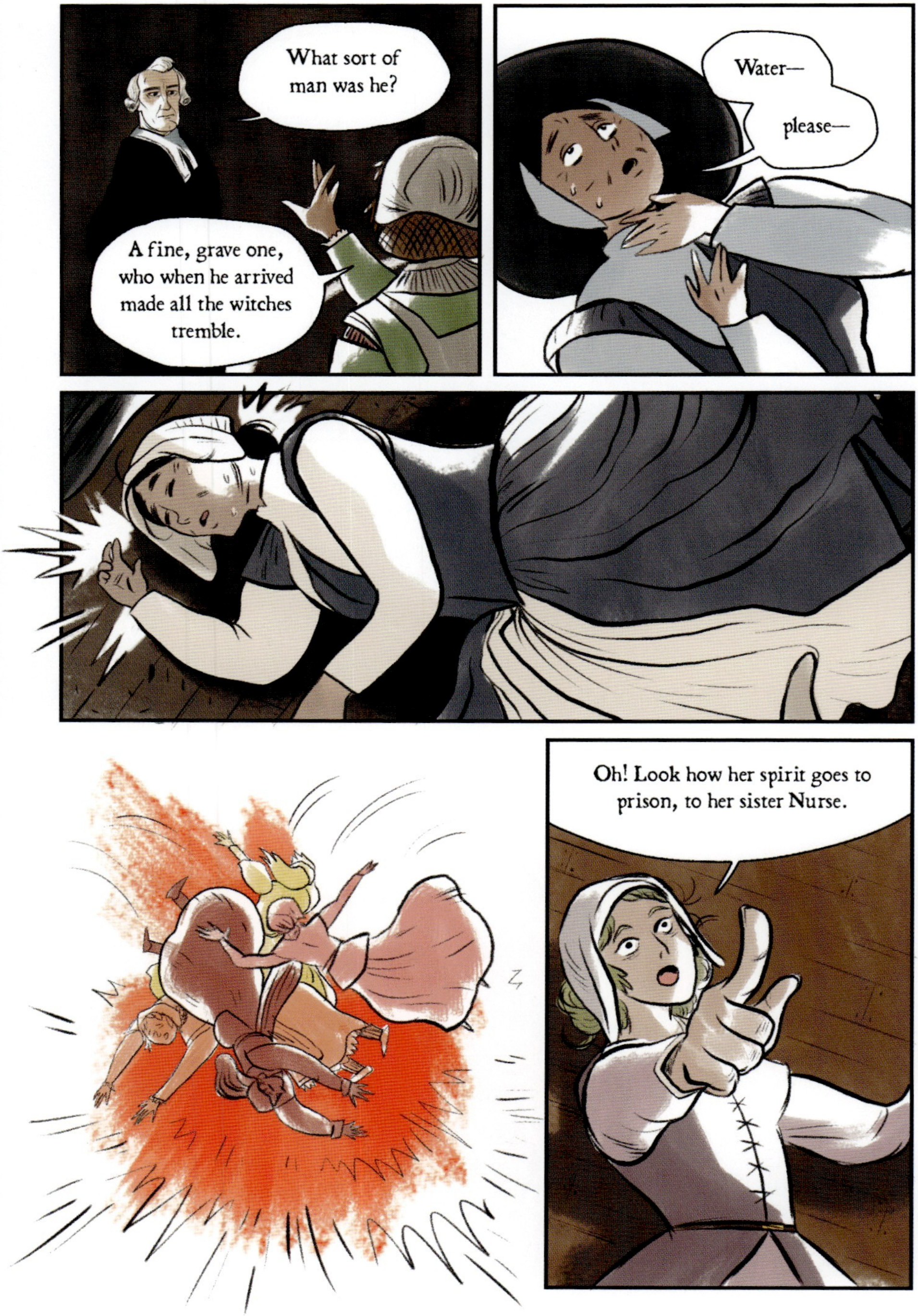
What sort of man was he?
A fine, grave one, who when he arrived made all the witches tremble.
Water— please—
Oh! Look how her spirit goes to prison, to her sister Nurse.

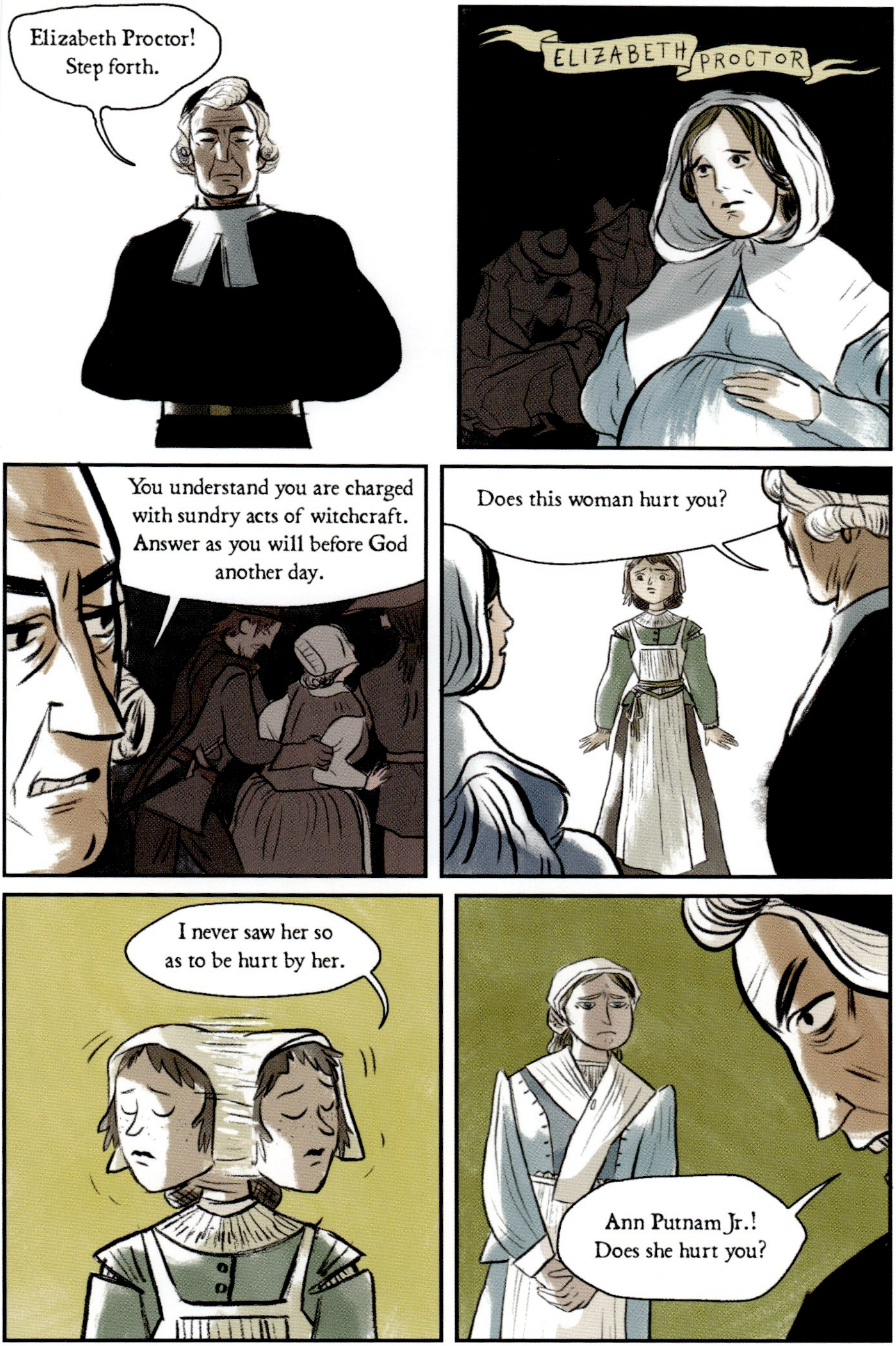
Elizabeth Proctor!
Step forth.
ELIZABETH PROCTOR
You understand you are charged with sundry acts of witchcraft. Answer as you will before God another day.
Does this woman hurt you?
I never saw her so as to be hurt by her.
Ann Putnam Jr.! Does she hurt you?

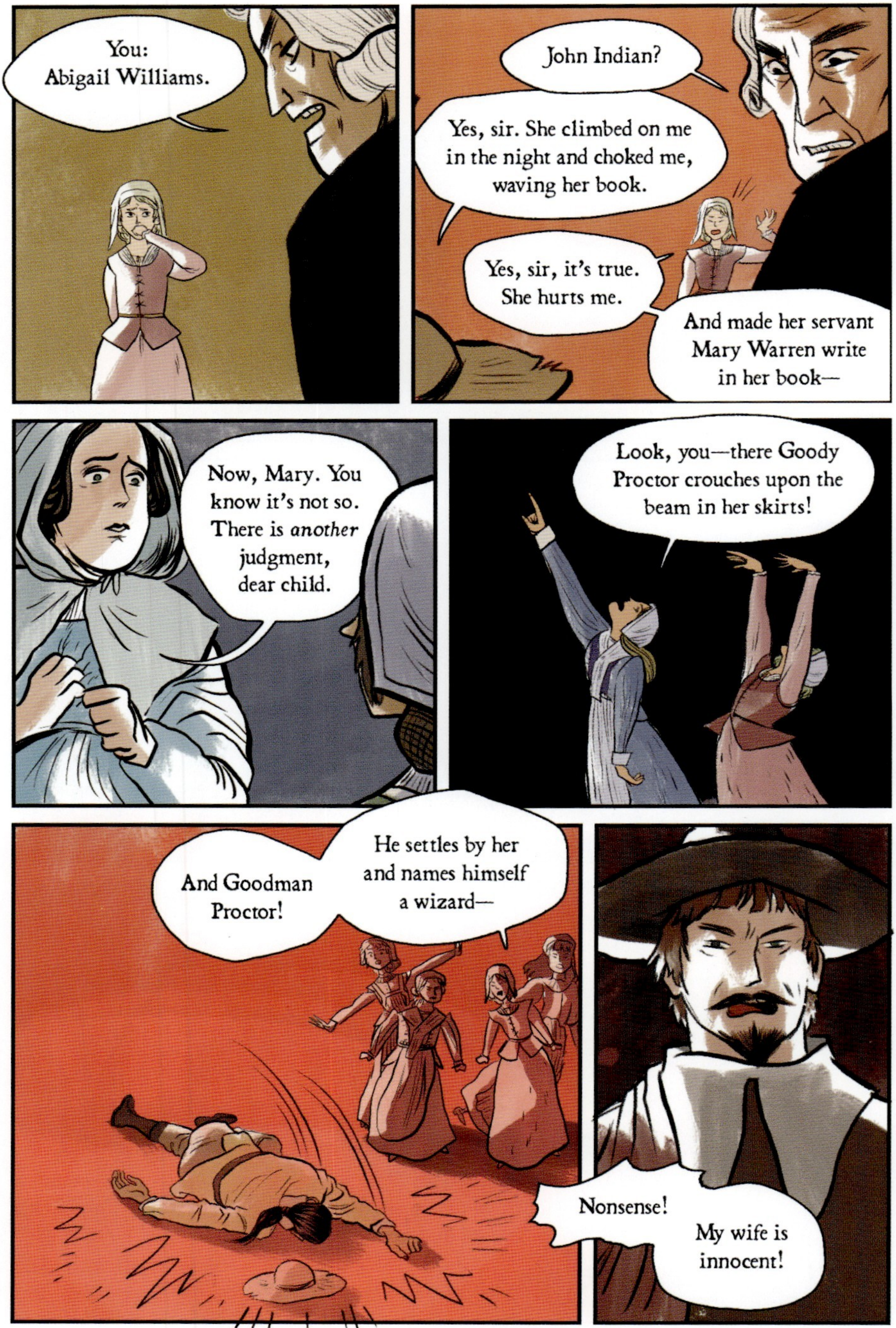
You: Abigail Williams.
John Indian?
Yes, sir. She climbed on me in the night and choked me, waving her book.
Yes, sir, it's true. She hurts me.
And made her servant Mary Warren write in her book—
Now, Mary. You know it's not so. There is *another* judgment, dear child.
Look, you—there Goody Proctor crouches upon the beam in her skirts!
And Goodman Proctor!
He settles by her and names himself a wizard—
Nonsense!
My wife is innocent!

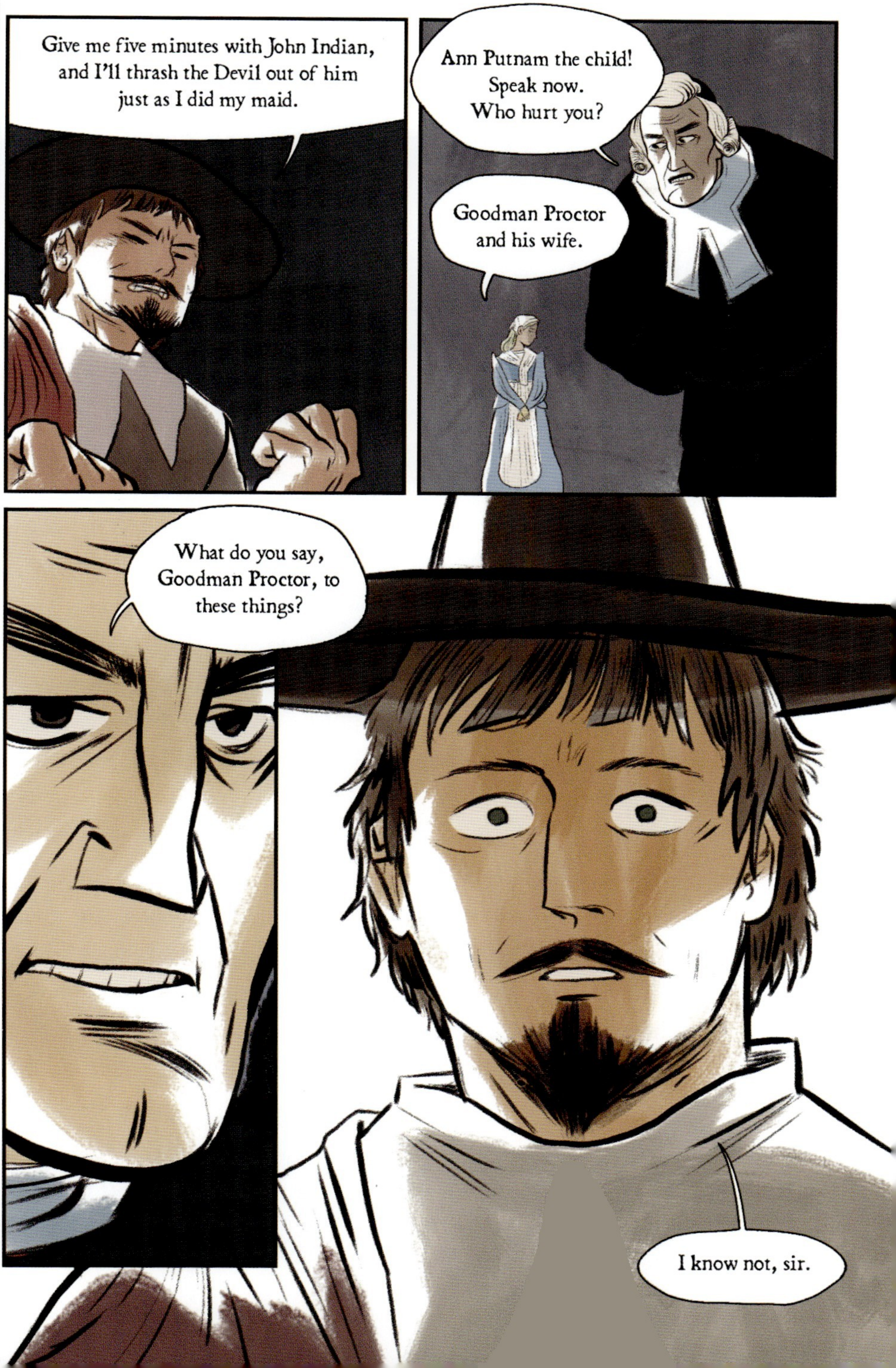
Give me five minutes with John Indian, and I'll thrash the Devil out of him just as I did my maid.
Ann Putnam the child! Speak now. Who hurt you?
Goodman Proctor and his wife.
What do you say, Goodman Proctor, to these things?
I know not, sir.

Part III

Spectral Evidence

The witch hunters of Salem were direct descendants of the first European settlers in the New World—men, women, and children who had braved the difficult passage across the Atlantic to flee religious persecution in Europe.

Some seventy years after the first Pilgrim landing and eighty years before the American Revolution, Massachusetts was a British colony divided by political unrest. In 1684, it had lost its charter—a document from the Crown of England granting a colony permission to exist—due to negligence and lax administration. Minister Increase Mather sailed to England to lobby for a new charter, but in the years preceding the witch trials, the colonists lived in fear of losing their hard-won autonomy to local English rule.

Salem Town and Salem Village also had different concerns—merchant versus agricultural—yet the village fell under legal and political jurisdiction of the town, which taxed it and set prices for its crops. Sharp factions formed between those who embraced the town's merchant life and those bound to the land.

Salem Village was so infected with rivalries that for years it couldn't agree on how to run its church. It hired several ministers in a row, including Deodat Lawson, who stayed for four years, and George Burroughs, who lasted three. Samuel Parris was an aggressive negotiator and unbending in his views. By the time he took the pulpit in 1689, he had divided his parish even more by openly siding with those who would see him ordained and complaining constantly about conditions at the parsonage.

Governor Phips and Increase Mather would return from England

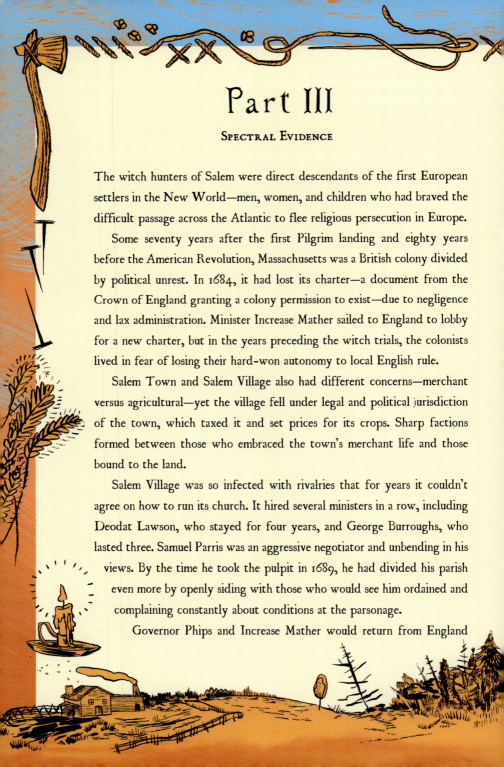

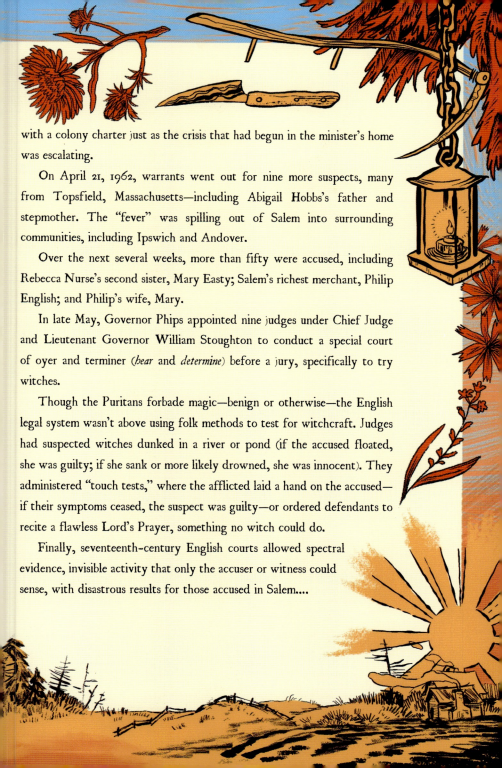

with a colony charter just as the crisis that had begun in the minister's home was escalating.

On April 21, 1962, warrants went out for nine more suspects, many from Topsfield, Massachusetts—including Abigail Hobbs's father and stepmother. The "fever" was spilling out of Salem into surrounding communities, including Ipswich and Andover.

Over the next several weeks, more than fifty were accused, including Rebecca Nurse's second sister, Mary Easty; Salem's richest merchant, Philip English; and Philip's wife, Mary.

In late May, Governor Phips appointed nine judges under Chief Judge and Lieutenant Governor William Stoughton to conduct a special court of oyer and terminer (*hear* and *determine*) before a jury, specifically to try witches.

Though the Puritans forbade magic—benign or otherwise—the English legal system wasn't above using folk methods to test for witchcraft. Judges had suspected witches dunked in a river or pond (if the accused floated, she was guilty; if she sank or more likely drowned, she was innocent). They administered "touch tests," where the afflicted laid a hand on the accused—if their symptoms ceased, the suspect was guilty—or ordered defendants to recite a flawless Lord's Prayer, something no witch could do.

Finally, seventeenth-century English courts allowed spectral evidence, invisible activity that only the accuser or witness could sense, with disastrous results for those accused in Salem....

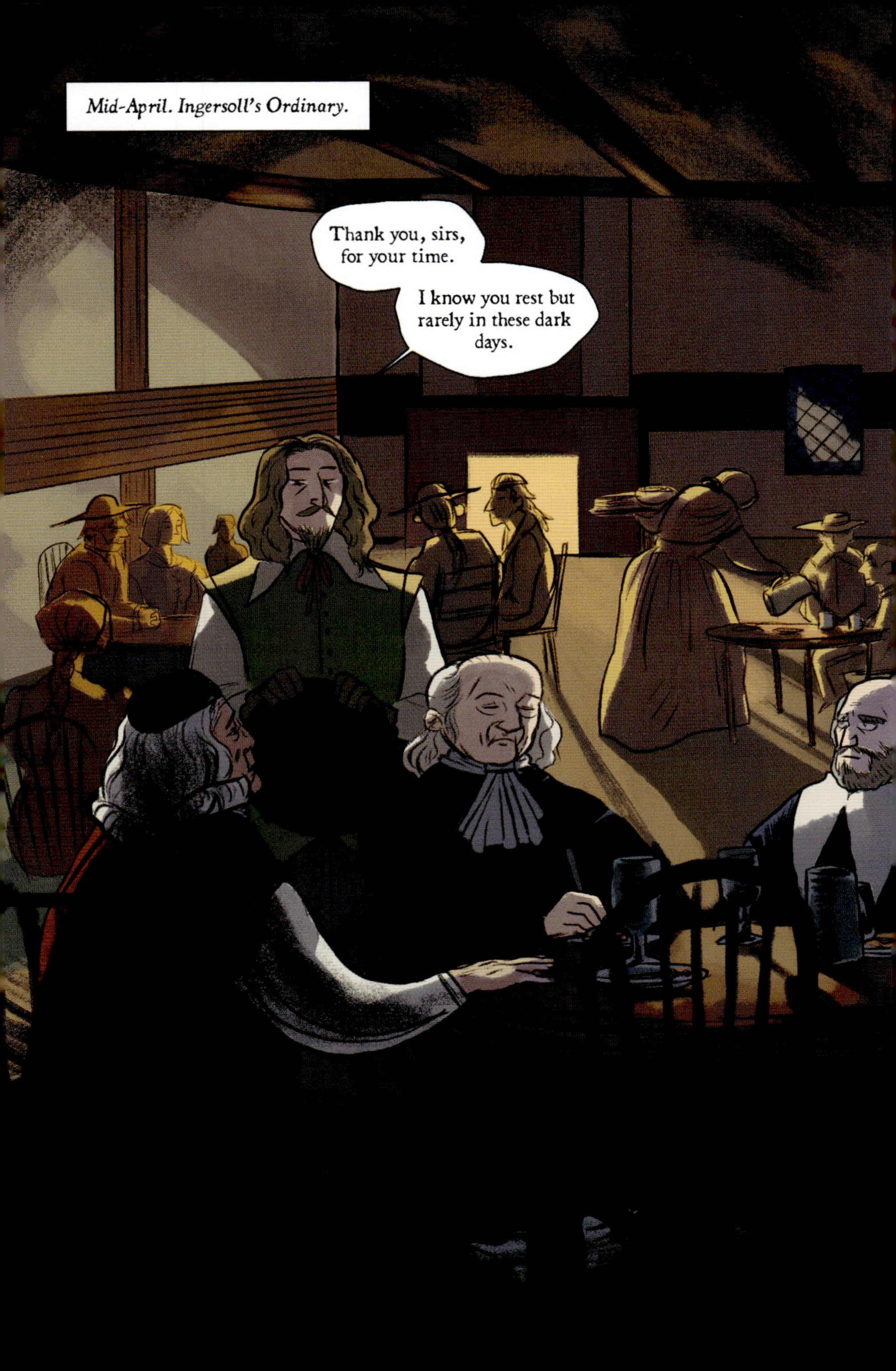
Mid-April. Ingersoll's Ordinary.
Thank you, sirs, for your time.
I know you rest but rarely in these dark days.

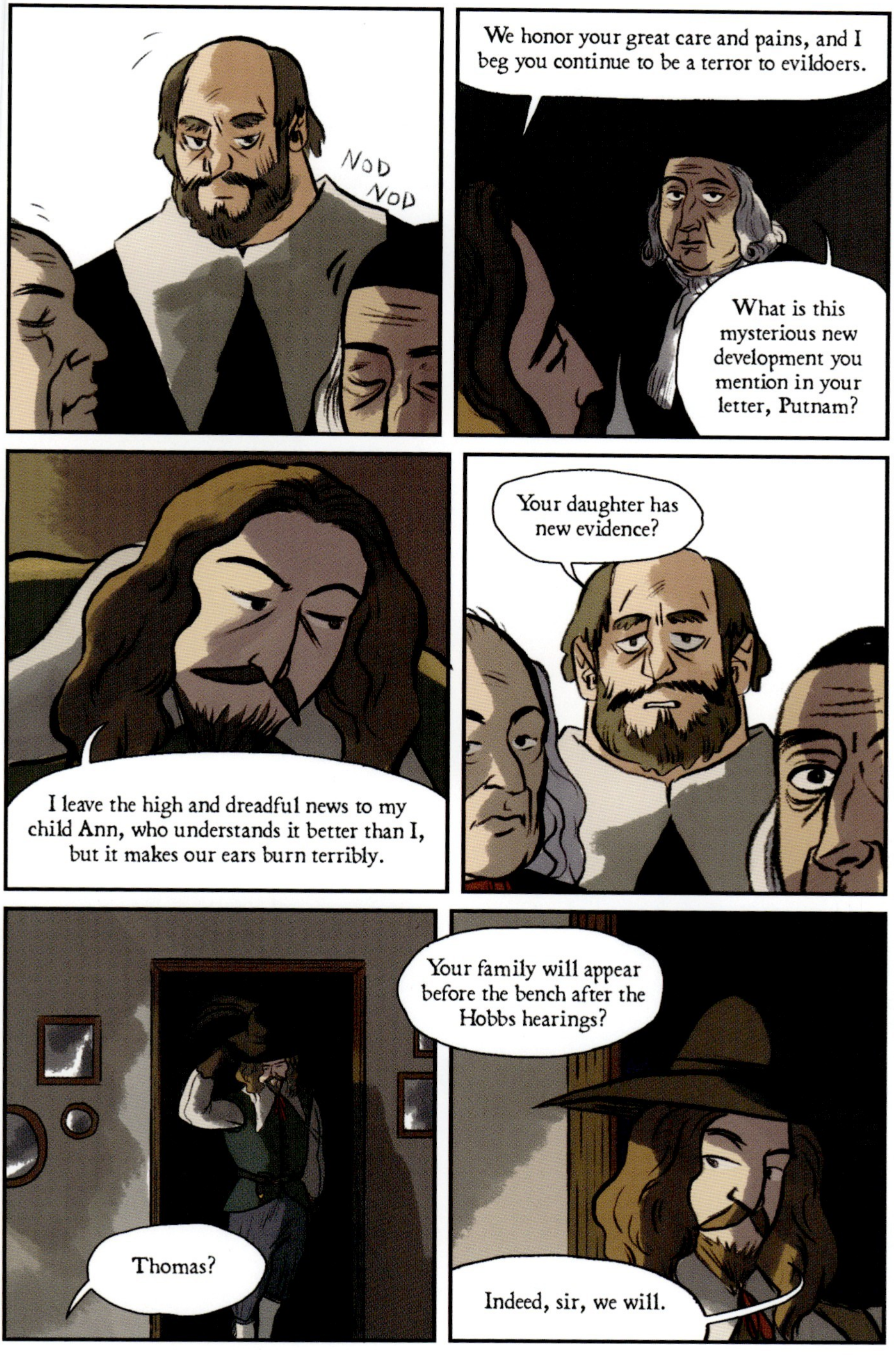
NOD
NOD
We honor your great care and pains, and I beg you continue to be a terror to evildoers.
What is this mysterious new development you mention in your letter, Putnam?
I leave the high and dreadful news to my child Ann, who understands it better than I, but it makes our ears burn terribly.
Your daughter has new evidence?
Thomas?
Your family will appear before the bench after the Hobbs hearings?
Indeed, sir, we will.

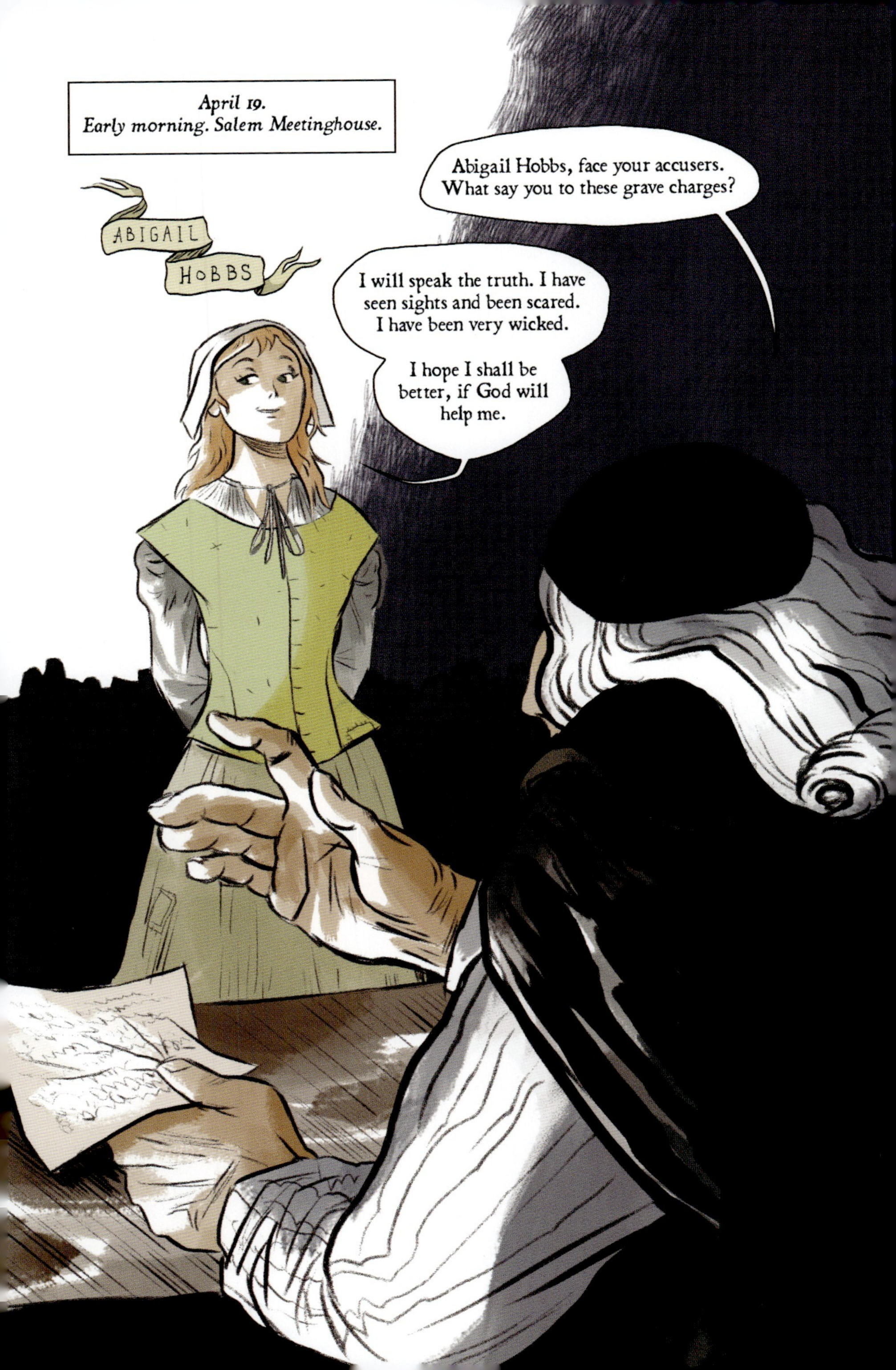
April 19.
Early morning. Salem Meetinghouse.
ABIGAIL HOBBS
Abigail Hobbs, face your accusers. What say you to these grave charges?
I will speak the truth. I have seen sights and been scared. I have been very wicked.
I hope I shall be better, if God will help me.

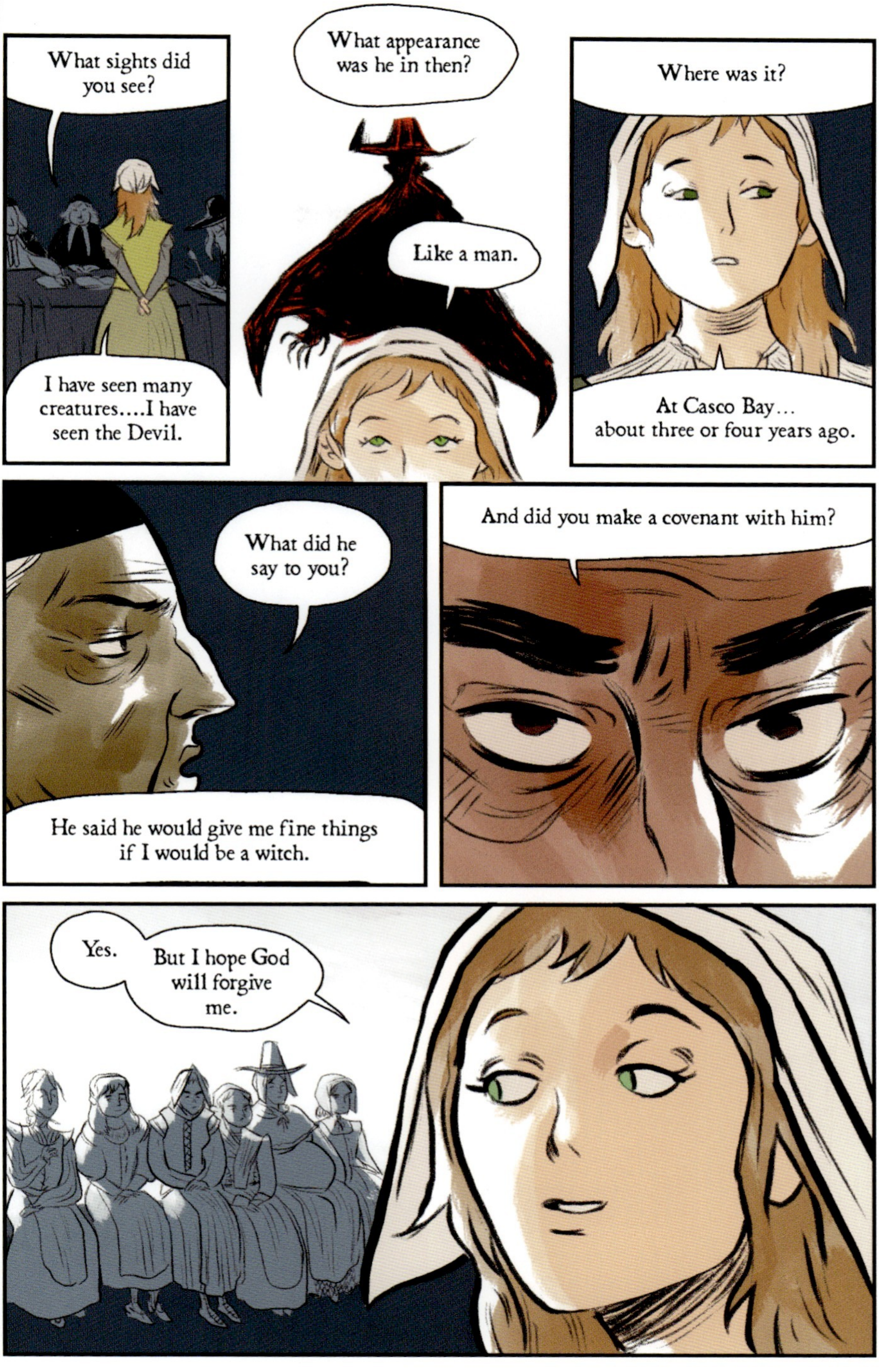
What sights did you see?
I have seen many creatures....I have seen the Devil.
What appearance was he in then?
Like a man.
Where was it?
At Casco Bay... about three or four years ago.
What did he say to you?
He said he would give me fine things if I would be a witch.
And did you make a covenant with him?
Yes.
But I hope God will forgive me.

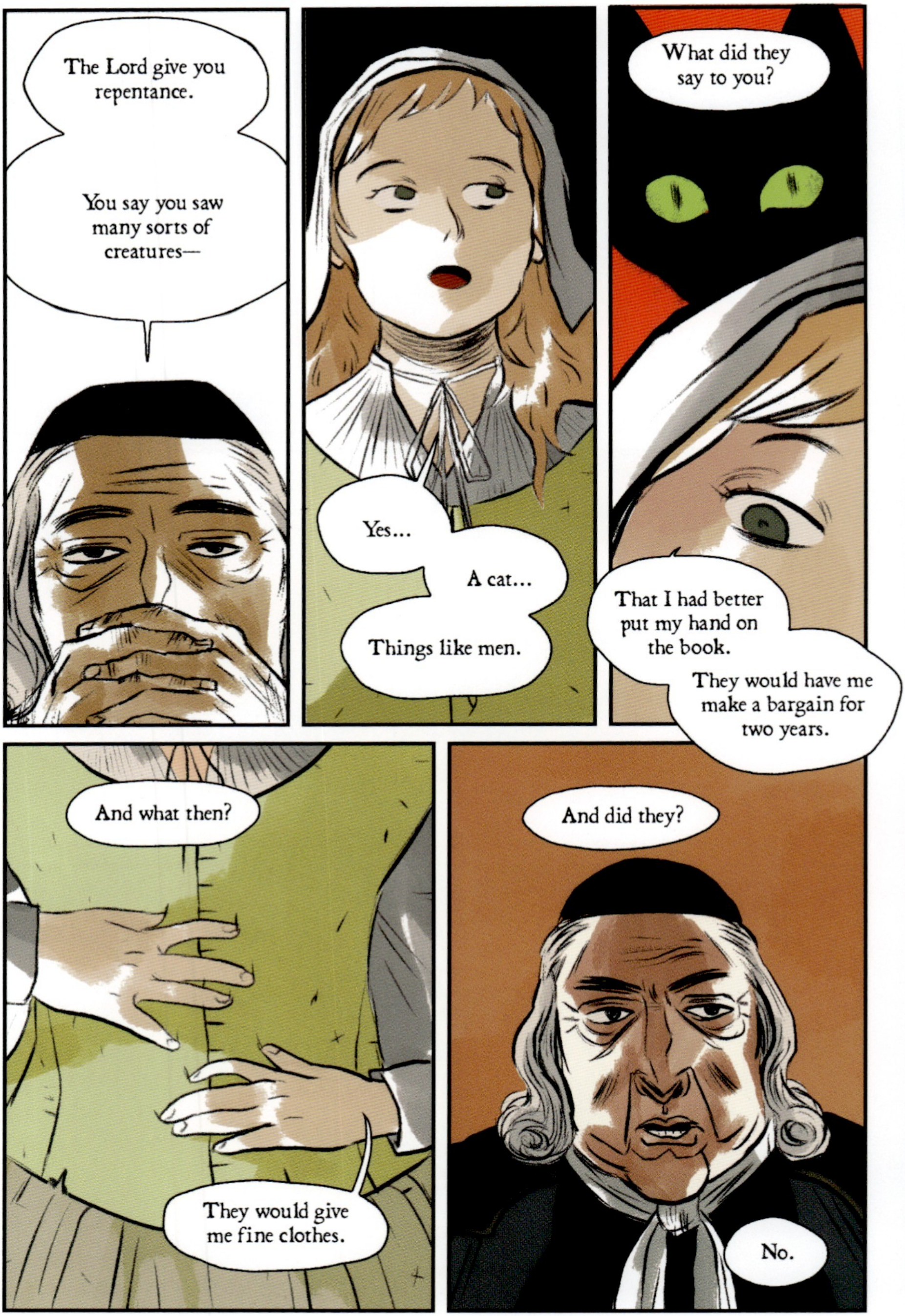
The Lord give you repentance.
You say you saw many sorts of creatures—
Yes...
A cat...
Things like men.
What did they say to you?
That I had better put my hand on the book.
They would have me make a bargain for two years.
And what then?
They would give me fine clothes.
And did they?
No.

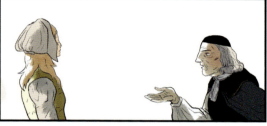

She is struck deaf! She cannot hear you, Excellency.

Sarah Good and Sarah Osborne stand on either side with fingers in her ears!

Now she is struck blind—

with her eyes quite open.

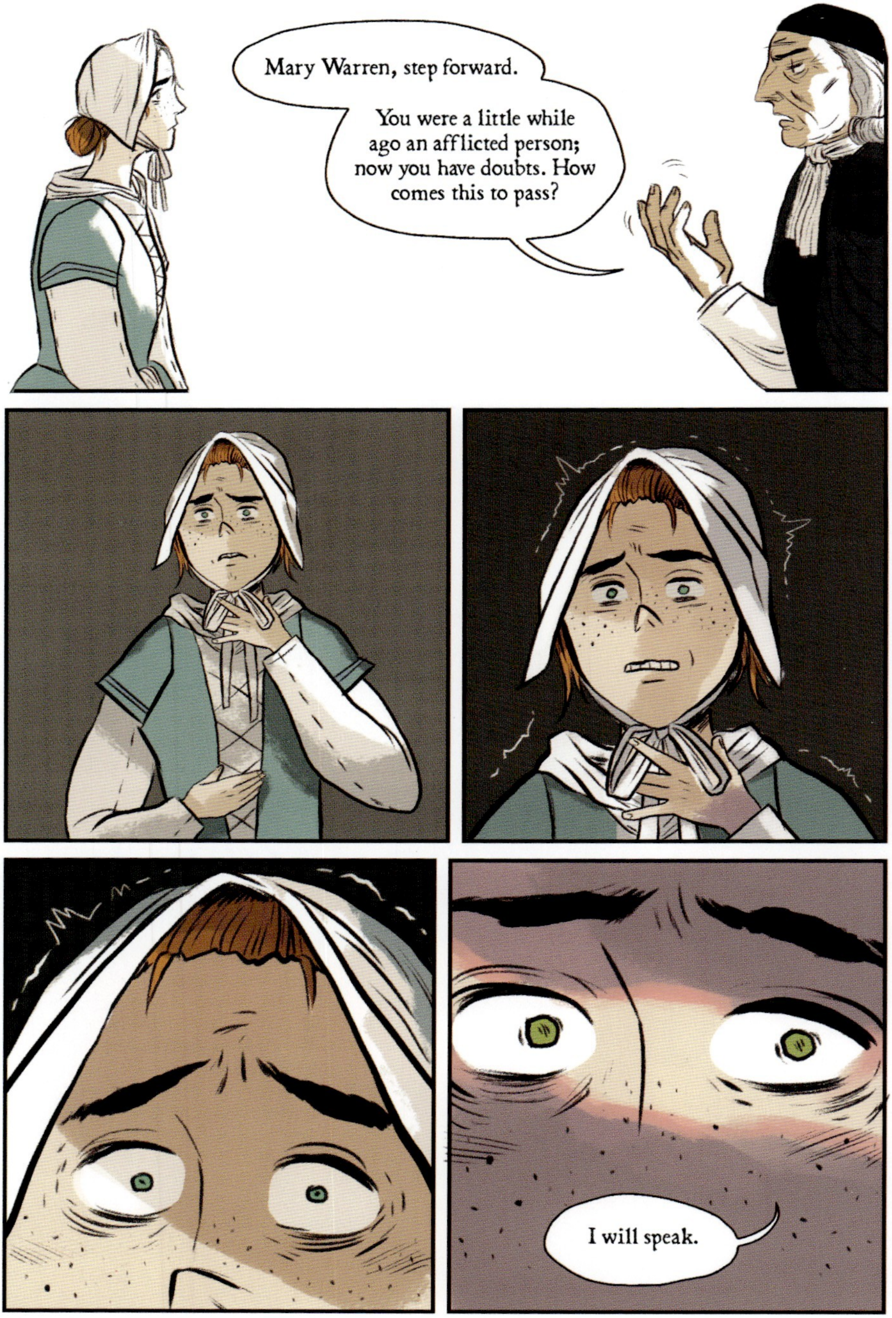
Mary Warren, step forward.
You were a little while ago an afflicted person; now you have doubts. How comes this to pass?
I will speak.

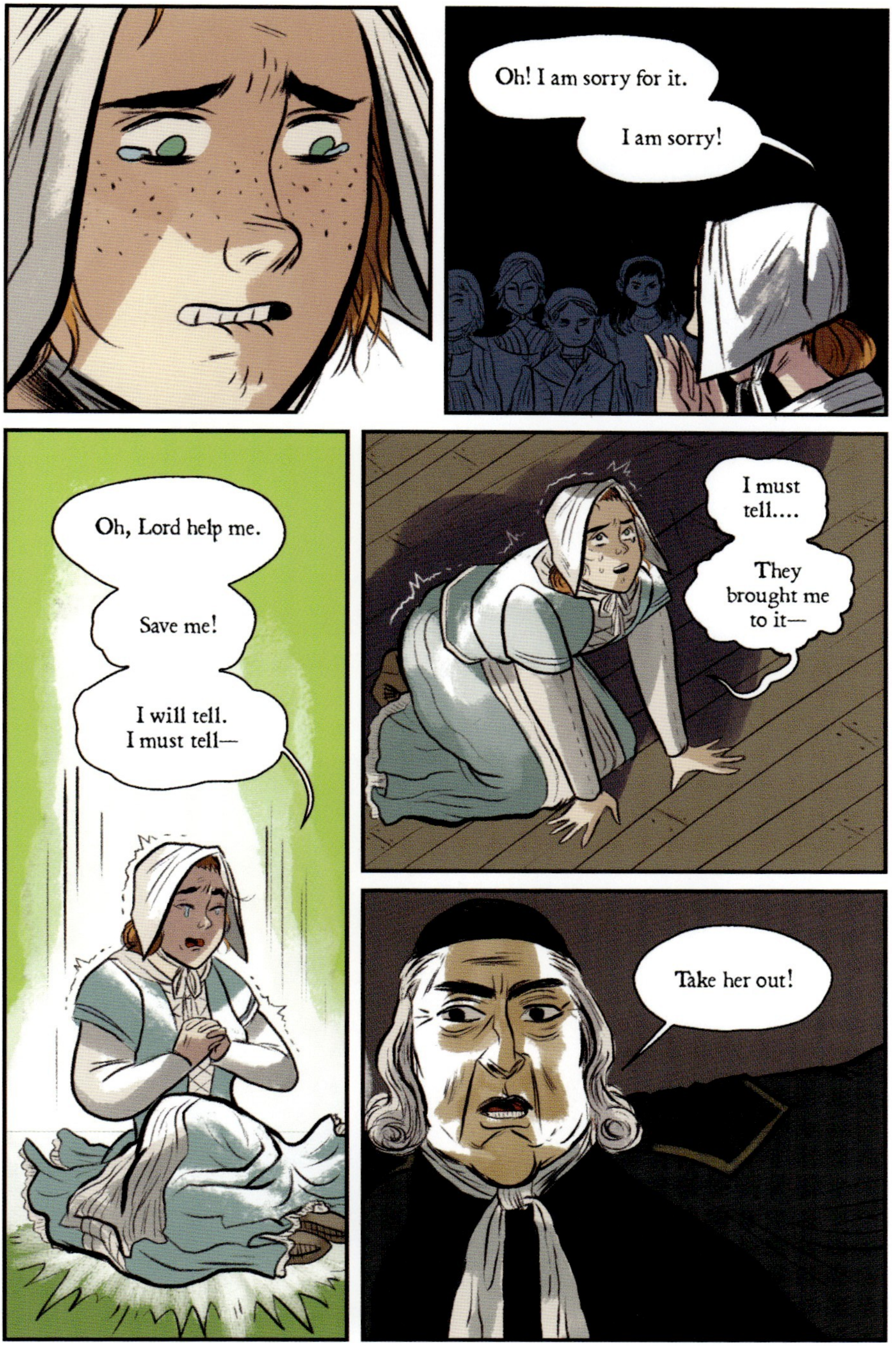
Oh! I am sorry for it.
I am sorry!
Oh, Lord help me.
Save me!
I will tell. I must tell—
I must tell....
They brought me to it—
Take her out!

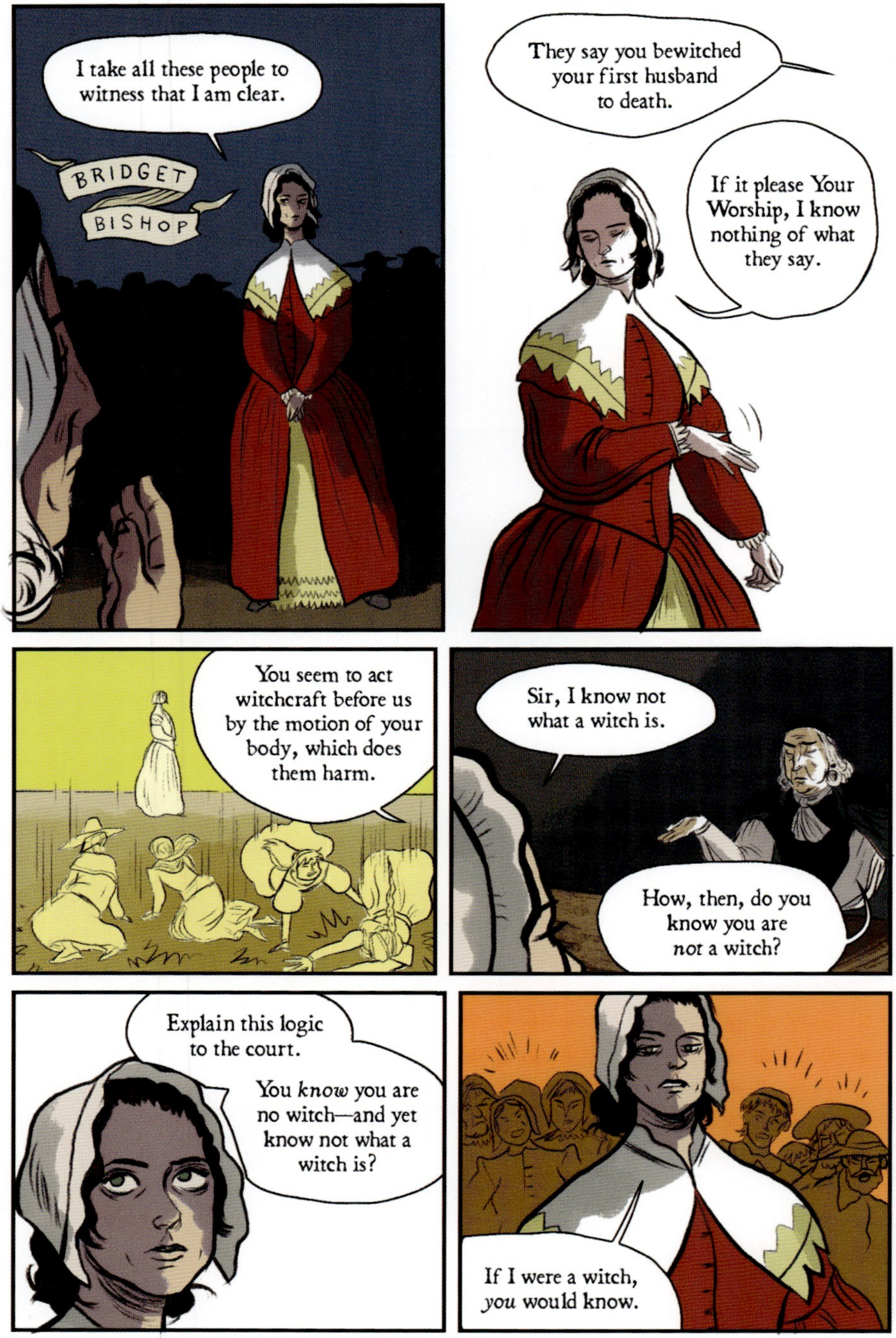
I take all these people to witness that I am clear.
BRIDGET BISHOP
They say you bewitched your first husband to death.
If it please Your Worship, I know nothing of what they say.
You seem to act witchcraft before us by the motion of your body, which does them harm.
Sir, I know not what a witch is.
How, then, do you know you are *not* a witch?
Explain this logic to the court.
You *know* you are no witch—and yet know not what a witch is?
If I were a witch, *you* would know.

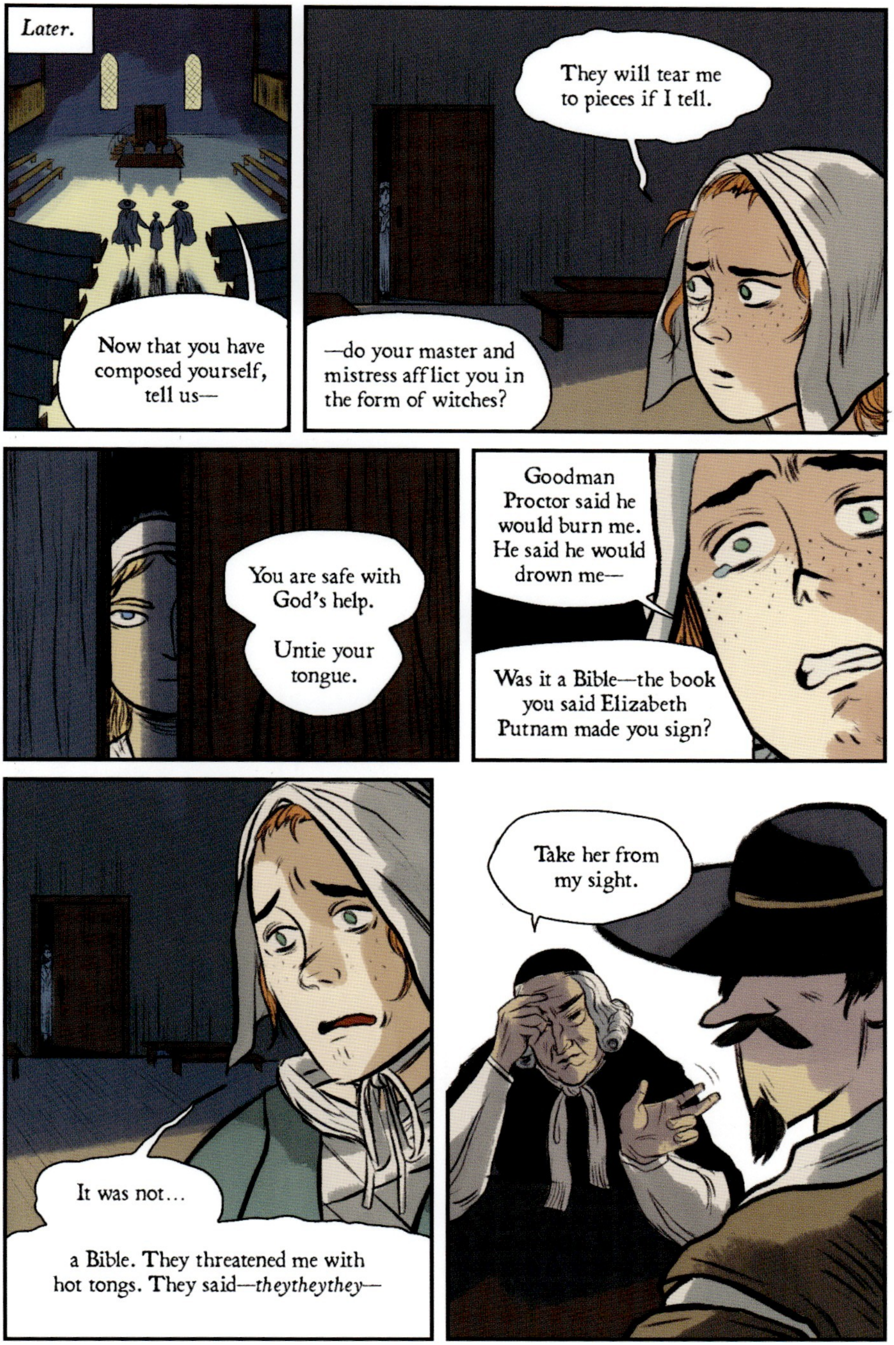
Later.
Now that you have composed yourself, tell us—
—do your master and mistress afflict you in the form of witches?
They will tear me to pieces if I tell.
You are safe with God's help.
Untie your tongue.
Goodman Proctor said he would burn me. He said he would drown me—
Was it a Bible—the book you said Elizabeth Putnam made you sign?
It was not...
a Bible. They threatened me with hot tongs. They said—*theytheythey*—
Take her from my sight.

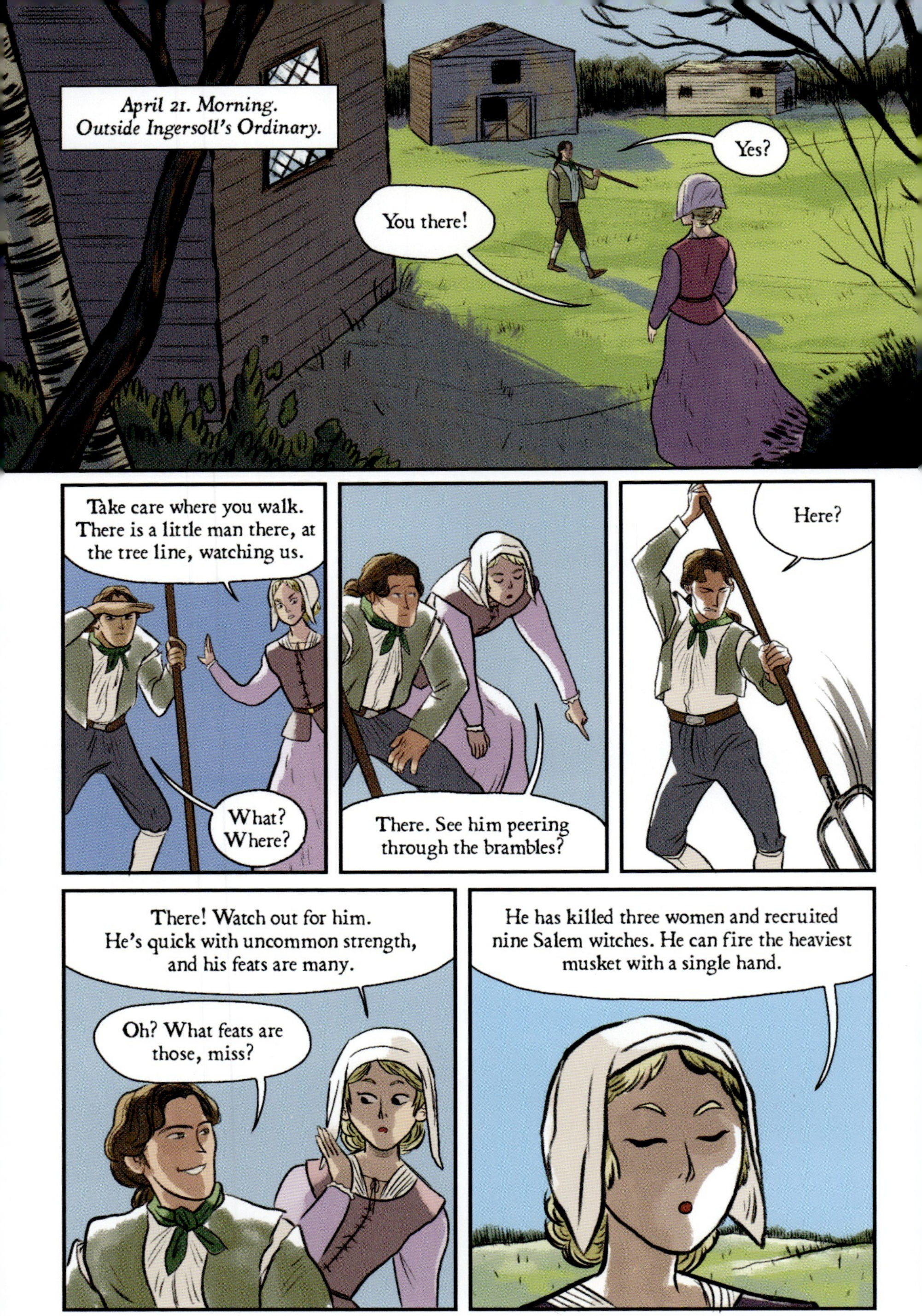
April 21. Morning.
Outside Ingersoll's Ordinary.
You there!
Yes?
Take care where you walk. There is a little man there, at the tree line, watching us.
What? Where?
There. See him peering through the brambles?
Here?
There! Watch out for him. He's quick with uncommon strength, and his feats are many.
Oh? What feats are those, miss?
He has killed three women and recruited nine Salem witches. He can fire the heaviest musket with a single hand.

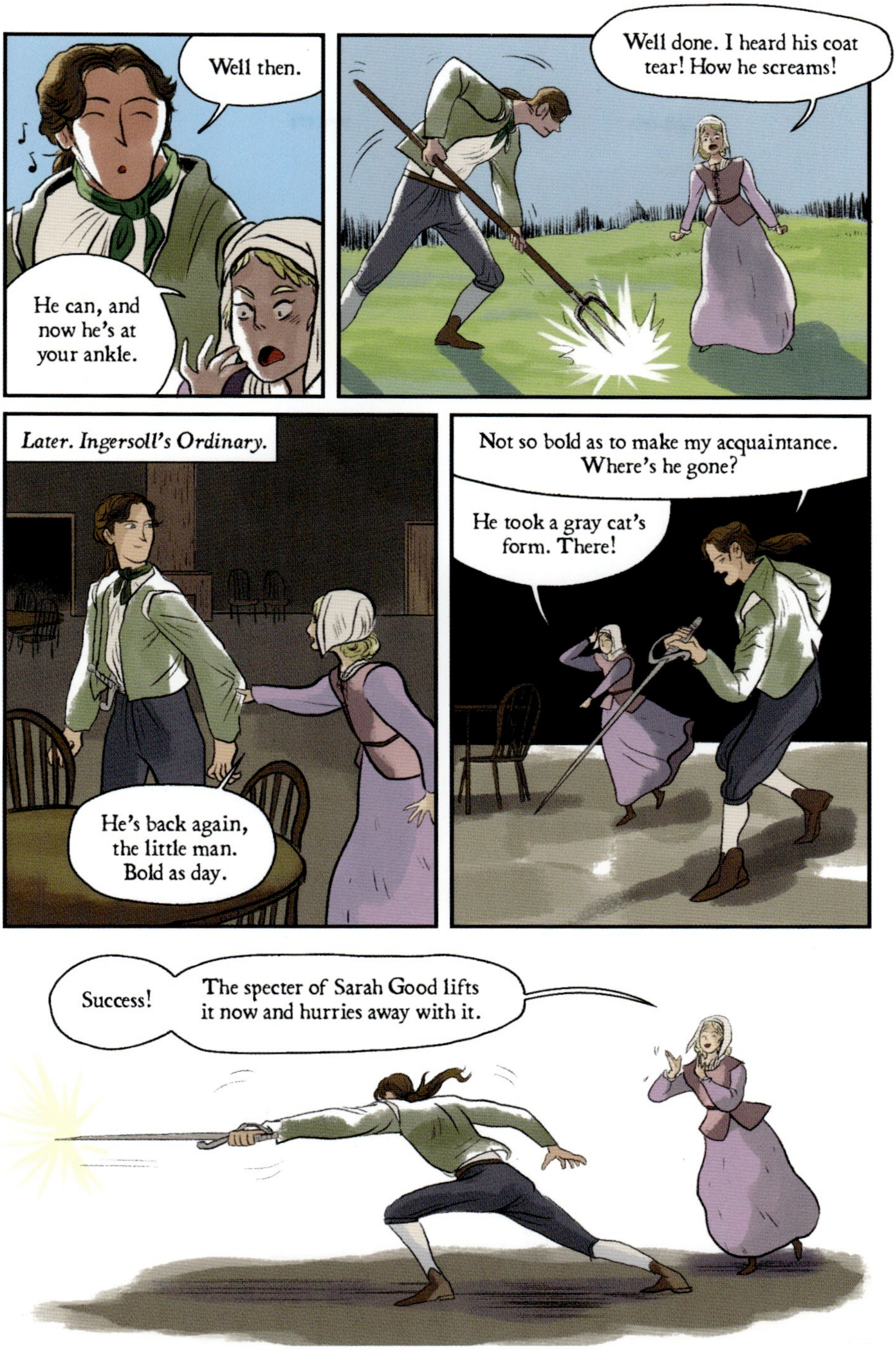
Well then.
He can, and now he's at your ankle.
Well done. I heard his coat tear! How he screams!
Later. Ingersoll's Ordinary.
He's back again, the little man. Bold as day.
Not so bold as to make my acquaintance. Where's he gone?
He took a gray cat's form. There!
Success!
The specter of Sarah Good lifts it now and hurries away with it.

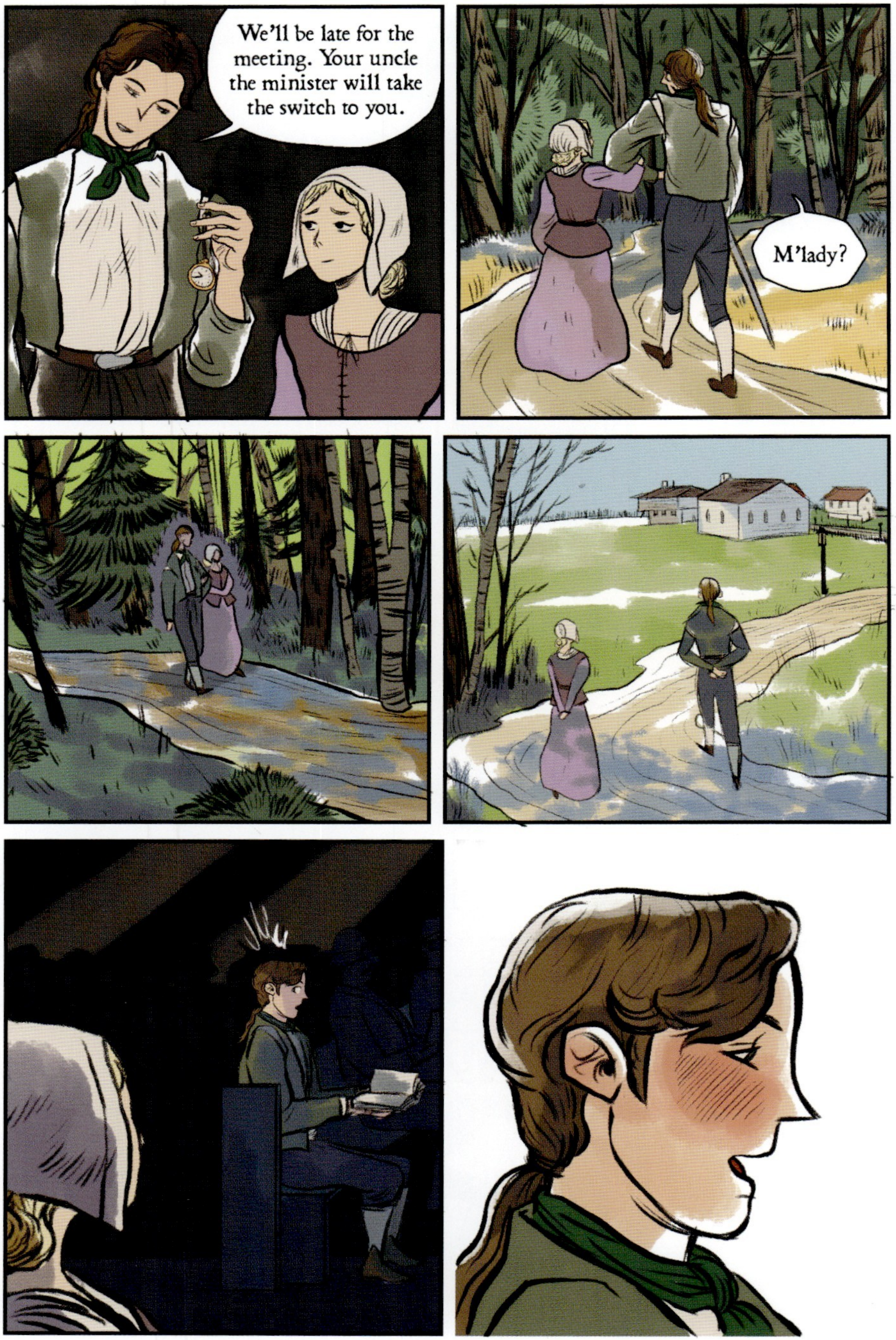

We'll be late for the meeting. Your uncle the minister will take the switch to you.
M'lady?

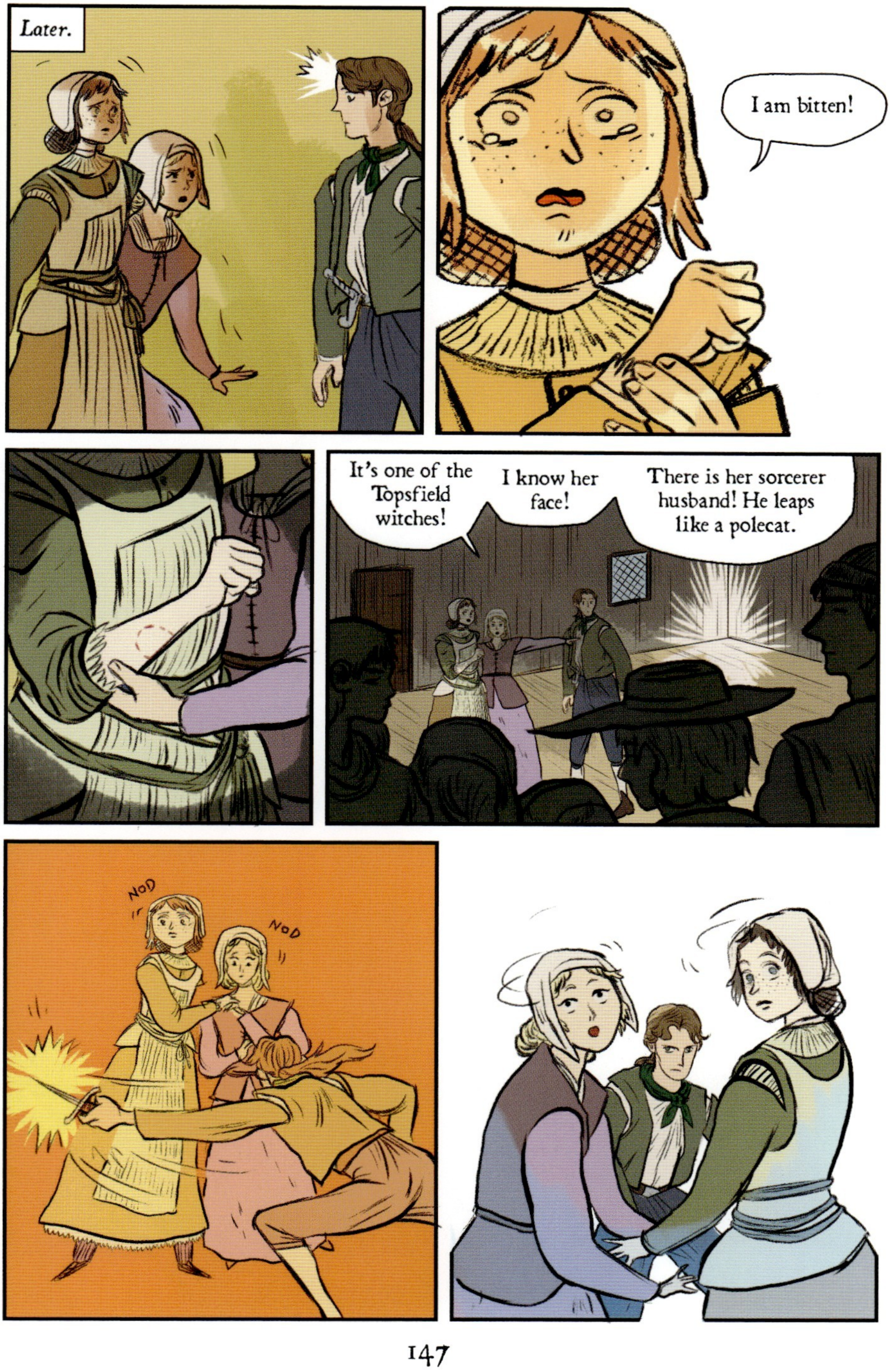
Later.
I am bitten!
It's one of the Topsfield witches!
I know her face!
There is her sorcerer husband! He leaps like a polecat.
NOD
NOD

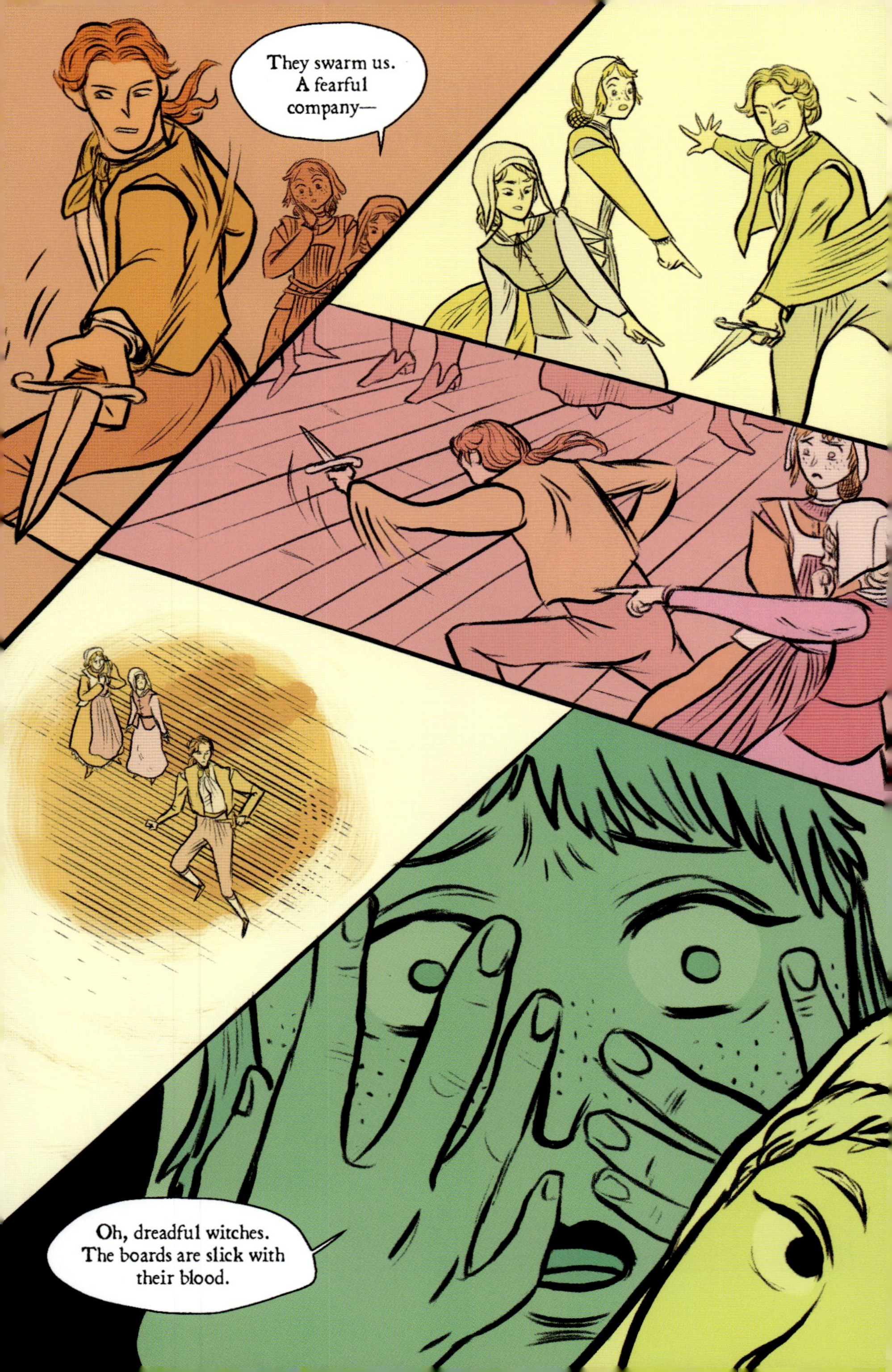
They swarm us. A fearful company—
Oh, dreadful witches. The boards are slick with their blood.

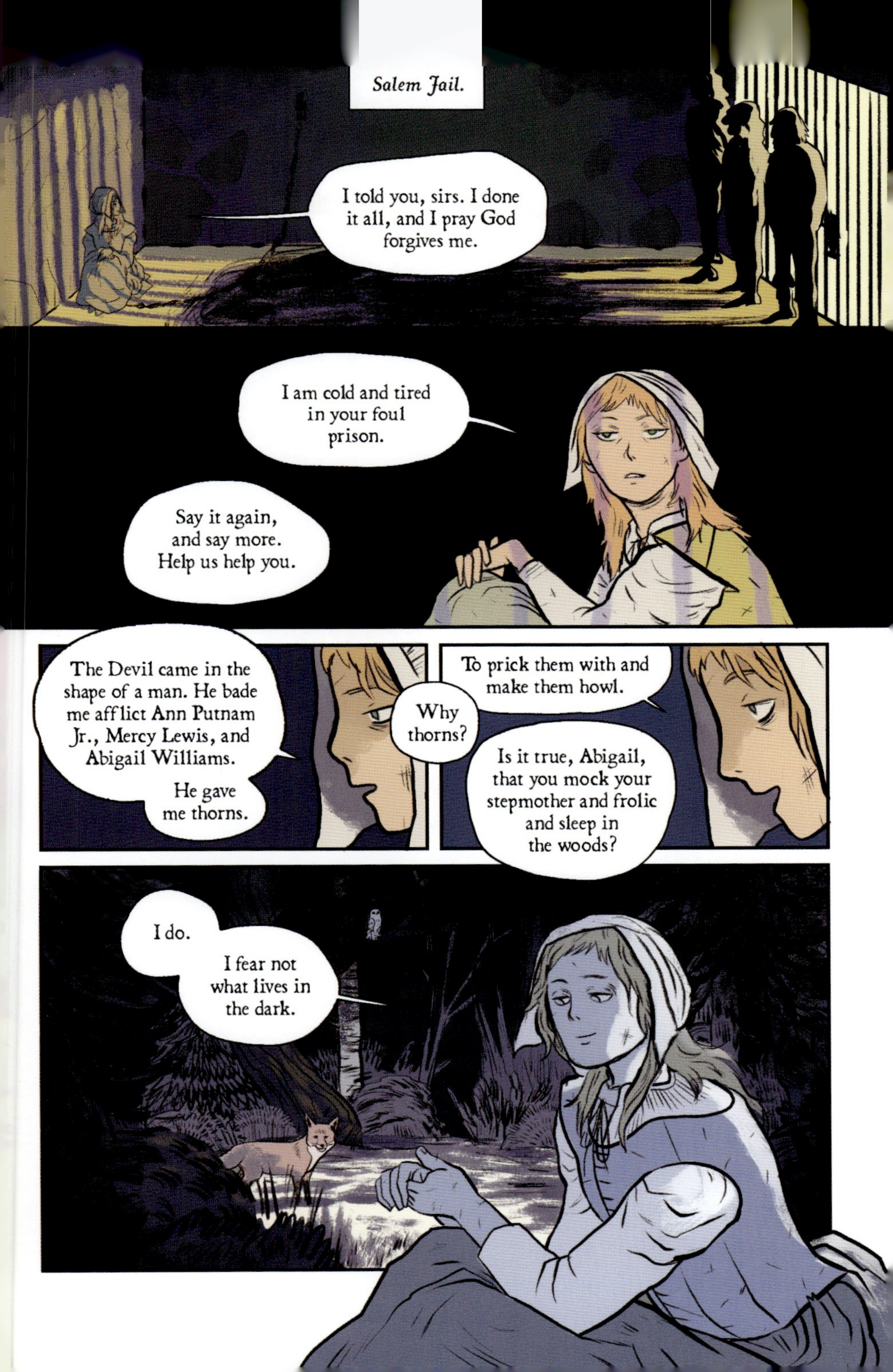
Salem Jail.
I told you, sirs. I done it all, and I pray God forgives me.
I am cold and tired in your foul prison.
Say it again, and say more. Help us help you.
The Devil came in the shape of a man. He bade me afflict Ann Putnam Jr., Mercy Lewis, and Abigail Williams.
He gave me thorns.
Why thorns?
To prick them with and make them howl.
Is it true, Abigail, that you mock your stepmother and frolic and sleep in the woods?
I do.
I fear not what lives in the dark.

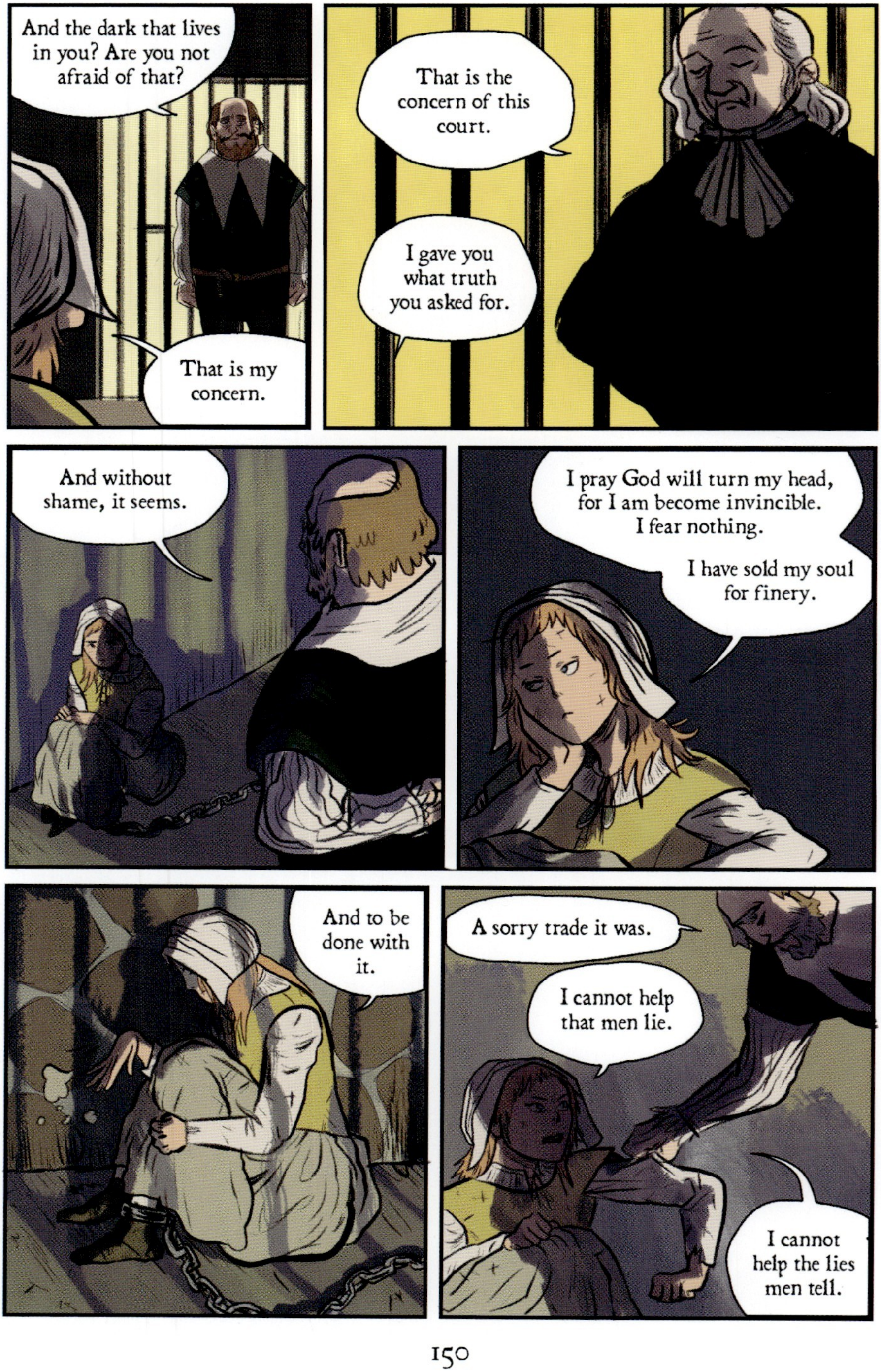
And the dark that lives in you? Are you not afraid of that?
That is my concern.
That is the concern of this court.
I gave you what truth you asked for.
And without shame, it seems.
I pray God will turn my head, for I am become invincible. I fear nothing.
I have sold my soul for finery.
And to be done with it.
A sorry trade it was.
I cannot help that men lie.
I cannot help the lies men tell.

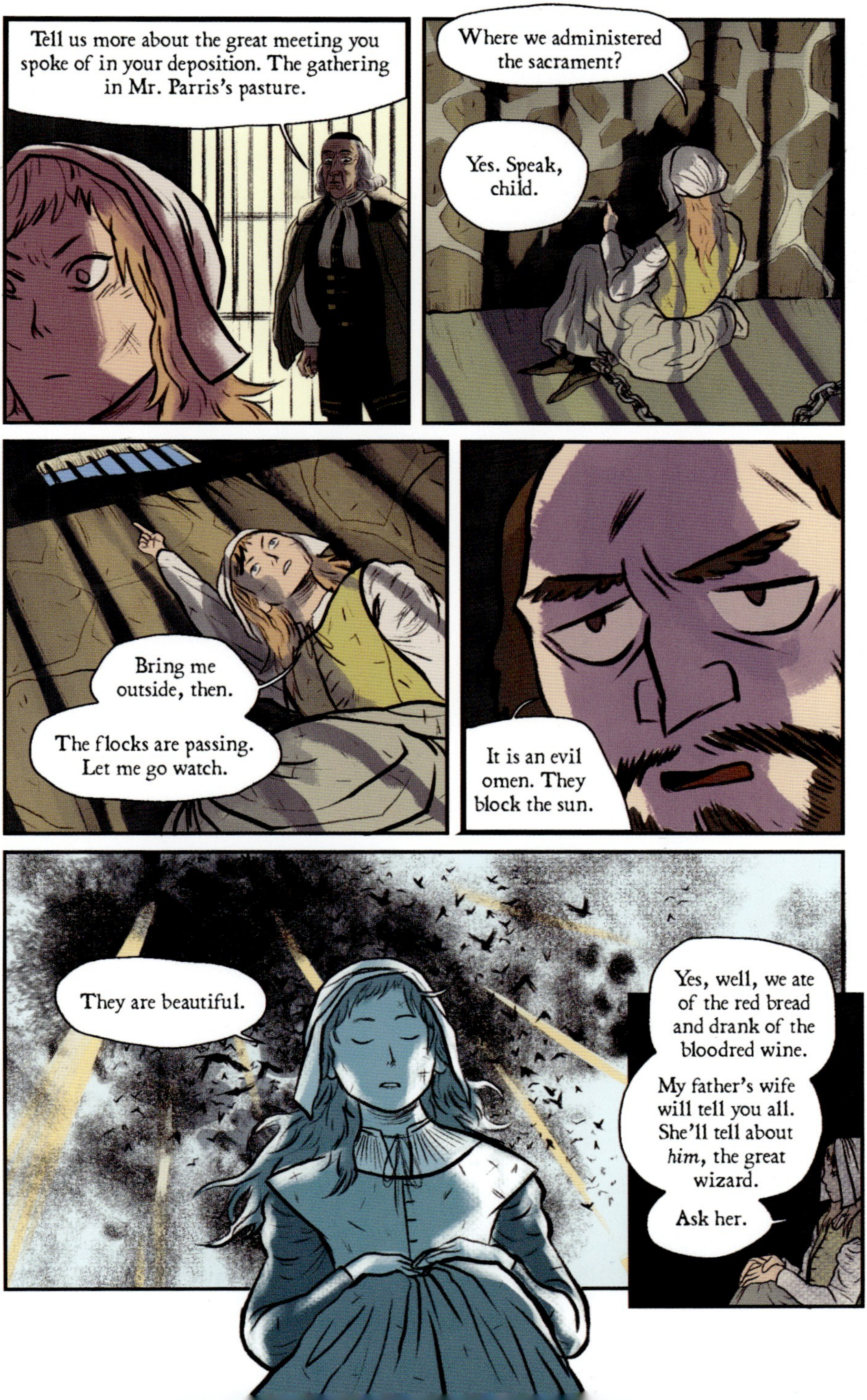
Tell us more about the great meeting you spoke of in your deposition. The gathering in Mr. Parris's pasture.
Where we administered the sacrament?
Yes. Speak, child.
Bring me outside, then.
The flocks are passing. Let me go watch.
It is an evil omen. They block the sun.
They are beautiful.
Yes, well, we ate of the red bread and drank of the bloodred wine.
My father's wife will tell you all. She'll tell about *him*, the great wizard.
Ask her.

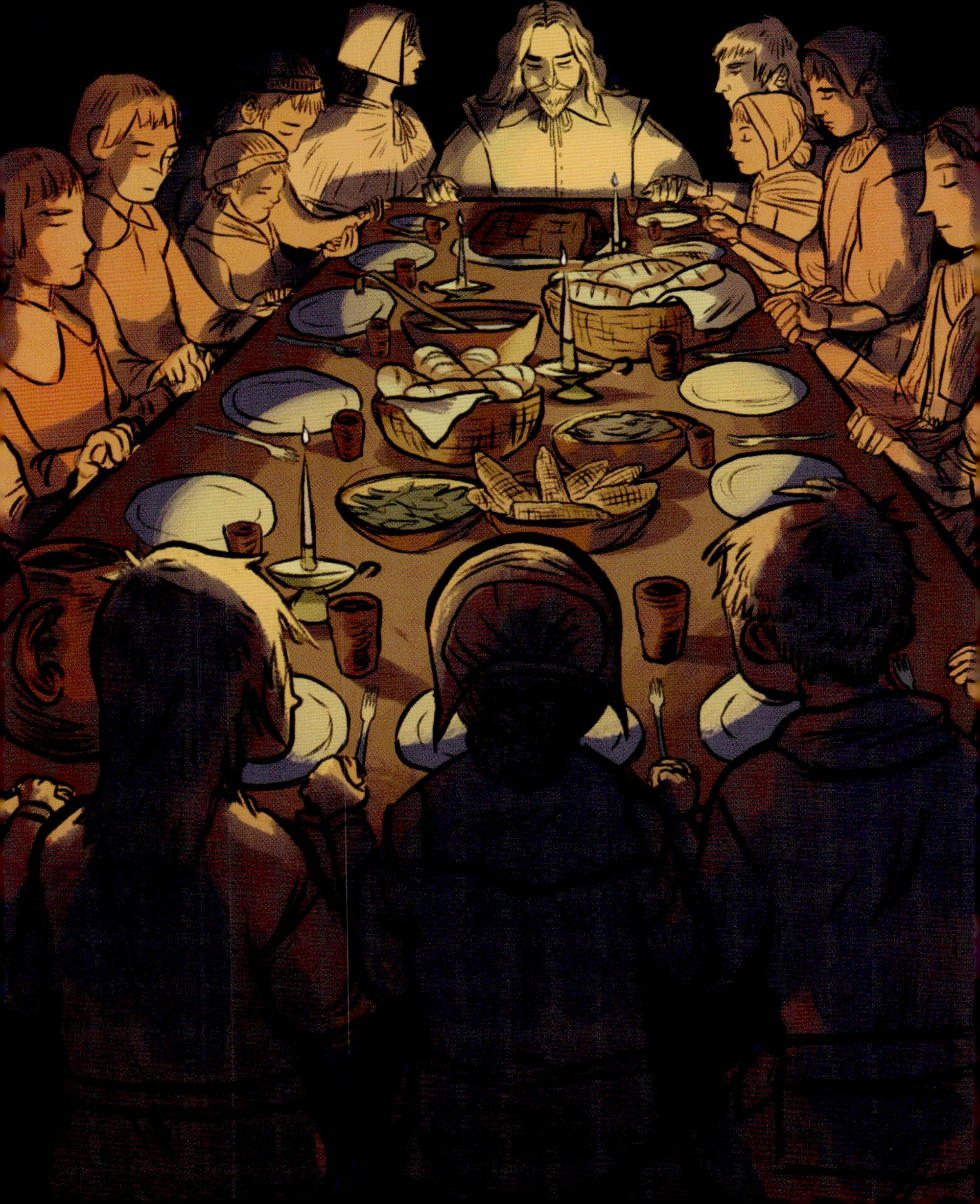
April 21. Evening.
The Putnam home.

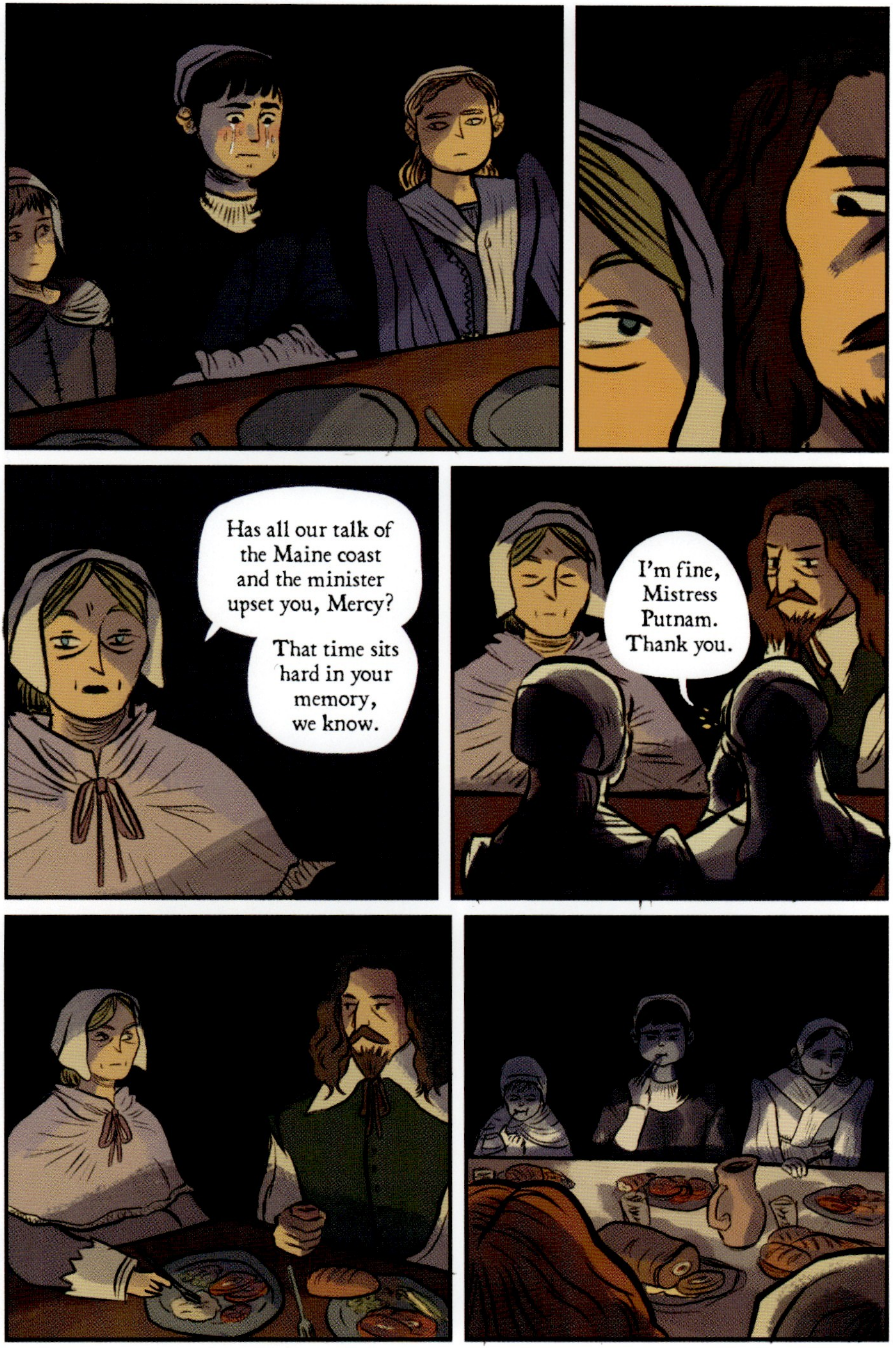
Has all our talk of the Maine coast and the minister upset you, Mercy?
That time sits hard in your memory, we know.
I'm fine, Mistress Putnam. Thank you.

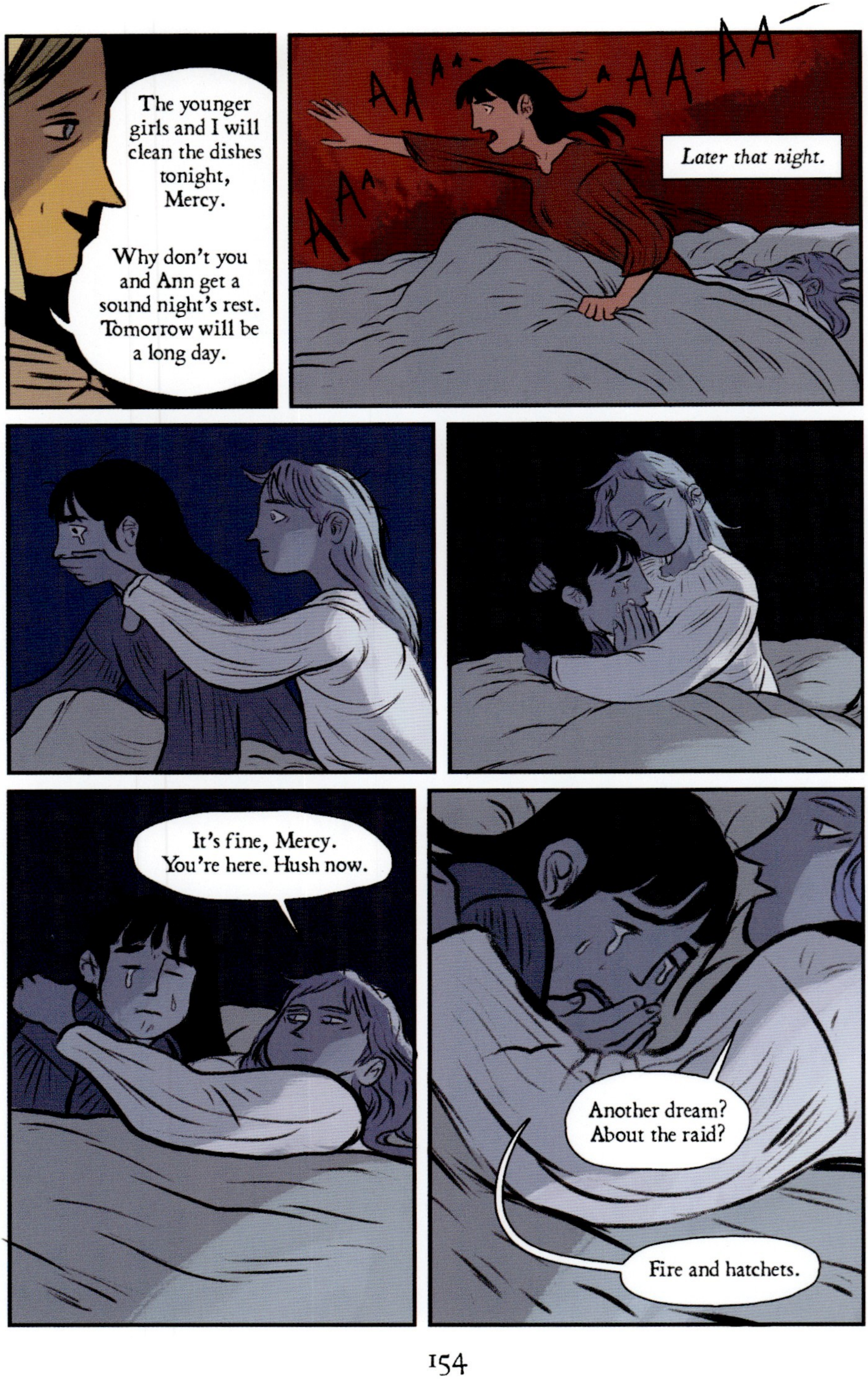
The younger girls and I will clean the dishes tonight, Mercy.
Why don't you and Ann get a sound night's rest. Tomorrow will be a long day.
AAAA-AA-AA-AA-AA-
Later that night.
It's fine, Mercy. You're here. Hush now.
Another dream? About the raid?
Fire and hatchets.

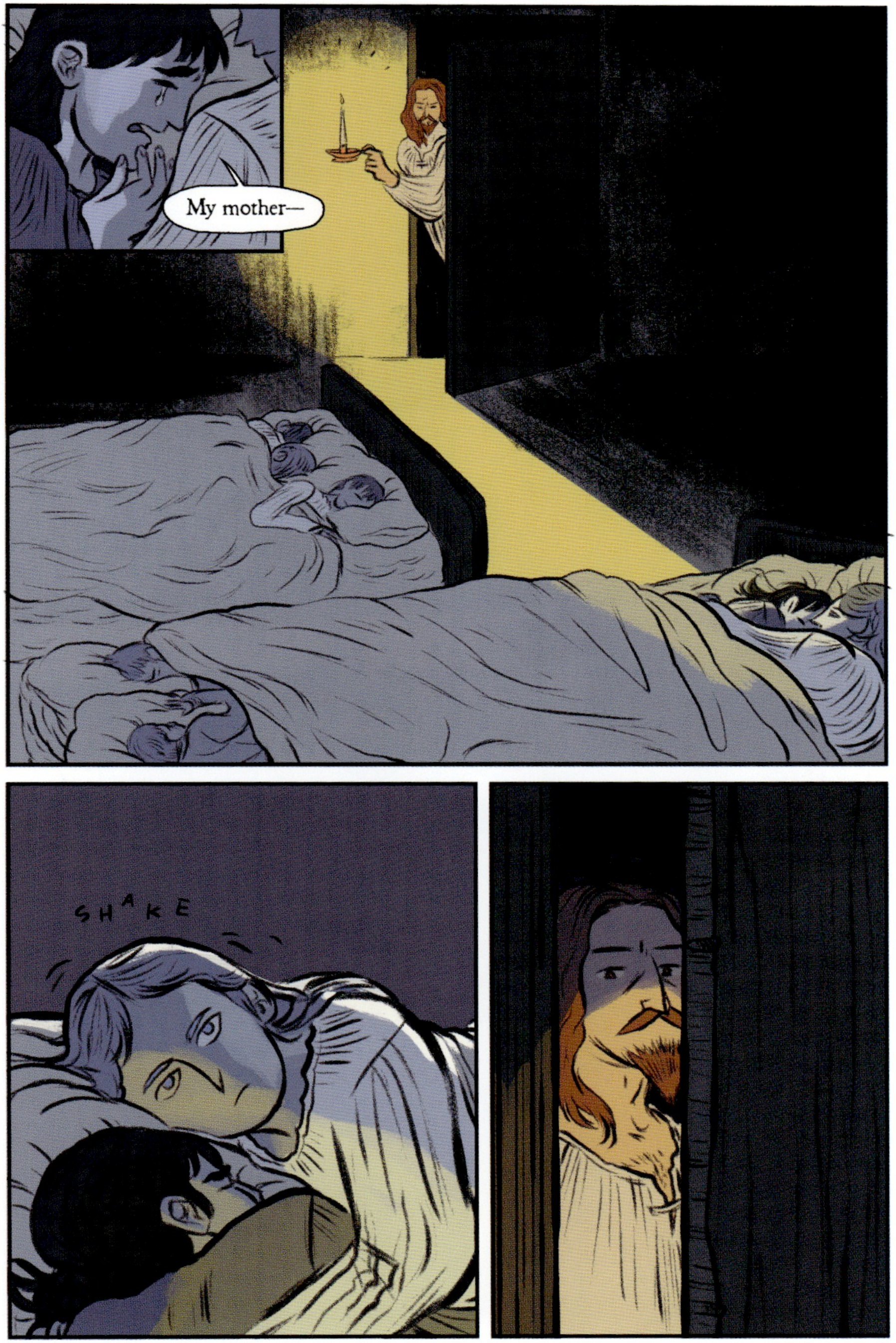
My mother—
SHAKE

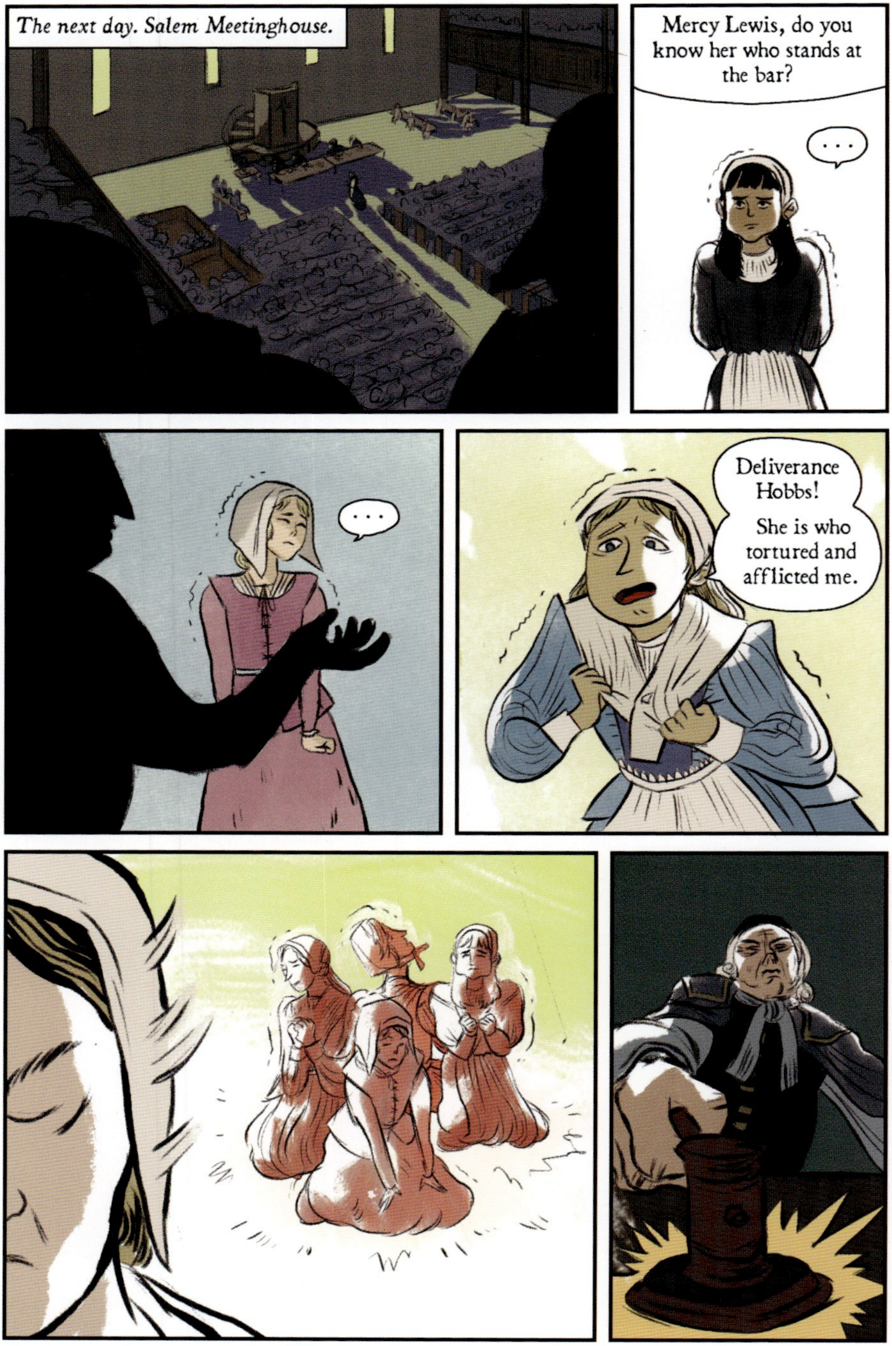

The next day. Salem Meetinghouse.
Mercy Lewis, do you know her who stands at the bar?
. . .
. . .
Deliverance Hobbs!
She is who tortured and afflicted me.

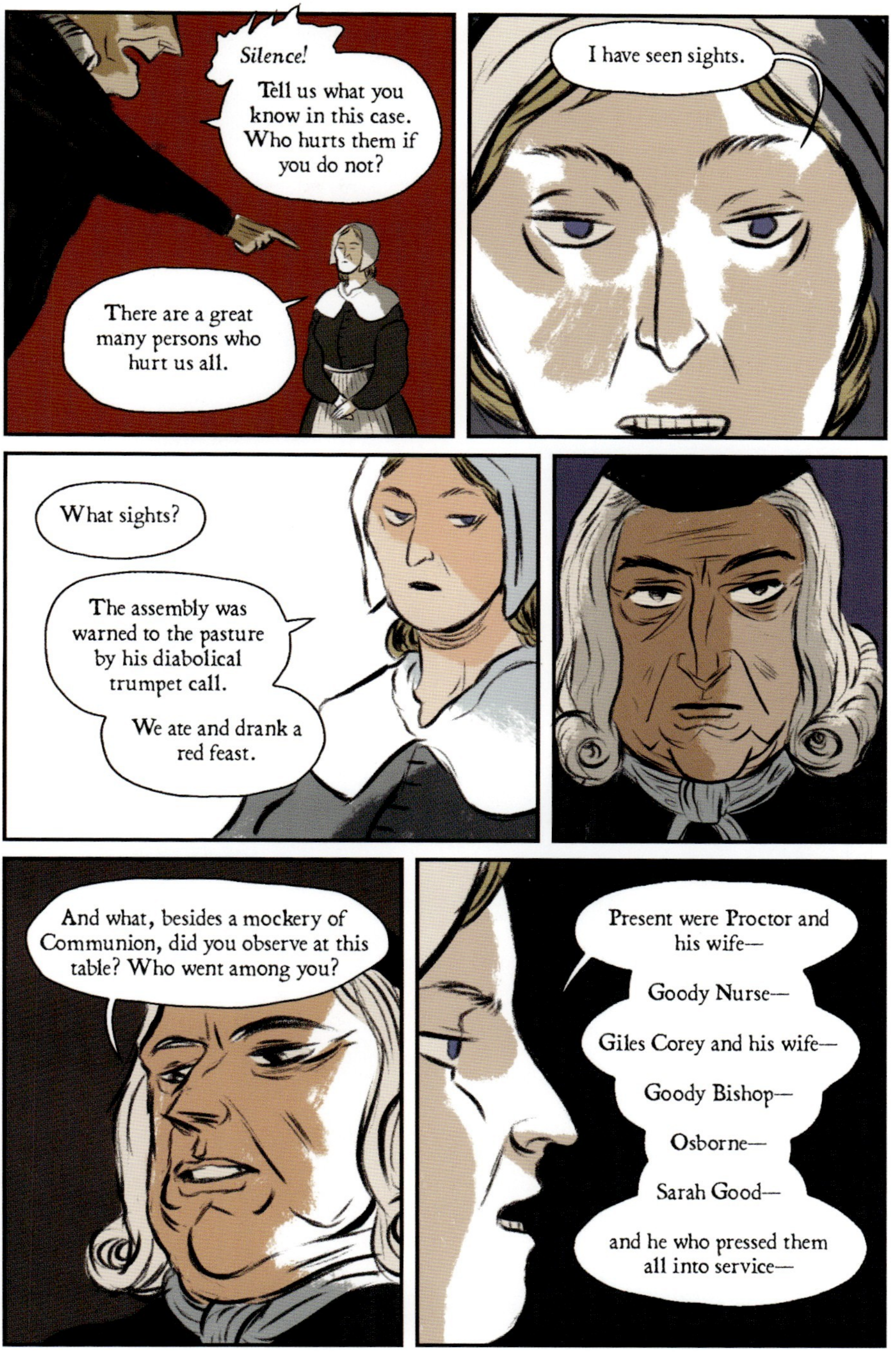
Silence!
Tell us what you know in this case. Who hurts them if you do not?
There are a great many persons who hurt us all.
I have seen sights.
What sights?
The assembly was warned to the pasture by his diabolical trumpet call.
We ate and drank a red feast.
And what, besides a mockery of Communion, did you observe at this table? Who went among you?
Present were Proctor and his wife—
Goody Nurse—
Giles Corey and his wife—
Goody Bishop—
Osborne—
Sarah Good—
and he who pressed them all into service—

And who is "he"?

A tall man in black. With a high-crowned hat.

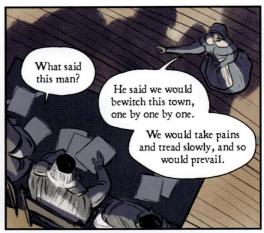

What said this man?

He said we would bewitch this town, one by one by one.

We would take pains and tread slowly, and so would prevail.

Later.

Thank you for waiting, Thomas. Ann, your father says you have new evidence?

My child came to me, two nights past, terrified and crying out, "Oh, dreadful, dreadful—here is a minister come—what, are *ministers* witches, too?"

Speak, Ann. What did you see?

I saw an apparition in a dark coat.

"What is your name?" I cried. "For if you are a wizard, I will complain of you, though you be a minister."

Immediately I was tortured by him, racked and choked for my refusal to write in his book. He almost tore me to pieces. I cried so loud!

How could he who teaches children to fear God persuade them to give their souls to the Devil?

"Oh, dreadful," I said. "Tell me your name that I may know who you are," and he spoke it.

The name?

Reverend George Burroughs.

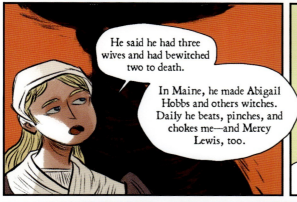

He said he had three wives and had bewitched two to death.

In Maine, he made Abigail Hobbs and others witches. Daily he beats, pinches, and chokes me—and Mercy Lewis, too.

He said one more thing.

Yes?

He said I was to hold him above a witch. He said he was a conjurer.

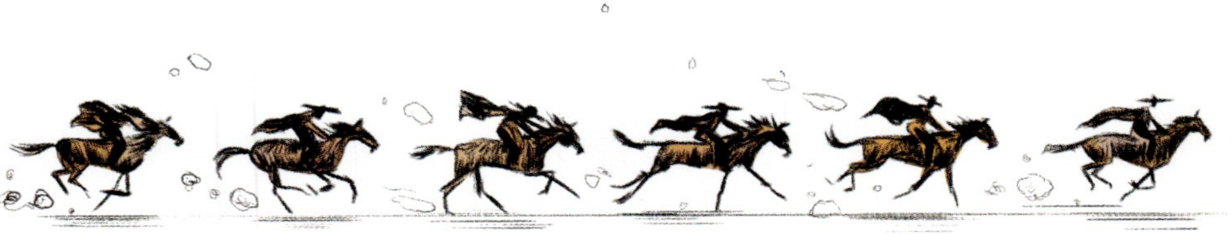

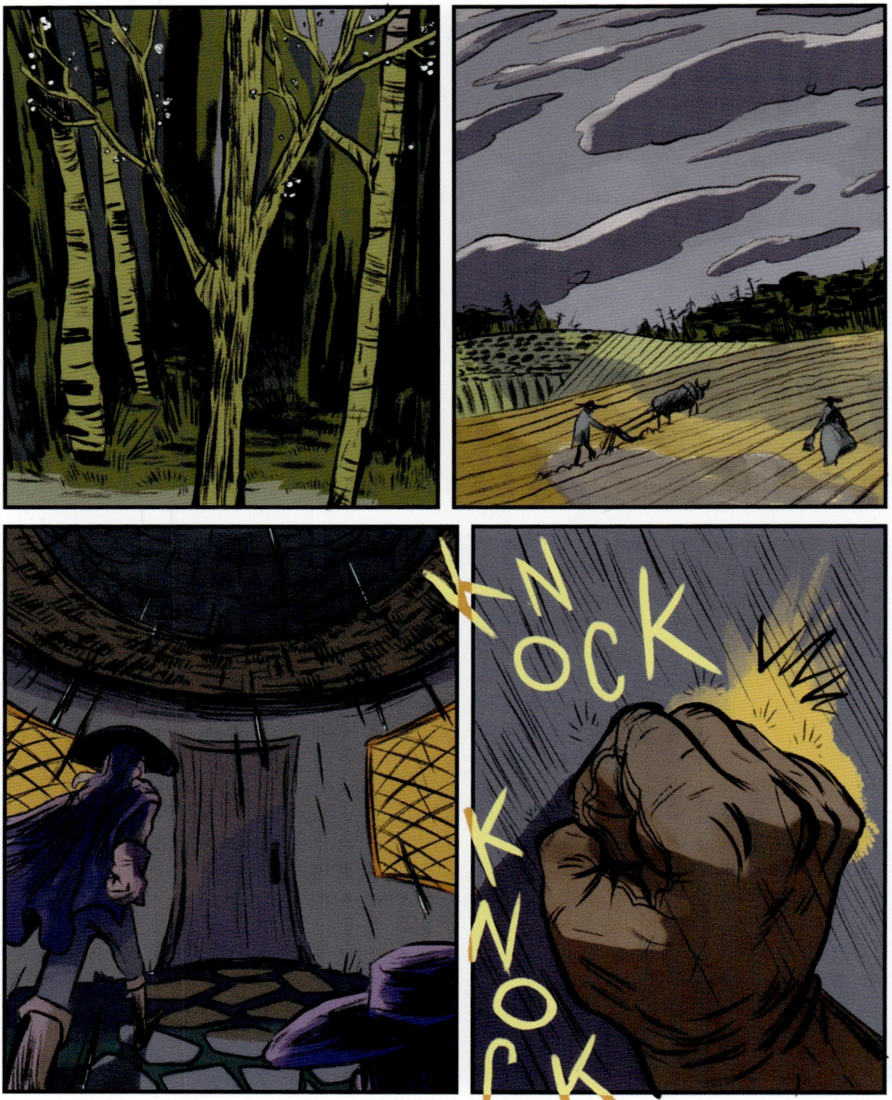
KNOCK
KNOCK

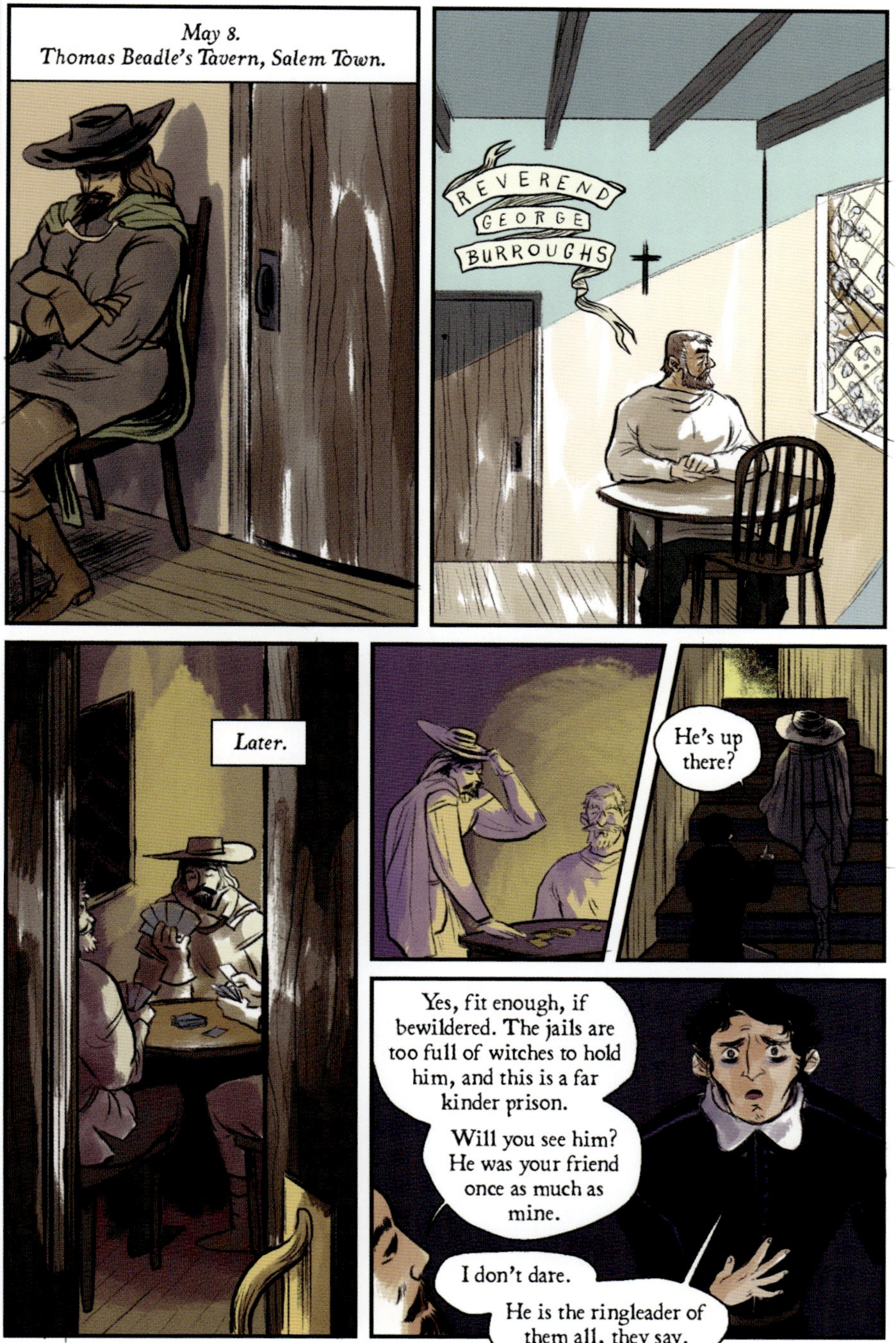
May 8.
Thomas Beadle's Tavern, Salem Town.
REVEREND GEORGE BURROUGHS
Later.
He's up there?
Yes, fit enough, if bewildered. The jails are too full of witches to hold him, and this is a far kinder prison.
Will you see him? He was your friend once as much as mine.
I don't dare.
He is the ringleader of them all, they say.

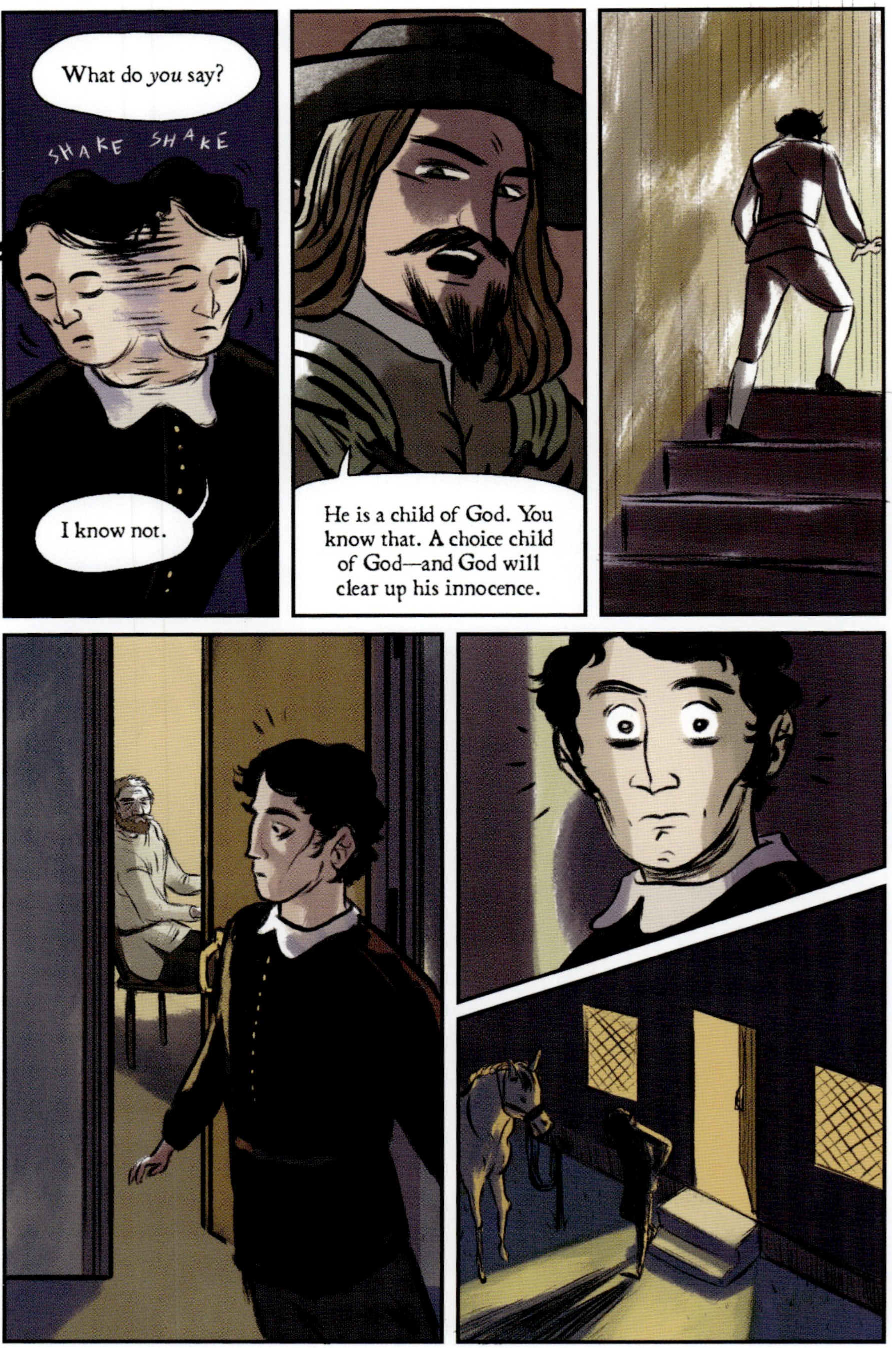
What do *you* say?
SHAKE SHAKE
I know not.
He is a child of God. You know that. A choice child of God—and God will clear up his innocence.

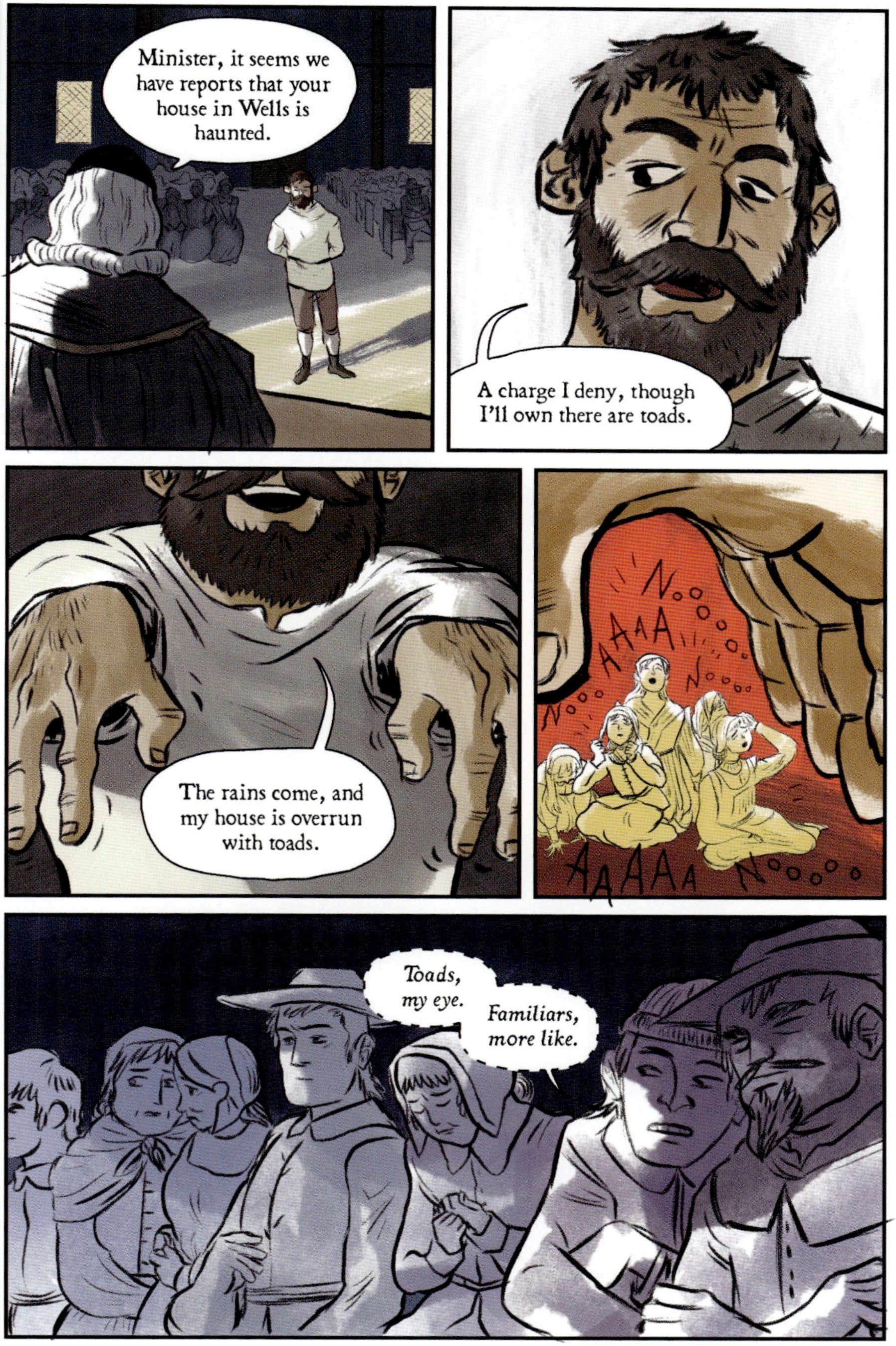
Minister, it seems we have reports that your house in Wells is haunted.
A charge I deny, though I'll own there are toads.
The rains come, and my house is overrun with toads.
NOOO AAAA NOOOO NOOOO AAAAA NOOOOO
Toads, my eye.
Familiars, more like.

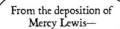

From the deposition of Mercy Lewis—

"On the 7th of May at evening, I saw the apparition of Mr. George Burroughs, whom I know very well, which did torture and command me, holding a fashion book.

"I could have it, he said, if I wrote in *his* book. He told me he could bewitch people from afar because he could raise the Devil. The Devil was his servant.

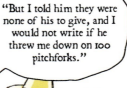

"He said that I should not witness against him—he would rack me all to pieces or kill me—but I told him I hoped my life was not in his power.

"On the 9th of May, Mr. Burroughs carried me up to an exceedingly high mountain and showed me all the kingdoms of the earth.

"He told me that he would give them all to me if I would write in his book, and if I would not, he would throw me down and break my neck.

"But I told him they were none of his to give, and I would not write if he threw me down on 100 pitchforks."

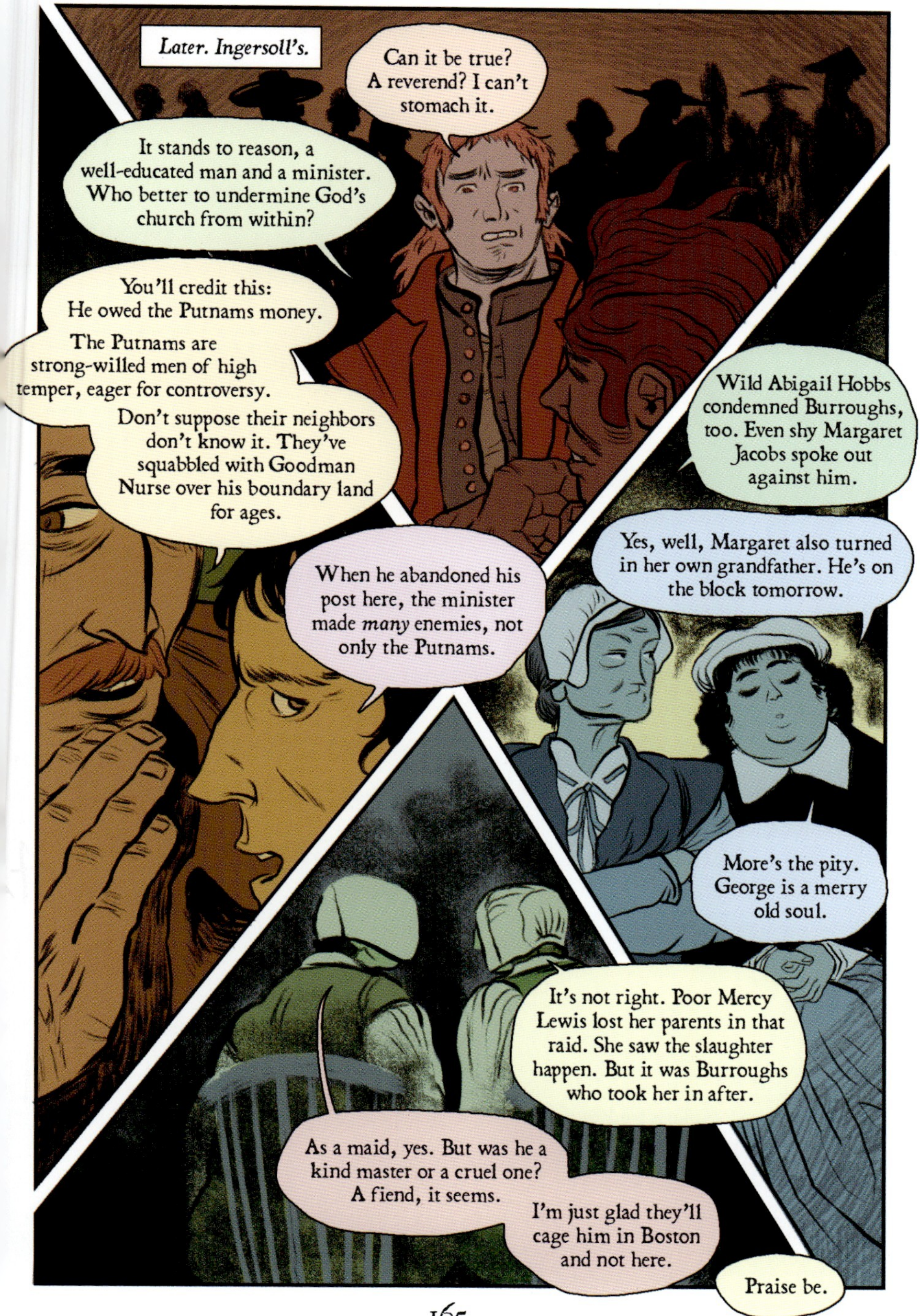
Later. Ingersoll's.
Can it be true? A reverend? I can't stomach it.
It stands to reason, a well-educated man and a minister. Who better to undermine God's church from within?
You'll credit this: He owed the Putnams money.
The Putnams are strong-willed men of high temper, eager for controversy.
Don't suppose their neighbors don't know it. They've squabbled with Goodman Nurse over his boundary land for ages.
When he abandoned his post here, the minister made *many* enemies, not only the Putnams.
Wild Abigail Hobbs condemned Burroughs, too. Even shy Margaret Jacobs spoke out against him.
Yes, well, Margaret also turned in her own grandfather. He's on the block tomorrow.
More's the pity. George is a merry old soul.
It's not right. Poor Mercy Lewis lost her parents in that raid. She saw the slaughter happen. But it was Burroughs who took her in after.
As a maid, yes. But was he a kind master or a cruel one? A fiend, it seems.
I'm just glad they'll cage him in Boston and not here.
Praise be.

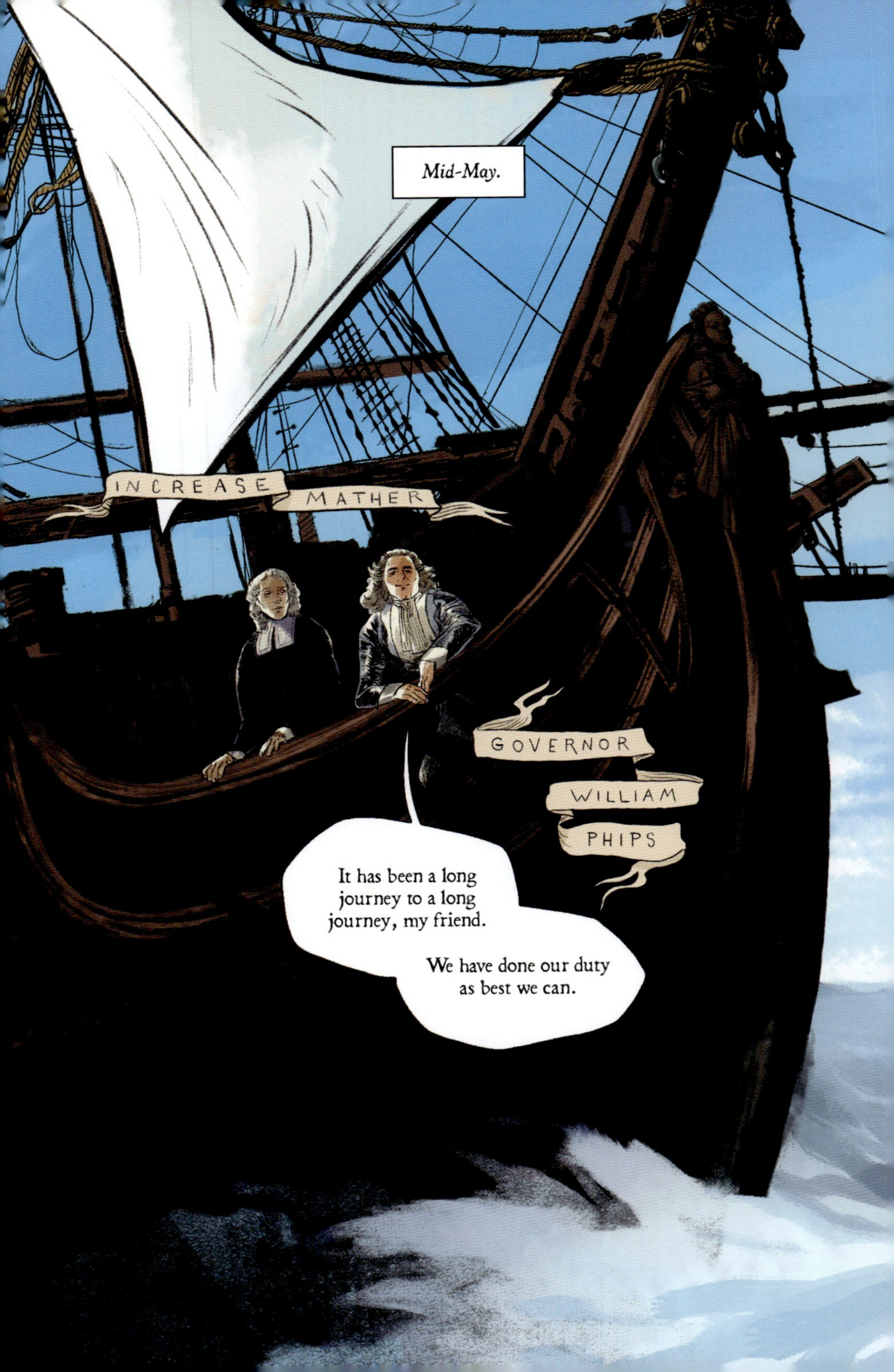
Mid-May.
INCREASE MATHER
GOVERNOR WILLIAM PHIPS
It has been a long journey to a long journey, my friend.
We have done our duty as best we can.

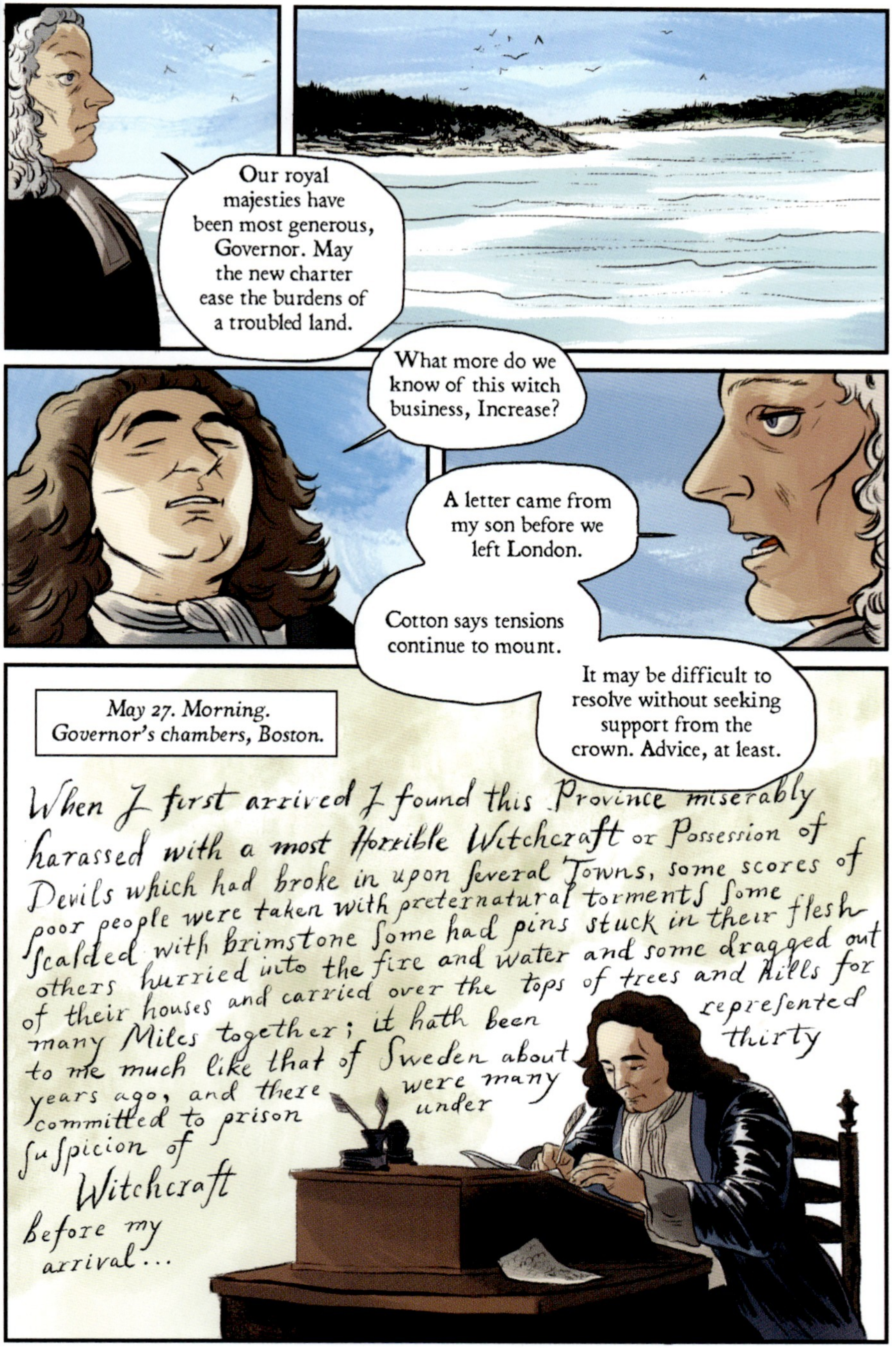

Our royal majesties have been most generous, Governor. May the new charter ease the burdens of a troubled land.
What more do we know of this witch business, Increase?
A letter came from my son before we left London.
Cotton says tensions continue to mount.
It may be difficult to resolve without seeking support from the crown. Advice, at least.
May 27. Morning.
Governor's chambers, Boston.
When I first arrived I found this Province miserably harassed with a most Horrible Witchcraft or Possession of Devils which had broke in upon several Towns, some scores of poor people were taken with preternatural torments some scalded with brimstone some had pins stuck in their flesh others hurried into the fire and water and some dragged out of their houses and carried over the tops of trees and hills for many Miles together; it hath been represented to me much like that of Sweden about thirty years ago, and there were many committed to prison under suspicion of Witchcraft before my arrival...

Enter.

JUDGE WILLIAM STOUGHTON

We commend you, sir, for taking immediate action.

Will our majesties be displeased that we govern swiftly in this instance?

Your reports persuade me that to delay is folly. I write them now. And then must away to the eastward on important matters.

I assure you these matters rival any in Maine, sir, and warrant your time and attention.

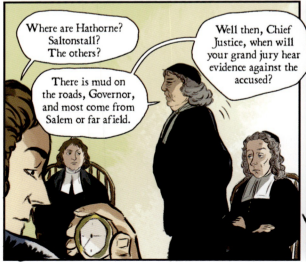

Where are Hathorne? Saltonstall? The others?

There is mud on the roads, Governor, and most come from Salem or far afield.

Well then, Chief Justice, when will your grand jury hear evidence against the accused?

KNOCK KNOCK KNOCK

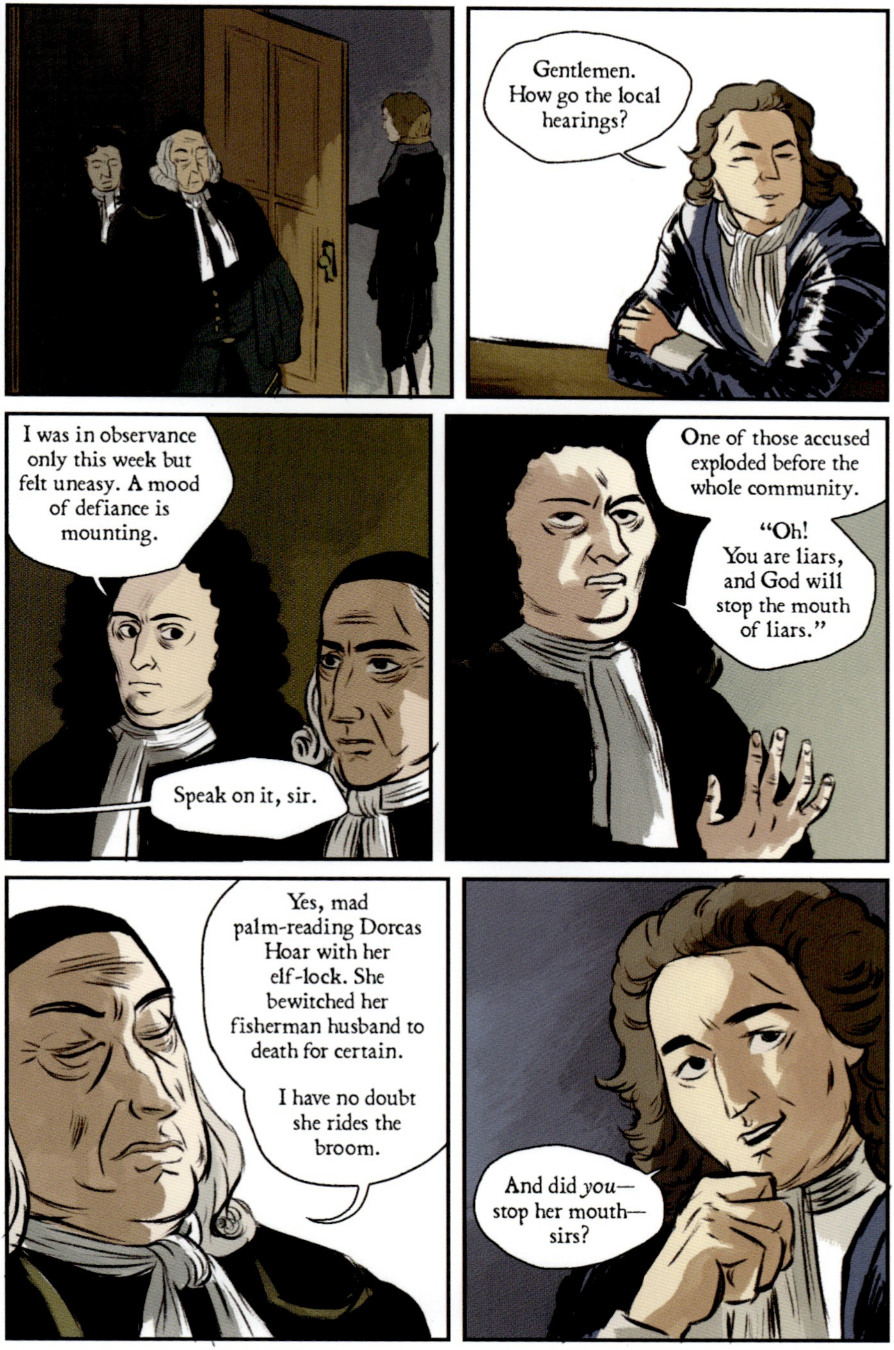
Gentlemen. How go the local hearings?
I was in observance only this week but felt uneasy. A mood of defiance is mounting.
Speak on it, sir.
One of those accused exploded before the whole community.
"Oh! You are liars, and God will stop the mouth of liars."
Yes, mad palm-reading Dorcas Hoar with her elf-lock. She bewitched her fisherman husband to death for certain.
I have no doubt she rides the broom.
And did *you*— stop her mouth— sirs?

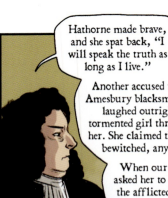

Hathorne made brave, and she spat back, "I will speak the truth as long as I live."

Another accused that day, an Amesbury blacksmith's widow, laughed outright when a tormented girl threw a glove at her. She claimed they were not bewitched, any of them.

When our worshipful Hathorne asked her to expound, she supposed the afflicted dealt in furtive black magic, like the biblical Witch of Endor, who also posed as a saint.

—Ahem—

Do we allow for the possibility of fraud?

The Devil is vigilant...and a liar to the bone. Your prudence is well founded, Judge Saltonstall, and I humbly beg the new court not to lay more stress upon pure specter testimony than it will bear.

But consider the source, won't you? When a case is sound, we must make a stern example of it.

You should also know of various petitions and objections speaking to the character of some of the accusers.

Some witnesses have suggested that the tormented...dissemble.

Others believe devout and credible women such as Rebecca Nurse and her sisters are innocent and speak out on it.

Further...a minister is charged.

Yes, shocking. But will you try these witches, Saltonstall, or make excuses for them?

Let justice be swift and severe.

But let it be just.

170

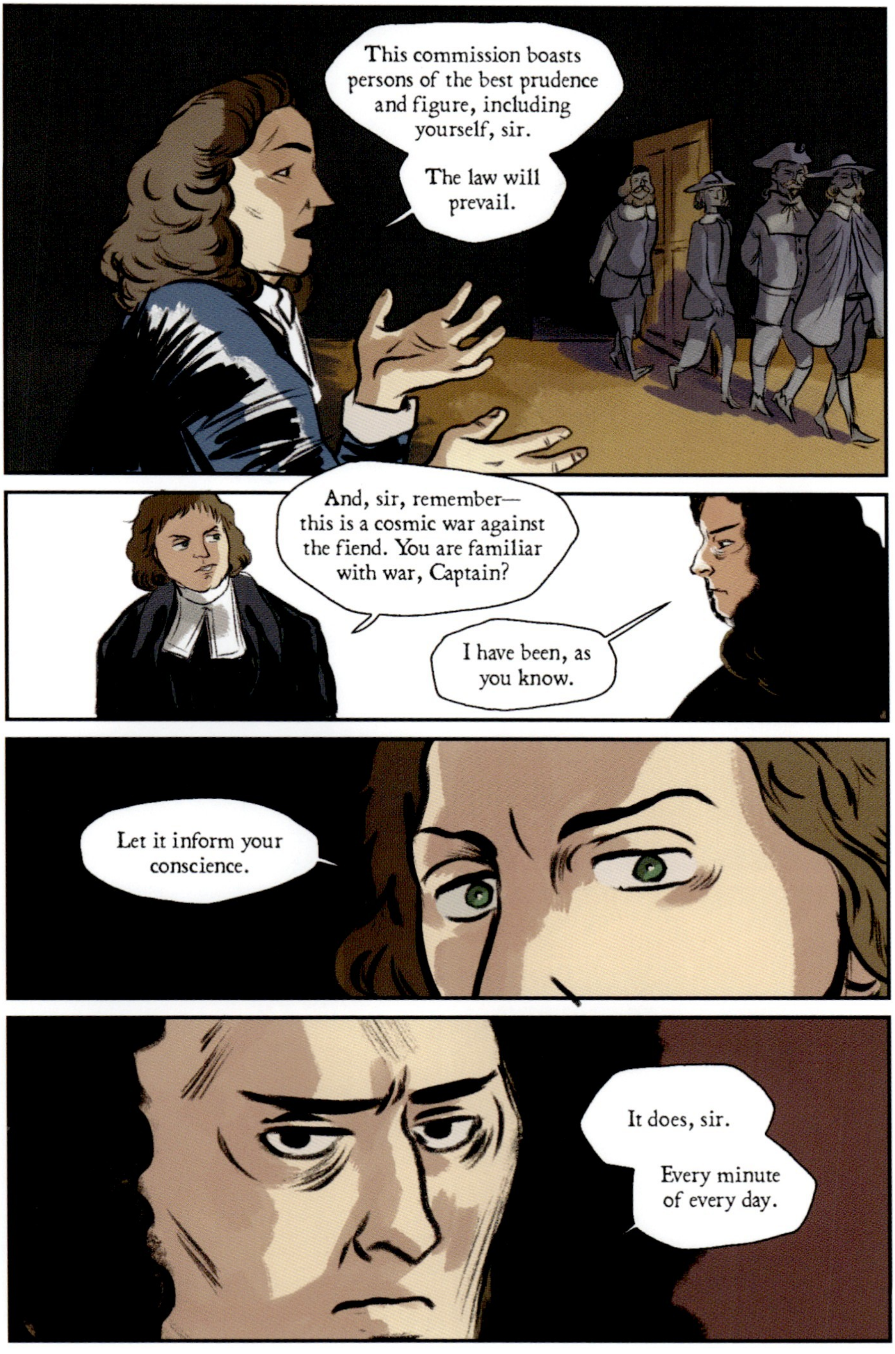
This commission boasts persons of the best prudence and figure, including yourself, sir.
The law will prevail.
And, sir, remember—this is a cosmic war against the fiend. You are familiar with war, Captain?
I have been, as you know.
Let it inform your conscience.
It does, sir.
Every minute of every day.

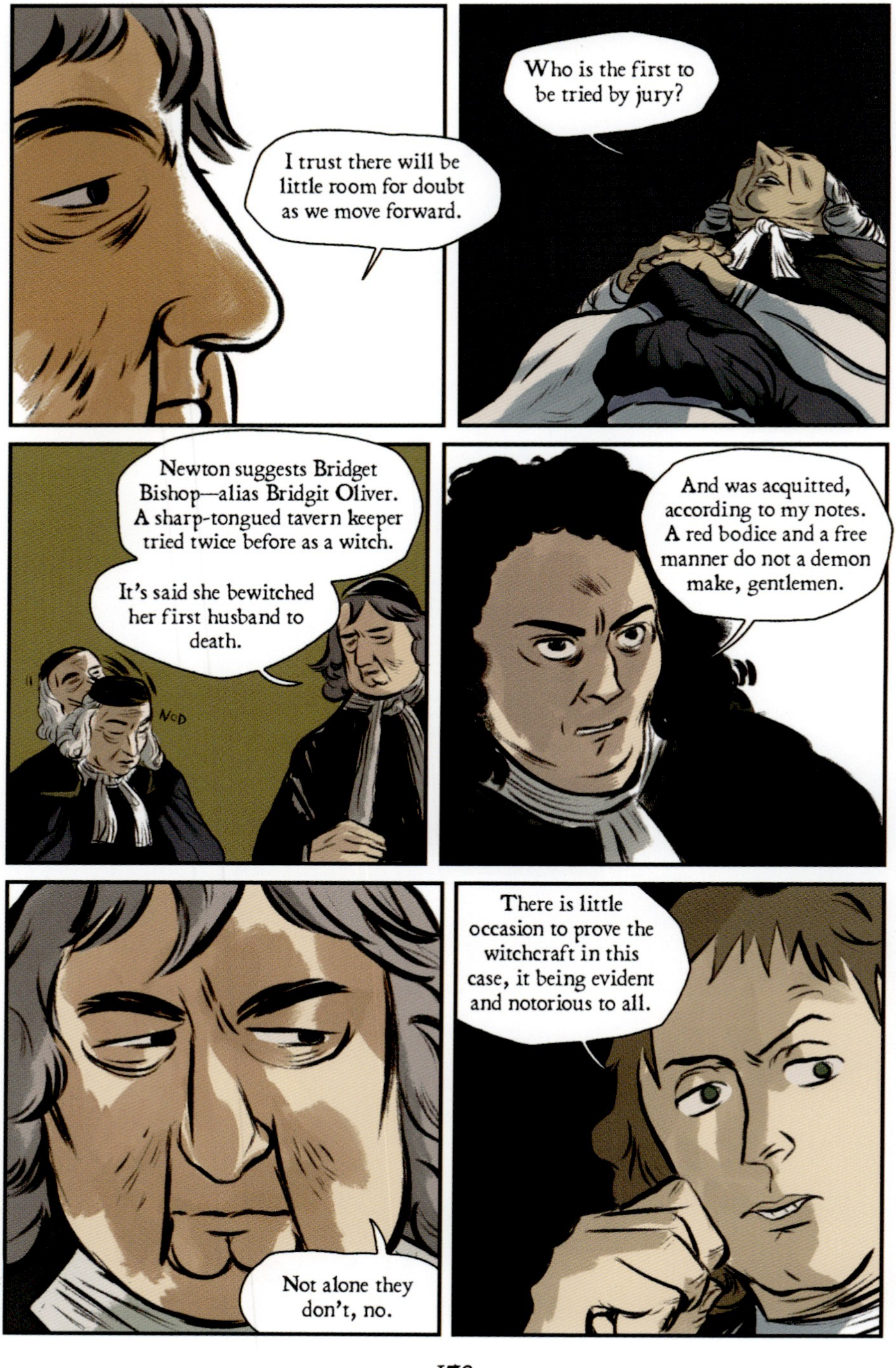

I trust there will be little room for doubt as we move forward.
Who is the first to be tried by jury?
Newton suggests Bridget Bishop—alias Bridgit Oliver. A sharp-tongued tavern keeper tried twice before as a witch.
It's said she bewitched her first husband to death.
NOD
And was acquitted, according to my notes. A red bodice and a free manner do not a demon make, gentlemen.
Not alone they don't, no.
There is little occasion to prove the witchcraft in this case, it being evident and notorious to all.

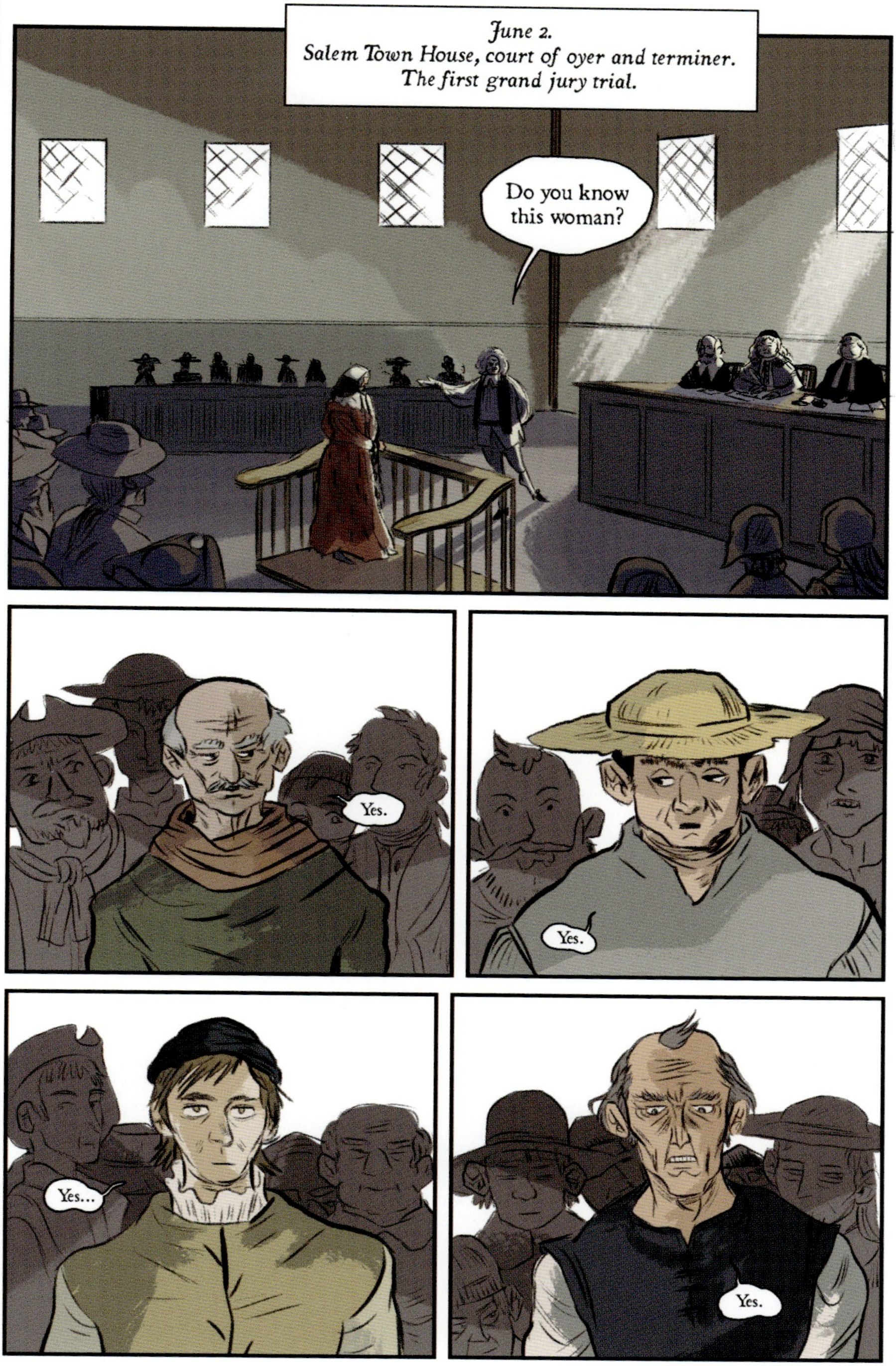
June 2.
Salem Town House, court of oyer and terminer.
The first grand jury trial.
Do you know this woman?
Yes.
Yes.
Yes...
Yes.

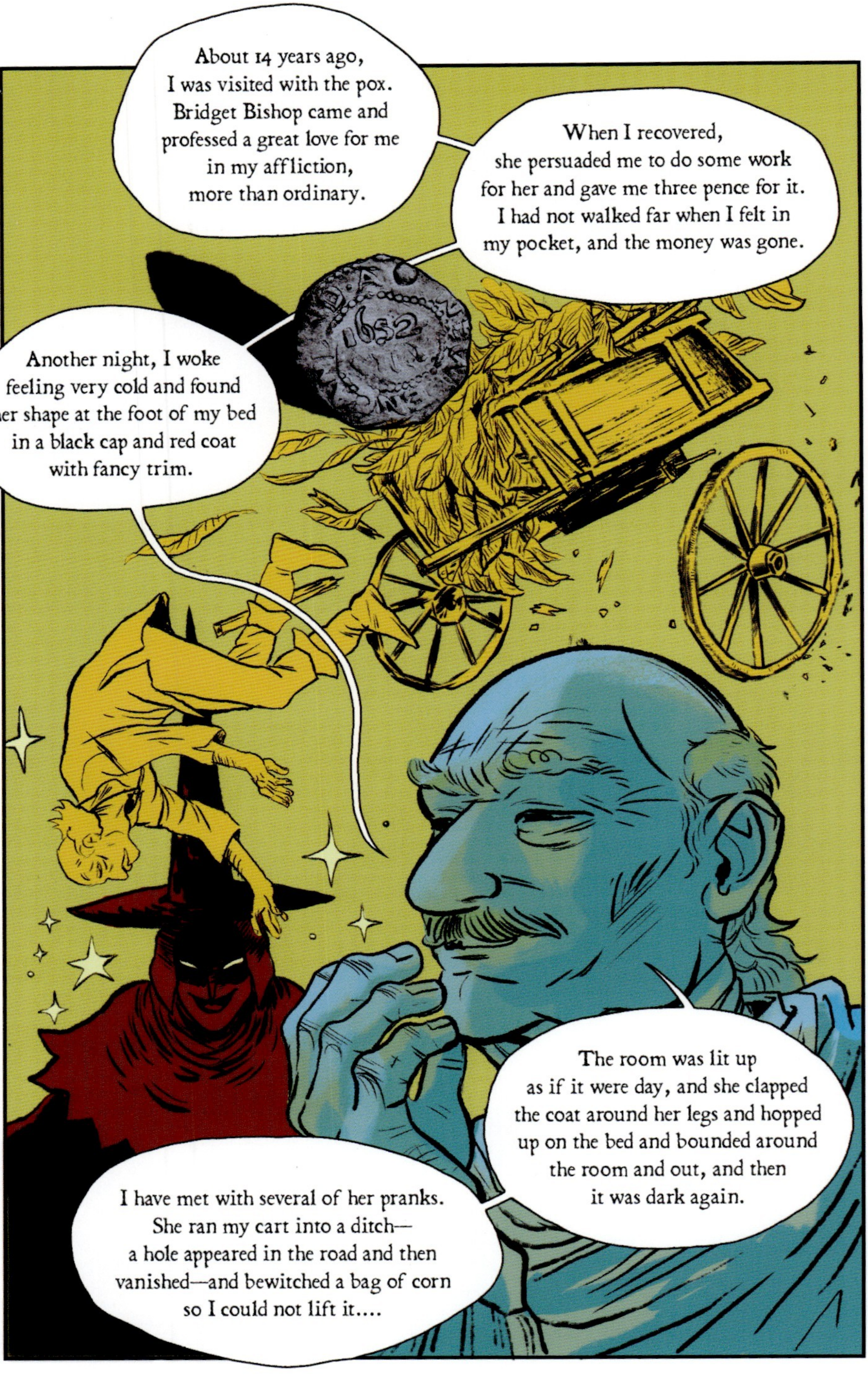
About 14 years ago, I was visited with the pox. Bridget Bishop came and professed a great love for me in my affliction, more than ordinary.
When I recovered, she persuaded me to do some work for her and gave me three pence for it. I had not walked far when I felt in my pocket, and the money was gone.
1652
Another night, I woke feeling very cold and found her shape at the foot of my bed in a black cap and red coat with fancy trim.
The room was lit up as if it were day, and she clapped the coat around her legs and hopped up on the bed and bounded around the room and out, and then it was dark again.
I have met with several of her pranks. She ran my cart into a ditch—a hole appeared in the road and then vanished—and bewitched a bag of corn so I could not lift it....

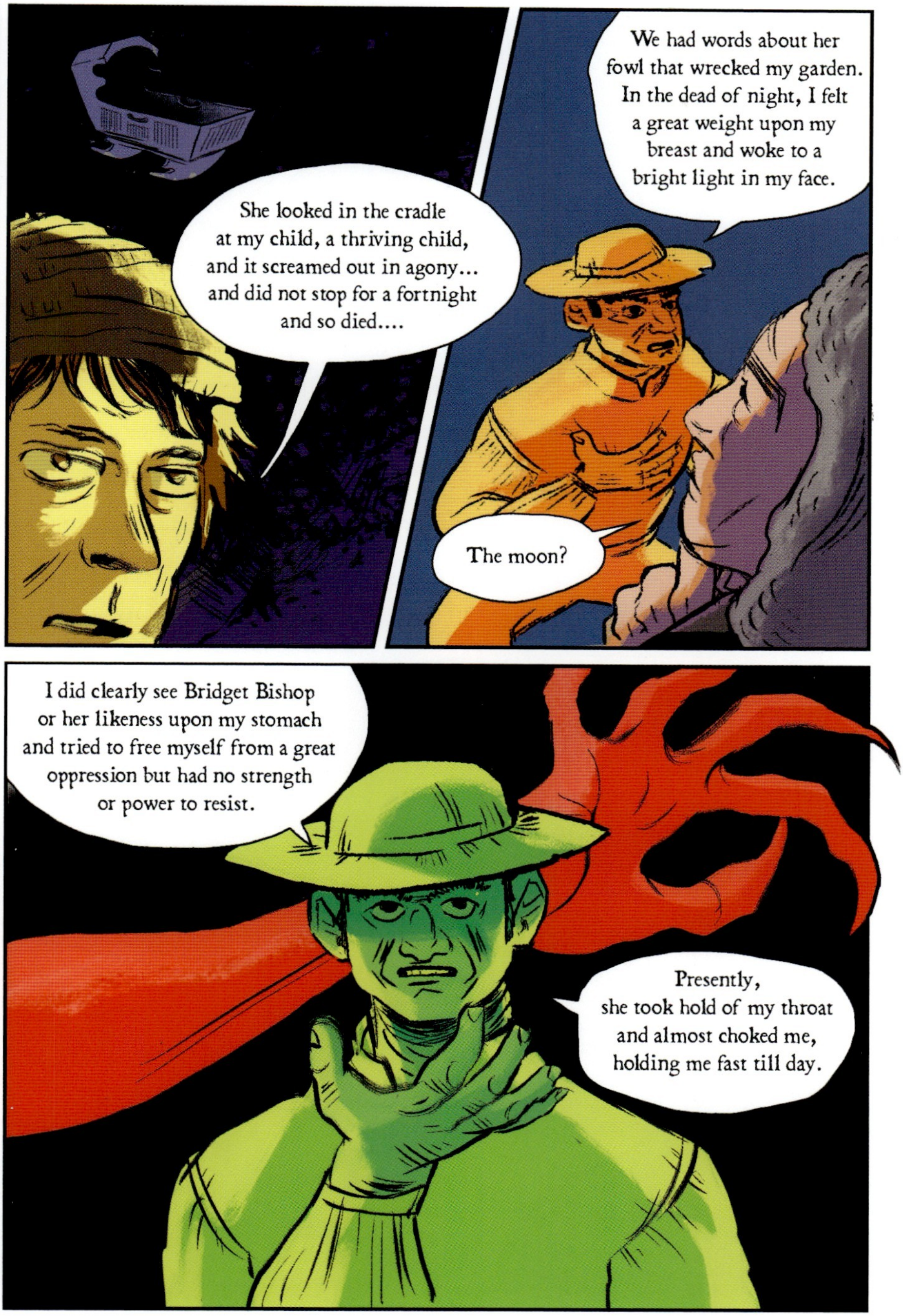
She looked in the cradle at my child, a thriving child, and it screamed out in agony... and did not stop for a fortnight and so died....
We had words about her fowl that wrecked my garden. In the dead of night, I felt a great weight upon my breast and woke to a bright light in my face.
The moon?
I did clearly see Bridget Bishop or her likeness upon my stomach and tried to free myself from a great oppression but had no strength or power to resist.
Presently, she took hold of my throat and almost choked me, holding me fast till day.

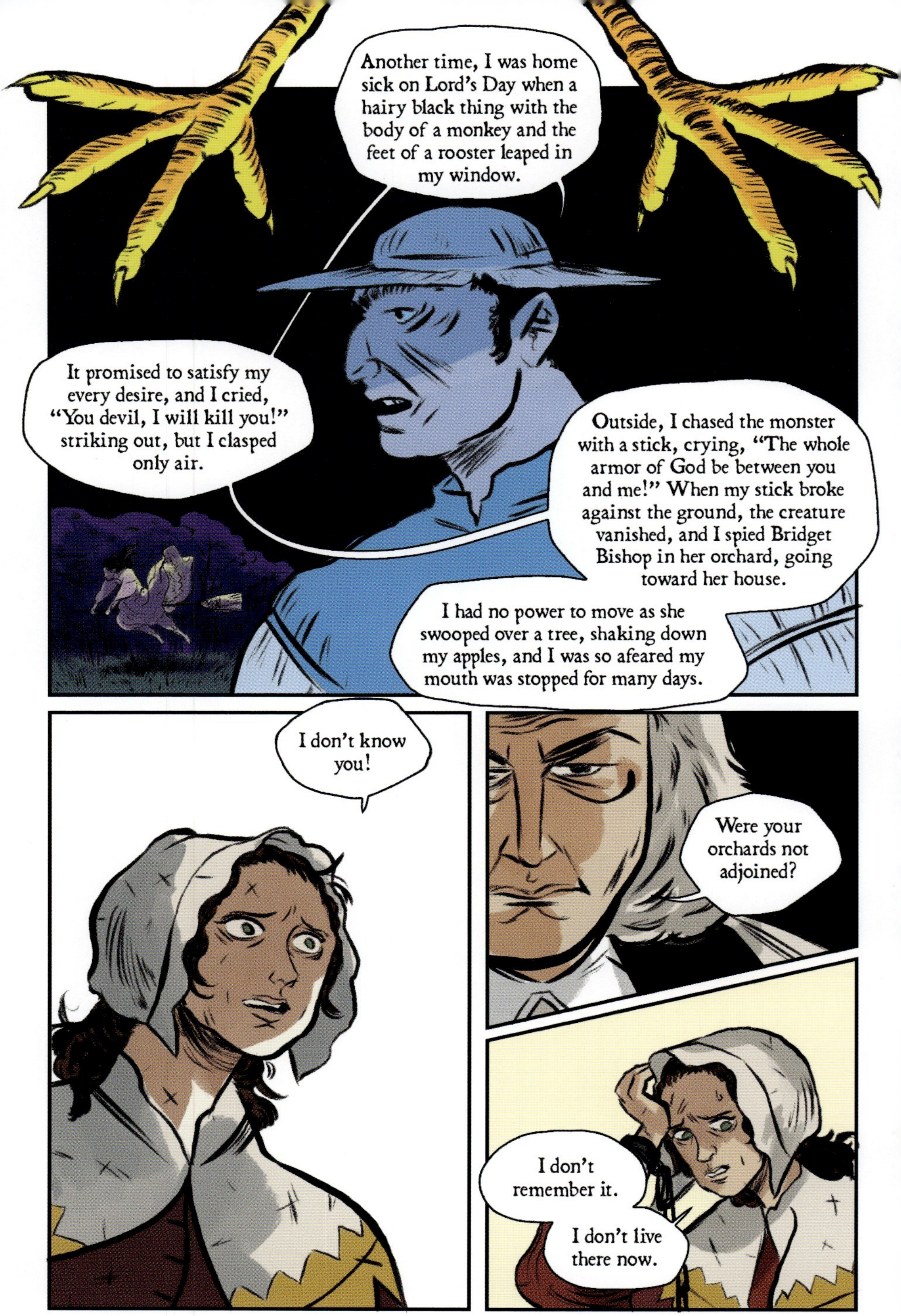
Another time, I was home sick on Lord's Day when a hairy black thing with the body of a monkey and the feet of a rooster leaped in my window.
It promised to satisfy my every desire, and I cried, "You devil, I will kill you!" striking out, but I clasped only air.
Outside, I chased the monster with a stick, crying, "The whole armor of God be between you and me!" When my stick broke against the ground, the creature vanished, and I spied Bridget Bishop in her orchard, going toward her house.
I had no power to move as she swooped over a tree, shaking down my apples, and I was so afeared my mouth was stopped for many days.
I don't know you!
Were your orchards not adjoined?
I don't remember it.
I don't live there now.

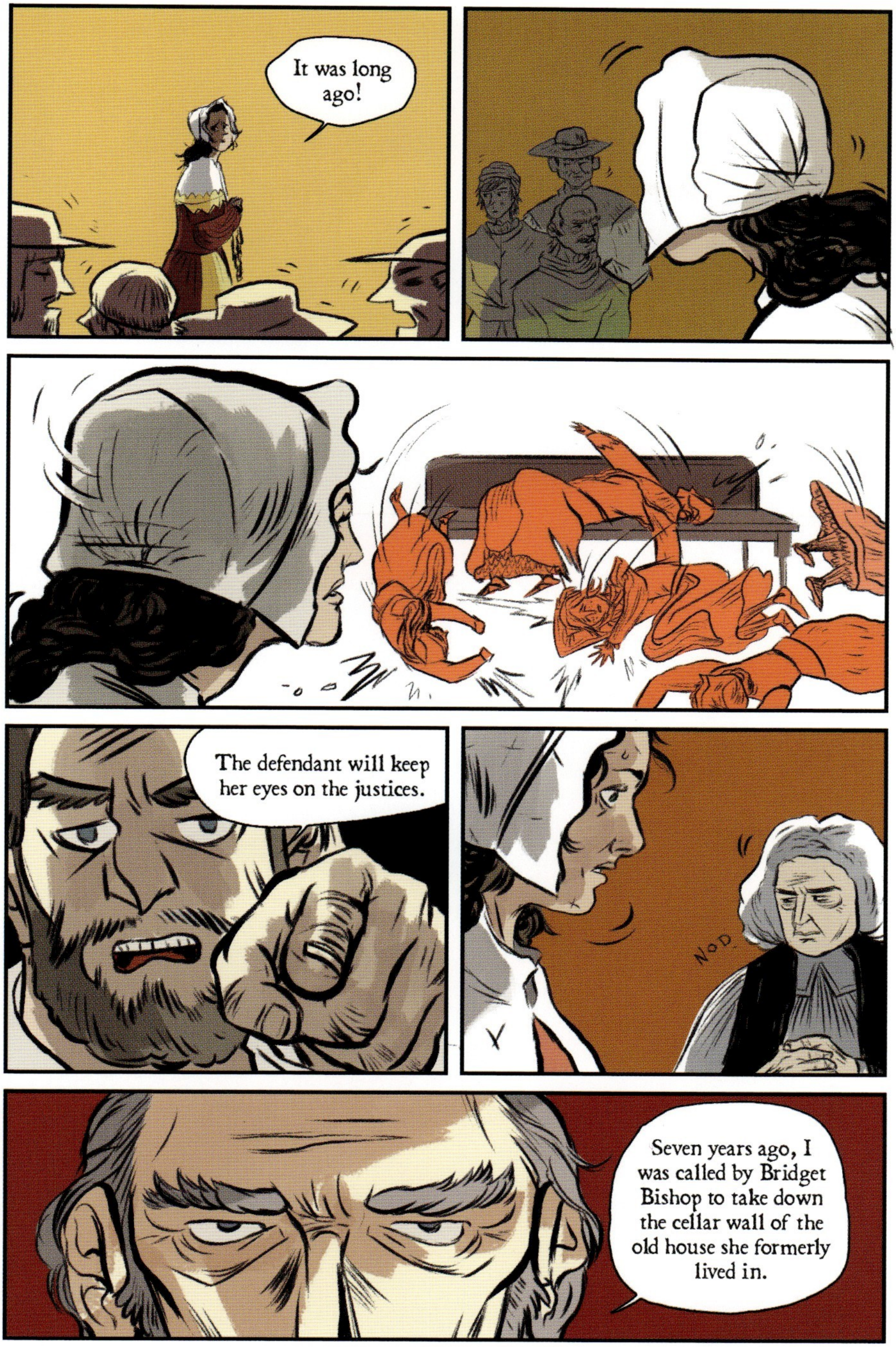
It was long ago!
The defendant will keep her eyes on the justices.
NOD
Seven years ago, I was called by Bridget Bishop to take down the cellar wall of the old house she formerly lived in.

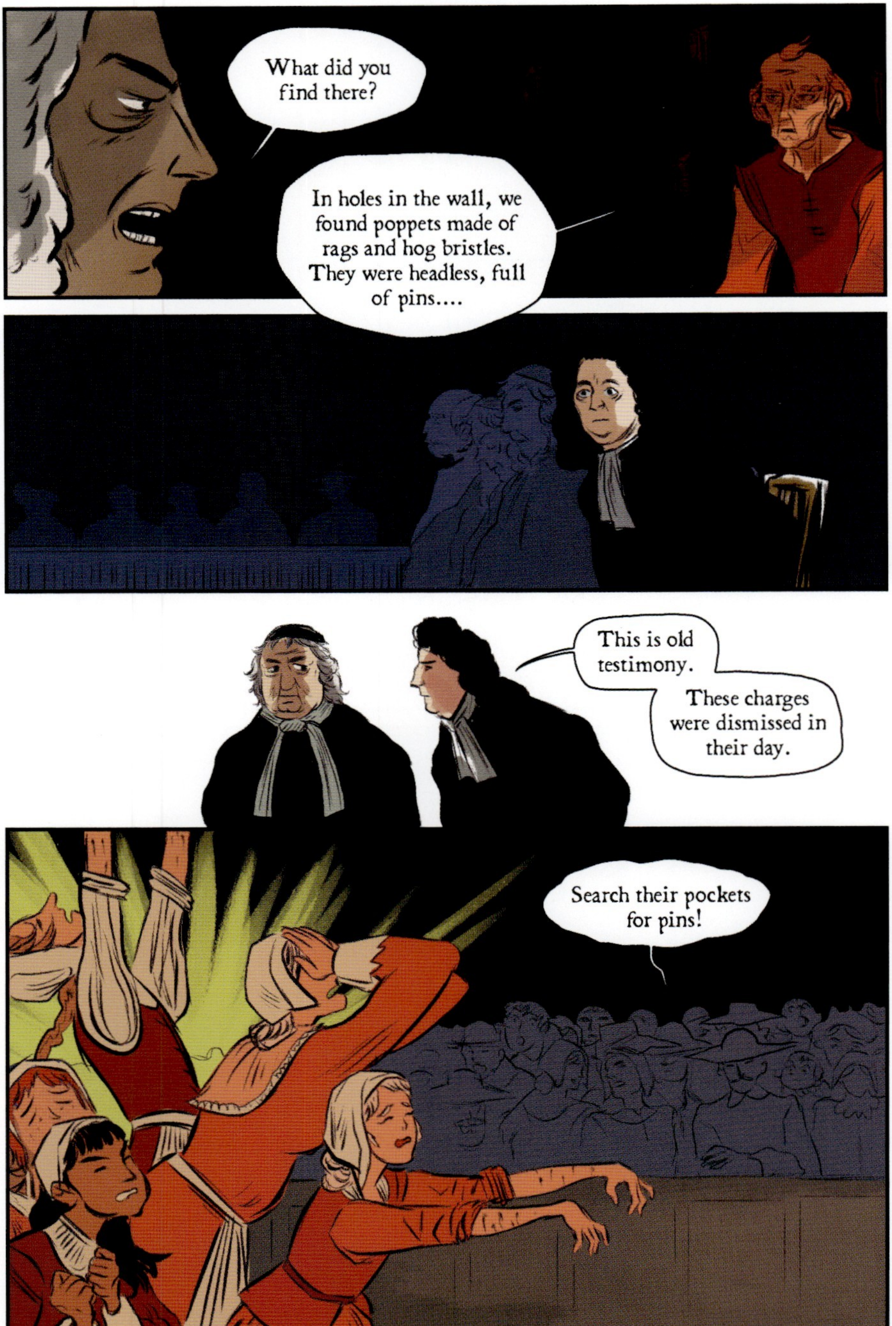
What did you find there?
In holes in the wall, we found poppets made of rags and hog bristles. They were headless, full of pins....
This is old testimony.
These charges were dismissed in their day.
Search their pockets for pins!

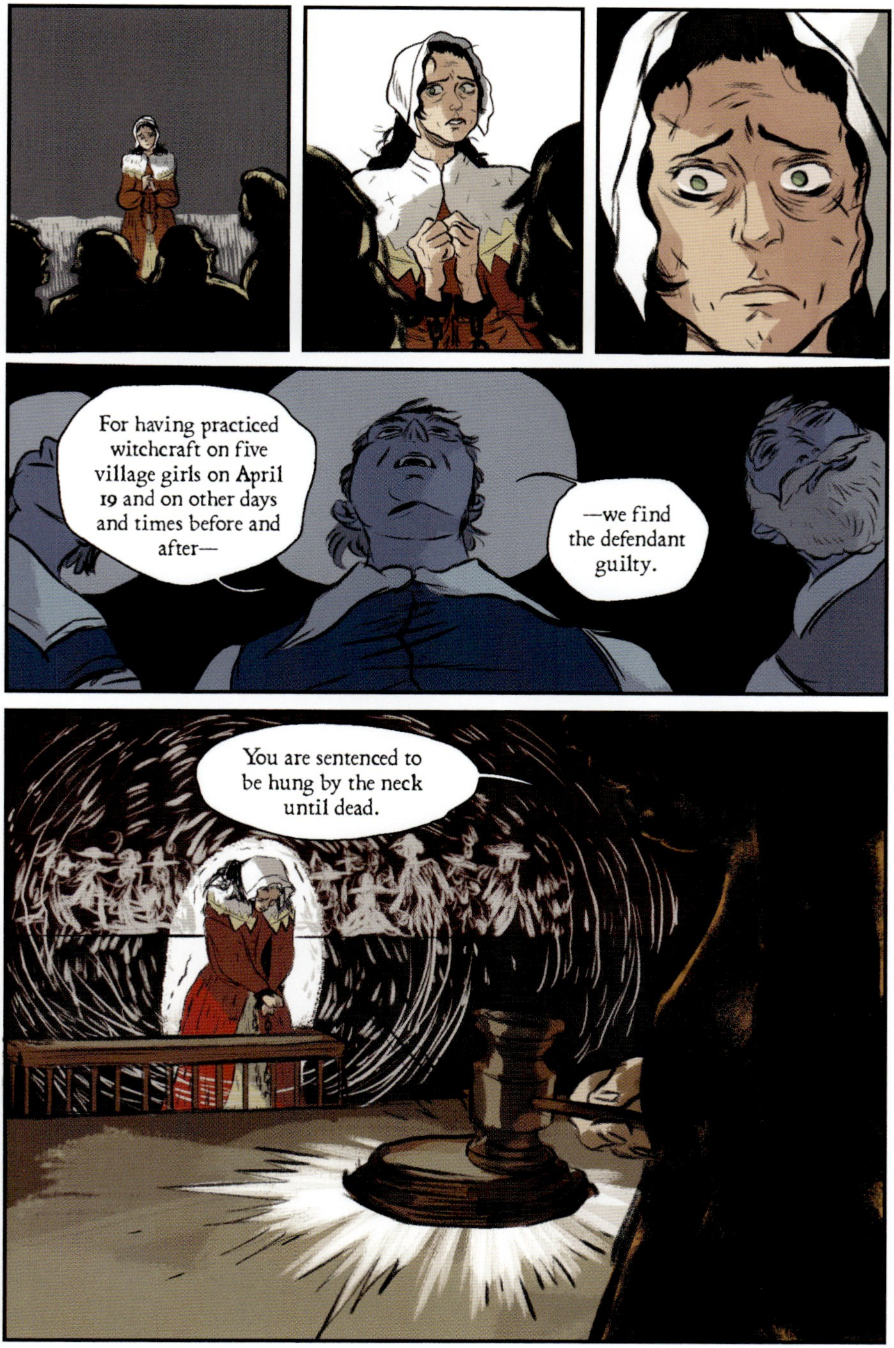
For having practiced witchcraft on five village girls on April 19 and on other days and times before and after—
—we find the defendant guilty.
You are sentenced to be hung by the neck until dead.

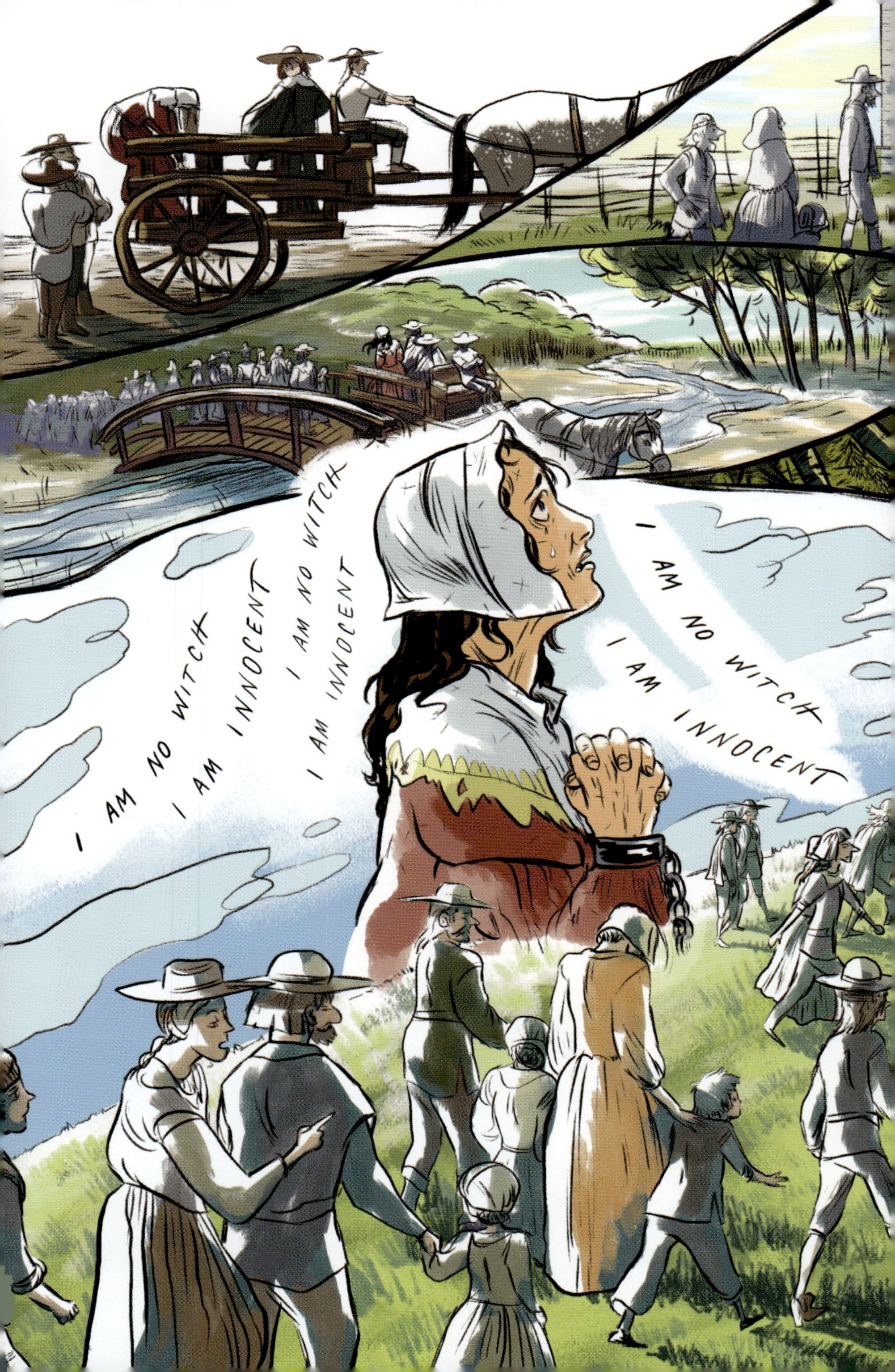
I AM NO WITCH
I AM INNOCENT
I AM NO WITCH
I AM INNOCENT
I AM NO WITCH
I AM INNOCENT

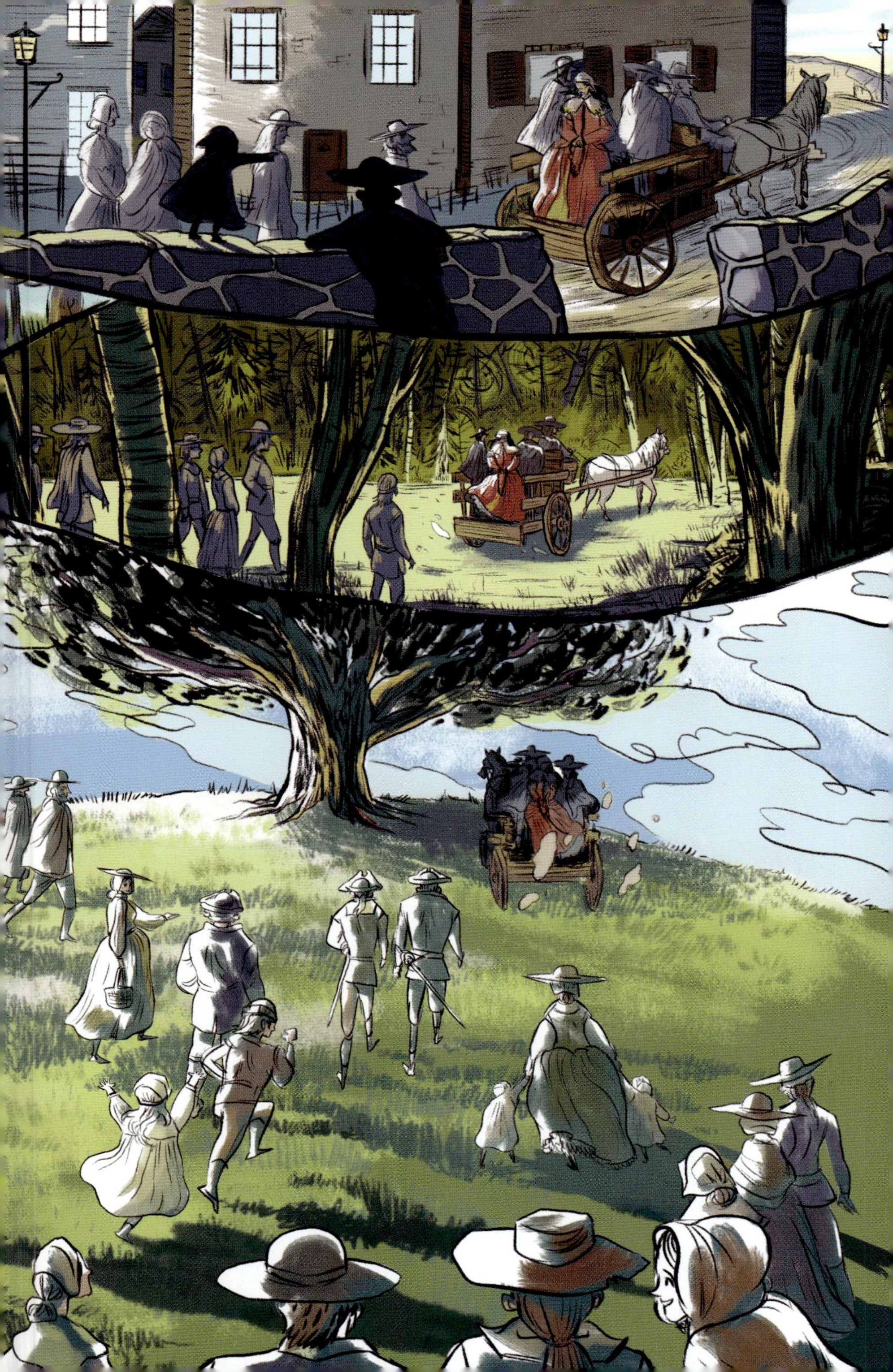

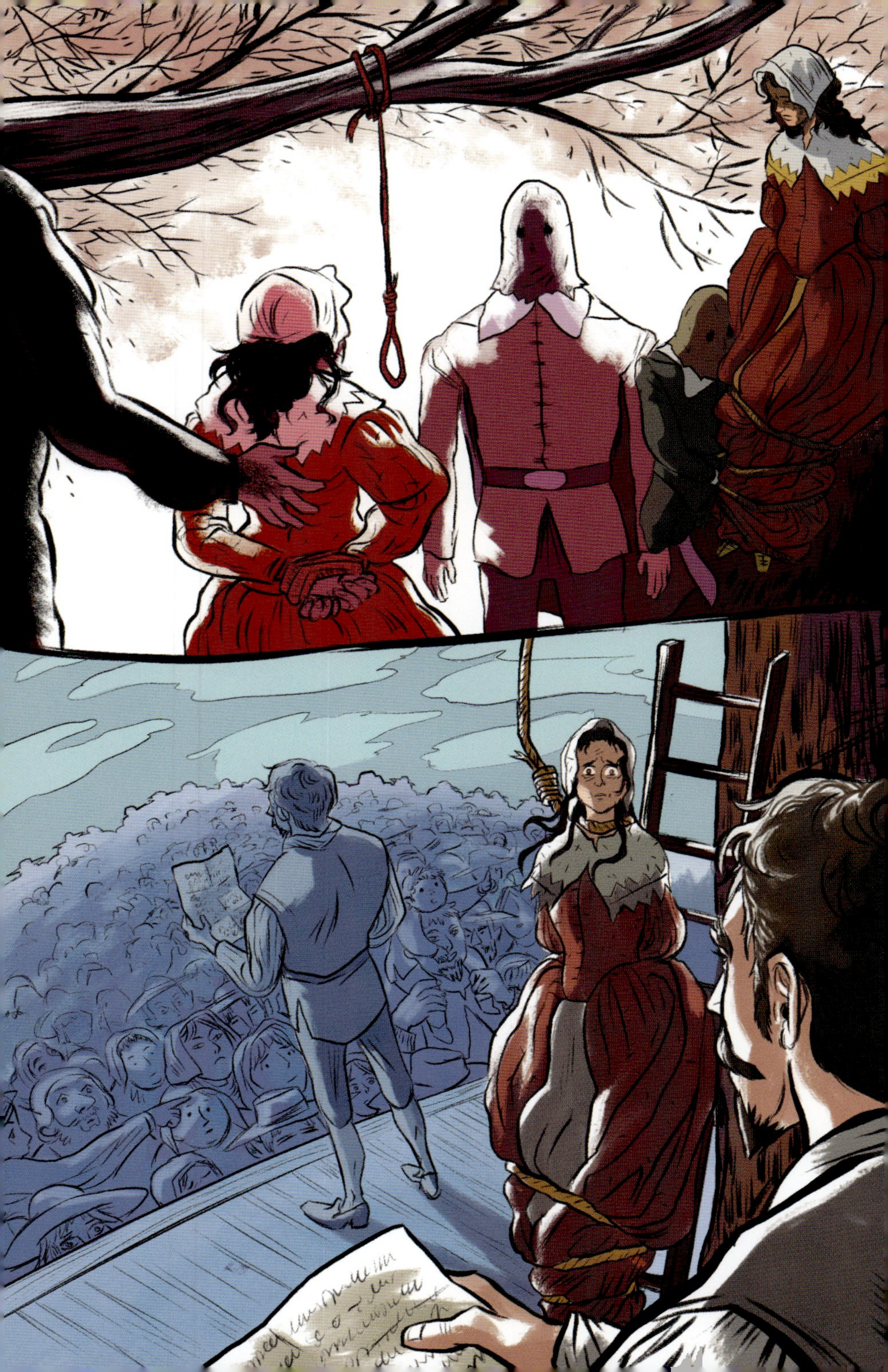

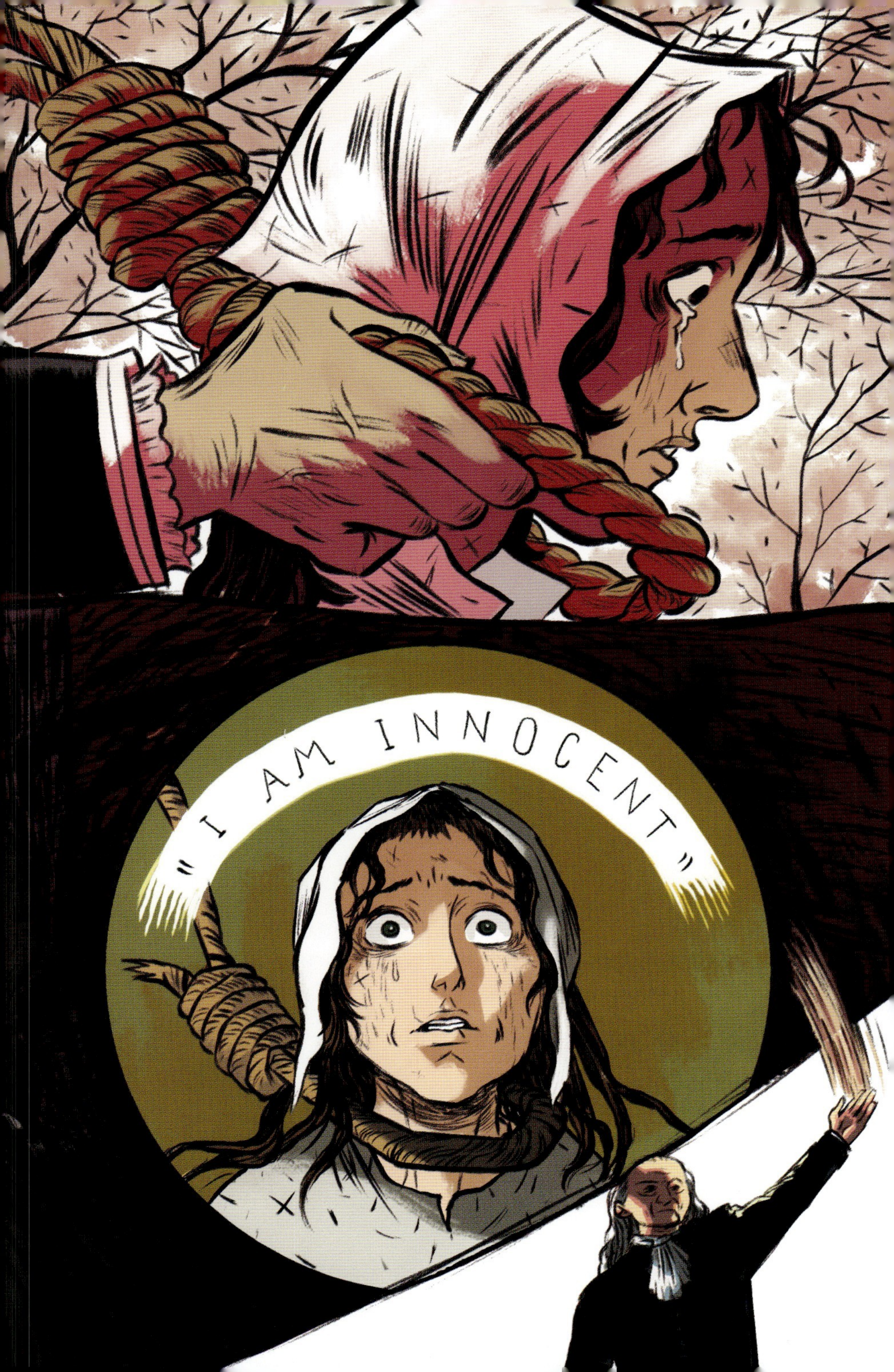
"I AM INNOCENT"

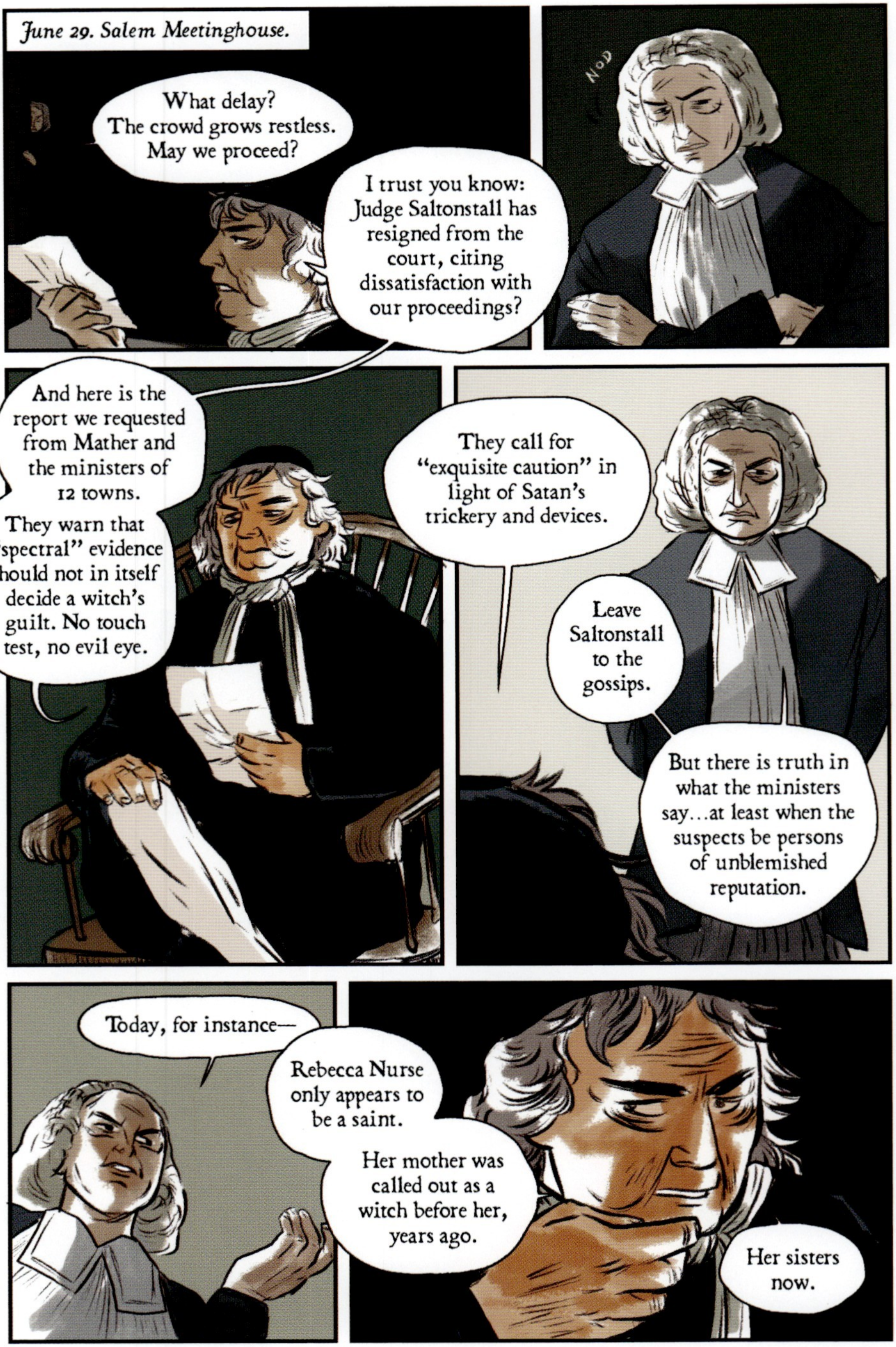
June 29. Salem Meetinghouse.
What delay? The crowd grows restless. May we proceed?
I trust you know: Judge Saltonstall has resigned from the court, citing dissatisfaction with our proceedings?
NOD
And here is the report we requested from Mather and the ministers of 12 towns.
They warn that "spectral" evidence should not in itself decide a witch's guilt. No touch test, no evil eye.
They call for "exquisite caution" in light of Satan's trickery and devices.
Leave Saltonstall to the gossips.
But there is truth in what the ministers say...at least when the suspects be persons of unblemished reputation.
Today, for instance—
Rebecca Nurse only appears to be a saint.
Her mother was called out as a witch before her, years ago.
Her sisters now.

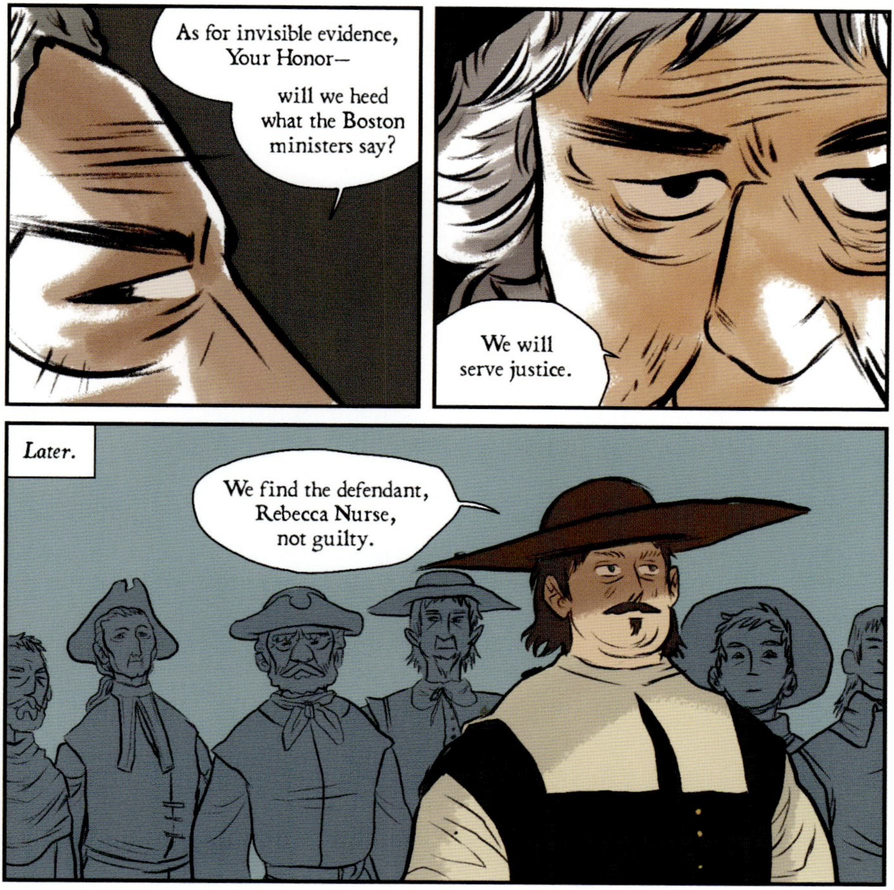
As for invisible evidence, Your Honor—
will we heed what the Boston ministers say?
We will serve justice.
Later.
We find the defendant, Rebecca Nurse, not guilty.

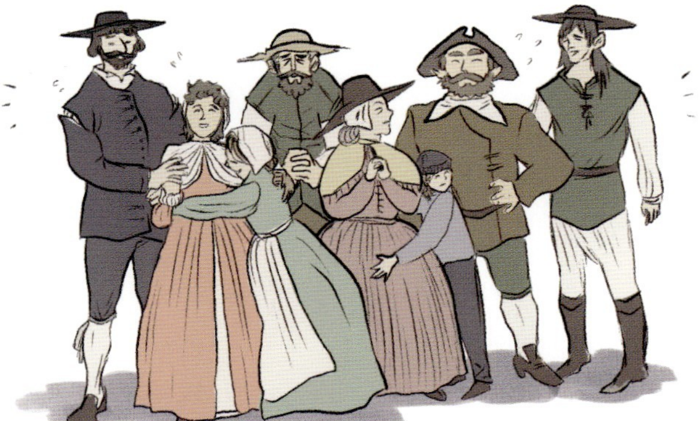

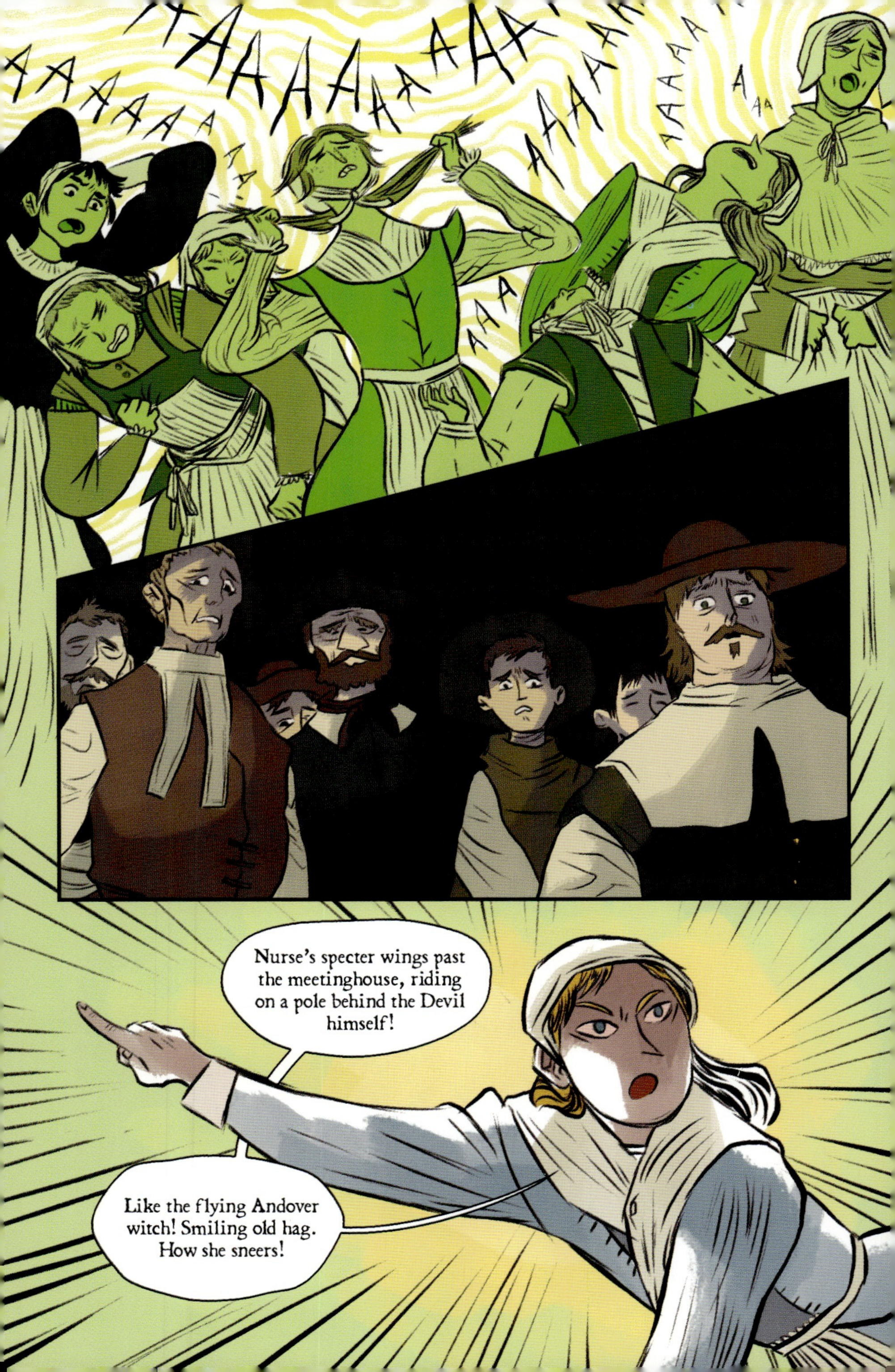
Nurse's specter wings past the meetinghouse, riding on a pole behind the Devil himself!
Like the flying Andover witch! Smiling old hag. How she sneers!

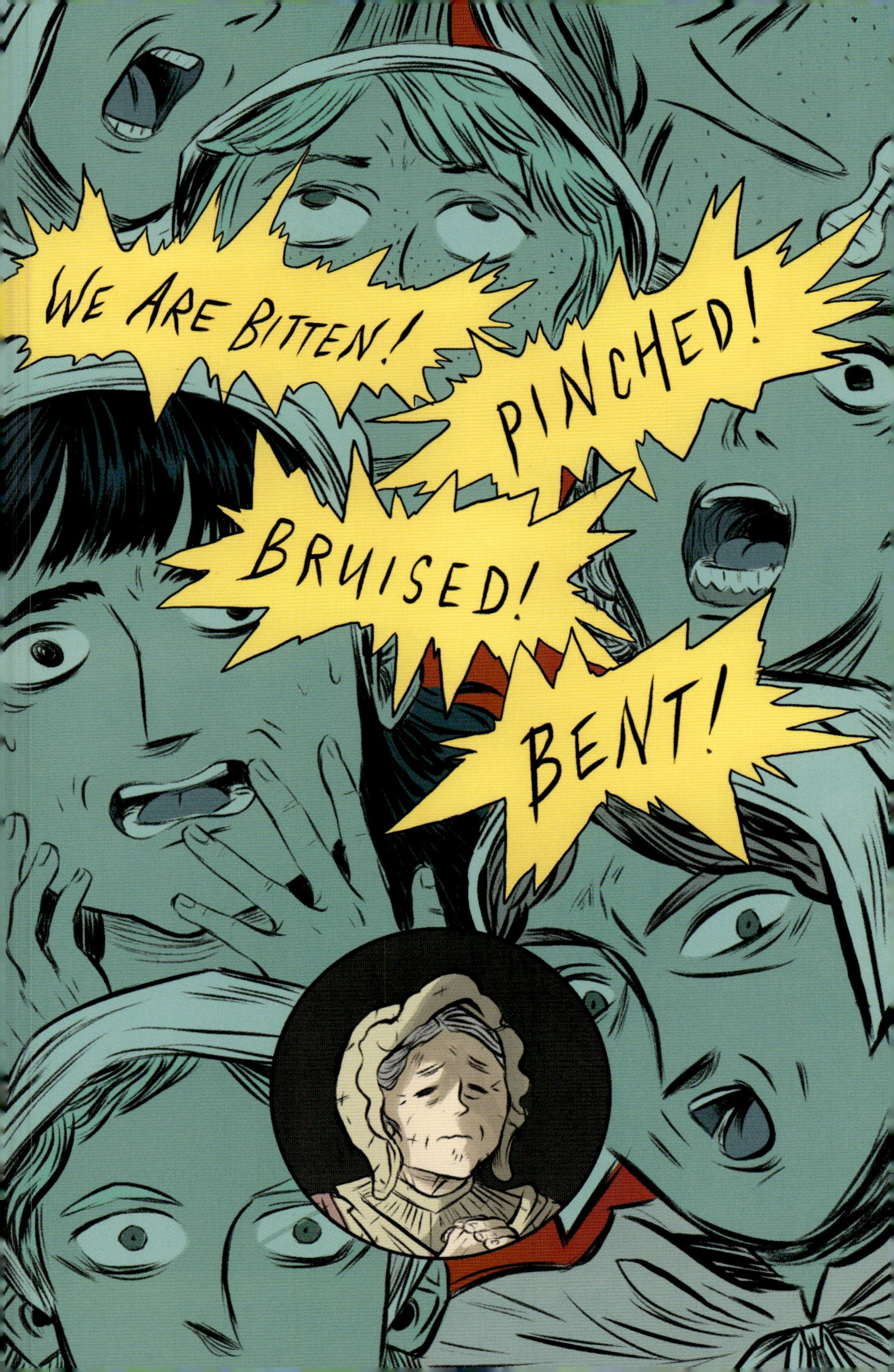
WE ARE BITTEN!
PINCHED!
BRUISED!
BENT!

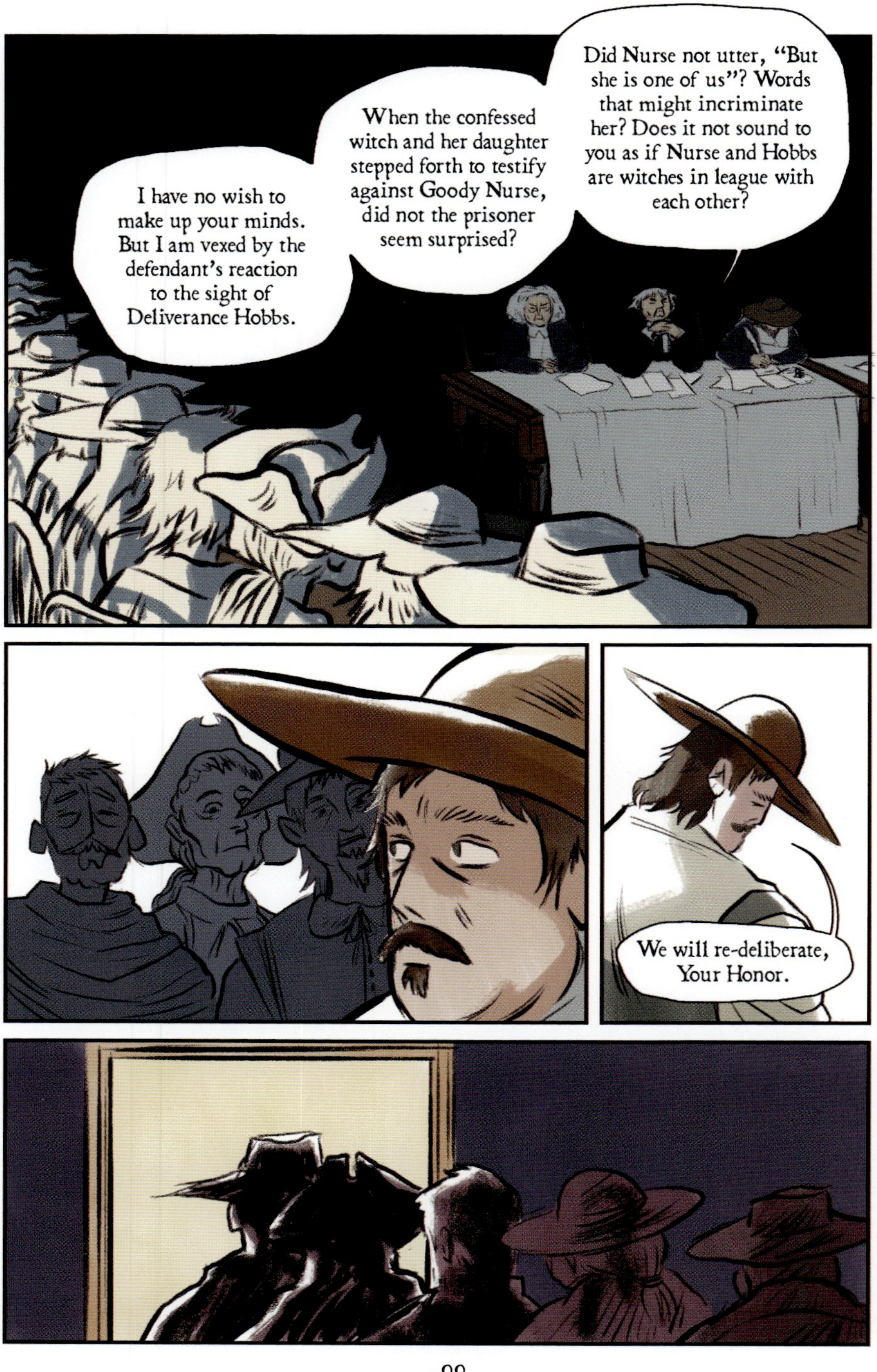
I have no wish to make up your minds. But I am vexed by the defendant's reaction to the sight of Deliverance Hobbs.
When the confessed witch and her daughter stepped forth to testify against Goody Nurse, did not the prisoner seem surprised?
Did Nurse not utter, "But she is one of us"? Words that might incriminate her? Does it not sound to you as if Nurse and Hobbs are witches in league with each other?
We will re-deliberate, Your Honor.

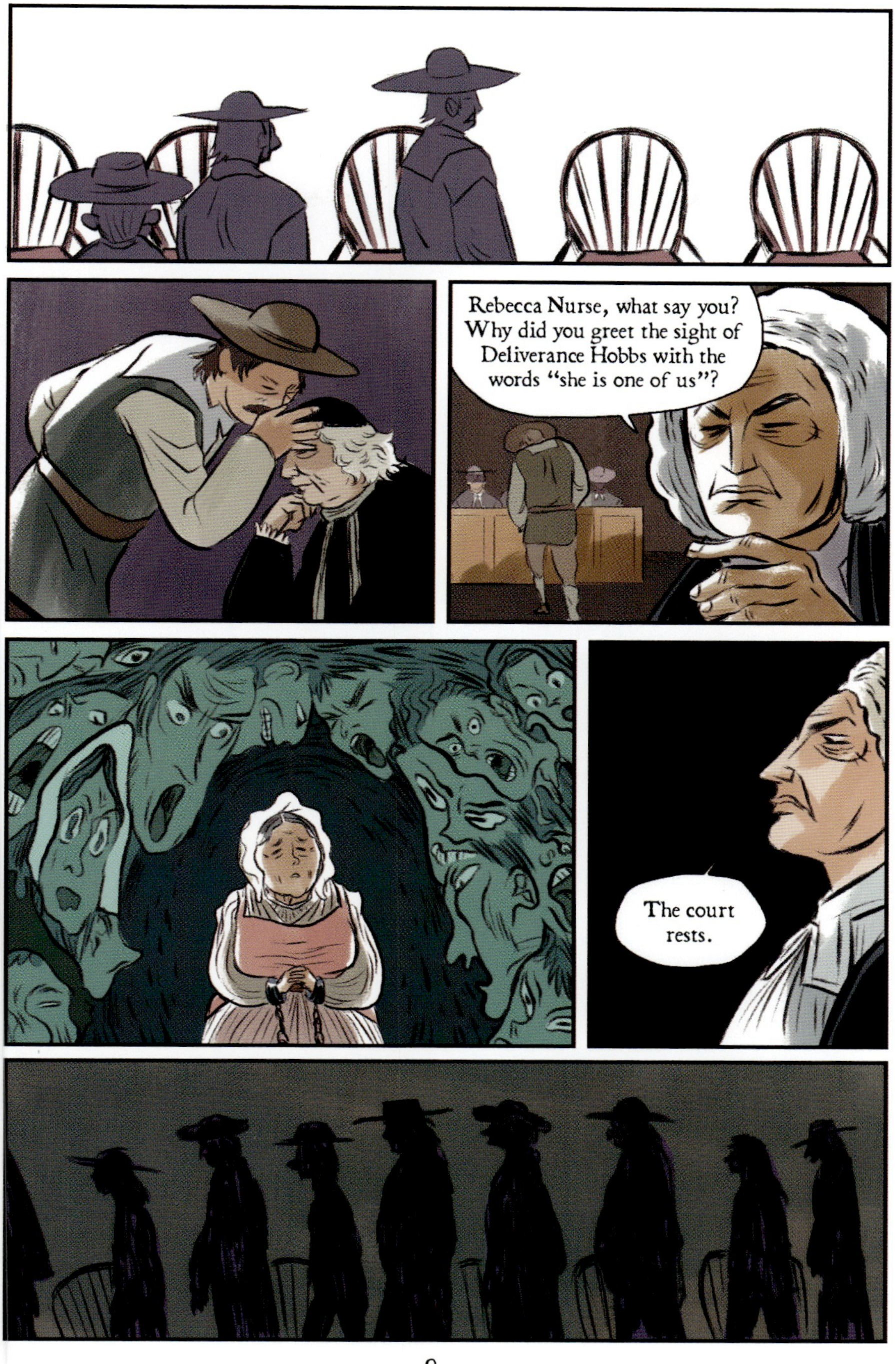
Rebecca Nurse, what say you? Why did you greet the sight of Deliverance Hobbs with the words "she is one of us"?
The court rests.

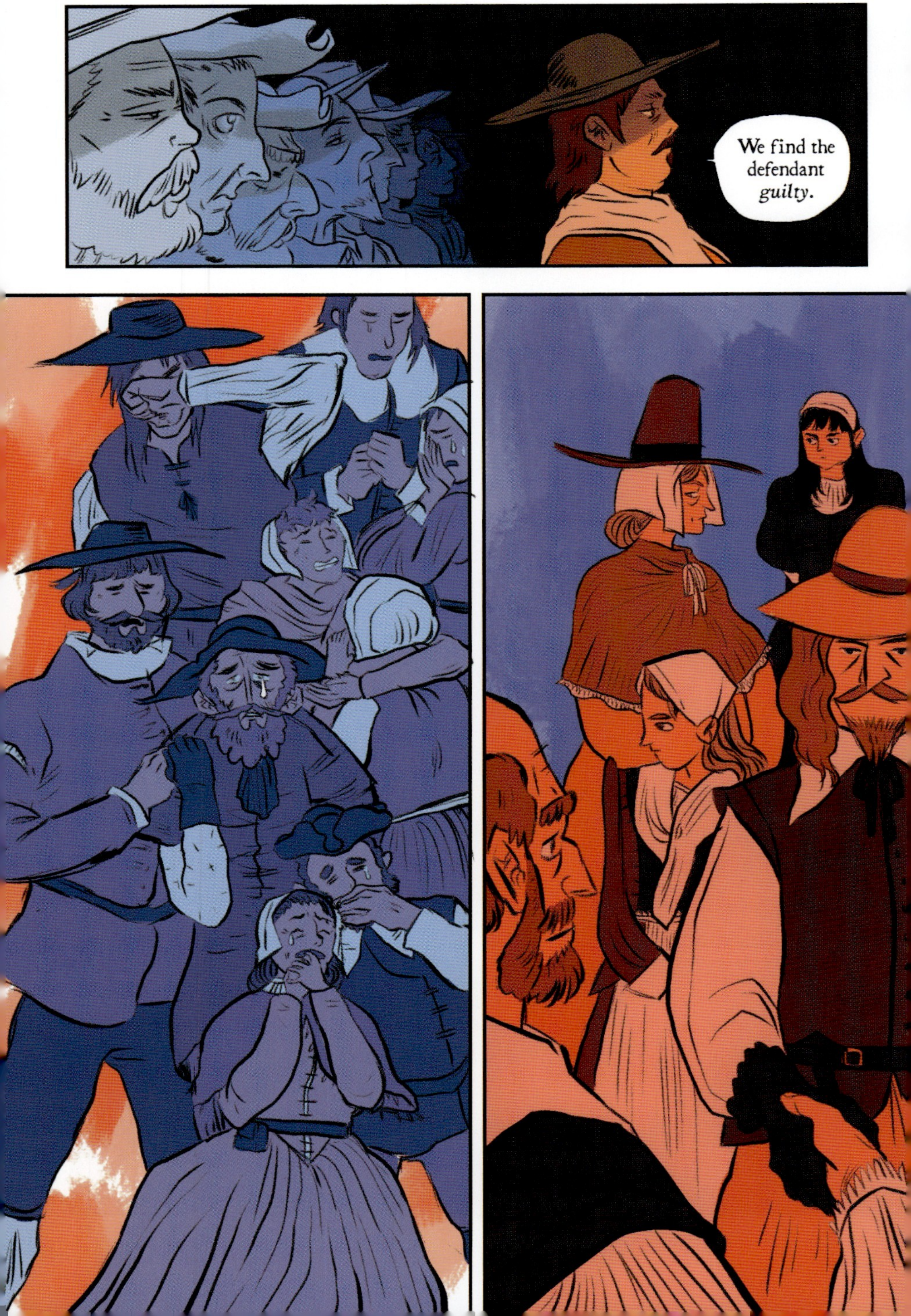
We find the defendant *guilty*.

Later. Dusk.

She couldn't *hear* the question, much less answer it.

Is it not obvious? She meant only that the Hobbs women had been her fellow prisoners.

How could they be called to testify against her?

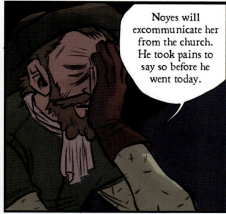

Noyes will excommunicate her from the church. He took pains to say so before he went today.

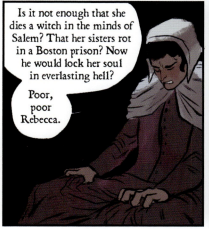

Is it not enough that she dies a witch in the minds of Salem? That her sisters rot in a Boston prison? Now he would lock her soul in everlasting hell?

Poor, poor Rebecca.

191

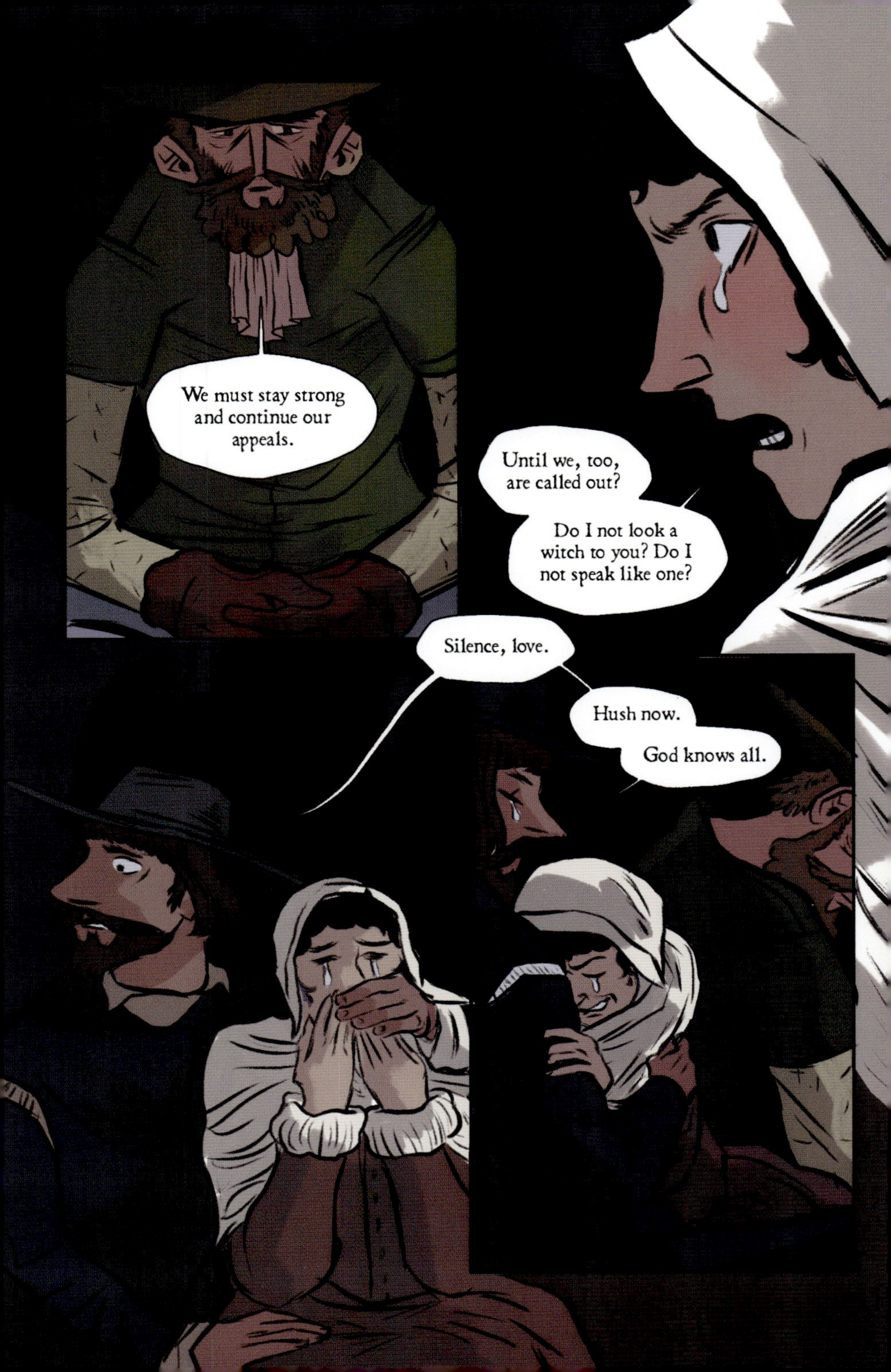
We must stay strong and continue our appeals.
Until we, too, are called out?
Do I not look a witch to you? Do I not speak like one?
Silence, love.
Hush now.
God knows all.

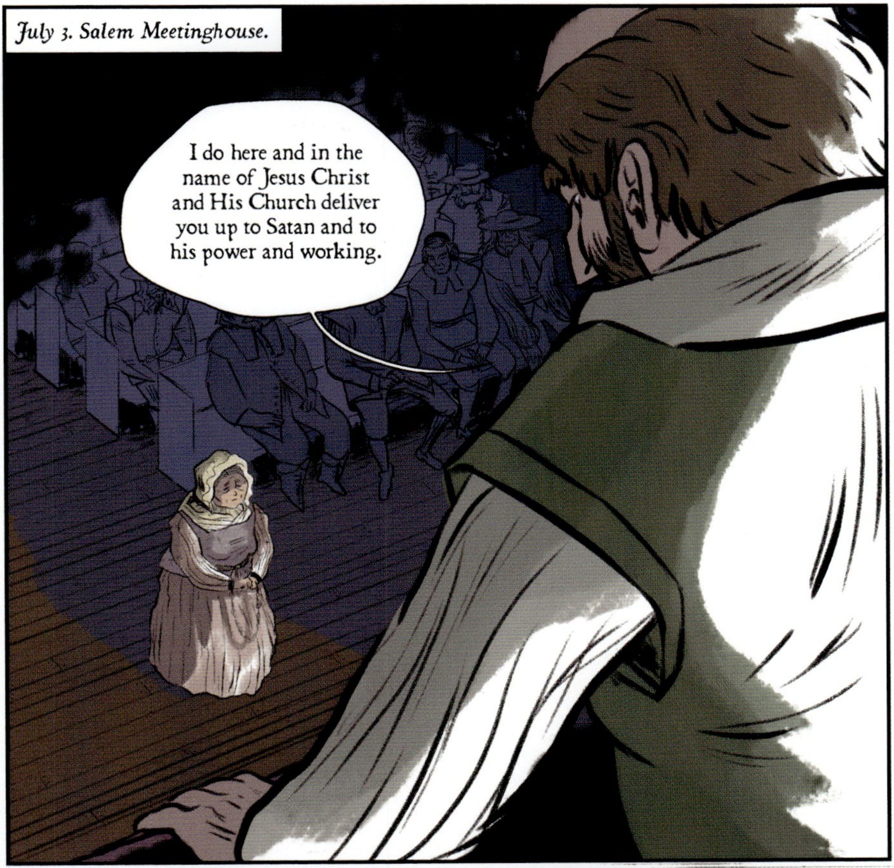
July 3. Salem Meetinghouse.
I do here and in the name of Jesus Christ and His Church deliver you up to Satan and to his power and working.

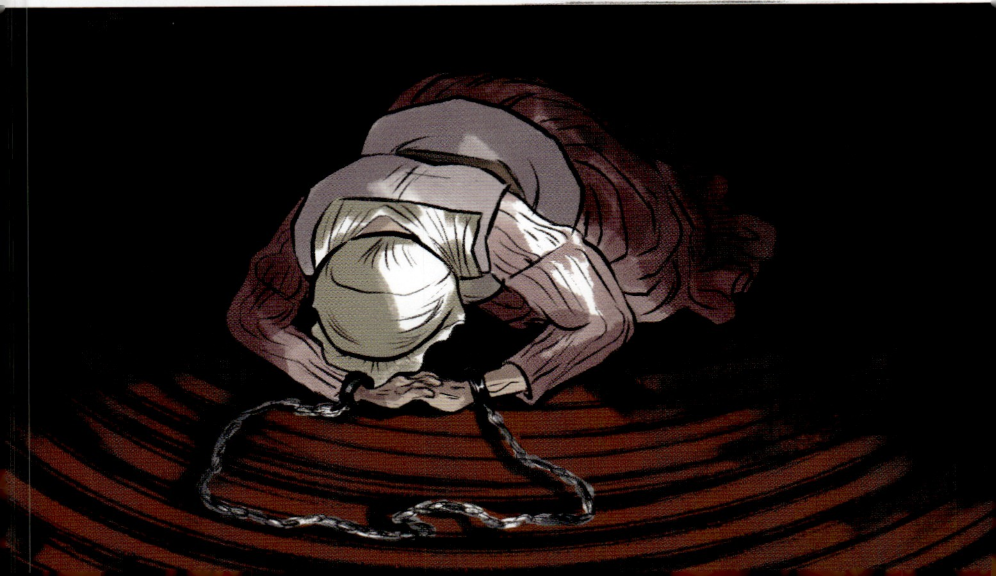

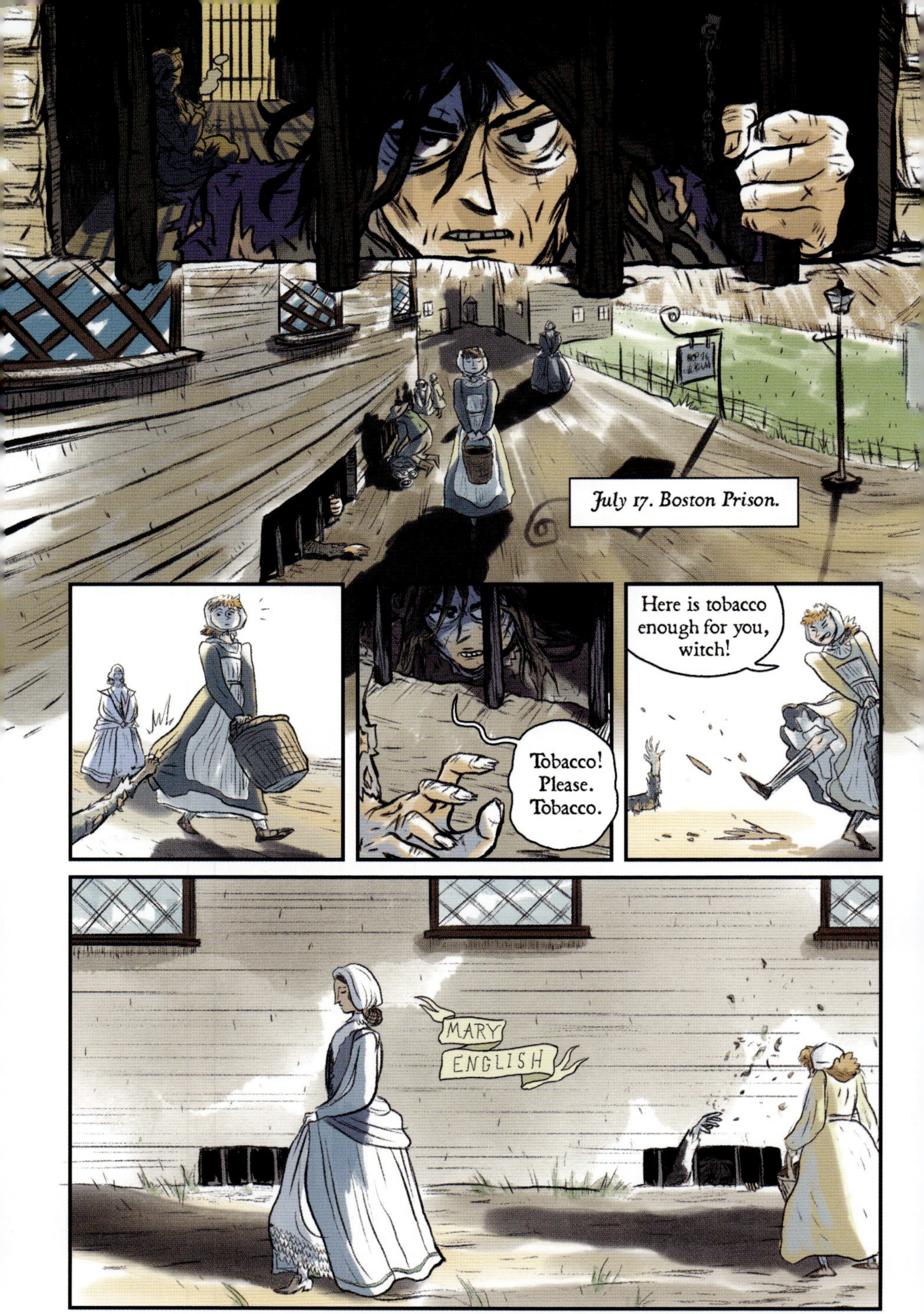
July 17. Boston Prison.
Tobacco! Please. Tobacco.
Here is tobacco enough for you, witch!
MARY ENGLISH

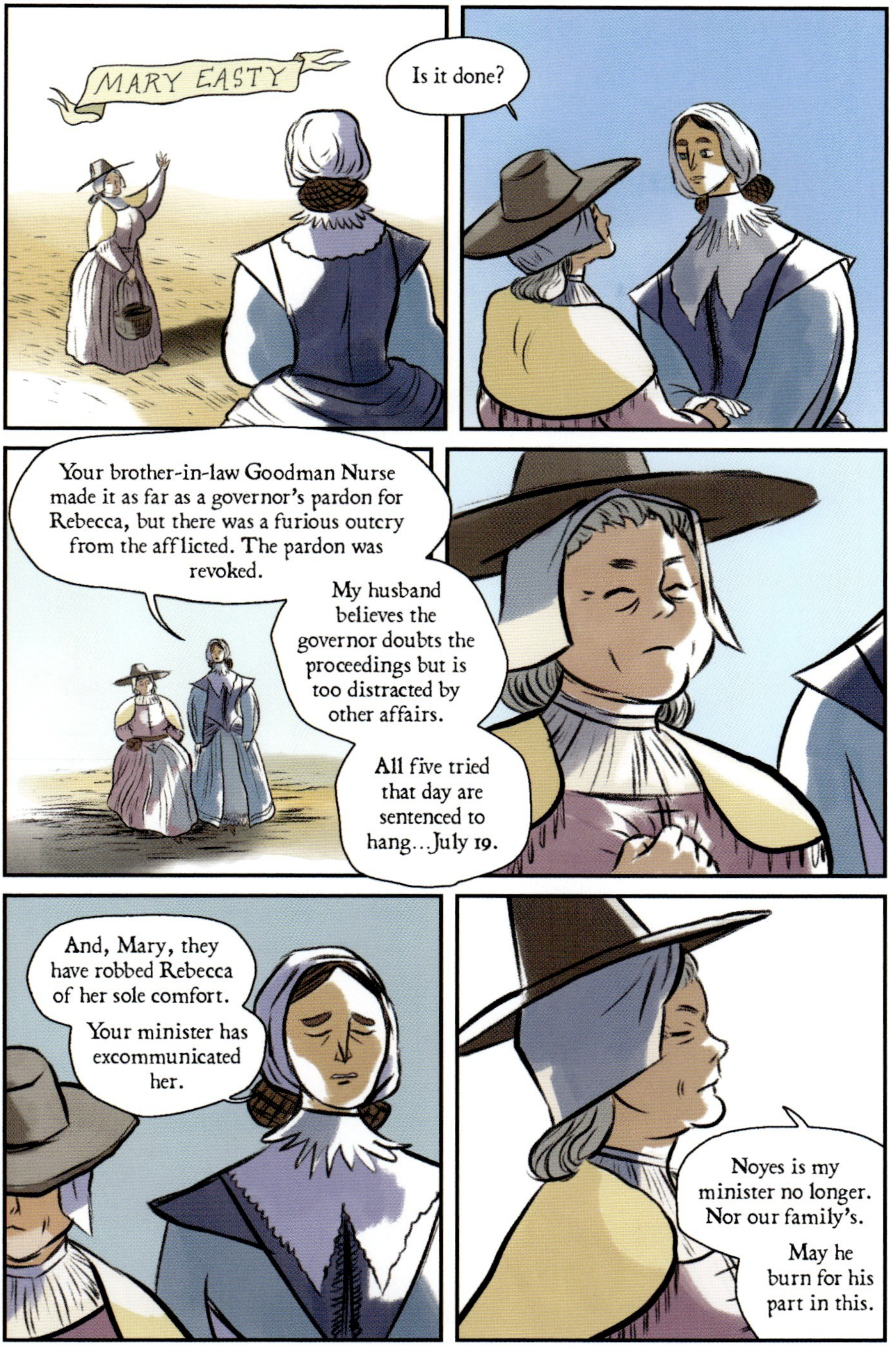
MARY EASTY
Is it done?
Your brother-in-law Goodman Nurse made it as far as a governor's pardon for Rebecca, but there was a furious outcry from the afflicted. The pardon was revoked.
My husband believes the governor doubts the proceedings but is too distracted by other affairs.
All five tried that day are sentenced to hang...July 19.
And, Mary, they have robbed Rebecca of her sole comfort.
Your minister has excommunicated her.
Noyes is my minister no longer. Nor our family's.
May he burn for his part in this.

I'm so sorry, Mary.

What we spoke of? You'll bear witness?

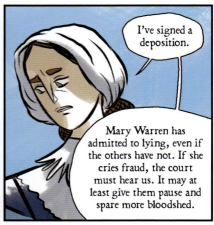

I've signed a deposition.

Mary Warren has admitted to lying, even if the others have not. If she cries fraud, the court must hear us. It may at least give them pause and spare more bloodshed.

The courts are deaf and blind, it seems, even to the thunder and lightning of God's displeasure.

But we must try.

I value your courage. More than I can say.

You heard Mary Warren confess it?

"When I was afflicted, I thought I saw the apparitions of 100 persons" were her words.

"But my head was distempered and could not tell what I saw."

To me, she said the magistrates were better off listening to Keyser's crazy daughter than the afflicted.

It is criminal, this "dissembling."

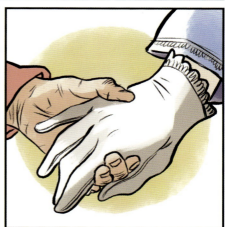

As is the fact that the land dispute between your two families has never entered testimony. Who accuses whom? The Putnams want for shame!

Philip and I will do what we can. You know that.

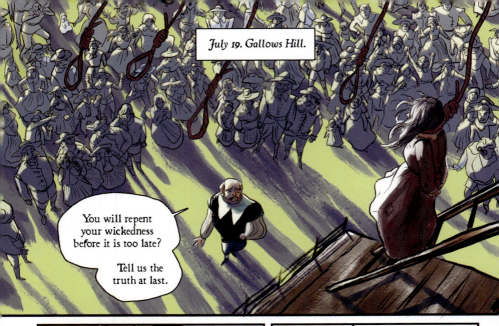

July 19. Gallows Hill.

You will repent your wickedness before it is too late?

Tell us the truth at last.

I am innocent.

It is high time you confessed!

You, sir, are a liar. I am no more a witch than you are a wizard.

And if you take away my life, God will give you blood to drink!

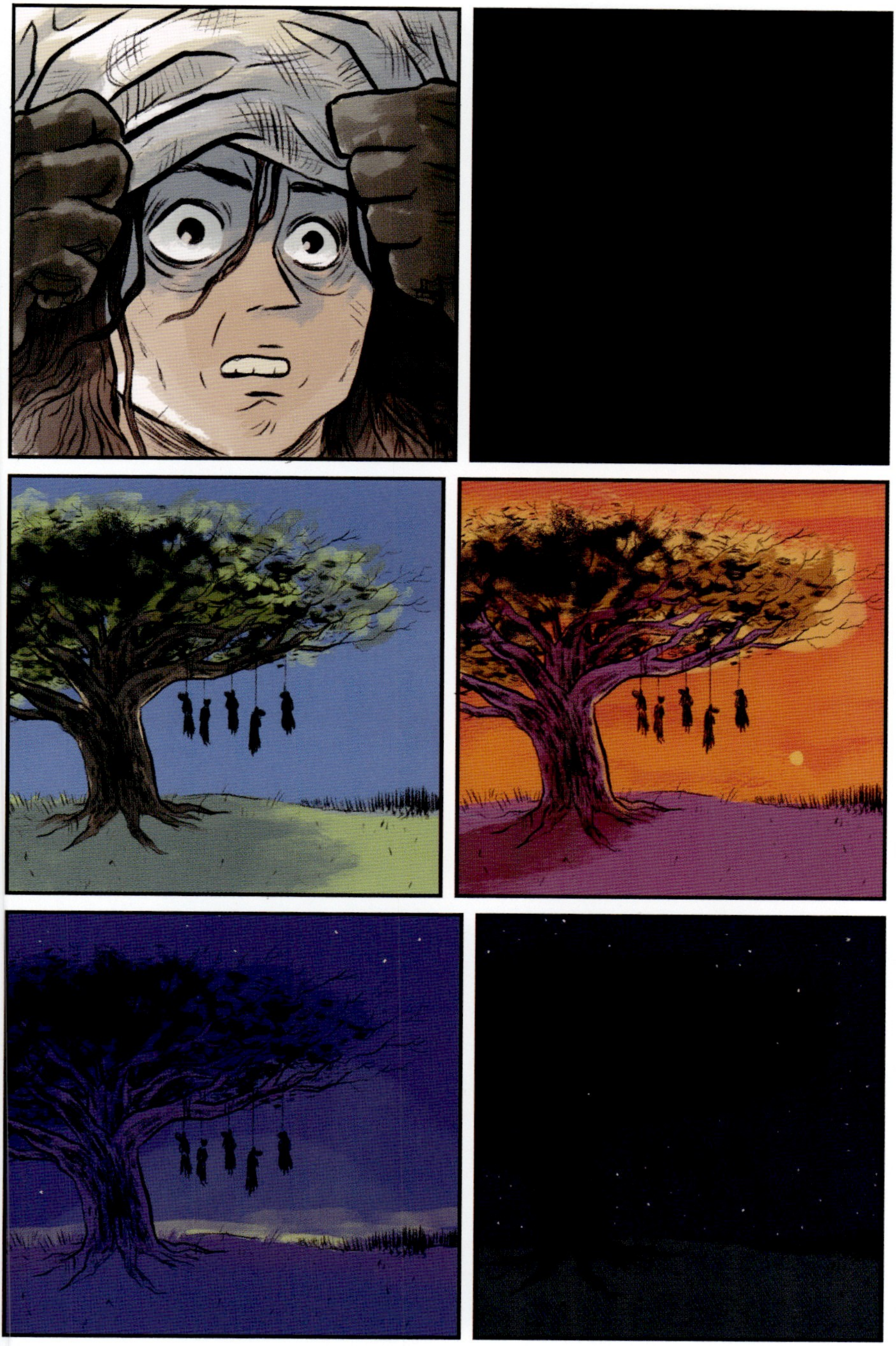

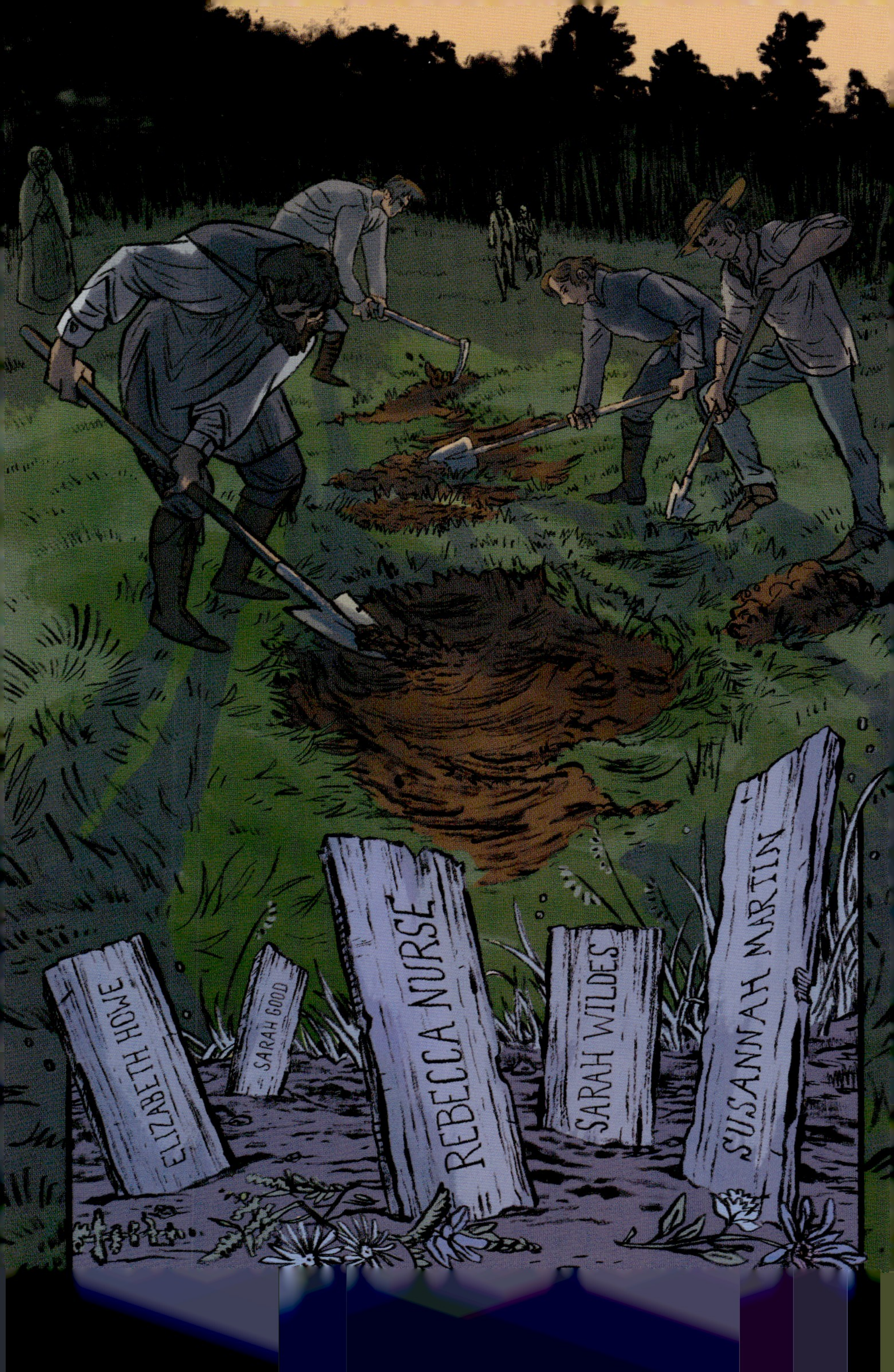
ELIZABETH HOWE
SARAH GOOD
REBECCA NURSE
SARAH WILDES
SUSANNAH MARTIN

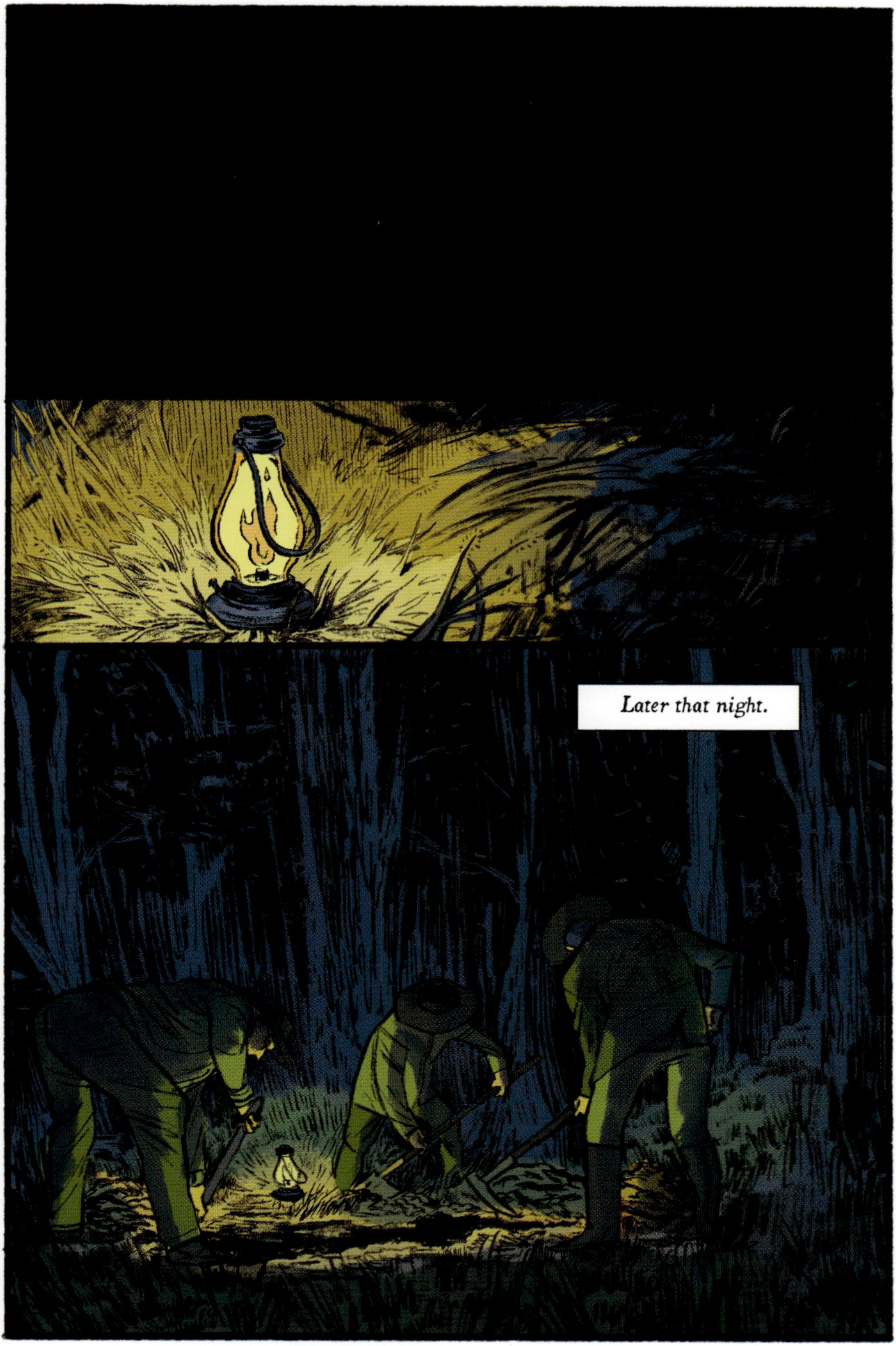
Later that night.

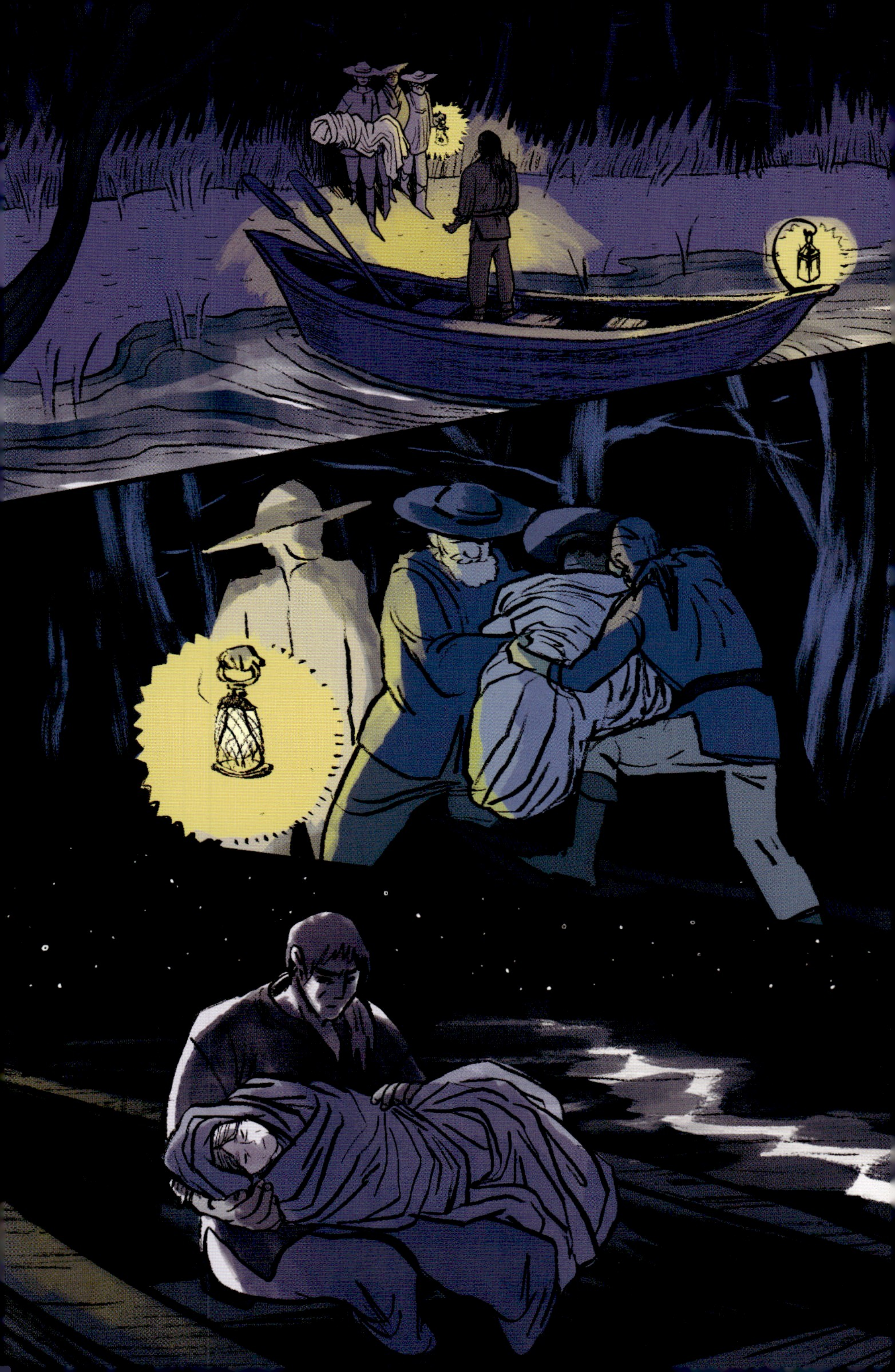

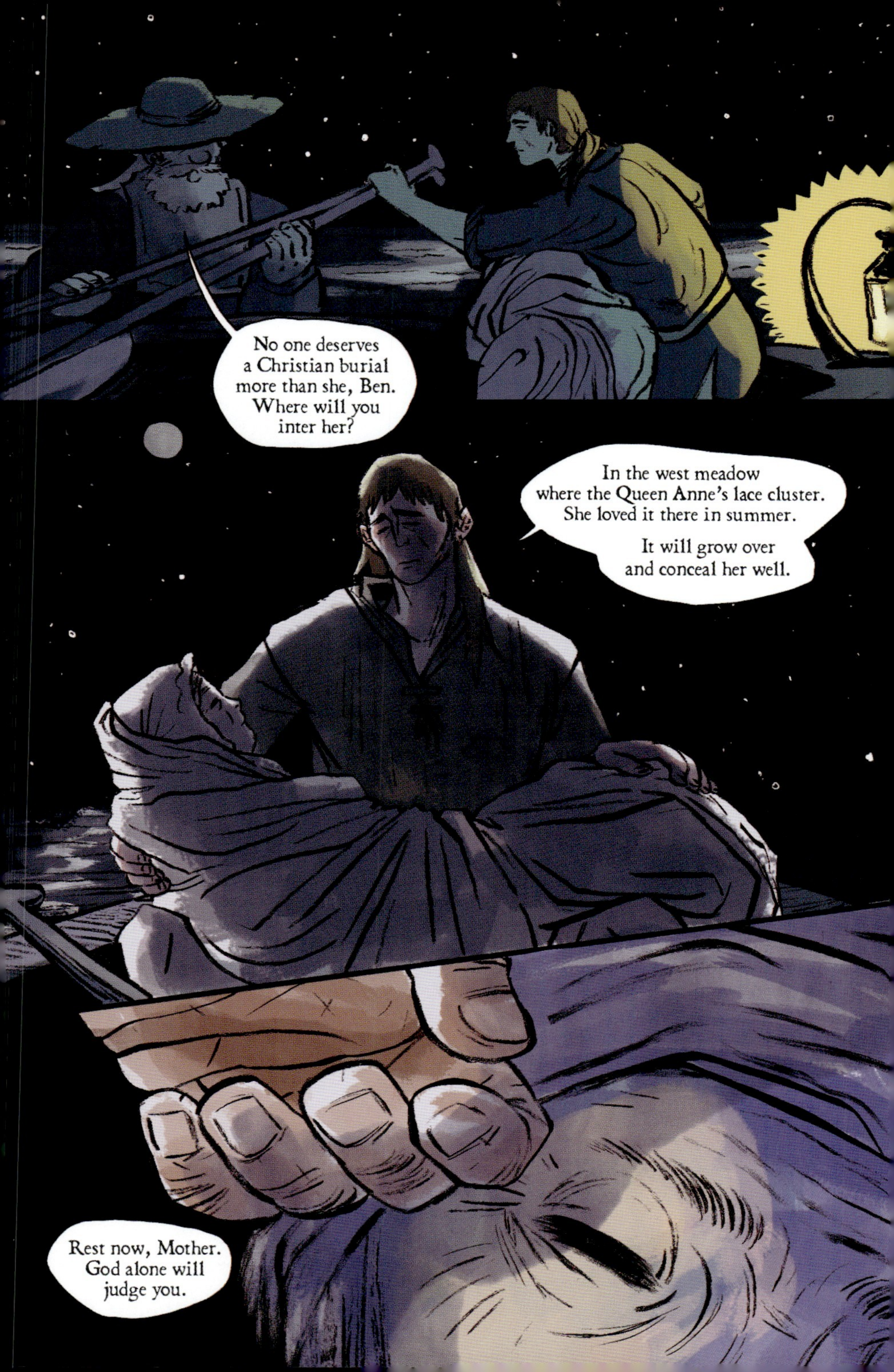
No one deserves a Christian burial more than she, Ben. Where will you inter her?
In the west meadow where the Queen Anne's lace cluster. She loved it there in summer.
It will grow over and conceal her well.
Rest now, Mother. God alone will judge you.

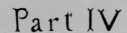

Part IV

A Delusion of Satan

How did the crisis in Salem—the "delusion"—spread so quickly and vehemently?

Conditions conspired: fear and stress brought on by epidemics, Native American raids, harsh weather, and stark living conditions; superstition, racism, and gender prejudice; political strife, biased leadership, feuds, and land disputes. There was also, of course, the dynamic of powerless, oppressed, and profoundly bored adolescent girls given sudden agency over life and death (a dynamic exploited by the adult men in their lives with agendas of their own).

But the physical symptoms that started it all remain a mystery. The girls' violent fits were, to all who witnessed them, terrifying and utterly convincing. Was it just gripping (and deadly) theater? Or could the early behaviors exhibited by Betty Parris and Abigail Williams (and the Goodwin children before them)—violent convulsions and contortions, trancelike states, the impulse to crawl into corners—have a physical explanation?

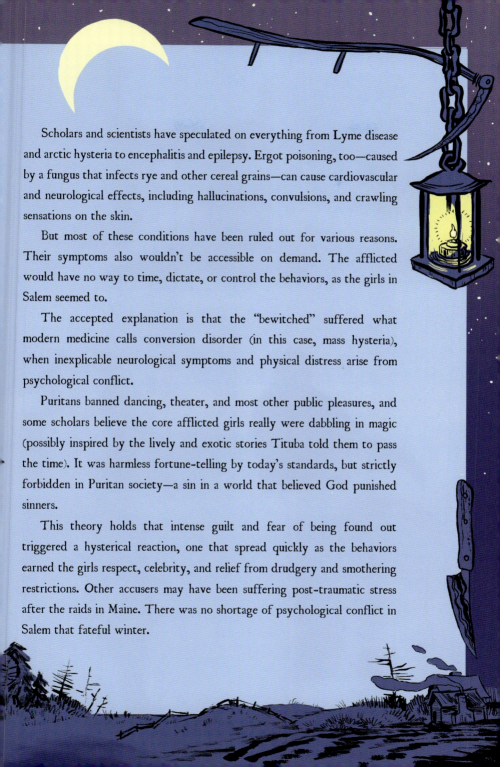

Scholars and scientists have speculated on everything from Lyme disease and arctic hysteria to encephalitis and epilepsy. Ergot poisoning, too—caused by a fungus that infects rye and other cereal grains—can cause cardiovascular and neurological effects, including hallucinations, convulsions, and crawling sensations on the skin.

But most of these conditions have been ruled out for various reasons. Their symptoms also wouldn't be accessible on demand. The afflicted would have no way to time, dictate, or control the behaviors, as the girls in Salem seemed to.

The accepted explanation is that the "bewitched" suffered what modern medicine calls conversion disorder (in this case, mass hysteria), when inexplicable neurological symptoms and physical distress arise from psychological conflict.

Puritans banned dancing, theater, and most other public pleasures, and some scholars believe the core afflicted girls really were dabbling in magic (possibly inspired by the lively and exotic stories Tituba told them to pass the time). It was harmless fortune-telling by today's standards, but strictly forbidden in Puritan society—a sin in a world that believed God punished sinners.

This theory holds that intense guilt and fear of being found out triggered a hysterical reaction, one that spread quickly as the behaviors earned the girls respect, celebrity, and relief from drudgery and smothering restrictions. Other accusers may have been suffering post-traumatic stress after the raids in Maine. There was no shortage of psychological conflict in Salem that fateful winter.

Mid-July. Governor's chambers.

KNOCK KNOCK

Will you assure me, William, that we are a civilized colony? Or are we an inquisition?

Who in the New World tortures boys to make witches of their mothers?

I am uncertain what ails you, Your Excellency.

We combat the scourge of witchcraft.

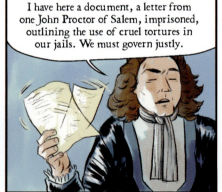

I have here a document, a letter from one John Proctor of Salem, imprisoned, outlining the use of cruel tortures in our jails. We must govern justly.

My sentiments exactly, Governor.

Tell me this, William. Do you not believe the Devil can impersonate an innocent? Do you think the fiend, with all his wiles, can't fool the likes of a few magistrates?

Do you suppose that forcing a mother's sons to condemn that mother by tying them neck and heels until the blood pours from their noses will aid our cause—or our majesties—at this time?

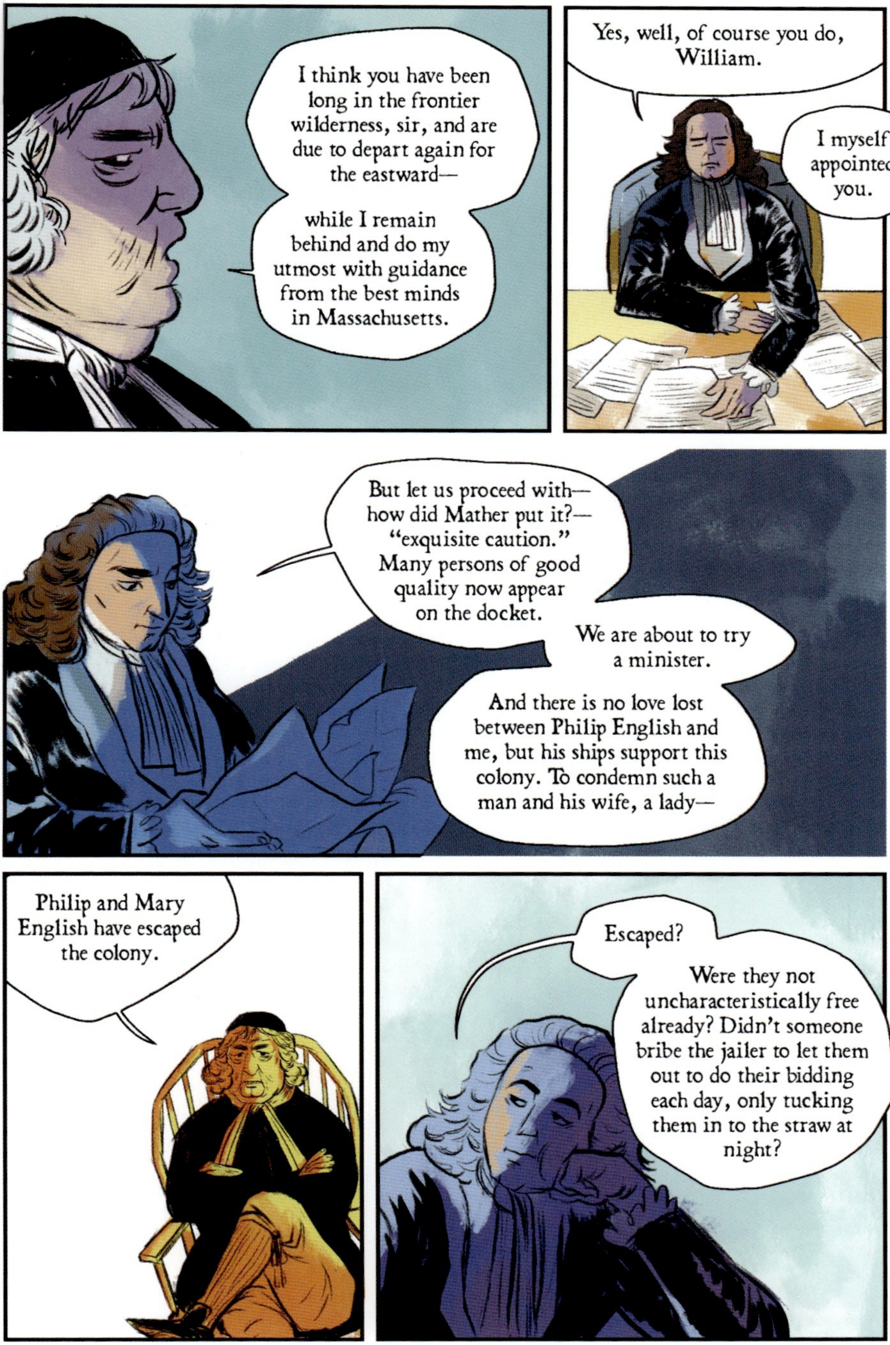
I think you have been long in the frontier wilderness, sir, and are due to depart again for the eastward—
while I remain behind and do my utmost with guidance from the best minds in Massachusetts.
Yes, well, of course you do, William.
I myself appointed you.
But let us proceed with—how did Mather put it?—"exquisite caution." Many persons of good quality now appear on the docket.
We are about to try a minister.
And there is no love lost between Philip English and me, but his ships support this colony. To condemn such a man and his wife, a lady—
Philip and Mary English have escaped the colony.
Escaped?
Were they not uncharacteristically free already? Didn't someone bribe the jailer to let them out to do their bidding each day, only tucking them in to the straw at night?

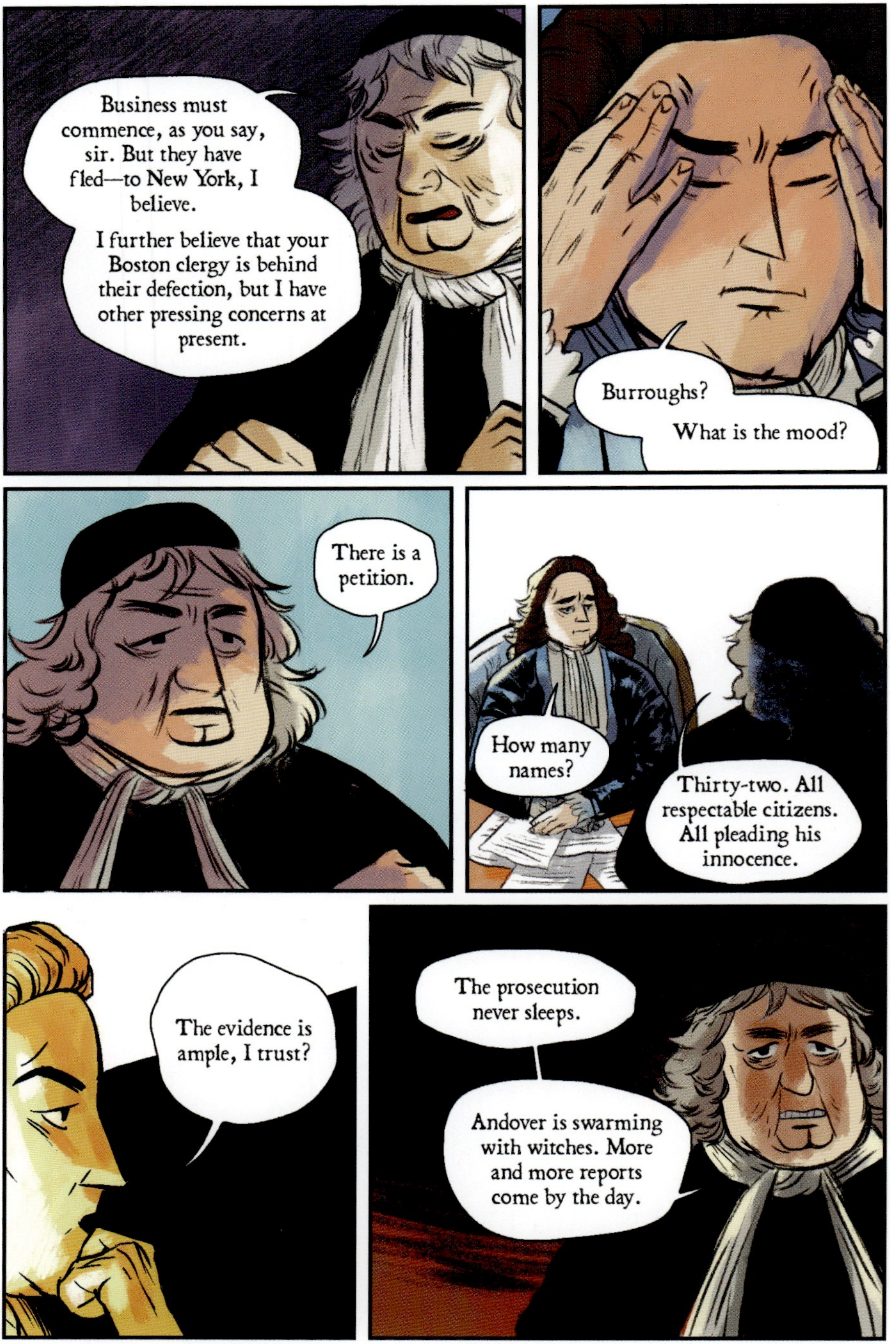
Business must commence, as you say, sir. But they have fled—to New York, I believe.
I further believe that your Boston clergy is behind their defection, but I have other pressing concerns at present.
Burroughs?
What is the mood?
There is a petition.
How many names?
Thirty-two. All respectable citizens. All pleading his innocence.
The evidence is ample, I trust?
The prosecution never sleeps.
Andover is swarming with witches. More and more reports come by the day.

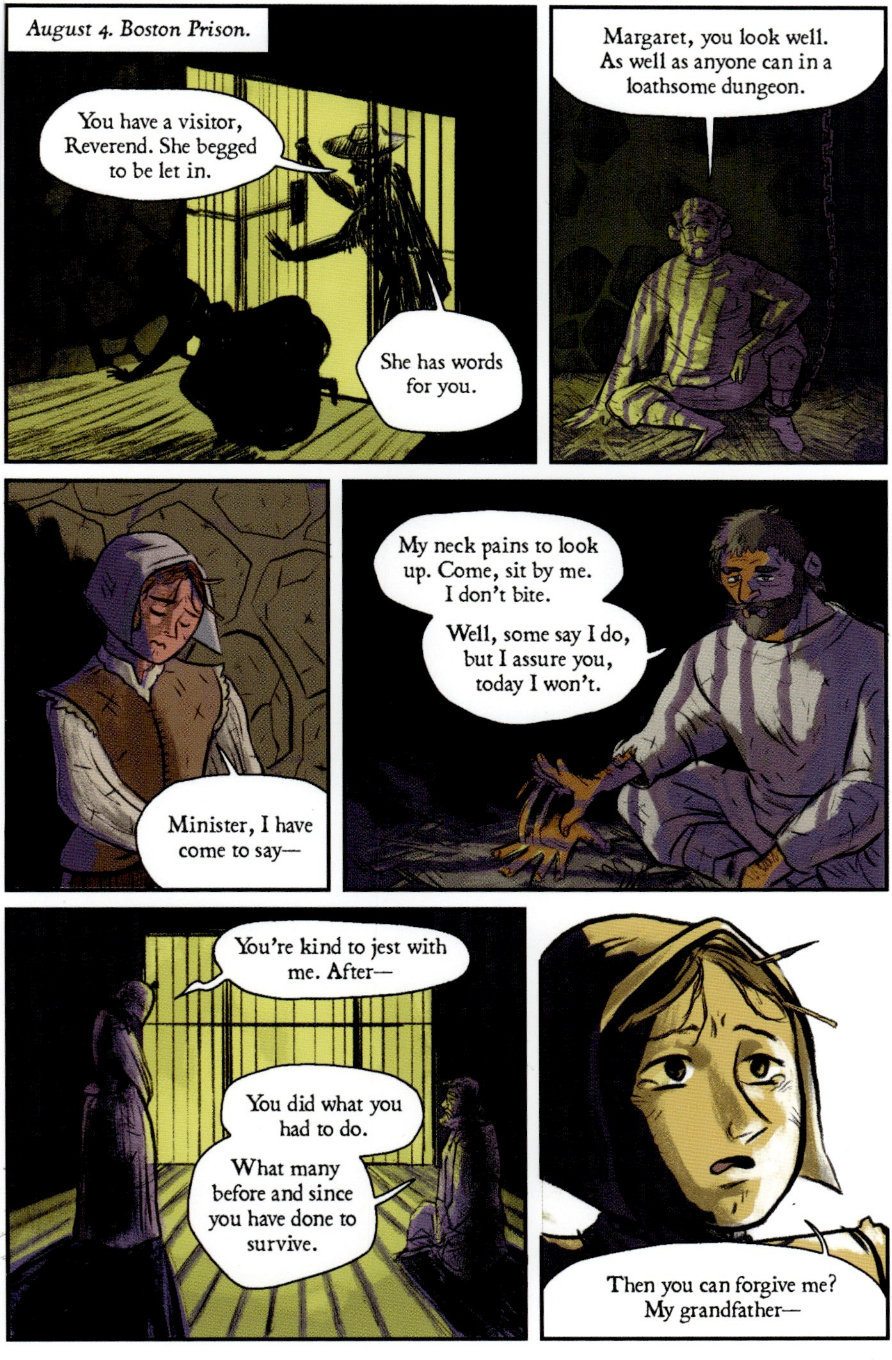
August 4. Boston Prison.
You have a visitor, Reverend. She begged to be let in.
She has words for you.
Margaret, you look well. As well as anyone can in a loathsome dungeon.
Minister, I have come to say—
My neck pains to look up. Come, sit by me. I don't bite.
Well, some say I do, but I assure you, today I won't.
You're kind to jest with me. After—
You did what you had to do.
What many before and since you have done to survive.
Then you can forgive me? My grandfather—

George will do likewise if he keeps his wits about him, and I'm sore pressed to imagine the old rascal parted from his wits.

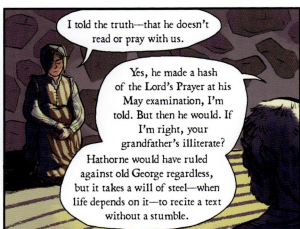

I told the truth—that he doesn't read or pray with us.

Yes, he made a hash of the Lord's Prayer at his May examination, I'm told. But then he would. If I'm right, your grandfather's illiterate? Hathorne would have ruled against old George regardless, but it takes a will of steel—when life depends on it—to recite a text without a stumble.

His trial—

We stand tomorrow, with four others.

They told me if I would not confess, I should be put down into the dungeon and would be hanged, but if I confessed, I should have my life.

But I have bad dreams. I've had such bad dreams—

We all have them, I trust, and a conscience sore with sin.

Have you told the jailer? Will they take a deposition?

I pray so. I begged him to have the magistrates hear me before your trial.

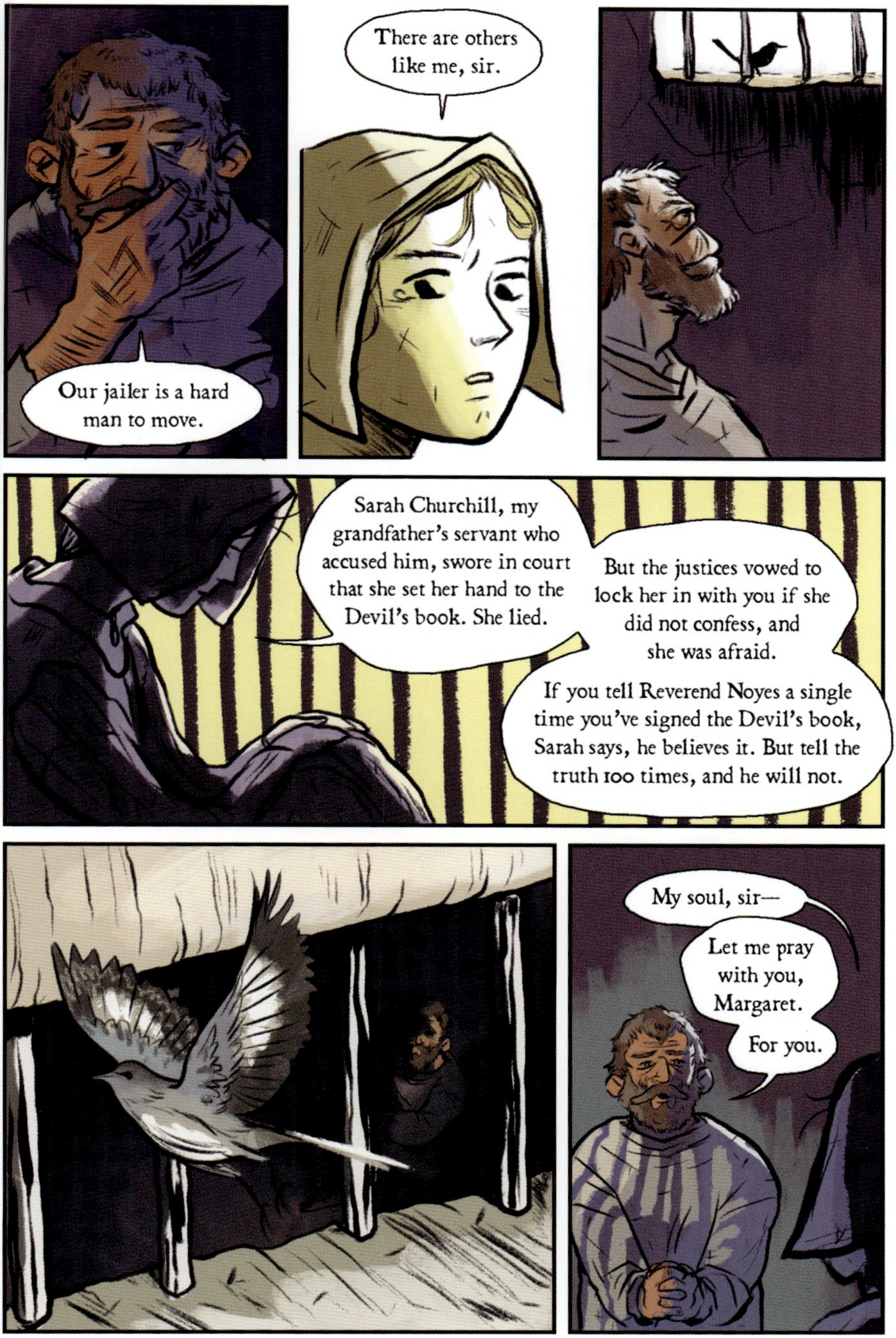
Our jailer is a hard man to move.
There are others like me, sir.
Sarah Churchill, my grandfather's servant who accused him, swore in court that she set her hand to the Devil's book. She lied.
But the justices vowed to lock her in with you if she did not confess, and she was afraid.
If you tell Reverend Noyes a single time you've signed the Devil's book, Sarah says, he believes it. But tell the truth 100 times, and he will not.
My soul, sir—
Let me pray with you, Margaret.
For you.

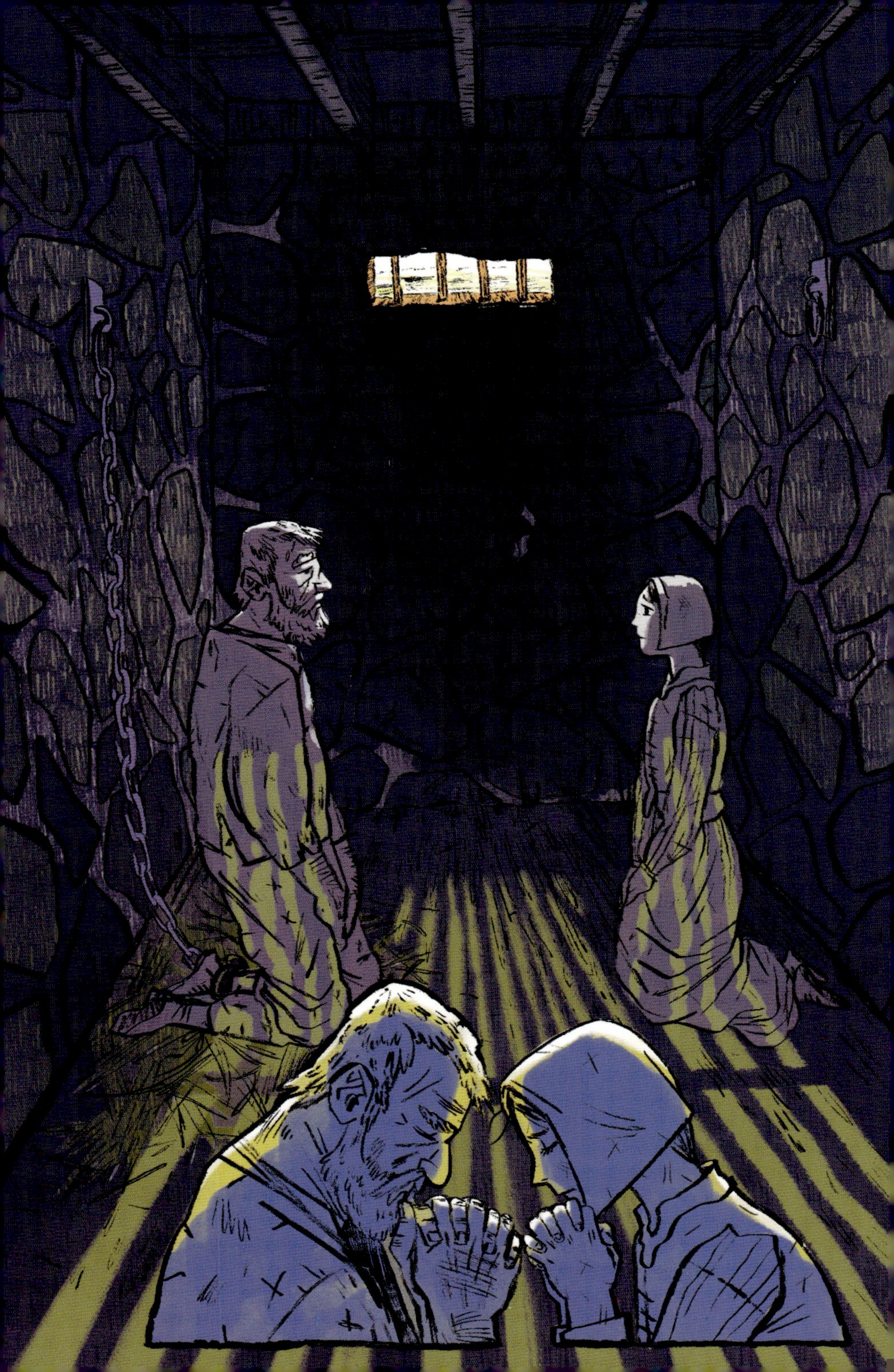

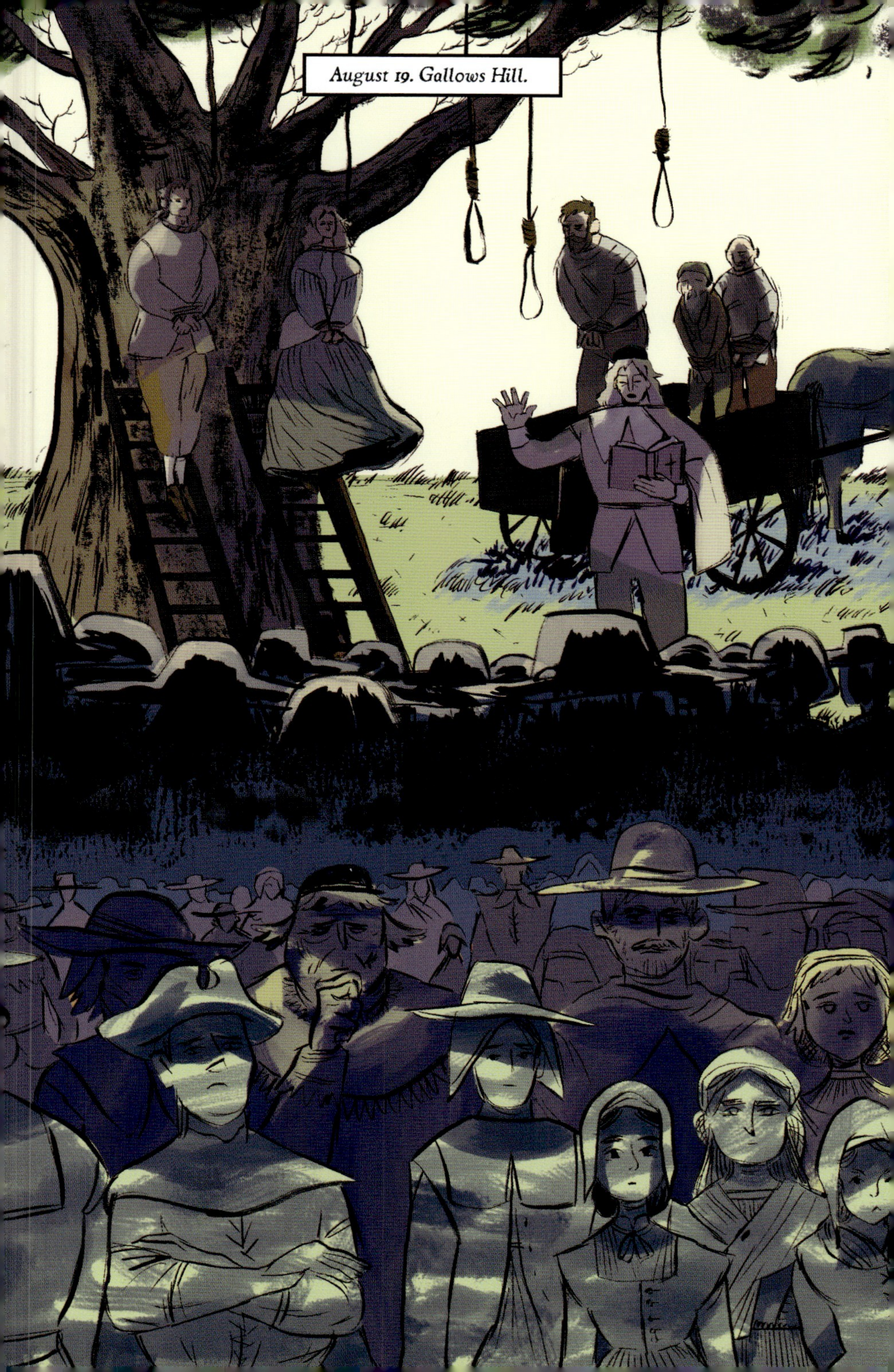
August 19. Gallows Hill.

God knows
I am innocent.

I pray God discover what witchcrafts are among us. I am clear and sinned against, but my soul forgives the sinners.

God keep me.

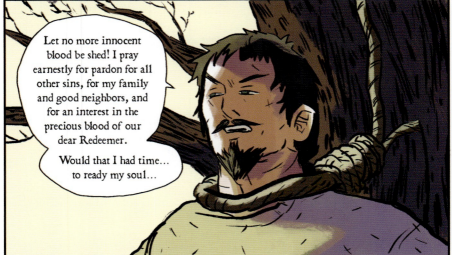

Let no more innocent blood be shed! I pray earnestly for pardon for all other sins, for my family and good neighbors, and for an interest in the precious blood of our dear Redeemer.

Would that I had time... to ready my soul...

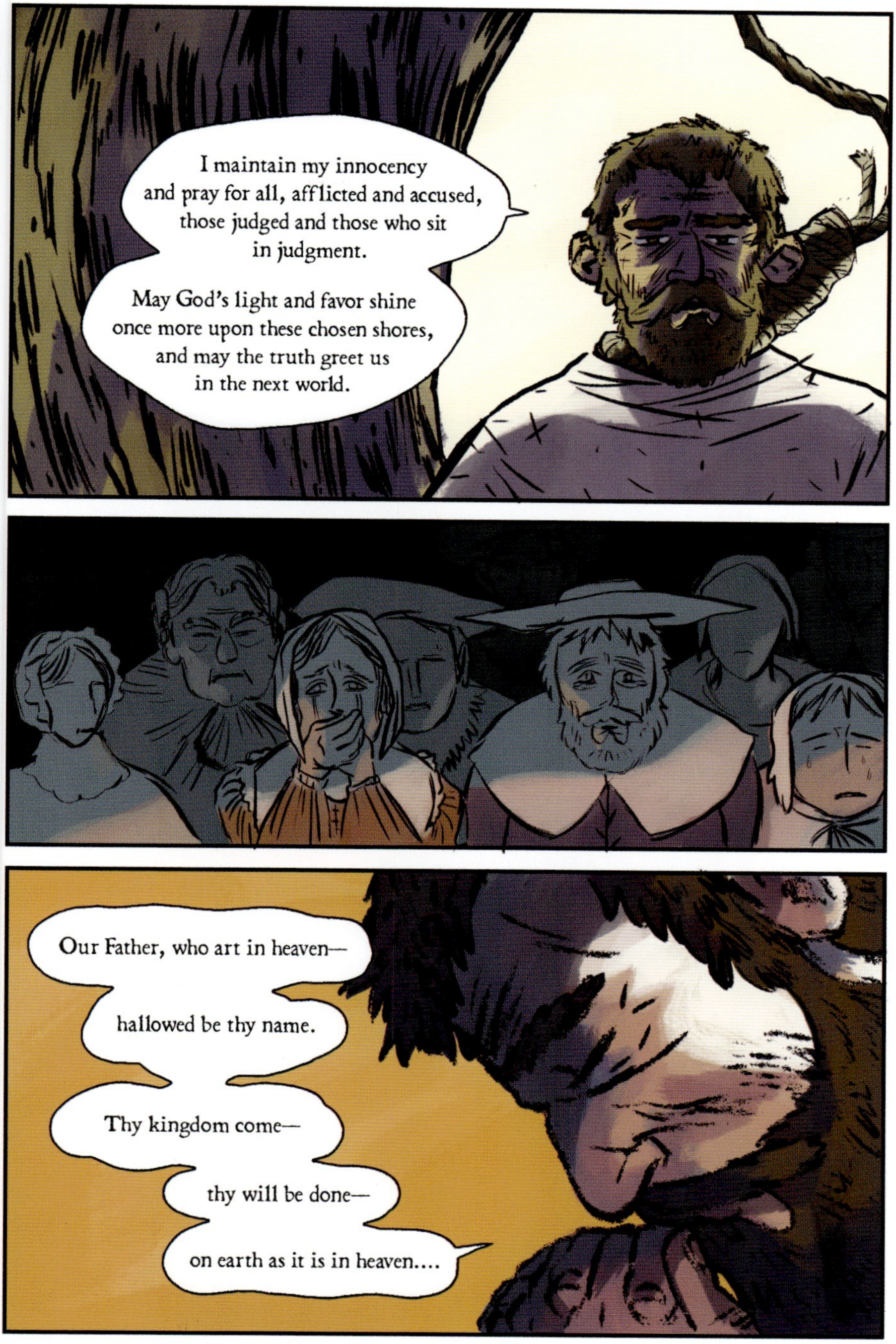
I maintain my innocency and pray for all, afflicted and accused, those judged and those who sit in judgment.
May God's light and favor shine once more upon these chosen shores, and may the truth greet us in the next world.
Our Father, who art in heaven—
hallowed be thy name.
Thy kingdom come—
thy will be done—
on earth as it is in heaven....

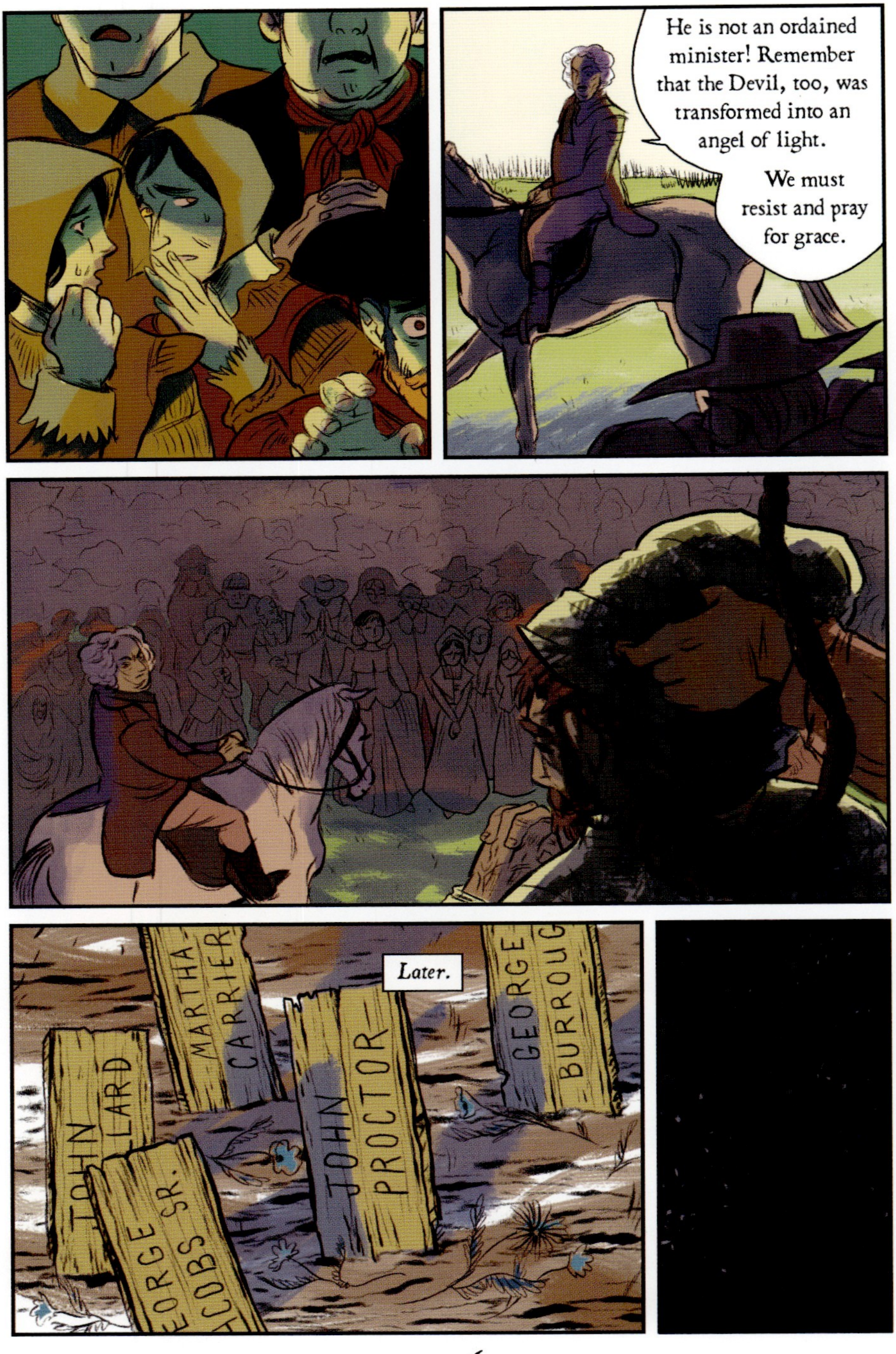
He is not an ordained minister! Remember that the Devil, too, was transformed into an angel of light.
We must resist and pray for grace.
Later.
JOHN
LARD
MARTHA
CARRIER
JOHN
PROCTOR
GEORGE
BURROUG
EORGE SR.
ACOBS

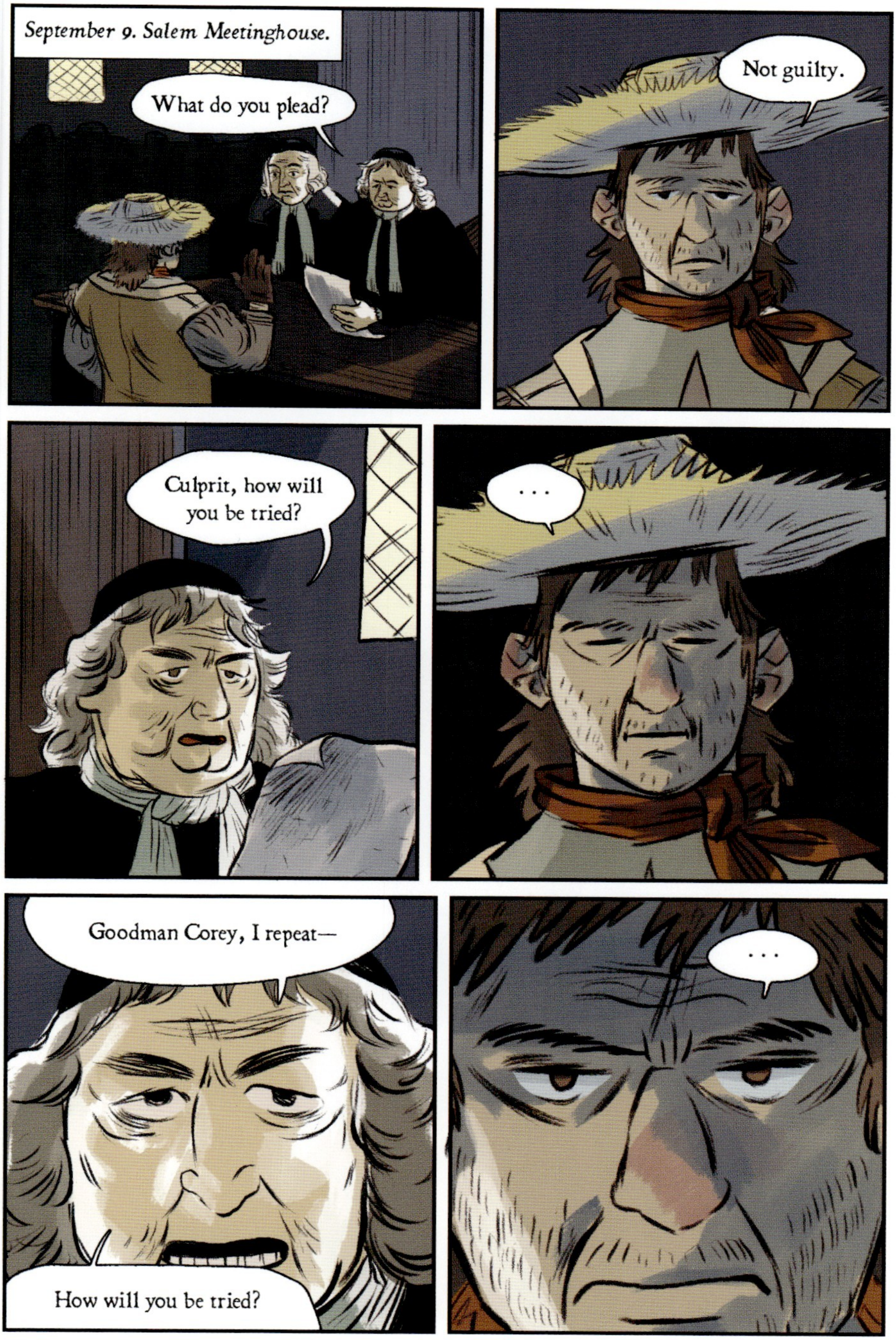
September 9. Salem Meetinghouse.
What do you plead?
Not guilty.
Culprit, how will you be tried?
. . .
Goodman Corey, I repeat—
How will you be tried?
. . .

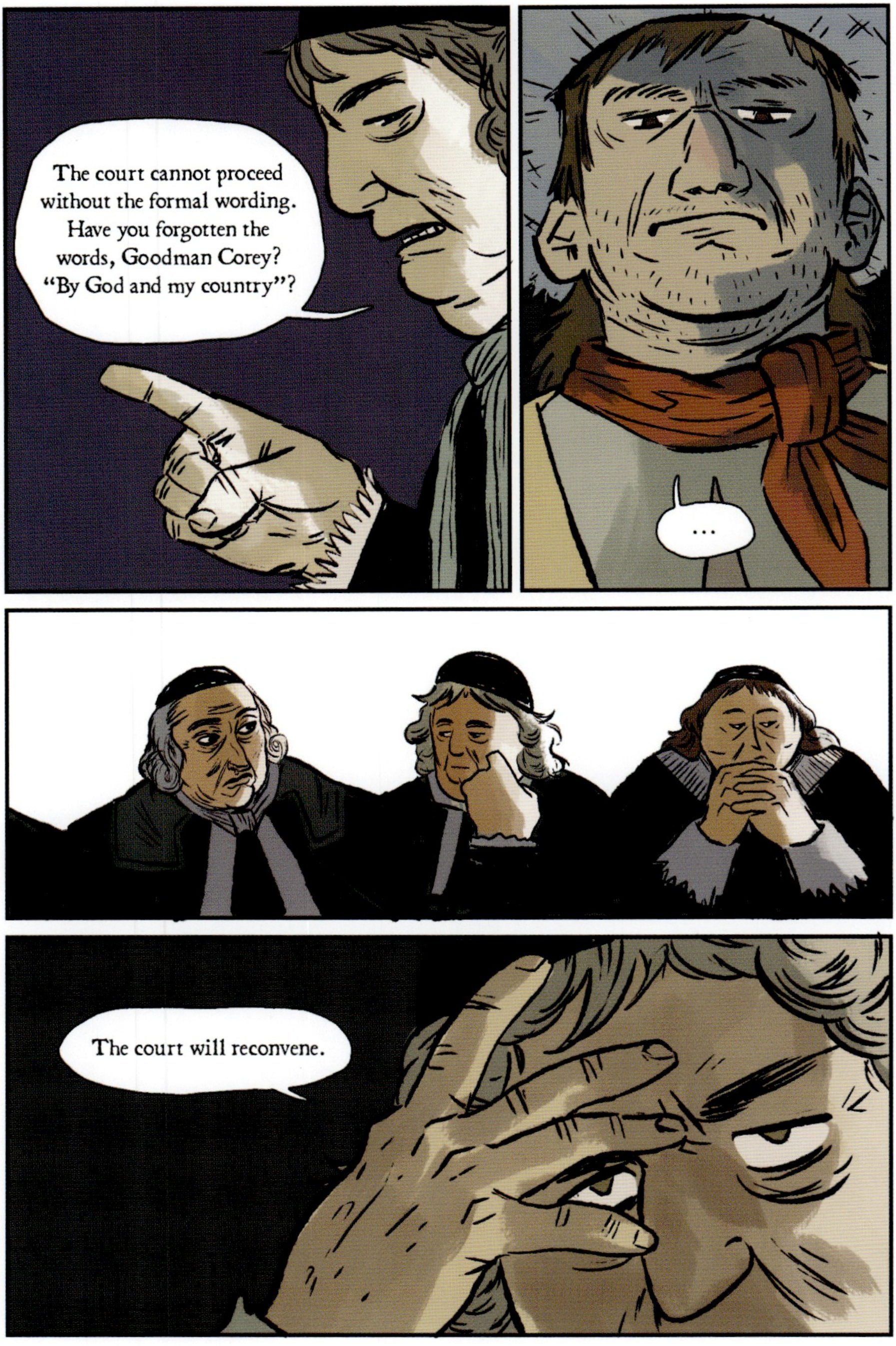
The court cannot proceed without the formal wording. Have you forgotten the words, Goodman Corey? "By God and my country"?
...
The court will reconvene.

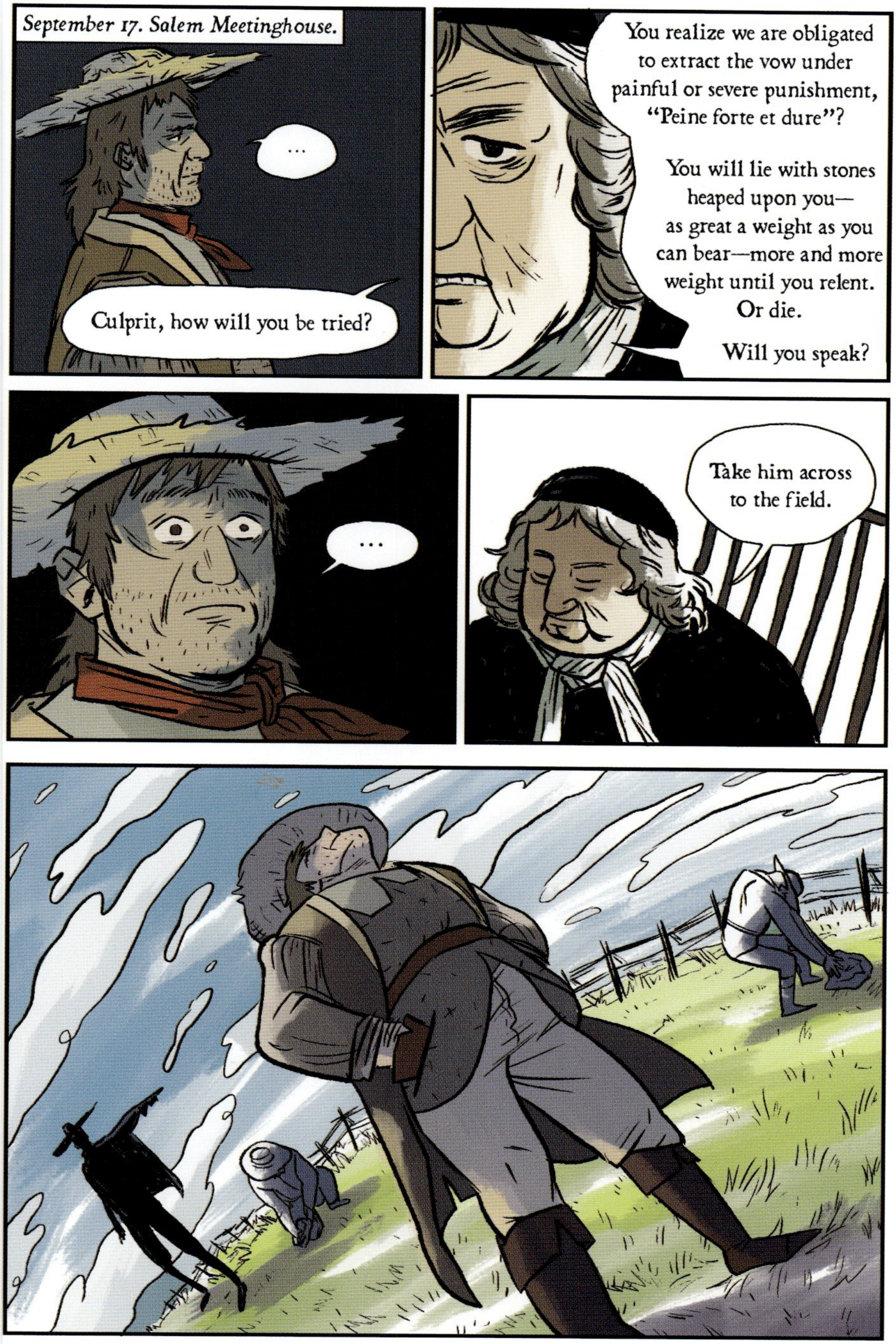
September 17. Salem Meetinghouse.
...
Culprit, how will you be tried?
You realize we are obligated to extract the vow under painful or severe punishment, "Peine forte et dure"?
You will lie with stones heaped upon you— as great a weight as you can bear—more and more weight until you relent. Or die.
Will you speak?
...
Take him across to the field.

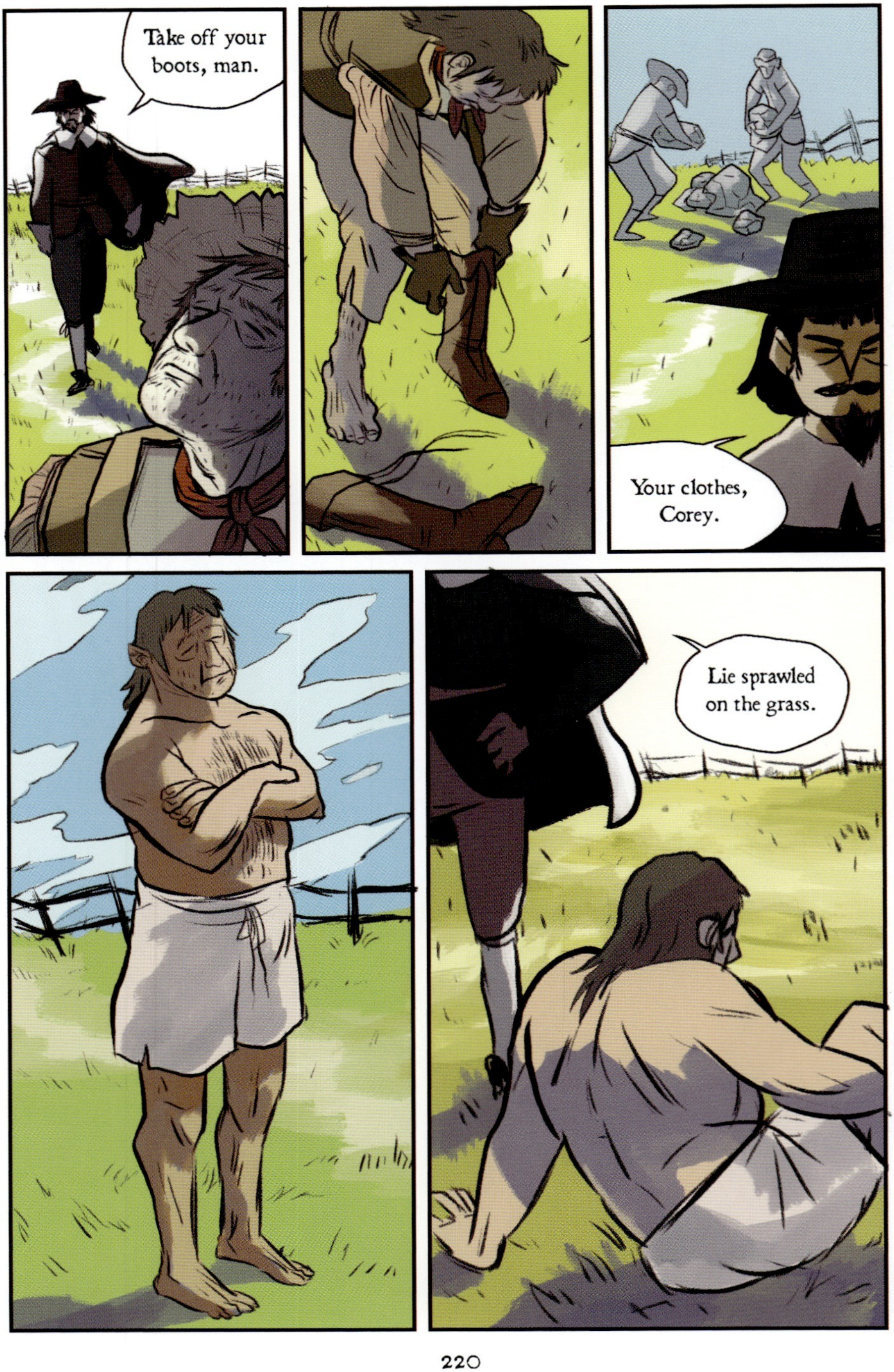
Take off your boots, man.
Your clothes, Corey.
Lie sprawled on the grass.

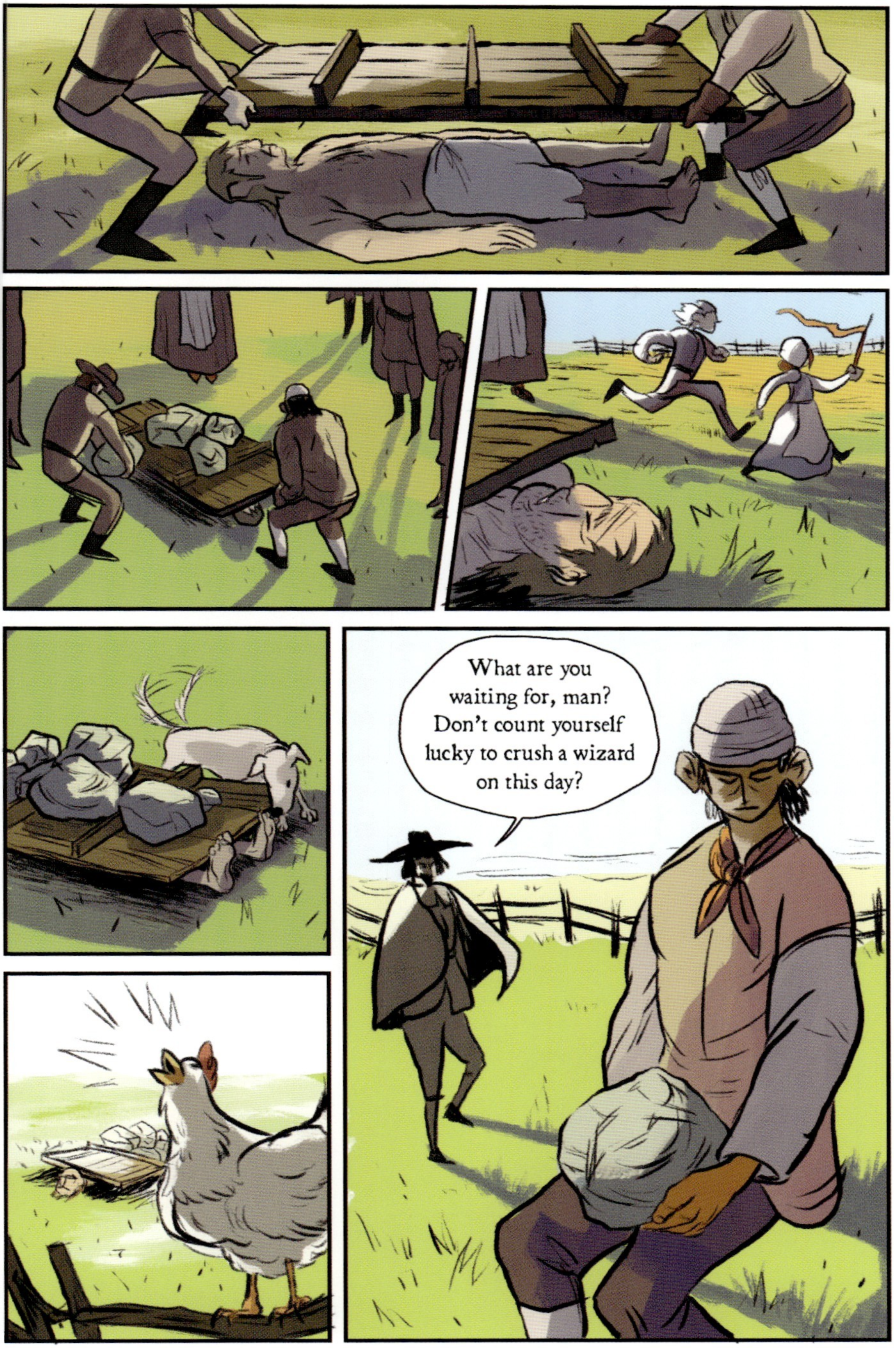
What are you waiting for, man? Don't count yourself lucky to crush a wizard on this day?

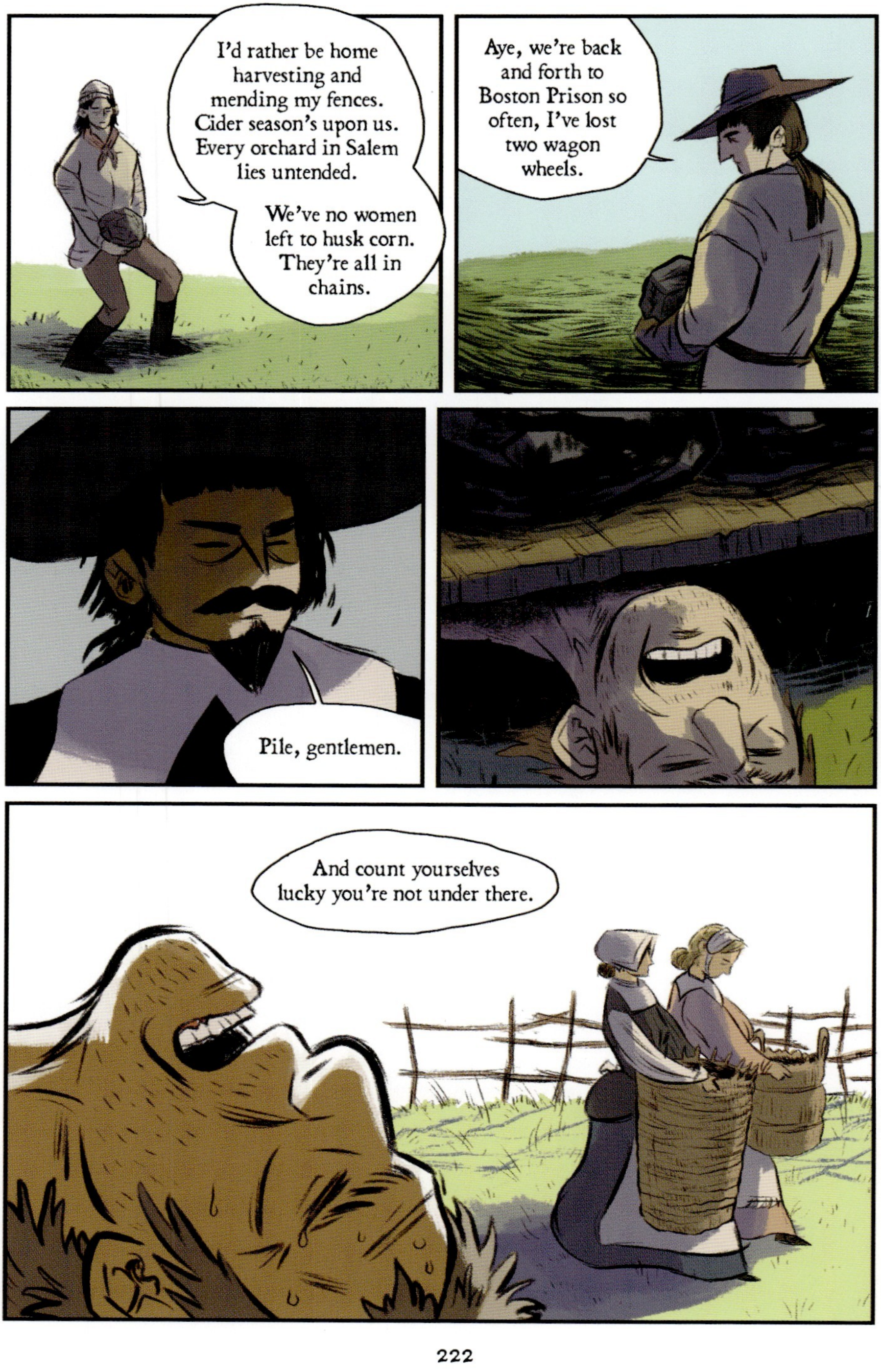
I'd rather be home harvesting and mending my fences. Cider season's upon us. Every orchard in Salem lies untended.
We've no women left to husk corn. They're all in chains.
Aye, we're back and forth to Boston Prison so often, I've lost two wagon wheels.
Pile, gentlemen.
And count yourselves lucky you're not under there.

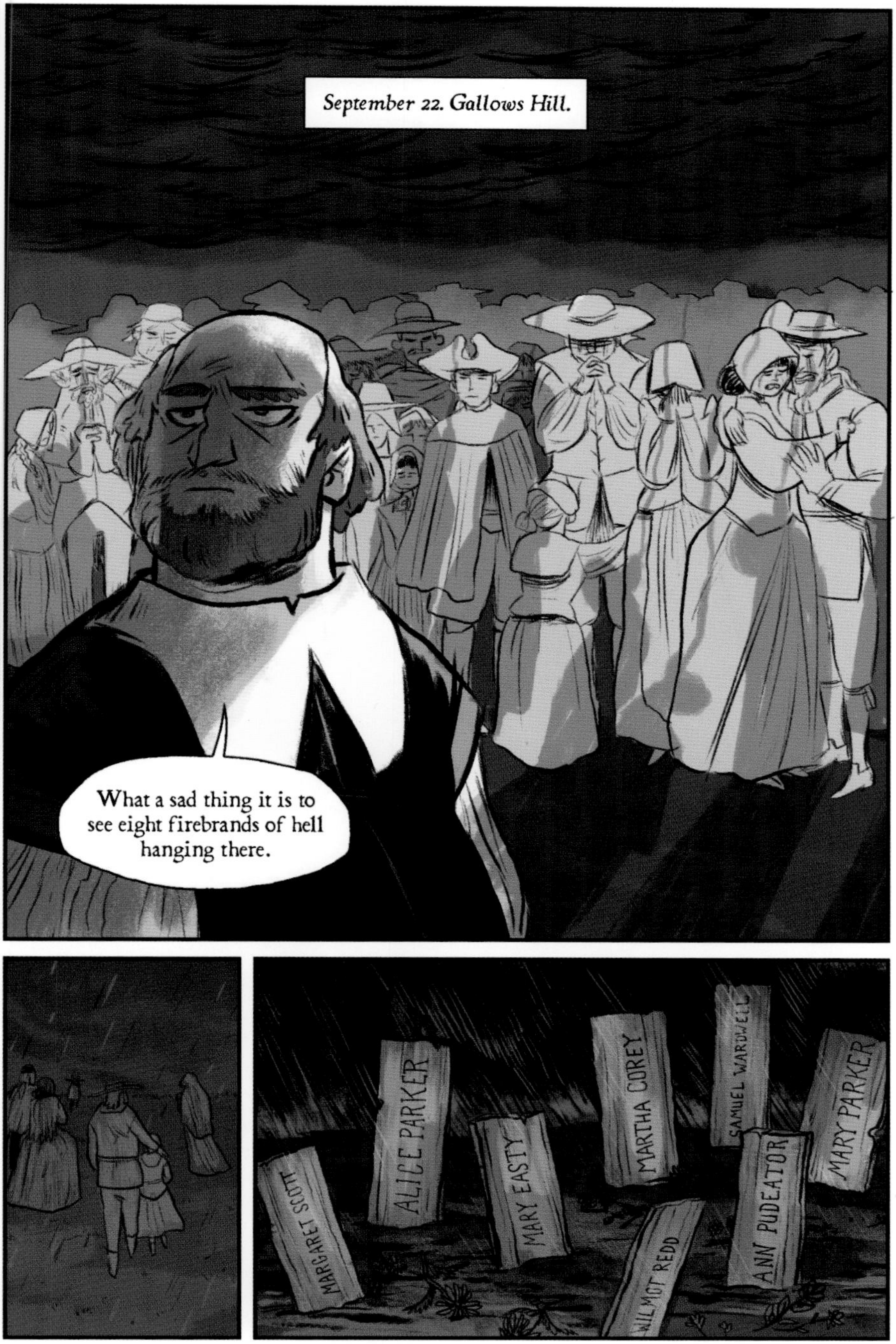

September 22. Gallows Hill.
What a sad thing it is to see eight firebrands of hell hanging there.
MARGARET SCOTT
ALICE PARKER
MARY EASTY
MARTHA COREY
WILMOT REDD
SAMUEL WARDWELL
ANN PUDEATOR
MARY PARKER

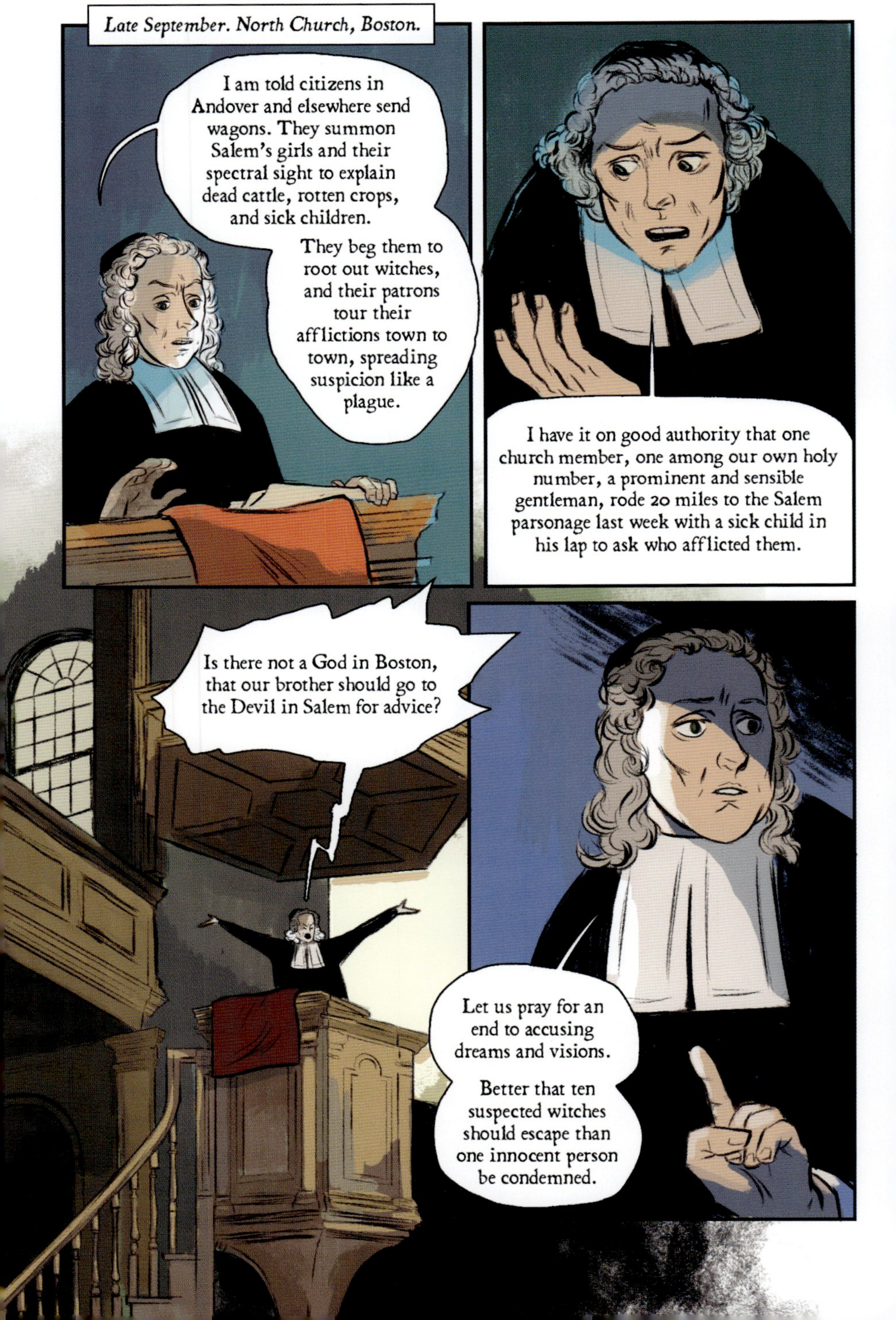
Late September. North Church, Boston.
I am told citizens in Andover and elsewhere send wagons. They summon Salem's girls and their spectral sight to explain dead cattle, rotten crops, and sick children.
They beg them to root out witches, and their patrons tour their afflictions town to town, spreading suspicion like a plague.
I have it on good authority that one church member, one among our own holy number, a prominent and sensible gentleman, rode 20 miles to the Salem parsonage last week with a sick child in his lap to ask who afflicted them.
Is there not a God in Boston, that our brother should go to the Devil in Salem for advice?
Let us pray for an end to accusing dreams and visions.
Better that ten suspected witches should escape than one innocent person be condemned.

Early October.
The governor's chambers, Boston.

Enough! I can no longer condone this. The court of oyer and terminer was devised to empty the jails, Stoughton. Instead, you have filled them.

I beg your patience—

When I returned from the Maine coast last week, I found vocal dissatisfaction with your proceedings.

Some 20 persons condemned and executed? And many of that number widely believed to be innocent?

Still you persist, despite all advice to the contrary, to credit invisible evidence.

We had sound testimony against those condemned. They were detestable witches, all.

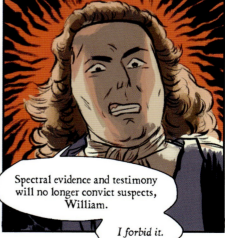

Spectral evidence and testimony will no longer convict suspects, William.

I forbid it.

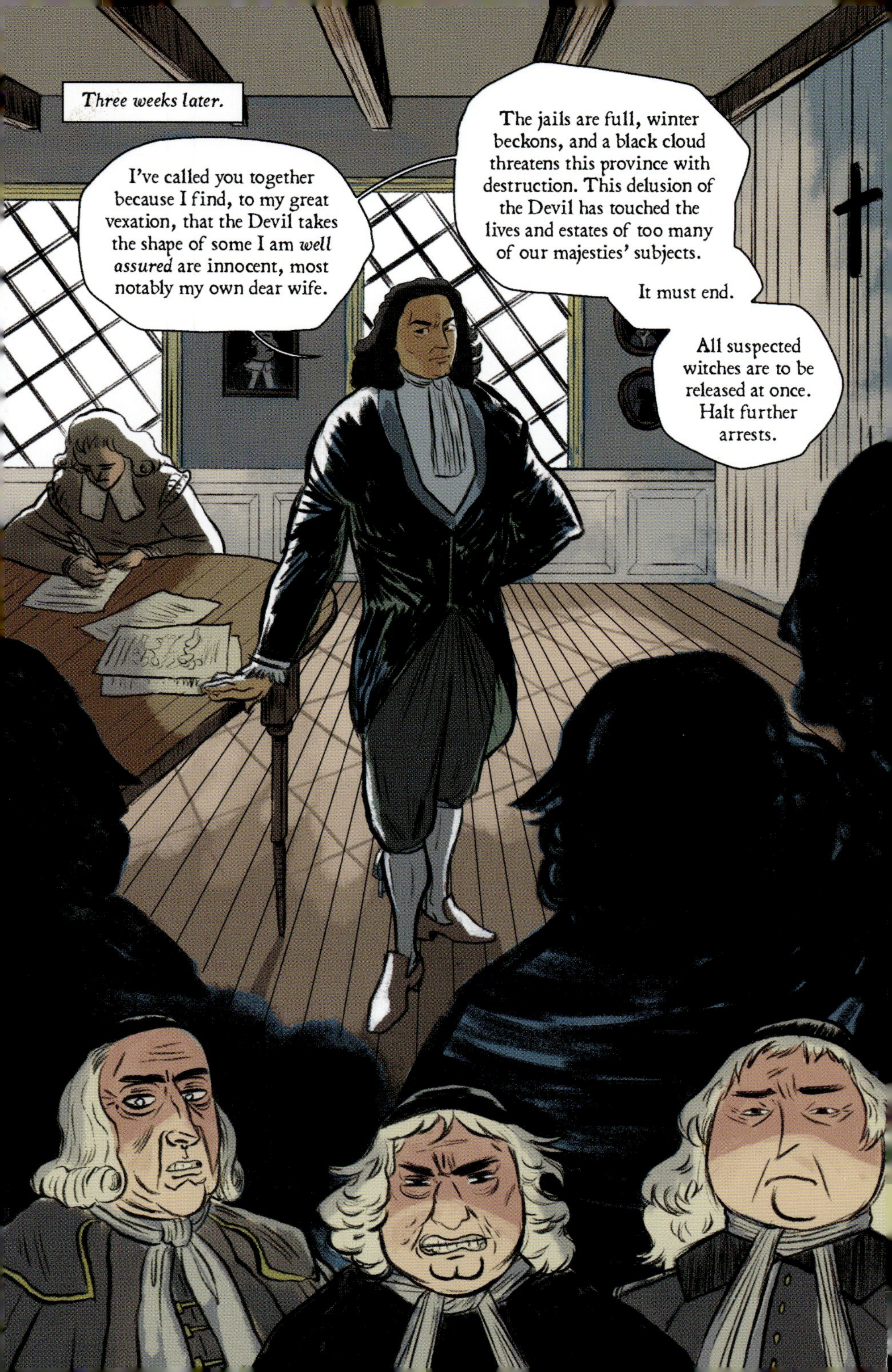
Three weeks later.
I've called you together because I find, to my great vexation, that the Devil takes the shape of some I am *well assured* are innocent, most notably my own dear wife.
The jails are full, winter beckons, and a black cloud threatens this province with destruction. This delusion of the Devil has touched the lives and estates of too many of our majesties' subjects.
It must end.
All suspected witches are to be released at once. Halt further arrests.

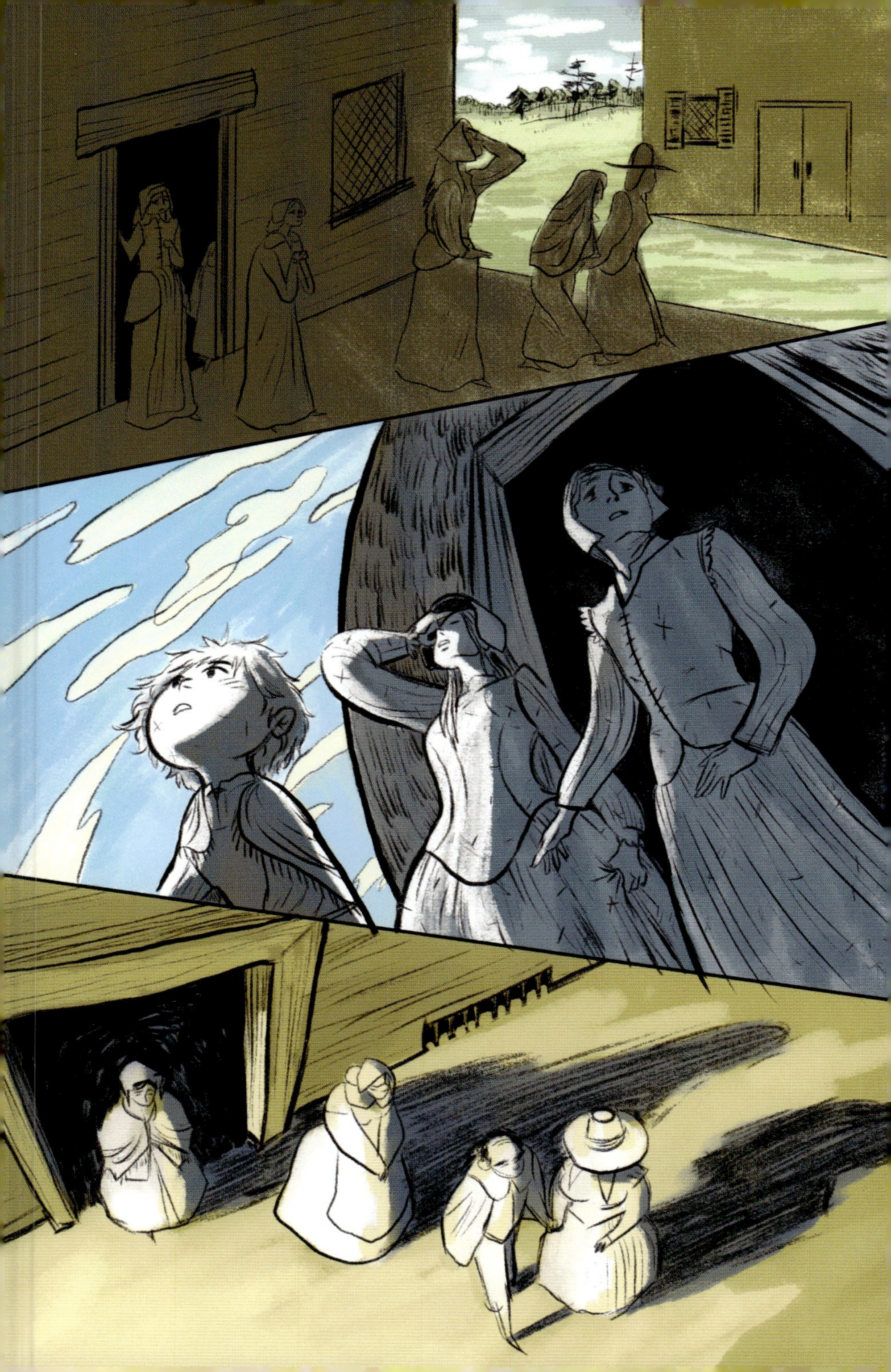

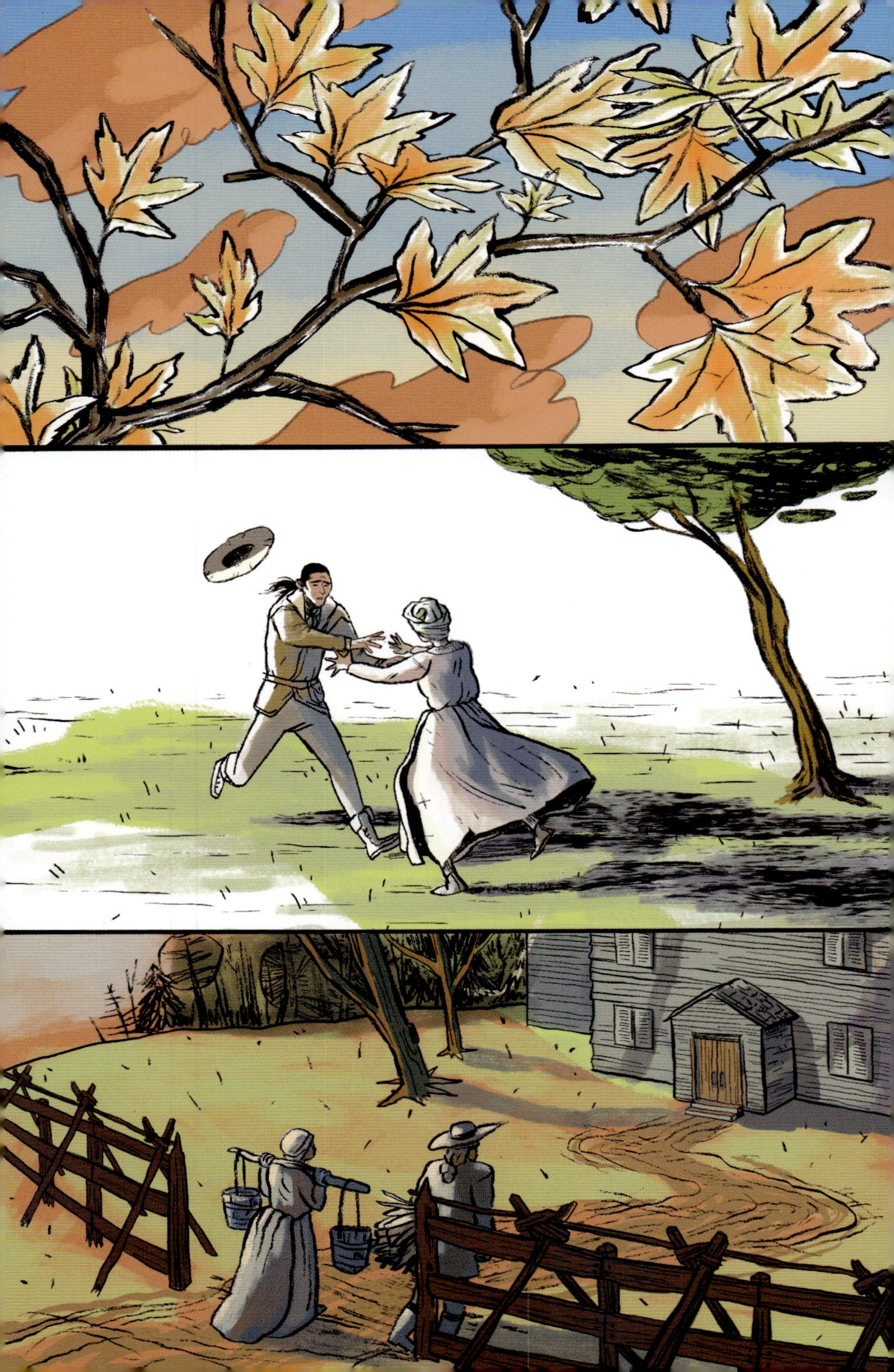

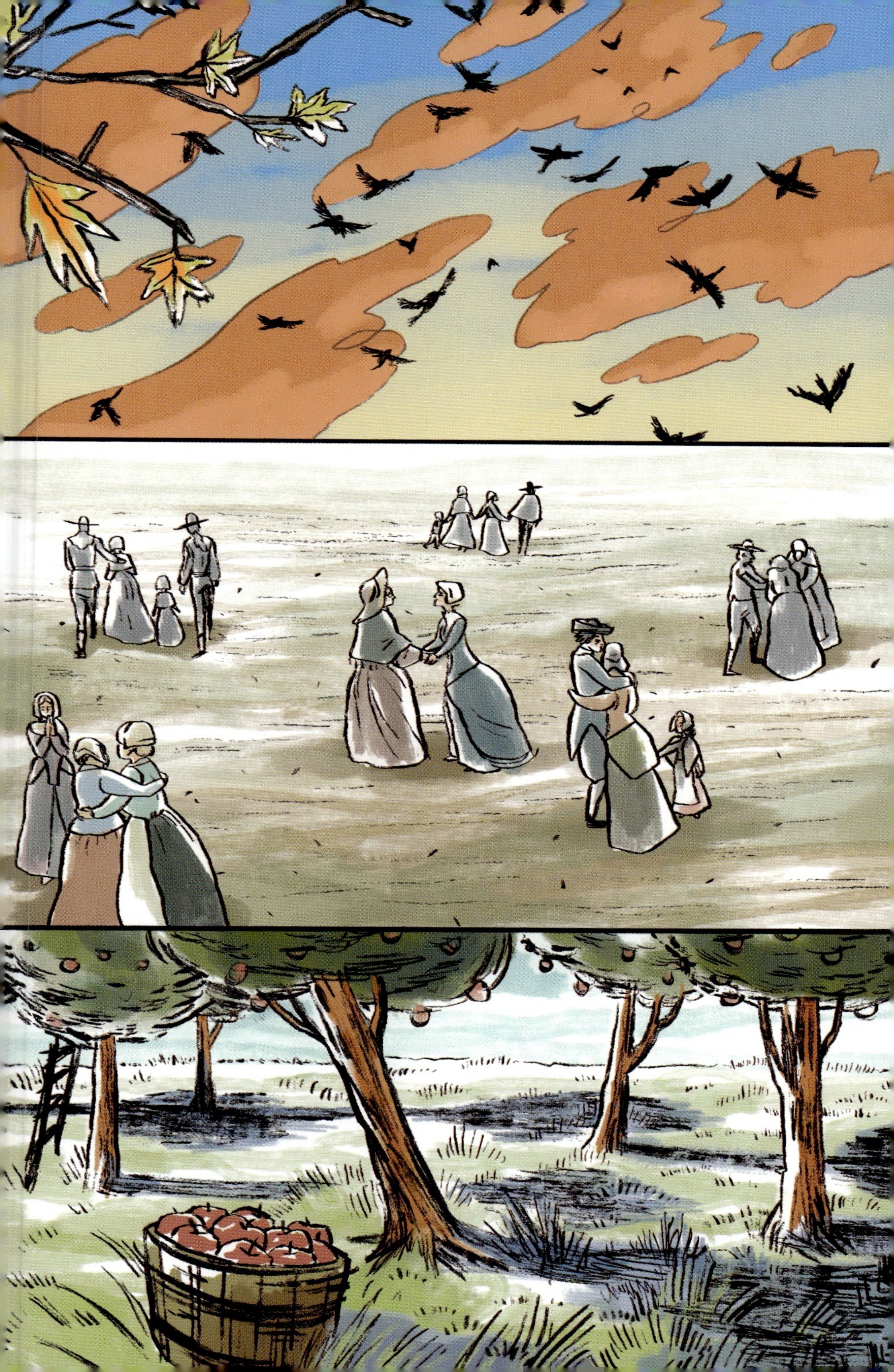

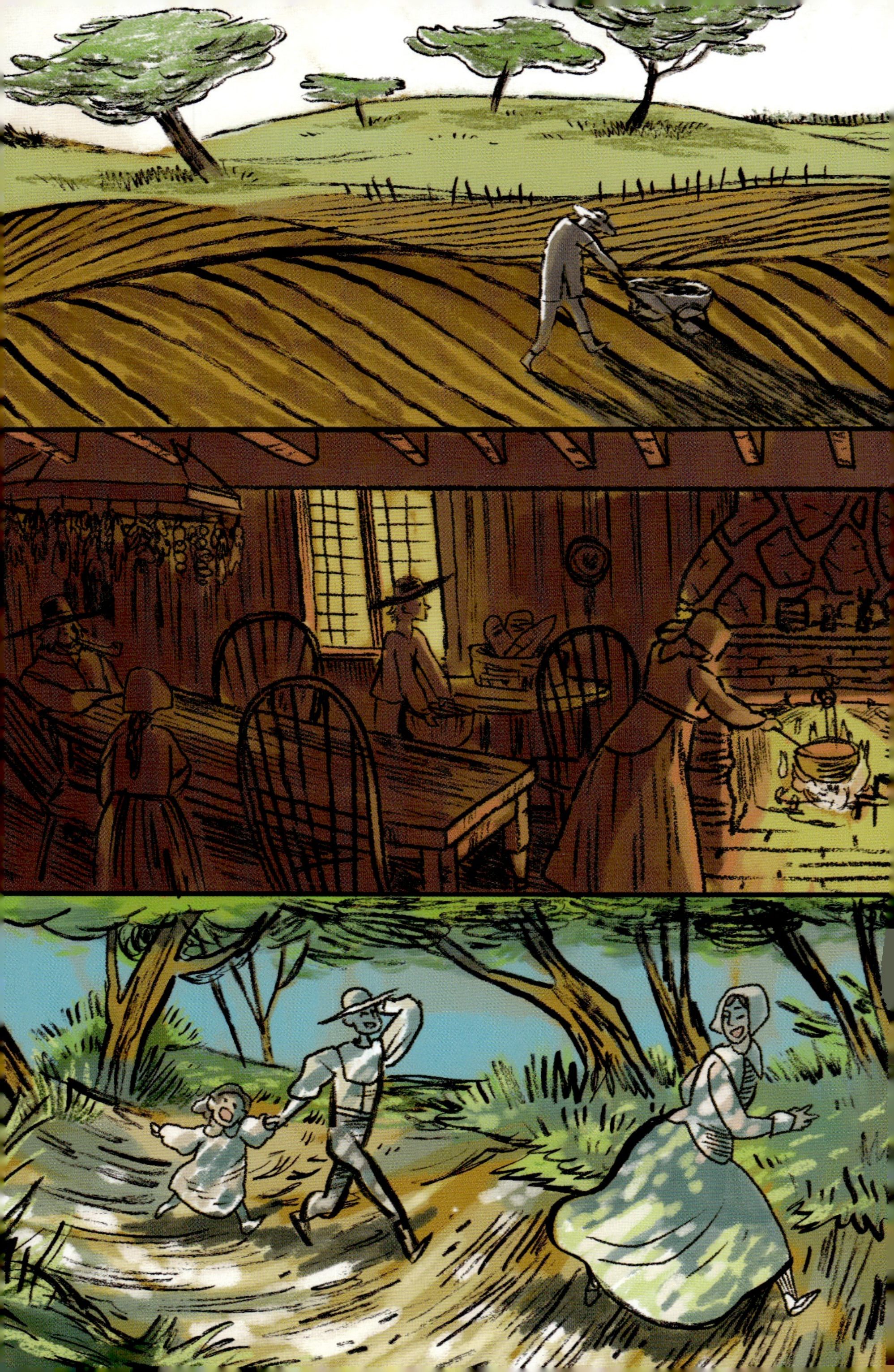

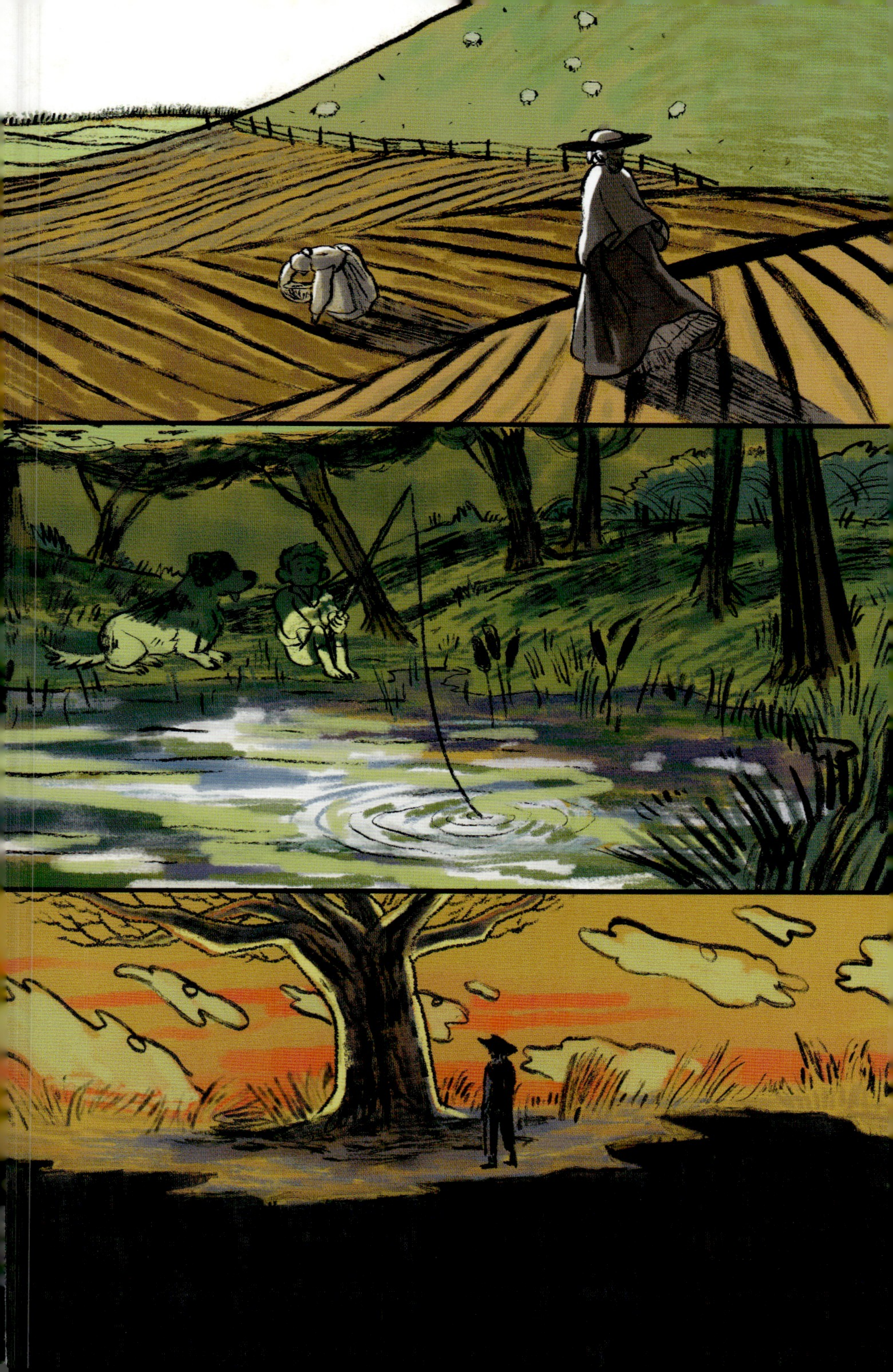

In May of 1693, Governor Phips pardoned
those confessed witches remaining in prison,
including Tituba.

In 1697, Minister Samuel Parris was driven out of Salem
and replaced by a progressive young pastor
named Joseph Green, who began to heal a community
still very much divided after the ordeal of the trials.
He urged forgiveness and a spirit of openness.

That January, the General Court ordered a day of fasting
and repentance, at which time oyer and terminer judge
Samuel Sewall publicly confessed his guilt and error.

Five years later, the General Court declared the Salem witch
trials of 1692 unlawful. (A 1711 legislative bill would restore
the rights and reputations of the accused witches
and pay their heirs reparations.)

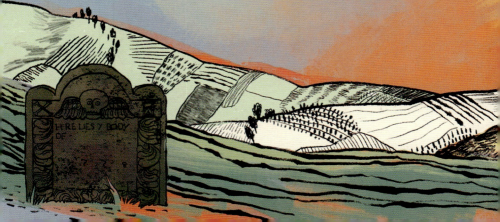

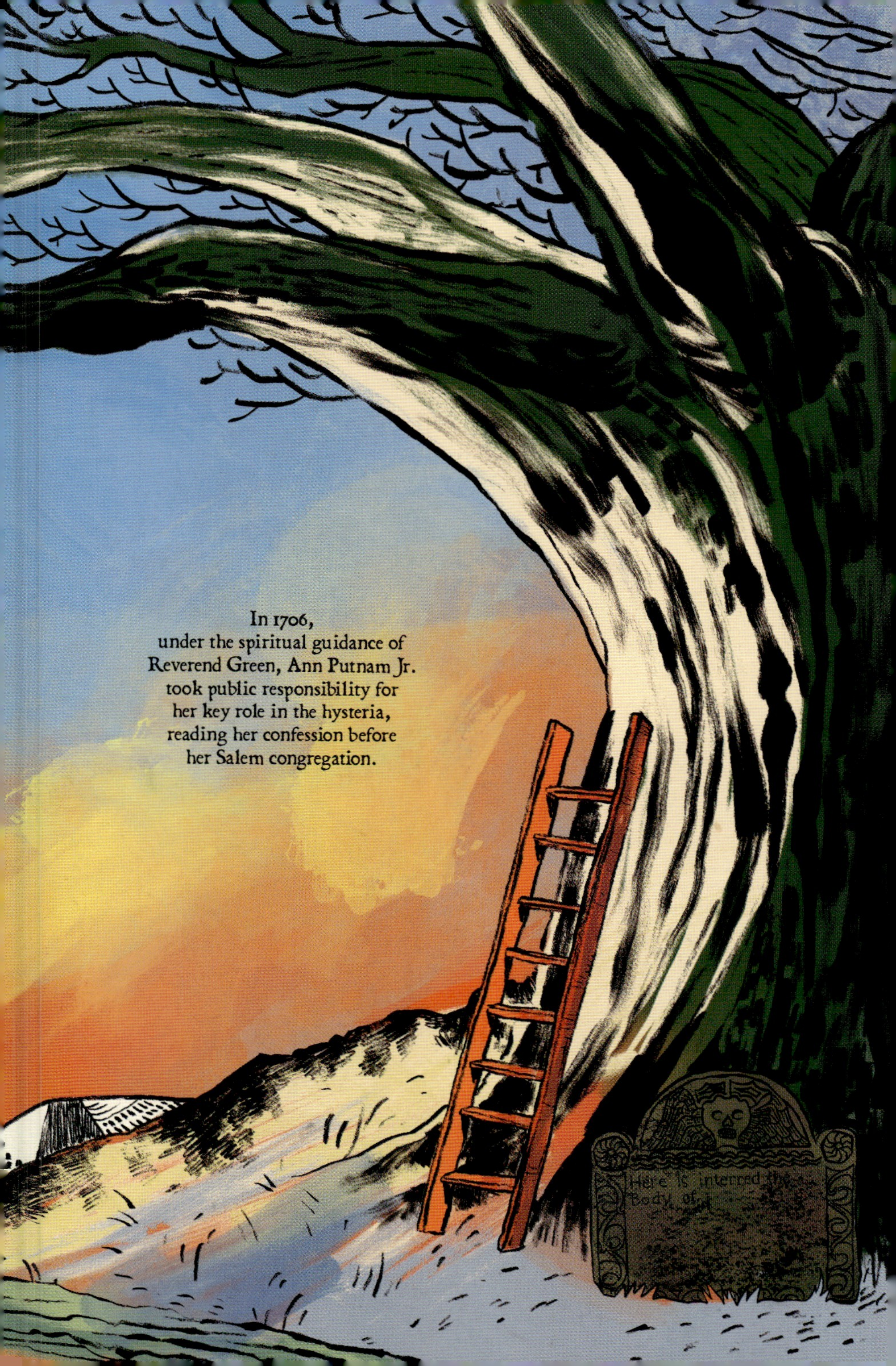
In 1706,
under the spiritual guidance of
Reverend Green, Ann Putnam Jr.
took public responsibility for
her key role in the hysteria,
reading her confession before
her Salem congregation.
Here is interred the
Body of

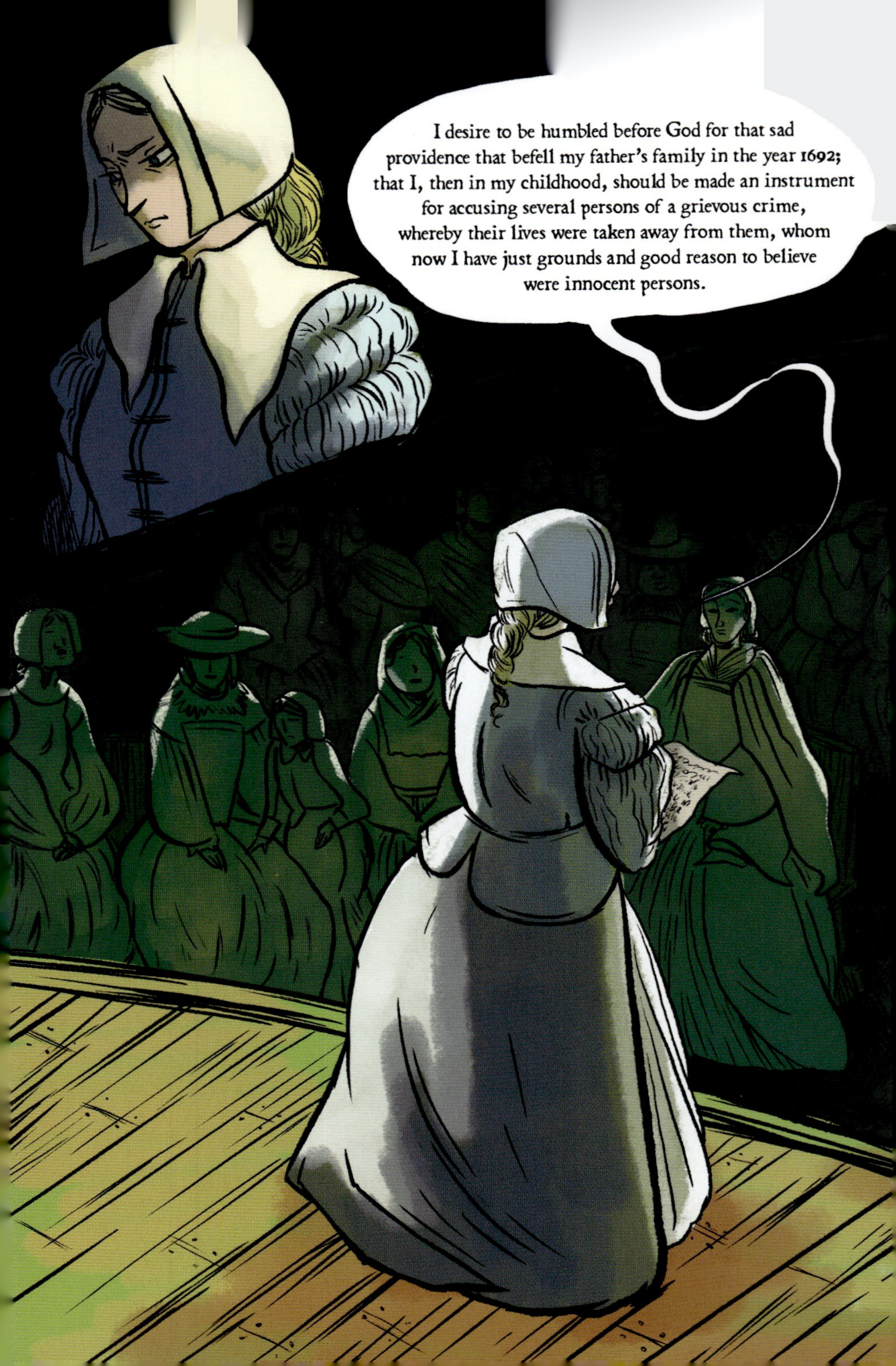
I desire to be humbled before God for that sad providence that befell my father's family in the year 1692; that I, then in my childhood, should be made an instrument for accusing several persons of a grievous crime, whereby their lives were taken away from them, whom now I have just grounds and good reason to believe were innocent persons.

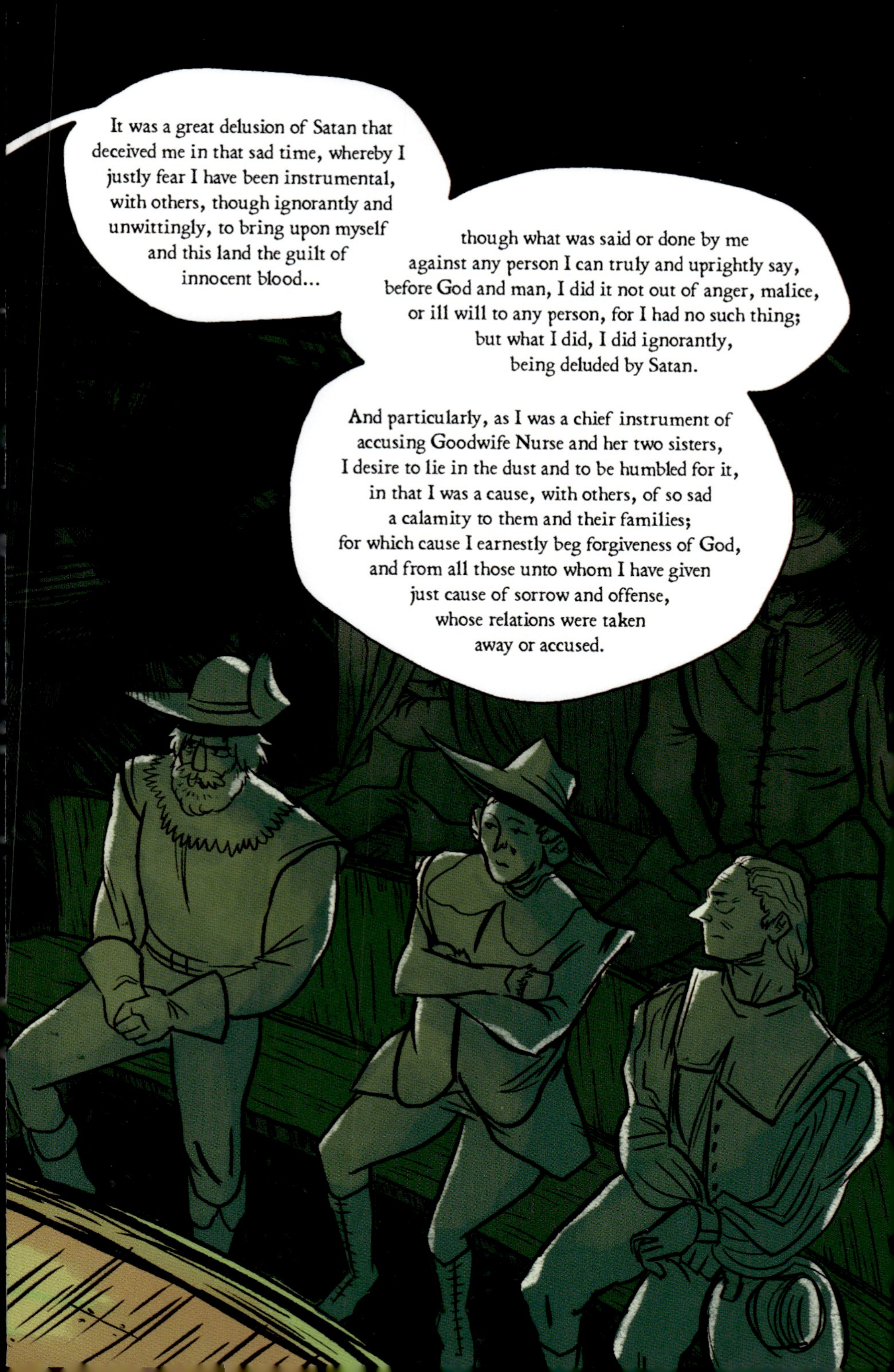
It was a great delusion of Satan that deceived me in that sad time, whereby I justly fear I have been instrumental, with others, though ignorantly and unwittingly, to bring upon myself and this land the guilt of innocent blood...
though what was said or done by me against any person I can truly and uprightly say, before God and man, I did it not out of anger, malice, or ill will to any person, for I had no such thing; but what I did, I did ignorantly, being deluded by Satan.
And particularly, as I was a chief instrument of accusing Goodwife Nurse and her two sisters, I desire to lie in the dust and to be humbled for it, in that I was a cause, with others, of so sad a calamity to them and their families; for which cause I earnestly beg forgiveness of God, and from all those unto whom I have given just cause of sorrow and offense, whose relations were taken away or accused.

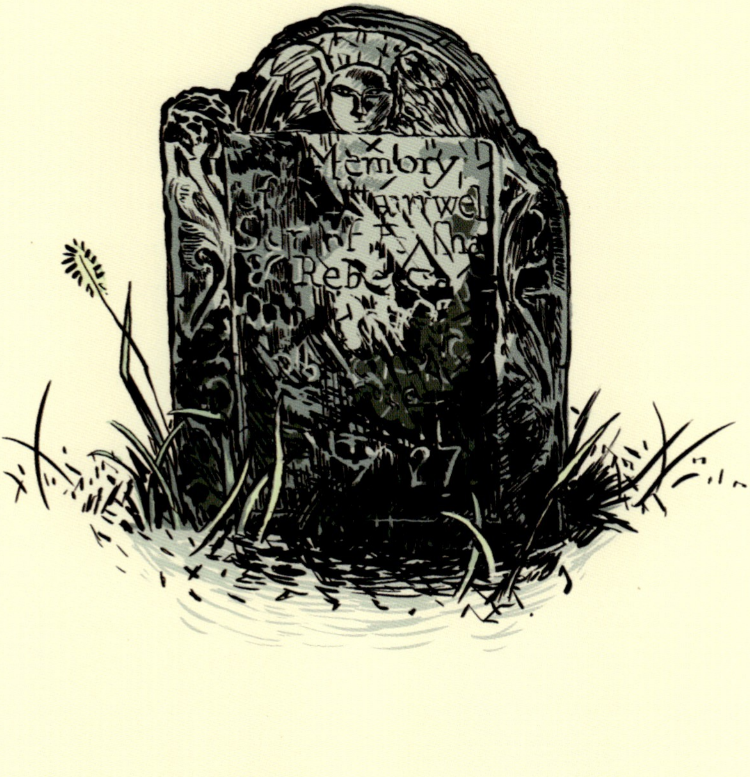
Memory

Author's Note

For narrative reasons, this book follows the fates of only some of the people involved in the Salem witch trials.

In addition to the books on the "For Further Reading" page, I owe a tremendous debt of gratitude to Benjamin C. Ray and the Salem Witch Trials Documentary Archive and Transcription Project at the University of Virginia (https://salem.lib.virginia.edu/). An online collection of primary source materials—including a new transcription of the court records, maps, and diaries—the project is indispensable to anyone studying this dark passage in American history. I drew heavily on these critical primary source documents, incorporating abridged text from court transcripts into dialogue wherever possible. I wanted those who lived this to speak, inasmuch as possible, for themselves, framed by my best understanding of their stories.

The official ordeal began in February 1692 and lasted through April of the following year. Besides the accused and afflicted, hundreds of people in the Massachusetts Bay Colony—neighbors, relatives, jurors, ministers, and magistrates—were ensnared in the legal proceedings.

The 160 accused people hailed from Salem Town, Salem Village, and two dozen other towns in the Massachusetts Bay Colony.

Most spent time in jail. Many were stripped of property and legal rights. Nearly fifty confessed to witchcraft to elude immediate trial and a possible conviction leading to execution.

Of the accusers, only Ann Putnam Jr. confessed.

Of the magistrates and judges who remained (Nathaniel Saltonstall stepped down), only one, Samuel Sewall, bore public responsibility.

More than twenty people died.

This book is dedicated to them.

Executed by Hanging on Gallows Hill

June 10

Bridget Bishop

July 19

Sarah Good
Elizabeth Howe
Susannah Martin
Rebecca Nurse
Sarah Wildes

August 19

George Burroughs
Martha Carrier
George Jacobs Sr.
John Proctor
John Willard

September 22

Martha Corey
Mary Easty
Alice Parker
Mary Parker
Ann Pudeator
Wilmot Redd
Margaret Scott
Samuel Wardwell

Giles Corey was tortured to death on September 19.

Sarah Osborne, Roger Toothaker, Lydia Dustin, and Ann Foster died in jail due to harsh conditions.

A number of others, including Sarah Good's infant, Mercy, are believed to have died in prison as well, though sources vary.

Works Consulted

Baker, Emerson W. *A Storm of Witchcraft: The Salem Trials and the American Experience.* New York: Oxford University Press, 2015.

Hill, Frances. *A Delusion of Satan: The Full Story of the Salem Witch Trials.* Boston: Da Capo Press, 1997.

Hill, Frances. *The Salem Witch Trials Reader.* Boston: Da Capo Press, 2000.

Karsen, Carol F. *The Devil in the Shape of a Woman: Witchcraft in Colonial New England.* New York: W. W. Norton, 1998.

Lawson, Deodat. "Christ's fidelity the only shield against Satans malignity. Asserted in a sermon delivered at Salem-village, the 24th of March, 1692. Being lecture-day there, and a time of public examination, of some suspected for witchcraft." Evans Early American Imprint Collection. Accessed October 21, 2022. https://quod.lib.umich.edu/e/evans/n00515.0001.001.

Norton, Mary Beth. *In the Devil's Snare: The Salem Witchcraft Crisis of 1692.* New York: Alfred A. Knopf, 2002.

Ray, Benjamin C., project dir. Salem Witch Trials Documentary Archive and Transcription Project. Accessed October 21, 2022. https://salem.lib.virginia.edu/.

Ray, Benjamin C. *Satan and Salem: The Witch-Hunt Crisis of 1692.* Charlottesville: University of Virginia Press, 2015.

Roach, Marilynne K. *The Salem Witch Trials: A Day-by-Day Chronicle of a Community Under Siege.* Lanham, MD: Taylor Trade Publishing, 2004.

Roach, Marilynne K. *Six Women of Salem: The Untold Story of the Accused and Their Accusers in the Salem Witch Trials.* Boston: Da Capo Press, 2013.

Schiff, Stacy. *The Witches: Suspicion, Betrayal, and Hysteria in 1692 Salem.* New York: Back Bay Books, 2016.

For Further Reading

Aronson, Marc. *Witch-Hunt: Mysteries of the Salem Witch Trials.* New York: Atheneum Books for Young Readers, 2003.

Crane, Jakob. *Lies in the Dust: A Tale of Remorse from the Salem Witch Trials.* Art by Timothy Decker. Yarmouth, ME: Islandport Press, 2014.

Roach, Marilynne K. *In the Days of the Salem Witchcraft Trials.* Boston: Sandpiper, 2003.

Schanzer, Rosalyn. *Witches! The Absolutely True Tale of Disaster in Salem.* Washington, DC: National Geographic Society, 2011.

Acknowledgments

I owe a tremendous debt of gratitude to Benjamin C. Ray, one of the leading contemporary scholars of the Salem witch trials and author of *Satan and Salem: The Witch-Hunt Crisis of 1692*, who generously read my draft and offered invaluable insights. Any errors that remain are entirely my own. In addition to Ray and his indispensable Salem Witch Trials Documentary Archive and Transcription Project, published in partnership with the Scholar's Lab of the University of Virginia Library and the Institute for Advanced Technology in the Humanities, I'm grateful to my friend and colleague Lisa Goodfellow for her careful reading.

Thanks to Patrice Caldwell, Heather Crowley, and Rotem Moscovich; to my agent, Jill Grinberg, and her team, especially the tirelessly gracious Sophia Seidner; to the other extraordinary team at Little, Brown Ink: dream editor Andrea Colvin, Megan McLaughlin, Jake Regier, Aria Balraj, and Kimberly Stella; and to Duffy—for a vision beyond anything I could have hoped for or imagined.

—DN

Lisa Goodfellow

Deborah Noyes is an author of nonfiction and fiction for young readers and adults, including *Lady Icarus*, *Ten Days a Madwoman*, *A Hopeful Heart*, *The Magician and the Spirits*, and *The Ghosts of Kerfol*. She also compiled and edited the short story anthologies *Gothic!*, *The Restless Dead*, and *Sideshow*.

Em White

M. Duffy resides in Richmond, Virginia, with their husband, Kyle, and four cats. Rev, a female orange tabby, leads their clowder of familiars. Every drawing is personally supervised by Rev's keen eye. Duffy is a cartoonist, printmaker, educator, and officiant. They think storytelling is the coolest, most human thing ever and intend to do it until the day they die.